CLINICAL WORK WITH SUBSTANCE-ABUSING CLIENTS

THE GUILFORD SUBSTANCE ABUSE SERIES

HOWARD T. BLANE and THOMAS R. KOSTEN, Editors

Clinical Work with Substance-Abusing Clients

Edited by
Shulamith Lala Ashenberg Straussner

FOREWORD BY FRANCES L. BRISBANE

THE GUILFORD PRESS
New York London

© 1993 The Guilford Press
A Division of Guilford Publications, Inc.
72 Spring Street, New York, NY 10012

Printed in the United States of America

This book is printed on acid-free paper.

Last digit is print number: 9 8 7 6 5 4 3

Library of Congress Cataloging-in-Publication Data

Clinical work with substance-abusing clients / edited by Shulamith
    Lala Ashenberg Straussner.
        p.   cm. — (The Guilford substance abuse series)
    Includes bibliographical references and index.
    ISBN 0-89862-193-3
    1. Substance abuse—Treatment.   2. Social work with alcoholics.
3. Social work with narcotics addicts.   I. Straussner, Shulamith
Lala Ashenberg.   II. Series.
    [DNLM: 1. Social Work—United States.   2. Substance Abuse—
therapy.   3. Substance Dependence—therapy.   WM 270 C6418]
RC564.C57   1993
616.86′06—dc20
DNLM/DLC
for Library of Congress   92-1574
                                                                  CIP

Contributors

ARMIN R. BAIER, JR., JD, CSW, Parallax Center, Inc., New York, New York

CAROLE S. BARABANDER, BCD, CSW, ACSW, CEAP, Employee assistance program consultant and psychotherapist in private practice, Maplewood, New Jersey

VINCENT CASOLARO, CSW, CAC, CEAP, Inter-Care, Ltd., New York, New York

JENNIFER DAVIS, MSW, CSW, Social Work Department, St. Luke's-Roosevelt Hospital Center, New York, New York

BEVERLY FEIGELMAN, MSW, ACSW, Psychotherapist in private practice and affiliate, Department of Social Work Services, Long Island Jewish Medical Center, New Hyde Park, New York

WILLIAM FEIGELMAN, PhD, Department of Sociology, Nassau Community College, Garden City, New York

ELLEN GRACE FRIEDMAN, MSW, ACSW, Methadone Maintenance Treatment Program, Beth Israel Medical Center, New York, New York; School of Social Work, New York University, New York, New York

EDA G. GOLDSTEIN, DSW, CSW, ACSW, School of Social Work, New York University, New York, New York

KATHY B. GORDON, DSW, Private practice, New York, New York

MURIEL GRAY, PhD, LCSW, CAC, School of Social Work, University of Maryland at Baltimore, Baltimore, Maryland

ROBERTA MARKOWITZ, ACSW, Oakwood Psychotherapy Center, White Plains, New York

JEFFREY R. MCINTYRE, CAC, LCSW, Cogswell Associates, Cambridge, Massachusetts; Graduate School in Psychology and Counseling, Lesley College, Cambridge, Massachusetts; Family Therapy Extern Training Program, Harvard Medical School at The Cambridge Hospital, Cambridge, Massachusetts

DAVID M. OCKERT, DSW, CSW, Parallax Center, Inc., New York, New York

PHILIP O'DWYER, MA, CSW, CAC, Brookfield Clinics, Garden City, Michigan

Lois Orlin, MSW, CSW, Social Work Department, St. Luke's-Roosevelt Hospital Center, New York, New York

Patricia A. Pape, LCSW, CSADC, Pape & Associates, Wheaton, Illinois

Shelley Scheffler, CSW, School of Social Work, New York University, New York, New York

Fran M. Silverman, MSW, ACSW, Department of Social Work and Home Care Services, Beth Israel Medical Center, New York, New York

Robert J. Smith, CSW, CAC, CEAP, Inter-Care, Ltd., New York, New York

Betsy Robin Spiegel, ACSW, Private practice, New York, New York; School of Social Work, New York University, New York, New York; Center for the Advancement of Group Studies, New York, New York

Shulamith Lala Ashenberg Straussner, DSW, CSW, CEAP, School of Social Work, New York University, New York, New York

Diane Pincus Strom, MSW, ACSW, Department of Social Work Services, Bronx-Lebanon Hospital Center, Bronx, New York

Elizabeth Zelvin, MSW, ACSW, CSW, CAC, Women's Alcoholism Treatment Program, Coney Island Hospital, Brooklyn, New York

Foreword

In almost 20 years of educating social work students about alcohol and other drug problems, I have been unable to find a book on clinical interventions as comprehensive as this one. The individual authors not only provide overviews of a vast range of important clinical issues, but also carefully document their claims. Most of the authors are practitioners and they explore in detail what they do in their clinical work. Moreover, they teach the method and techniques that frame their approaches. Because the authors have many years of experience, clinicians who use the suggested interventions will not be trying to implement untested theory.

Much of the book's content is new, and more traditional issues are explored in a fresh way, challenging the reader to think about the subject in new ways. An example is Zelvin's chapter on treating the partners of substance abusers. In spite of the major focus in recent years on children of chemically dependent parents, many professionals have increasingly abandoned the relatives of the chemically addicted. This chapter reminds us that the spouse of a chemically dependent person is still a very much affected individual and may continue to require intervention and treatment. Zelvin further broadens the category of persons affected by others' addictions by using the term "partner," which includes not only one's spouse, but also others significantly close to the chemical abuser.

A similar approach of adding new knowledge to an "old debate" is carefully explored in Friedman's chapter on methadone maintenance in the treatment of addiction. Methadone maintenance is used more often than any other form of treatment for narcotic addiction, and it is therefore important for readers to understand this much maligned form of treatment. In fact, the professional debate about the value of methadone (one drug treating addiction to another drug) has raged for so long that many clinicians have forgotten their obligation to share treatment options with their clients so that they may participate in choosing the one most suited to their situation. The continued widespread use of methadone maintenance is indicative that this option is appropriate for some clients.

Since the explosion of crack cocaine and other stimulants, the general public has become aware of drug addiction as a menace to individuals, families, and the country as a whole. Most important for today's clinicians is the fact that crack, cocaine, and other stimulant users require a treatment protocol that is unique not only to each individual but also to each category of drugs. Not unlike working with alcohol and other drug users, there should be a thorough assessment of stimulant-abusing clients before determining the proper treatment approach. Although not much is known about the long-term physical and psychological effects of crack, some very important information is provided in the excellent chapter by Ockert and Baier on assessment and treatment of clients dependent on cocaine and other stimulants.

Social work students and clinicians, student nurses and nurse practitioners, addiction counselors, and others in health and human services who have not identified themselves as working with chemically dependent individuals and families would especially benefit from Straussner's carefully compiled and professionally crafted introductory chapter. Many clinicians do not realize the need to treat the addiction, even when they are involved in working with chemically addicted clients. Without a general knowledge of the problems facing the chemically dependent, each "Band-Aid" they apply to their clients' problems will last only until the next chemical episode. In fact, the problems associated with alcoholism, drug abuse, and other addictions are major causes of and contributing factors to the problems that bring many people to a variety of human service agencies not specifically identified as treating chemically dependent clients. Frequently, the myriad of problems caused by alcohol and drug abuse are treated without making a connection to the root cause. This state-of-the-art chapter provides clinicians with the tools to remedy this gross assessment and treatment oversight.

This book truly fills a void in our knowledge and offers helpful techniques for treating alcohol and other drug abusers. It does not rehash old problems or invite us again to read about the difficulty involved in treating this population. It does not leave us feeling powerless to have an impact on the lives of our clients. This fine book gives clinicians answers—the tools needed to treat these problems and to heal their clients. Knowing that help is available, as explicated in this book, clinicians as well as students can approach their clients with a positive attitude, one of hope for the clients and faith in the clinicians' professional ability to make treatment work.

FRANCES L. BRISBANE, PhD
Dean, School of Social Welfare
State University of New York at Stony Brook

Preface

The impetus for this book was my unsuccessful search for a basic textbook about clients with alcohol and, especially, other drug abuse problems that would address the clinical practice issues encountered by social work students in a variety of settings. I was also made aware of the need for such a book by numerous experienced social work and other mental health clinicians who were asking for my consultation in order to better assess and treat their growing number of clients with drug and alcohol problems and their family members. It is hoped that this book will be useful to both beginning and experienced clinicians treating such clients.

The contributors are all clinicians with extensive experience with substance-abusing clients. Unfortunately, time and space limitations made it impossible to address other topics initially considered, such as the impact of social policy on practice; working with substance abusers in school settings, community mental health services, and family and children's services; and substance-abusing special populations, such as ethnic and racial minorities, gays and lesbians, and the elderly.

The book is organized into five sections:

Section I provides an overview of the impact of alcohol and other drugs on individuals and discusses basic clinical practice issues.

Section II discusses assessment and intervention with substance abusers in such settings as medical and psychiatric facilities, private practice, and the workplace.

Section III addresses clinical work in specialized substance abuse facilities, such as those focusing on interventions, alcoholism treatment, methadone maintenance, and the 12-step programs.

Section IV deals with assessment and intervention with families of substance abusers, including partners and children.

Section V deals with treatment issues for such populations as adolescents, women, the homeless, cocaine and other stimultant abusers, those with borderline personality disorders, and those with AIDS. This section also addresses relapse prevention, an area receiving growing recognition by clinicians treating drug and alcohol abusers.

I wish to thank all the contributors who were willing to make the numerous revisions requested of them. I also want to express my appreciation to Barbara Dane for her helpful critique of my own chapter and to Kitty Moore of The Guilford Press for her ongoing support and availability, And, as always, I want to express my love and gratitude to my family—Joel, Adam, and Sarina—all of whom helped in their own unique ways.

SHULAMITH LALA ASHENBERG STRAUSSNER

Contents

WITH FAMILIES OF SUBSTANCE ABUSERS

10. Family Treatment of Substance Abuse 171
    Jeffrey R. McIntyre

    An Overview of the Chemically Dependent Family Process, 171
    The Process of Recovery, 173
    Basic Issues in Assessment, 174
    Treatment, 179
    Conclusion, 192
    References, 193

11. Treating the Partners of Substance Abusers 196
    Elizabeth Zelvin

    How the Partner Is Affected, 197
    Treating the Codependent Partner, 202
    Addictions and Other Pathologies of the
       Codependent Partner, 209
    The Recovering Relationship, 210
    Summary, 212
    References, 213

12. Dynamics and Treatment Issues with Children of Drug and
    Alcohol Abusers 214
    Roberta Markowitz

    Etiology and Dynamics, 214
    Coping Mechanisms, 219
    Treatment, 223
    Working with Young Children of Substance Abusers, 224
    Treating Adult Children of Alcoholics, 225
    Conclusion, 228
    References, 228

SECTION V. SPECIAL ISSUES
AND SPECIAL POPULATIONS

13. Treating the Adolescent Substance Abuser 233
    Beverly Feigelman and William Feigelman

    Historical Perspectives, 233
    Current Substance Use among Adolescents, 234
    What Attracts Adolescents to Substance Use?, 235
    Stages of Adolescent Alcohol and Drug Use, 236
    Warning Signals, 238
    Motivation, 238
    Treatment Approaches for Adolescents, 241

CLINICAL WORK WITH SUBSTANCE-ABUSING CLIENTS

An Introduction to Clinical Practice with Substance-Abusing Clients

I

Assessment and Treatment of Clients with Alcohol and Other Drug Abuse Problems: An Overview

SHULAMITH LALA ASHENBERG STRAUSSNER

The courage to be is rooted in the God who appears
when God has disappeared in the anxiety of doubt.
—PAUL TILLICH, *The Courage to Be*

From the infant born to a woman addicted to crack cocaine to the elderly alcoholic who needs nursing home care, the abuse of alcohol and other drugs is a major health and social problem affecting every segment of our society. The direct or indirect impact of substance abuse and dependence is experienced by social workers and other clinicians in all types of settings and requires each worker to have some familiarity with the various substances and with the assessment and treatment needs of those abusing them. The purpose of this chapter is to provide an overview of the impact of alcohol and other drugs on individuals and to discuss the issues related to clinical assessment and intervention with clients who abuse alcohol and/or other drugs and their families.

DEFINITION OF TERMS

Every day millions of Americans use alcohol and other psychoactive substances; however, not everyone experiences a problem due to such use. It is therefore helpful to conceptualize alcohol and other drug use as ranging on a continuum from nonproblematic experimental and social use to pathological abuse to dependence or addiction.

While there is no generally accepted distinction that differentiates between the "use" and "abuse" of alcohol and/or other drugs, the revised third edition of the American Psychiatric Association's (APA, 1987) *Diagnostic and Statistical Manual of Mental Disorders* (DSM-III-R) defines "abuse" as the continued use of psychoactive substances despite experiencing social, occupational, psychological, or physical problems; recurrent use in situations in which use is physically hazardous, such as driving while intoxicated; and a minimal duration of disturbance of at least 1 month. The APA (1987, pp. 167–168) further differentiates "psychoactive substance abuse" from substance dependence," which it defines as the existence of at least three of the following nine symptoms:

1. Substance often taken in larger amounts or over a longer period than the person intended
2. Persistent desire or one or more unsuccessful efforts to cut down or control substance use
3. A great deal of time spent in activities necessary to get the substance, take the substance, or recover from its effects
4. Frequent intoxication or withdrawal symptoms when expected to fulfill major role obligations at work, school, or home, or when substance use is physically hazardous
5. Important social, occupational, or recreational activities given up or reduced because of substance use
6. Continued substance use despite knowledge of having a persistent or recurrent social, psychological, or physical problem that is caused or exacerbated by the use of the substance
7. Marked tolerance; need for markedly increased amounts of the substance in order to achieve intoxication or desired effect, or markedly diminished effect with continued use of the same amount
8. Characteristic withdrawal symptoms
9. Substance often taken to relieve or avoid withdrawal symptoms

In essence, substance dependence, which may vary in severity from mild to severe, refers to compulsive use of a chemical and continued use despite adverse consequences.

The terms "alcoholism" and "drug addiction" are synonymous with substance dependence. These terms imply the existence of an initial increase of tolerance to the drugs, that is, that more and more of the substance is required to achieve the same effect. Once dependence or addiction develops, the individual cannot wait too long between doses without experiencing craving and, depending on the substance, physical withdrawal symptoms. The potential for addiction of different substances varies greatly; for example, narcotics or crack cocaine have a much higher potential for addiction than alcohol or marijuana. Both alcoholism and drug addiction imply a progressive deterioration of the individual's social, physical, and mental status best exemplified in the well-known Jellinek chart, named after the man who first described the various symptoms and the downhill progression of the typical alcoholic (Jellinek, 1952).

Although, technically, alcohol is classified as a mood-altering drug or chemical compound (Levin, 1990), traditionally, due to a combination of political, historical, economic, and possibly racial factors, alcohol abuse and alcoholism were viewed as phenomena that were distinct from and more acceptable than abuse of and addiction to other drugs. During the 1970s, however, clinicians treating alcoholics became aware that many patients, especially women and younger men, tended to abuse and become dependent not only on alcohol (in addition to caffeine and nicotine) but also on other sedative–hypnotics, such as minor tranquilizers and sleeping pills. Thus the term "chemical dependency" began to be used to indicate the harmful use of alcohol and other sedative–hypnotics, while terms such as "drug abuse," "substance abuse," and "addiction" were relegated to illicit substances such as heroin, amphetamines, and marijuana.

The growing use of cocaine during the early 1980s changed the clinical picture as well as the vocabulary in the field. Due to a lack of treatment facilities, numerous middle-class cocaine abusers, who also tended to use alcohol to cope with the side effects of cocaine, were being referred to alcoholism treatment facilities (Washton & Gold, 1987). Moreover, methadone patients who tended to increase their drinking as they gave up heroin were also coming to these facilities. Thus, in spite of the omission of alcohol from most "war on drugs" legislation and the separate federal funding streams for alcohol and drug programs, the line separating "alcoholics/chemical dependents" from "drug abusers" had started to erode and the treatment for both groups began to converge. National surveys of treatment facilities show that by 1989, 81% of treatment programs were treating both alcohol and other drug abusers, compared to 50% of programs in 1983 (Zimmerman, 1991).

The change in client population has become reflected in the change in nomenclature. By the end of the 1980s, the Division of Communication programs in the federal Office of Substance Abuse Prevention (OSAP) recommended the use of the terms "alcohol and other drug use" and "abuse," while the APA (1987) used the category of "psychoactive substance use disorders" as a catchall term for dysfunctional use of all mood-altering chemicals and further differentiated these disorders into psychoactive substance abuse and substance dependence. Thus the terms "alcohol and other drug abuse" or "substance abuse/dependence" are gradually replacing the older terms of "alcoholism" and "substance/drug abuse" to indicate dysfunctional use and addiction to *all* mind- and mood-altering chemicals. It is the newer terminology that will be utilized throughout this chapter.

THE SCOPE AND IMPACT OF SUBSTANCE ABUSE

The abuse of alcohol and other drugs impacts on individuals, families, communities, and society as a whole. Below is a brief overview of the scope and the impact of substance abuse as it relates to clinical practice.

Scope of Alcohol-Related Problems

According to government estimates, there are 10.5 million adults suffering from alcohol dependence and an additional 7.2 million alcohol-abusing individuals in the United States. It is further estimated that by 1995 there will be 11.2 million alcohol-dependent Americans (U.S. Department of Health and Human Services [USDHHS], 1990).

Alcohol abuse is associated with a wide variety of illnesses and social problems: A minimum of 3 out of every 100 deaths are attributed to alcohol-related causes, including liver and pancreas diseases, cancer, and cardiovascular problems (Williams, Grant, Hartford, & Noble, 1989). Nearly half of all violent deaths (accidents, suicides, and homicides), particularly of men below age 34, are alcohol related (USDHHS, 1990), and alcohol has been found to be a consistent factor in reports of child abuse, including incest (Straussner, 1989), domestic violence (Hindman, 1979; Wright, 1985), and date rape among young adults (New York State Division of Alcoholism and Alcohol Abuse [NYSDAAA], 1988).

Alcohol abuse and dependence vary according to age and gender as well as ethnic and racial factors. Among young adults (ages 18–29), white males have been found to have the highest risk for alcohol problems, while black men have the highest rates among the middle-aged and elderly population and are at higher risk for alcohol-related diseases as well as personal and social problems (Herd, 1989). Socioeconomic factors also correlate with race and gender: Limited education and poverty are related to alcohol dependence in black males but not in white males (USDHHS, 1990). Among Hispanic men, the rate of alcohol abuse increases sharply for men in their 30s but declines thereafter, with Mexican-American men and women having higher rates of both abstention and alcohol abuse than men and women of Puerto Rican or Cuban origin (USDHHS, 1990). American Indian and Alaska Native groups, as a whole, have very high rates of alcohol abuse and dependence (USDHHS, 1990), while Asian-Americans, a term that encompasses an extremely diverse population, have a lower level of alcohol abuse and dependence than other racial and ethnic groups, a finding accounted for by their physiological sensitivity to the effects of alcohol, the so-called flushing response (Sue, 1987).

The overall national ratio of alcoholic men to women is approximately 5 to 2, although this may vary in large urban areas, where the ratio of men to women may approach 2 to 1. Women at highest risk for alcohol abuse and dependence are usually in their 20s or 30s, those who are unmarried but living with a partner, and those in a relationship with an alcohol-abusing man (USDHHS, 1990).

Scope of Problems Related to Other Drugs

Due to previously mentioned social and political factors, it is difficult to obtain corresponding data regarding abuse and dependence of drugs other than alcohol. National drug use surveys conducted by the Research Triangle Institute for the National Institute on Drug Abuse (NIDA) provide data on frequency of drug use, not necessarily the biopsychosocial impact on individuals. Based on a study of all available research, the Committee for the Substance Abuse Coverage Study of the Institute of Medicine (Gerstein & Harwood, 1990) estimated that approximately 2.5 million Americans are drug-dependent and another 3 million are drug abusers, for a total comprising 2.7% of the U.S. population over 12 years of age. An estimated 105,000 pregnant women annually are in need of drug treatment (Gerstein & Harwood, 1990).

Household surveys have found that black women are more likely than black men, or women in any other racial or ethnic group, to be using crack cocaine (USDHHS, 1989).

While the proportion of high school and college students using any illicit drug dropped steadily from 1980 to 1987, according to a government publication "this nation's high school students and other young adult show a level of involvement with illicit drugs which is greater than can be found in any other industrialized nation in the world" (Johnston, O'Malley, & Bachman, 1988, p. 14). Nearly two-thirds of high school students use at least one illicit drug before graduation, and at least 1 in 20 high school seniors smokes marijuana on a daily or near-daily basis (Johnston et al., 1988).

About one-fifth of all adolescent and adult drug abusers/dependents are under the supervision of the criminal justice system. Of those arrested for serious crimes in major urban areas during 1988, 75% tested positive for illicit drugs (USDHHS, 1991b).

It is estimated that there are between 500,000 and 1 million chronic intravenous drug abusers (IVDAs) in the United States; about 25% of them are HIV-seropositive, with approximately 28% of all reported AIDS cases today occurring among this risk group (USDHHS, 1991b). Intravenous drug abuse or sexual contact with IVDAs account for over 80% of AIDS cases in women, and 80% of pediatric patients with AIDS have an IVDA parent (USDHHS, 1991b). Over half of all adults with IVDA-related AIDS cases today are African-American, and nearly a third are of Hispanic origins (USDHHS, 1991b).

In addition to AIDS, the use of dirty, shared, and reused needles results in various systemic infections. Illnesses such as anemia, tuberculosis, heart disease, diabetes, pneumonia, and hepatitis are also common among heroin abusers, while cocaine use affects the cardiovascular system, resulting in blockages in blood circulation, abnormal heart rhythms, and strokes. Prostitution, a frequent means of support for drug-dependent women, leads to a high incidence of sexually transmitted diseases (L. P. Finnegan, 1985).

Prenatal Impact of Alcohol and Other Drugs

A unique issue among women who abuse alcohol and/or drugs is the prenatal impact of these substances upon their children. The impact of fetal exposure to alcohol and other drugs is determined by many factors, including the type of substance, the gestation age of the fetus at exposure, the route and duration of exposure, the dosage and frequency of drug intake, other substances consumed simultaneously, and environmental factors (L. P. Finnegan, 1985; Nadel, 1985). Substances used by the mother are transmitted to the fetus during pregnancy and may result in the birth of an addicted baby or, depending on the substance used, in permanent physiological and brain damage (for a fuller discussion, see Straussner, 1989).

During 1985 an estimated 50,000 babies were born affected by prenatal alcohol exposure leading to fetal alcohol syndrome (FAS) and related defects (Brody, 1986), while heroin-addicted women gave birth to an estimated 10,000 children during a corresponding time frame (Deren, 1986). A recent study indicated that the "cost of hospital care for babies born to cocaine-addicted mothers is $504 million a year more than it would be if the babies were born healthy ("Care of Babies," 1991, p. B-4).

While the impact of paternal drug and alcohol use has yet to be identified, authorities are increasingly taking a harsher view regarding parental responsibilities for damages caused to the fetus and to the newborn due to maternal abuse of drugs and alcohol. In many states, children who are born addicted or test positive to illicit substances are legally viewed as being abused, and hospital workers are required to report such cases to local child welfare agencies (Straussner, 1989). Unfortunately, treatment of substance-abusing mothers is not always required or readily available.

THEORIES OF ADDICTION

Research and clinical data reveal no single etiological factor that accounts for why some people become dependent on a substance and others do not. Among the factors frequently cited are those discussed below.

Biochemical and Genetic Factors

Studies on twins, half-siblings, and adopted children of alcoholics (Goodwin, 1984; Goodwin, Schulsinger, Hermansen, Guze, & Winokur, 1973; Schuckit, Goodwin, & Winokur, 1972) as well as newer research on markers of inherited susceptibility (Porjesz & Begleiter, 1985; Tabakoff et al., 1988) point to the presence of a genetic factor in the intergenerational transmission of alcoholism, especially in males (Goodwin et al., 1974; Straussner, 1985); while neurochemical studies point to the importance of biochemical factors in narcotic and cocaine abuse (Carroll, 1985; USDHHS, 1991b).

Familial Factors

Studies of the backgrounds of alcoholics and opiate addicts in treatment indicate that they are more likely to have experienced early separation from one or both parents and tended to receive inadequate care during childhood (Kaufman, 1985). Many were physically or sexually abused during childhood (Black & Mayer, 1980) and/or grew up in families with high incidences of multigenerational abuse of alcohol or other drugs (Carroll, 1985). Substance abuse has also been viewed as serving as an important stabilizing force in dysfunctional families (Alexander & Dibb, 1975; Steinglass, Weiner, & Mendelson, 1971).

Psychological Factors

Psychological explanations of substance abuse encompass various perspectives, including classical and modern psychoanalytic theory, developmental and personality theories, and behavioral and conditioning theories.

According to the classical psychoanalytic view, the individual uses a substance as a defense against unacceptable sexual and aggressive drives. In a letter to his friend Fliess, Freud described addictions to "alcohol, morphine, tobacco, etc." as a "substitute and replacement" for the "primal addiction," masturbation (Freud, 1897/1954), and in his description of the case of Dr. Schreber, Freud (1911/1958) posited alcoholism as a defense against homosexuality. Other early psychoanalysts viewed alcoholism as the result of a fixation in and regression to the oral stage of development (Abraham, 1908/1979), as a response to underlying neurotic conflict between dependence and anger (Fenichel, 1945), and/or as a self-destructive, slow suicide (Menninger, 1938).

Modern psychoanalysts, focusing on object relations, ego, and self psychology, view the abuse of alcohol and other drugs as an individual's attempt at dealing with poor ego development (Khantzian, 1981; Wurmser, 1978), as regression to or fixation at pathological narcissism (Kernberg, 1975), or as an effort to overcome a deficiency in the sense of self (Kohut, 1971, 1977; Levin, 1987). According to this view, alcohol and other drugs provide a "sense of internal homeostasis which substitutes for the basic lack of a sense of integration of self" (Kaufman, 1985, p. 14).

Other psychological perspectives view the abuse of alcohol and other drugs as:

- Attempts to "medicate" preexisting emotional problems, such as affective, anxiety, or somatoform disorders, as well as to cope with borderline, narcissistic, or antisocial personality disorders (Waldinger, 1986) or even psychosis (Soika, 1983)
- Efforts to diminish anxieties about self-assertion and to obliterate unacceptable feelings of anger and hostility (Kaufman, 1985)
- Ways of expressing unacceptable dependency needs
- Efforts to compensate for feelings of inferiority or powerlessness (McClelland, Davis, Kalin, & Wanner, 1972)
- Related to such personality characteristics as novelty seeking, field dependence, low frustration tolerance, high level of impulsivity, or inability to endure anxiety or tension

According to learning and behavioral theories, substance abuse is a conditioned behavioral response resulting from positive reinforcement following initial alcohol or other drug use. Although drug use may have originally been motivated by a desire for its pleasurable effects, the aversive consequence of taking a substance may be equally as reinforcing under certain environmental conditions (Barrett, 1985). Moreover, withdrawal signs could be conditioned to environmental cues. Expectancy, modeling, imitation, and identification may also play a role in substance abuse (Marlatt, Baer, Donovan, & Kivlahan, 1988).

Environmental and Cultural Factors

Numerous environmental, cultural, and economic factors have been linked to substance use and abuse, such as the increasing availability of various substances; a paucity of alternatives to a meaningful life or source of income, particularly among minority populations in urban ghettos; the influence of peer groups and the mass media; and social acceptance, even cultural idealization, of various substances (Carroll, 1985; Kaufman, 1985).

Studies of female substance abusers, in particular those in lower socioeconomic classes, show a high correlation between substance abuse by women and by their spouses or boyfriends (Straussner, Kitman, Straussner, & Demos, 1980), positing the hypothesis of women's emotional as well as economic dependence on men as a factor in substance abuse (Straussner, 1985).

Multifactorial Perspective

Each theory of substance abuse has implications for both prevention and treatment; however, the etiology of alcohol and other drug abuse remains debatable. Most likely, substance abuse and dependence result from a combination of factors, including biochemical, genetic, familial, environmental, and cultural ones, as well as personality dynamics. Therefore, as pointed out by Pattison and Kaufman (1982), it may be best to view substance abuse as a multivariate syndrome in which multiple patterns of dysfunctional substance abuse occur in various types of people with multiple prognoses requiring a variety of interventions.

PSYCHOPHARMACOLOGY

Regardless of which theory of addiction one subscribes to, every individual taking a mind-altering substance in sufficient quantity will experience a physiological reaction or a state of intoxication. Moreover, many substances, if taken in large doses over a long period of time, will lead to addiction or physiological dependence regardless of the individual's predisposing characteristics. Thus it is important to understand the physiological impact of drugs on the human brain and body.

Of the various ways of categorizing the numerous substances available today, the most useful classification is based on their effect on the central nervous system (Straussner, 1989).

Central Nervous System Depressants

This category includes alcoholic beverages, barbiturates, and nonbarbiturate sedative-hypnotics (antianxiety and sleeping medications) such as Amytal, Luminal, Tuinal, Doriden, Quaalude, Placidyl, Noludar, Nembutal, and Seconal; benzodiazepines (minor tranquilizers) such as Miltown, Librium, Valium, Xanax, Ativan, Restoril, Tranxene, Dalmane, and Serax; anesthetics such as chloroform, ether, and nitrous oxide; volatile solvents such as toluene, xylene, and benzene; and low doses of cannabinoids such as marijuana and hashish.

These drugs slow down, or sedate, the excitable brain tissues. Such sedation affects the brain centers that control speech, vision, and coordination and alters the individual's ability to exercise judgment. The individual also experiences increased agitation and excitability when coming off these drugs—a withdrawal effect commonly known as a hangover.

Individuals under the influence of alcohol or other central nervous system (CNS) depressants are likely to have poor judgment, which is often manifested in inappropriate and even destructive behavior. While low doses of a CNS depressant, particularly alcohol, block the usual inhibitions, making the person appear to be relaxed or stimulated, high doses slow down the heart rate and respiration, produce lethargy and stupor, and may result in death. Numerous descriptions of deaths among young people resulting from ingestion of massive amounts of alcohol in short periods of time have been reported in the popular press.

Another dangerous situation arises from the potentiating effect of combining two or more substances within this category. Thus a combination of alcohol with Valium or any other sedative–hypnotic is a common cause of purposeful or accidental overdose, particularly among women (Straussner et al., 1980).

Central Nervous System Stimulants

This category includes substances such as amphetamines ("speed," "crank"), cocaine and crack, drugs such as Dexedrine and Ritalin, and caffeine and nicotine. In varying degrees, these drugs increase or speed up the function of excitable brain tissues, resulting in energized muscles, increased heart rate and blood pressure, and decreased appetite.

While low doses of amphetamines are commonly used by individuals wishing to stay awake, such as students and truck drivers, the individual will experience exhaustion and "crash," or fall asleep, when coming off these drugs. Large doses of such stimulants as amphetamines and cocaine can produce acute delirium and psychosis. The psychotic symptoms can at times be difficult to distinguish from schizophrenia and may include hallucinations, paranoia, and hypersexuality. The abuse of cocaine may also lead to a variety of other toxic effects, including severe feelings of depression and sudden heart attacks. Suicidal and violent behavior under the influence of amphetamines and the more potent forms of cocaine, such as freebase or crack, have been noted by researchers and clinicians (Wetli, 1987).

Narcotics or Opiates

These drugs decrease pain by binding to specific receptors in certain brain areas. This category includes opium and its derivatives, such as morphine, heroin, codeine, and paragoric, as well as synthetic drugs such as methadone (Dolophine), Demerol, Darvon, Prinadol, Lomotil, and Talwin.

The use of opiates generally tends to have a sedative and tranquilizing effect. However, unlike the users of sedative substances, narcotic users do not usually experience poor motor coordination or loss of consciousness. The opiate-using individual is likely to experience a state of stuporous inactivity and dwell in daydreaming fantasies. Due to the physical agitation caused by withdrawal and the psychological panic related to anticipation of withdrawal symptoms, antisocial behaviors may occur during drug-seeking behavior or opiate withdrawal.

Psychedelics/Hallucinogens

These drugs produce gross distortions of thoughts and sensory processes, thereby inducing a psychosis-like state, often with visual hallucinations. Included in this category are the "alphabet drugs," such as LSD, PCP, DOM, or STP, mescaline, psilocybin, and large or highly potent doses of cannabinoids or marijuana.

Psychedelics are less physiologically addictive than other substances; however, they may precipitate psychosis in vulnerable individuals. They also result in feelings of extreme anxiety and misperception of reality. This is particularly true for users of phencyclidine (PCP; angel dust), who frequently experience distorted body image, depersonalization, depression, and hostility that may be expressed through violence (Waldinger, 1986).

It is important to note that the marijuana used today is much more potent than that used during the 1960s and 1970s. Frequent use of marijuana by adolescents and young adults has been correlated with the development of the so-called amotivational syndrome, characterized by passivity and lack of ambition leading to poor school and work performance and personality deterioration.

Combinations and Designer Drugs

Various combinations of drugs—such as heroin and cocaine (commonly referred to as speedball); cocaine and alcohol or marijuana; cocaine and PCP; methadone and alcohol or cocaine; tranquilizers and alcohol; and so forth—are frequently used to either counteract the side effects of any one drug or to synergistically increase the impact of the drugs. Such polydrug abuse, which increased during the 1980s, is more likely to be seen among younger people. Also commonly used among young people are the so called designer, or look-alike, drugs, such as Ecstasy (or Adam), MPTP, and China White, which are synthesized in clandestine laboratories and resemble highly potent doses of amphetamines or narcotics in their impact.

As can be seen from the above discussion, different substances have a differential impact on a person's mood and behavior regardless of the their personality. Thus familiarity with the impact of the various substances on a person's behavior and thinking process is a crucial aspect of clinical assessment and treatment.

CLINICAL INTERVENTIONS

Clinical interventions with substance abusers, as with all clients, begins with a comprehensive assessment followed by appropriate interventive approaches that include some or all of the following:

- Identifying the kinds of substances being abused and the degree of physical and psychological dependence
- Assessing the degree to which these substances interfere with daily life
- Identifying appropriate community resource
- Motivating the abuser to obtain appropriate treatment
- Helping the substance abuser achieve recovery
- Monitoring ongoing recovery
- Helping family members and significant others understand substance abuse and its impact on them

Assessment

Assessment is an ongoing, interactive process comprised of a number of important tasks, including: (1) determining a formal diagnosis, (2) ascertaining the severity and impact of substance abuse on individuals and those around them, (3) establishing a baseline of the patient's status for future comparison, (4) providing a guide to treatment planning and the patient's progress, and (5) evaluating the impact of environmental influences and appropriate preventative efforts. A comprehensive patient assessment may include a medical examination, clinical interviews, collateral information, and data obtained through a variety of formal instruments (USDHHS, 1991a).

The first task in assessing people who abuse drugs or alcohol is to avoid stereotyping them, since there are tremendous variations in the background and characteristics of substance abusers, in the kinds of substances being abused, and in the impact of these chemicals on the users and on their significant others. Nonetheless, there are certain characteristics and behavioral patterns that are common to many substance abusers and provide basic assessment clues.

All clients whose behavior is highly volatile and unpredictable or whose history indicates interpersonal, occupational, financial, and/or legal problems should be questioned about possible substance abuse. While some individuals may readily admit to being substance abusers, others may not. It is often helpful to obtain factual information from family members or other relevant sources, as well as to rely on behavioral clues such as a runny nose, the wearing of long sleeves in the summer to cover up needle marks, or the smell of alcohol on the breath—especially early in the day.

Due to the biopsychosocial impact of substance abuse, alcohol and other drug abusers tend to rely excessively on such defense mechanisms as denial, projection, and rationalization (Griffin, 1991). Since defense mechanisms are unconscious, substance abusers are often unaware of the full impact of the substance abuse on their lives. Thus it is up to the worker to ask the "right" questions in order to form an appropriate assessment.

Since most people in this society drink, it is less ego-threatening to start with questions about drinking before moving to data about illicit drugs. It is also important to obtain information about the onset of substance use. Clinically, it is helpful to conceptualize the person as developmentally arrested at the age at which the substance abuse (not just use) first began, regardless of current chronological age, since there are profound developmental differences between an individual who started abusing alcohol and/ or smoking marijuana heavily at age 13 and one who did so at age 23.

The following set of questions can be used as part of an initial assessment (Straussner, 1989):

1. What do you usually drink?
2. How much do you drink a day/week?
3. How old were you when you had your first drink?
4. How old were you when you started drinking on a regular basis?
5. Are you now drinking more/less than a year ago? (testing for increase/decrease in tolerance)
6. Have you ever used ___?/How much? /How often?/When started?/ Date of last use?/Source of supply?/Method of use (i.e., smoking, injecting, etc.)?
   a. marijuana
   b. heroin
   c. methadone
   d. cocaine/crack
   e. amphetamines/uppers
   f. sleeping medication (what kind?)
   g. tranquilizers/downers (what kind?)

     h. other medication/drugs obtained from family/friends or on
       the street
     i. other medication/drugs obtained from a doctor

7. Have you ever tried to stop drinking/drug use? What happened?
8. Have you ever been in treatment for substance abuse? Where?/
   When?/What happened?
9. Have you ever attended AA or NA (or any other self-help group)?
   How did you feel there?
10. Does/Did your mother/father drink too much?
11. Does/Did your mother/father use drugs (what kind)?
12. Does your spouse/boyfriend/girlfriend drink a lot/use drugs? What
    kind?
13. Has anyone ever complained about your use of alcohol/drugs?
14. Do you think that you have a problem with drugs/alcohol?

Answers to the above questions can provide a rough assessment of
substance abuse. A growing number of clinicians are also finding the CAGE
test (Ewing, 1984; Mayfield, McLeod, & Hall, 1974) of particular value in
making a quick, preliminary assessment. While originally designed to assess
alcohol abuse, it can also be used to assess other substance abuse. CAGE is
named for the four symptoms, capitalized below, that it assesses (the items in
parenthesis have been modified by this author): "Have you ever felt you
should CUT down on your drinking?" (or other drugs?); "Have people
ANNOYED you by criticizing your drinking?" (or "Have people been ANGRY at
you due to your use of alcohol/drugs?"); "Have you ever felt bad or GUILTY
about your drinking?" (or "drug use"); and "Have you ever had a drink first
thing in the morning, an EYE OPENER, to steady your nerves or to get rid of a
hangover (or "took a pill/drug to get rid of shakes or to stop feeling sick?").
Positive ("yes") response to one question is suggestive of substance abuse;
positive responses to two or more questions suggest substance dependence.
      It is crucial that these and any other assessment questions be asked in a
matter-of-fact, nonpejorative manner. The clinician needs to remember that
once individuals start abusing such substances as alcohol, opiates, or cocaine, they often become addicted to them. They *cannot* just stop using them
through willpower alone. They should not be made to feel guilty or condemned for being dependent on a chemical any more than a client would be
condemned for having an uncontrolled medical condition. It is also essential
to be attuned to the severe feelings of worthlessness and self-hate and
expectations of scorn and rejection that often lie beneath the grandiose self-
presentation of many substance abusers.
      Also important in assessment is the differential biopsychosocial effects
of various substances. The use of an illicit substance such as crack, with its
30-second high and immediately recurring craving, will have different emo-

tional, legal, financial, and social sequelae than the drinking of legally obtained bottles of Scotch.

Lastly, it is important to be cognizant of the fact that substance abuse is a "family disease" (Straussner, Weinstein, & Hernandez, 1979)—that while a client may not be the one who abuses alcohol or other drugs, he or she may be the spouse or child of a substance abuser and thus a part of a substance-abusing family system. Assessing the impact of familial substance abuse on their mental health and daily functioning is an important intervention with all clients, regardless of their presenting problems.

Clinicians unsure about their assessment regarding substance abuse should refer the client to an appropriate community agency, such as the local alcoholism council or a substance abuse clinic. Just as clinicians may refer a client to a physician for an assessment of a possible physical problem, they need to feel comfortable making referrals for assessment of a substance abuse problem. It is a proper professional response for a worker in a non-substance-abuse setting to tell a client that "I am concerned about your use of ____ (alcohol, drugs etc.) and want you to go to ____ for an evaluation (or checkup)" or "While I believe you when you tell me that you do not have a problem with drugs/alcohol, you must go to ____ for an evaluation before we can make any further plans regarding your treatment."

An important area of assessment is differentiating between substance abuse and other psychopathology. Individuals with a diagnosis of "psychoactive substance use disorder" may also be dually diagnosed with another major psychiatric (Axis I on DSM III-R) diagnosis and/or have an underlying personality disorder (Axis II) necessitating a comprehensive psychiatric assessment in addition to assessment of their substance abuse. (For further discussion of dual diagnoses, see Chapters 3 and 15.)

Motivation for Treatment

A comprehensive assessment must include assessment of the client's motivation for treatment. As a rule, substance abusers do not enter treatment voluntarily. Due to the effects of alcohol and other drugs on the brain and the extensive use of denial and other defenses, substance abusers usually need other people to push them to treatment (Straussner, 1989). While a highly motivated client is generally more likely to make better use of treatment, recovery from substance abuse is not always dependent upon whether or not the initial contact with treatment was mandated. In fact, studies show that some individuals who are coerced into treatment may have an even better recovery rate than those who are not (Mark, 1988). The use of both instrumental and affective authority in getting a substance abuser to treatment has been found to be of value to individuals of all socioeconomic levels and ethnic backgrounds. It is the basis for the use of the family intervention approach (Johnson, 1986), for student (Griffin & Svendsen, 1986) and employee assistance programs (Trice & Beyer, 1984), for drunk-driving programs, and for various professional diversion programs, such as those for impaired physicians, nurses, and lawyers.

While the use of coercion may raise some ethical dilemmas, it is important to keep in mind that individuals who are addicted to a substance are unable to exercise a true freedom of choice in their decision-making process (King, 1986).

TREATMENT FACILITIES AND APPROACHES

An important task for social workers is to determine appropriate forms of treatment for clients with a substance abuse problem. In general, substance abusers need specialized treatment and workers need to be aware of the various treatment options available for these clients in their community, the most important of which are discussed below.

Detoxification

Detoxification is the first step in the treatment of those physically addicted to opioids, alcohol, barbiturates, other sedative–hypnotics, and amphetamines. It is not required for cocaine or crack abusers or for marijuana smokers. Physical dependence or addiction is defined primarily by signs of withdrawal or the presence of a set of symptoms that appear when the intake of a given substance is terminated. Frequently, these symptoms are opposite to the signs of acute intoxication. For example, the withdrawal symptoms from stimulants such as amphetamines include severe depression, while symptoms of withdrawal from sedative–hypnotics such as alcohol include extreme agitation and insomnia.

Although withdrawal from opiates has been given much publicity, it is not life-threatening, as it may be from severe alcohol, Valium, or barbiturate addiction. It has been compared to "a one-week bout with influenza" (Waldinger, 1986, p. 315).

Detoxification is generally carried out on a medical or psychiatric inpatient unit in order to allow for careful monitoring of physical status and to prevent potentially lethal withdrawal reactions. Inpatient detoxification treatment also increases the likelihood of a comprehensive assessment and a greater acceptance of further treatment. At times, detoxification is provided in outpatient settings or by physicians in private practice. Heroin addicts can be detoxified on an outpatient basis with the help of such chemicals as clondine or decreasing doses of methadone.

Rehabilitation Treatment Programs

Detoxification is usually only the beginning of a long and difficult course of recovery. When substance abusers give up their chemicals, they may experience a prolonged period of physiological and psychological withdrawal. Moreover, the lives of many substance abusers revolve around the process of obtaining drugs or alcohol; this provides a daily routine as well as relationships with other substance abusers that must be replaced if the individual is to maintain a drug-free existence. Furthermore, since substance abusers often medicate unpleasant feelings such as anxiety or depression, these feelings are likely to surface or worsen when the substance is taken away.

Therefore, short- and long-term inpatient and outpatient rehabilitation programs and drug-free residential communities are invaluable in helping substance abusers examine the impact of alcohol and/or other drugs upon their lives, their ability to relate to other people, and the necessary changes in their lifestyle that they must undertake if they want to recover from substance abuse. While cocaine and crack users do not require detoxification, they do require ongoing inpatient or outpatient counseling.

In order to serve the growing number of clients who do not need or do not have insurance coverage for a residential program, some facilities have established intensive outpatient rehabilitation programs. Also available in some communities are day treatment programs and part-time community residential facilities such as halfway and quarter-way houses and substance-free housing. Such programs and facilities are of particular value to those with limited social and vocational supports, such as a young adult crack or heroin addict or an elderly alcoholic.

The Use of Chemical and Nonchemical Substitutes: Methadone, Naltrexone, Antabuse, and Acupuncture

The utilization of methadone maintenance programs as a substitute for narcotics can lead to better prognosis for rehabilitation and allow narcotic addicts to avail themselves of such services as individual or group counseling and educational or vocational training; it can also help them improve the overall quality of their lives once the daily concern about obtaining drugs is alleviated. Moreover, the growing number of persons with HIV/AIDS among intravenous narcotic users is an important factor in referring clients to methadone maintenance programs. However, since methadone is more ad-dictive and more difficult to withdraw from than heroin and since metha-done maintenance programs vary greatly in their provision of supportive and social services, it is important to help clients determine whether a particular program is likely to be effective in meeting their particular needs.

While less extensively used than methadone, opioid antagonists such as naltrexone, which prevent addicts from experiencing the effects of narcotics, have been utilized by some clinicians (Waldinger, 1986). Unlike methadone, naltrexone has no narcotic effect of its own and is not physiologically addictive.

A chemical that is sometimes used to help alcoholics is disulfiram, commonly known as Antabuse. It is a medication that blocks the normal oxidation of alcohol so that acetaldehyde, a byproduct of alcohol, accumu-lates in the bloodstream and causes unpleasant, and at times even life-threatening, symptoms, such as rapid pulse and vomiting. This serves as a conscious deterrent to drinking while using Antabuse.

Although short-term use of the above drugs has been supported by many clinicians and researchers, the value of long-term utilization of any one of these chemical substitutes is questionable. They should be viewed as useful adjuncts to other forms of treatment for highly impulsive drug- and alcohol-abusing individuals but not as total treatment by themselves (Straussner, 1989).

A growing number of substance abuse settings are incorporating acu-puncture treatment during both the withdrawal process and the early phase of rehabilitation treatment. While research data are limited, acupuncture appears to be useful in alleviating withdrawal and craving symptoms of such substances as alcohol, heroin, and cocaine (Eckholm, 1986).

Outpatient Individual Therapy or Counseling

Generally, outpatient individual psychodynamically oriented psychotherapy is not recommended until the person is quite secure in his or her abstinence from chemicals, since the anxiety aroused during treatment may lead to the resumption of alcohol or drug use. Moreover, due to the impact of the chemicals on the brain and the possibility of blackouts (memory loss while intoxicated), individual counseling or therapy with an active substance abuser is frequently contraindicated (Levinson & Straussner, 1978). How-ever, if a client has stopped using substances or is making serious efforts to abstain from drug and alcohol use, ego-supportive counseling (Goldstein, 1984) or a self-psychological approach (Levin, 1987) can be particularly useful.

Since chronic substance abusers usually substitute a chemical for human contact, a crucial part of treatment is the establishment of a nonthreatening relationship with a caring and consistently reliable individual. The goal of individual treatment is to enhance patients' self-image and provide needed ego support so that they can begin to examine their use of chemicals and their current feelings and behavior.

The view of substance abuse as a disease is invaluable in helping drug and alcohol abusers to alleviate their frequently extreme feelings of guilt without absolving them from responsibility for their future behavior. This perspective also diminishes the usually negative countertransferential reactions of workers.

Group Interventions

Group counseling and group activities appear to be the treatment of choice for many substance abusers. Group therapy with other recovering substance abusers is useful in providing peer interaction and peer support, as well as in confronting substance-abusing patients with the consequences of their attitudes and behavior. The value of separate groups for substance-abusing women has been noted by many clinicians (Nichols, 1985).

Activity groups, such as cooking, program planning, sports, art, and so forth, allow for social interaction, the development of a variety of essential life skills, and sublimation of self- and other-destructive feelings (Brandler & Roman, 1991). Psychodrama groups are particularly helpful in concretizing and expressing repressed feelings and in dealing with unresolved dynamics of "unfinished business" (Blume, 1985; Buchbinder, 1986).

Self-help groups or "12-step" programs, such as Alcoholics Anonymous (AA), Narcotics Anonymous, Pills Anonymous, and Cocaine Anonymous, have proven to be particularly helpful and are free and available in every community. These groups provide continuously available support and help to replace drinking and drugging companions with a new group of peers with whom the substance abuser can identify. Self-help groups allow members not only to receive help but also to give help to others, thereby enhancing self-esteem.

It is strongly recommended that all clinicians attend a few "open" meetings of the various self-help groups, especially AA. At times, it may be helpful to escort a substance-abusing patient to a meeting or to encourage the client to call, in the presence of the worker, the main number of the self-help group (available in the phone book) and ask for help. Workers can also request a 12-step group to arrange for an institutional meeting for clients at the worker's agency.

In addition to 12-step groups, other self-help groups for substance abusers, such as Women for Sobriety, Rational Recovery, Social Workers Helping Social Workers, and Double Trouble/Recovery groups for the dually diagnosed, can be utilized where appropriate.

Psychoeducational Approaches

The value of didactic education as an effective interventive strategy has long been recognized in alcoholism treatment facilities, but only recently has this approach been utilized in other substance abuse settings.

Didactic lectures and discussion on such topics as the signs and symptoms of substance abuse and addiction, the addiction cycle for specific substances (such as cocaine, with its euphoric binges and depressive crashes), relapse prevention, the impact of substance abuse on the family, effective communication skills, coping with stress, human sexuality, and assertiveness training provide cognitive, non-ego-threatening understanding of the dynamics of substance abuse and what the individual and the family can do to help themselves. Such a psychoeducational approach can also be provided in settings that are not specifically connected to substance abuse and can include individual, group, or family treatment modalities.

Social Supports

Substance-abusing patients usually experience various social problems. Thus the provision of financial and social supports—including adequate housing, vocational rehabilitation programs, and legal assistance—is an essential aspect of helping this population.

STAGES OF TREATMENT

Treatment of clients with substance-abuse problems, as of any other client population, is an ongoing process that can be conceptualized as having a beginning, a middle or working phase, and an ending or termination stage.

Beginnings consist of assessing current substance use, focusing on the steps needed to achieve abstinence, and establishing a working relationship. As pointed out by Washton (1991), although a strong confrontational style has been institutionalized and traditionally encouraged in the addiction treatment field, such an approach tends to drive away the less motivated patient. Treatment studies show that although "patient characteristics did not differentiate between dropouts and treatment completers, clinicians with high dropout rates were characteristically more aggressive, controlling and critical while those with low dropouts tended to be more introspective, accepting and nurturing" (Washton, 1991, p. 8).

In addition to acceptance and nurturing, clinicians treating substance abusers may need to "lend one's ego" to a substance abuser whose judgment and reality testing have been impaired by use of chemicals as well as dysfunctional maturation. Direct advice-giving and limit-setting may be crucial during this stage, as is the use of collaterals both to obtain information and to provide emotional and economic support for the client.

An important aspect of beginning treatment is educating the clients to the psychophysiological impact of various substances so that they can, for example, differentiate between a depression caused by withdrawal from a stimulant and one due to unexpressed rage at a loved one. Workers also need to help clients make proper use of self-help groups, since such groups can provide advice and support between sessions and/or upon termination of treatment. (See Chapter 9 for further discussion of 12-step programs.) The beginning stage of treatment may also require extensive interdisciplinary collaborations and referrals. Finally, the worker must pay close attention to the use of self and transferential and countertransferential reactions. Interventions should be guided by clients' needs and abilities, not by workers' needs to rescue clients or by their anger at clients for not living up to workers' expectations.

Once a client is able to achieve abstinance, the work, with the same or a different clinician, moves into middle phase of treatment. During this stage issues such as psychological mourning for the lost substance (Goldberg, 1985), grief, depression, guilt, shame, and a sense of loss over wasted years need to be addressed. For some, the middle phase may involve dealing with early life traumas, including physical and sexual abuse, or confusion about sexuality and role identity; examining and modifing dysfunctional patterns of defense and coping mechanisms and improving interpersonal relationships may also be part of the work at this time. During this phase, clients need to learn how to both accept and prevent slips (relapse prevention; see Chapter 19) as well as and how to develop the ego function of adoptive regression, that is, how to relax, play, and have fun without alcohol or other drugs. Lastly, they need help in learning how to forgive themselves and others.

The final phase of treatment, the process of termination, may require helping patients cope with separation and loss without regressing to the use of substances.

SPECIAL TREATMENT ISSUES AND SPECIAL POPULATIONS

Space limitations preclude a comprehensive discussion of the numerous treatment issues and the unique treatment needs of various substance-abusing populations. For example, clinicians need to take into account the life cycle stages of clients (Carter & McGoldrick, 1980) and to realize that both assessment and intervention with an alcohol-abusing 17-year-old male will differ from that with a 67-year-old alcohol-abusing man. The issue of gender also has to be addressed differentially (see Chapter 14), as does that of patients with dual disorders (Chapter 3).

Treatment of minorities, particularly African-American clients, needs to take into account that "to survive in a brutalizing, inhospitable world, minorities have a higher tolerance for emotional pain. So they become an enabling community that tolerates addiction" (O'Connell, 1991, p. 13). Minorites are more likely to enter treatment through the courts than through formal intervention processes or 12-step programs, and they are more likely to access treatment much later and thus have a more difficult recovery process (O'Connell, 1991).

Ethnocultural norms and values need to be taken into account in treatment planning and relapse prevention with each client, as do issues of sexual identity and sexual behavior, including safe sex. The special needs of substance abusing gay and lesbian clients need to be addressed (Finnegan & McNally, 1987). While attention needs to be devoted to AIDS among intravenous drug abusers, it is important to be aware that the incident of AIDS is also very high among alcoholics, many of whom are HIV positive or have lost a close friend to this illness. Lastly, we need to remember that substance abuse, "like many other medical problems, is a chronic disorder in which recurrences are common and repeated periods of treatment are frequently required" (USDHHS, 1991b, p. 4).

IMPACT OF SUBSTANCE ABUSE ON THE FAMILY

Life with a substance-abusing family member is typically full of inconsistency and unpredictability, resulting in a chronic state of crisis. Legal and financial problems, serious illnesses, and various accidents are common occurrences impacting on family life. When the substance abuser is a parent, dysfunctional cross-generational alliance and role reversal (with children assuming parental roles and responsibilities) are frequently seen (Straussner et al., 1979). Child neglect and, in more disturbed families, violence between parents, child abuse, and incest are some of the consequences and correlates of substance abuse, particularly alcohol abuse (Straussner 1989). Neonatal crack and alcohol addictions and subsequent developmental and emotional impairments are growing national problems.

The impact of substance abuse on the family has additional intergenerational repercussions: The sons of alcoholic fathers are four times more likely to become alcoholics, while the daughters of alcoholics are three times more likely to become alcoholics. Moreover, the daughters of alcoholics are also more likely to marry alcoholics (Straussner, 1985). Although less documented, intergenerational repercussion also exist for families with parental opiate addiction. Studies of children of narcotic addicts indicate that they are more likely to be abusing drugs and/or alcohol than their peers (Sowder & Burt, 1980).

Intervention with Family Members

Couples and family therapy, including multifamily groups (Kaufman, 1985), are effective modalities for families with substance abusers who are already chemically free or working on their recovery.

It is also beneficial to refer family members to such self-help groups as Al-Anon, Pill-Anon, Co-Anon, or Nar-Anon. These groups help adult family members examine their own role in the "enabling" behavior (Levinson & Straussner, 1978) that allows for the continuous perpetuation of the problems and to obtain support from others in the same circumstances. These groups are particularly useful for parents and spouses of substance abusers.

Adolescent children of alcohol- and narcotic-abusing parents may benefit from such self-help groups as Alateen and Narateen. Adult Children of Alcoholics (ACOA) groups have been found to be extremely helpful for mature adolescents and adult children of alcoholics and are increasing rapidly throughout the country, as are Codependency Anonymous (Coda) groups aimed at helping people identify and work on their unmet dependency needs.

Intervention with latency-aged and adolescent children of substance abusers must focus not only on how to say "no" to their own substance use and abuse but also on helping the child recognize and understand familial substance abuse and its impact on them and other family members. Extensive literature written directly for children and adolescents can be obtained from Al-Anon and Nar-Anon and is extremely valuable in helping children to begin to understand what has happened to them and, hopefully, prevent the pattern from repeating itself in the next generation.

Clinicians must also be aware of their own countertransferential reaction to families of substance abusers, particularly in view of the fact that many in the helping professions are themselves affected by familial substance abuse.[1]

CONCLUSION

Helping substance-abusing clients and their families is a difficult, challenging, yet frequently highly rewarding task. It is a task that requires a variety of

---

[1] A 1987 survey of all first-year graduate students at a major school of social work found that 27% had a substance-abusing parent and 15% had a substance-abusing sibling. Interestingly, while the parents tended to be alcoholics, the siblings tended to be cocaine or heroin abusers (Straussner, 1987).

treatment modalities and interventive approaches and calls upon the worker to be a good diagnostician, a therapist, an educator, an advocate, and an educated consumer of never-ending research data. Most of all, it requires a clinician who is sensitive to the impact of substance abuse on the individual and on others, who can appreciate the strengths and the courage that these clients present, and who can provide hope for a better tomorrow.

REFERENCES

Abraham, K. (1979). The psychological relations between sexuality and alcoholism. In *Selected papers on psychoanalysis*. New York: Brunner/Mazel. (Original work published 1908)

Alexander, B. K., & Dibb, G. S. (1975). Opiate addicts and their parents. *Family Process, 14*, 499–514.

American Psychiatric Association. (1987). *Diagnostic and statistical manual of mental disorders* (3rd ed., rev.). Washington, DC: Author.

Barrett, R. J. (1985). Behavioral approaches to individual differences in substance abuse: Drug-taking behavior. In M. Galizio & S. Maisto (Eds.), *Determinants of substance abuse treatment: Biological, psychological, and environmental factors*. New York: Plenum.

Black, R., & Mayer, J. (1980). Parents with special problems: Alcoholism and opiate addictions. In C. H. Kempe & R. Helfer (Eds.), *The battered child*. Chicago: University of Chicago Press.

Blume, S. B. (1985). Psychodrama and the treatment of alcoholism. In S. Zimberg, J. Wallace, & S. Blume (Eds.), *Practical approaches to alcoholism psychotherapy*. New York: Plenum.

Brandler, S., & Roman, C. P. (1991). *Group work: Skills and strategies for effective interventions*. New York: Haworth.

Brody, J. E. (1986, January 15). Personal health. *New York Times*, p. C-6.

Buchbinder, J. (1986) Gestalt therapy and its application to alcoholism treatment. *Alcoholism Treatment Quarterly, 13*(2), 49–67.

Care of babies for cocaine is put at $504 million a year. (1991, September 19). *New York Times*, p. B-4.

Carroll, C. R. (1985). *Drugs in modern society*. Dubuque, IA: Brown.

Carter, E. A., & McGoldrick, M. (1980). The family life cycle and family therapy: An overview. In E. A. Carter & M. McGoldrick (Eds.), *The family life cycle: A framework for family therapy*. New York: Gardner.

Deren, S. (1986). Children of substance abusers: A review of the literature. *Journal of Substance Abuse Treatment, 3*, 77–94.

Eckholm, E. (1986, November 20). Acupuncture in medicine is still a disputed method. *New York Times*, pp. B-1, B-16.

Ewing, J. A. (1984). Detecting alcoholism: The CAGE questionnaire. *Journal of the American Medical Association, 252*, 1905–1907.

Fenichel, O. (1945). *The psychoanalytic theory of neurosis*. New York: Norton.

Finnegan, D. G., & McNally, E. B. (1987). *Dual identities: Counseling chemically dependent gay men and lesbians.* Center City, MN: Hazelden Foundation.

Finnegan, L. P. (1985). Focus on illicit drugs. *Drug and Alcohol Dependence, 9*(6), 9.

Freud, S. (1954). Letter 79, December 22, 1897. In *The origins of psycho-analysis: Letters to Wilhelm Fliess, drafts and notes: 1887-1902* (M. Bonaparte, A. Freud, & E. Kris, Eds.; E. Mosbacher & J. Strachey, Trans.). London: Imago. (Original work published 1897).

Freud, S. (1958). Psycho-analytic notes on an autobiographical account of a case of paranoia. In *Standard Edition* (Vol. 12). London: Hogarth. (Original work published 1911)

Gerstein, D. R., & Harwood, H. J. (Eds.). (1990). *Treating drug problems* (Vol. 1). Washington, DC: National Academy Press.

Goldberg, M. (1985). Loss and grief: Major dynamics in the treatment of alcoholism. In D. Cook, S. L. A. Straussner, & C. Fewell (Eds.), *Psychosocial issues in the treatment of alcoholism.* New York: Haworth.

Goldstein, E. (1984). *Ego psychology and social work treatment.* New York: Free Press.

Goodwin, D. W. (1984). Studies of familial alcoholism: A review. *Journal of Clinical Psychiatry, 45*(2), 14-17.

Goodwin, D. W., Schulsinger, F., Moller, N., Hermansen, L., Winokur, G., & Guze, S. B. (1974). Drinking problems in adopted and nonadopted sons of alcoholics. *Archives of General Psychiatry, 31,* 164-169.

Goodwin, D. W., Schulsinger, F., Hermansen, L., Guze, S. B., & Winocur, G. (1973). Alcohol problems in adoptees raised apart from alcoholic biological parents. *Archives of General Psychiatry, 28,* 238-243.

Griffin, R. E. (1991). Assessing the drug involved client. *Families in Society: Journal of Contemporary Human Services, 72*(2), 87-94.

Griffin, T., & Svendsen, R. (1986). *Student assistance program.* Minneapolis, MN: Hazelden Foundation.

Herd, D. (1989). The epidemiology of drinking patterns and alcohol related problems among U.S. blacks. In *The epidemiology of alcohol use and abuse among U.S. minorities* (USDHHS NIAAA Monograph No. 18, Pub. No. (ADM)89-1435). Washington, DC: U.S. Government Printing Office.

Hindman, M. (1979). Family violence: An overview. *Alcohol Health and Research World, 4*(1), 2-11.

Jellinek, E. M. (1952). Phases of alcohol addiction. *Quarterly Journal of Studies on Alcohol, 13,* 673-684.

Johnson, V. E. (1986), *Intervention: How to help someone who doesn't want help.* Minneapolis, MN: Johnson Institute Books.

Johnston, L., O'Malley, P., & Bachman, J. (1988). *Illicit drug use, smoking and drinking by America's high school students, college students and young adults: 1975-1987.* Rockville, MD: National Institute on Drug Abuse.

Kaufman, E. (1985). *Substance abuse and family therapy.* New York: Grune & Stratton.

Kernberg, O. (1975). *Borderline conditions and pathological narcissism.* New York: Aronson.

Khantzian, E. J. (1981). Some treatment implications of ego and self-disturbances in alcoholism. In M. H. Bean & N. E. Zimberg (Eds.), *Dynamic approaches to the understanding and treatment of alcoholism.* New York: Free Press.

King, B. (1986). Decision making in the intervention process. *Alcoholism Treatment Quarterly, 3*(3), 5–22.

Kohut, H. (1971). *The analysis of the self: A systematic approach to the psychoanalytic treatment of narcissistic personality disorders.* New York: International Universities Press.

Kohut, H. (1977). Preface. In *Psychodynamics of drug dependence* (NIDA Research Monograph No. 12). Washington, DC: U.S. Government Printing Office.

Levin, J. D. (1987). *Treatment of alcoholism and other addictions: A self psychology approach.* Northvale, NJ: Aronson.

Levin, J. D. (1990). *Alcoholism: A bio-psycho-social approach.* New York: Hemisphere.

Levinson, V., & Straussner, S. L. A. (1978). Social workers as "enablers" in the treatment of alcoholics. *Social Casework, 59*(1), 14–20.

Mark, F. (1988). Does coercion work? The role of referral source in motivating alcoholics in treatment. *Alcoholism Treatment Quarterly, 5*(3), 5–22.

Marlatt, G. A., Baer, J. S., Donovan, D. M., & Kivlahan, D. R. (1988). Addictive behaviors: Etiology and treatment. *Annual Review of Psychology, 39*, 223–252.

Mayfield, D., McLeod, G. N., & Hall, P. (1974). The CAGE questionnarie: Validation of a new alcoholism screening instrument. *American Journal of Psychiatry, 131*(10), 1121–1123.

McClelland, D. C., Davis, W., Kalin, R., & Wanner, E. (1972). *The drinking man: Alcohol and human motivation.* New York: Free Press.

Menninger, K. (1938). *Man against himself.* New York: Harcourt Brace.

Nadel, M. (1985). Offspring with fetal alcohol effects: Identification and intervention. In D. Cook, S. L. A. Straussner, & C. Fewell (Eds.), *Psychosocial issues in the treatment of alcoholism.* New York: Haworth.

New York State Division of Alcoholism and Alcohol Abuse. (1988). *Alcohol problems prevention/intervention programs: Guidelines for college campuses.* Albany, NY: Author.

Nichols, M. (1985). Theoretical concerns in the clinical treatment of substance abusing women: A feminist analysis. In D. Cook, S. L. A. Straussner, & C. Fewell (Eds.), *Psychosocial issues in the treatment of alcoholism.* New York: Haworth.

O'Connell, T. (1991). Treatment of minorities. *Drug and Alcohol Dependence, 15*(10), 13.

Pattison, E. M., & Kaufman, E. (1982). Alcoholism syndrome, definition and models. In E. M. Pattison & E. Kaufman (Eds.), *Encyclopedic handbook of alcoholism.* New York: Gardner.

Porjesz, B., & Begleiter, H. (1985). Human brain electrophysiology and alcoholism. In R. E. Tarter & D. H. van Thiel (Eds.), *Alcohol and the brain.* New York: Plenum.

Schuckit, M., Goodwin, D. W., & Winokur, G. (1972). A study of alcoholism in half-siblings. *American Journal of Psychiatry, 128*, 1132–1136.

Soika, S. H. (1983). Mental illness and alcoholism: Implications for treatment. In D. Cook, C. Fewell, & J. Riolo (Eds.), *Social work treatment of alcohol problems.* New Brunswick, NJ: Rutgers Center for Alcohol Studies.

Sowder, B., & Burt, M. (1980). *Children of heroin addicts: An assessment of health, learning, behavioral and adjustment problems.* New York: Praeger.

Steinglass, P., Weiner, S., & Mendelson, J. H. (1971). A systems approach to alcoholism: A model and its clinical application. *Archives of General Psychiatry*, 24, 401–408.

Straussner, S. L. A. (1985). Alcoholism in women: Current knowledge and implications for treatment. In D. Cook, S. L. A. Straussner, & C. Fewell (Eds.), *Psychosocial issues in the treatment of alcoholism*. New York: Haworth.

Straussner, S. L. A. (1987). *Substance abuse training for MSW students: Survey findings*. Unpublished study.

Straussner, S. L. A. (1989). Intervention with maltreating parents who are drug and alcohol abusers. In S. Ehrenkranz, E. Goldstein, L. Goodman, & J. Seinfeld (Eds.), *Clinical social work with maltreated children and their families: An introduction to practice*. New York: New York University Press.

Straussner, S. L. A., Kitman, C., Straussner, J. H., & Demos, E. (1980). The alcoholic housewife: A psychosocial analysis. *Focus on Women*, 1(1), 15–32.

Straussner, S. L. A., Weinstein, D., & Hernandez, R. (1979). Effects of alcoholism on the family system. *Health and Social Work*, 4(4), 111–127.

Sue, D. (1987). Use and abuse of alcohol by Asian Americans. *Journal of Psychoactive Drugs*, 19(1), 57–66.

Tabakoff, B., Hoffman, P. L., Lee, J. M., Saito, T., Willard, B., & De Leon-Jones, F. (1988). Differences in platelet enzyme activity between alcoholics and controls. *New England Journal of Medicine*, 318, 134–139.

Tillich, P. (1952). *The courage to be*. New Haven, CT: Yale University Press.

Trice, H. M., & Beyer, J. M. (1984). Work related outcomes of the constructive-confrontation strategy in a job based alcoholism program. *Journal of Studies on Alcohol*, 45, 393–404.

U.S. Department of Health and Human Services. (1989). *Substance abuse among blacks in the U.S.* (NIDA Capsules). Washington, DC: U.S. Government Printing Office.

U.S. Department of Health and Human Services. (1990). *Seventh special report to the U.S. Congress on alcohol and health*. Washington, DC: U.S. Government Printing Office.

U.S. Department of Health and Human Services (1991a). *Assessing alcoholism* (Alcohol Alert, NIAAA, No. 12 PH 294). Washington, DC: U.S. Government Printing Office.

U.S. Department of Health and Human Services. (1991b). *Drug abuse and drug abuse research: The third triennial report to Congress from the Secretary, Department of Health and Human Services*. Washington, DC: U.S. Government Printing Office.

Waldinger, R. J. (1986). *Fundamentals of psychiatry*. Washington, DC: American Psychiatric Press.

Washton, A. M. (1991). Attitudes shape treatment. *Drug and Alcohol Dependence*, 15(8), 8.

Washton, A. M., & Gold, M. S. (1987). Recent trend in cocaine abuse as seen from the "800-Cocaine" hotline. In A. M. Washton & M. S. Gold (Eds.), *Cocaine: A clinician's handbook*. New York: Guilford.

Wetli, C. V. (1987) Fatal reactions to cocaine. In A. M. Washton & M. S. Gold (Eds.), *Cocaine: A clinician's handbook*. New York: Guilford.

Williams, G. D., Grant, B. F., Hartford, T. C., & Noble, J. (1989). Population projections using DSM III criteria: Alcohol abuse and dependence 1990–2000. *Alcohol Health and Research World, 13*(4), 366–370.

Wright, J. (1985). Domestic violence and substance abuse: A cooperative approach toward working with dually affected families. In E. Freeman (Ed.), *Social work practice with clients who have alcohol problems.* Springfield, IL: Thomas.

Wurmser, L. (1978). *The hidden dimension: Psychodynamics in compulsive drug use.* New York: Aronson.

Zimmerman, R. (1991). Alcohol, drug separation draws controversy. *Drug and Alcohol Dependence, 15*(3), 13.

Issues in Assessment and Intervention with Substance Abusers in Various Settings

II

Assessment and Intervention with Drug and Alcohol Abusers in Medical Facilities

Fran M. Silverman

HOSPITALS TODAY

Today's general hospital is a far cry from days gone by. Previously, most patients were admitted directly by their private physician; hospitals, though busy, were not filled to maximum bed capacity. The length of stay was not a driving force motivating discharge planning, since insurance companies paid for each day regardless of the number of days in the hospital or the diagnosis.

Currently the health care environment is one in which most admissions enter the hospital through the emergency room. Patients arrive in acute distress and in medical and psychosocial crises. Many patients, particularly in the inner city, do not have private doctors and do not receive ongoing medical care. When hospitalization occurs, their medical condition is quite serious. Lengths of stay are rising, since patients are sicker and there are fewer resources available to them upon discharge. Hospitals run at almost 100% capacity (Greater New York Hospital Association, 1990). Reimbursement systems pay for days related to a diagnosis and not necessarily for an entire length of stay. Any rise in length of stay or decrease in the number of patients is financially disadvantageous for hospitals (Greater New York Hospital Association, 1988).

These factors create stress among the health care teams, since they are treating larger numbers of patients with limited resources and staff. Hospitals today can afford neither to augment staffing nor to divert patients to other facilities.

A high percentage of current admissions consist of individuals who have drug and/or alcohol problems as comorbid conditions to the medical condition for which they have been admitted (Moore et al., 1989). Studies conducted in the early 1980s found that 14% of medical patients suffered from alcohol or other substance abuse disorders (Coulehan, Zettler-Segal, Block, McClelland, & Schulberg, 1987; Sherin, Piotrowski, Panek, & Doot, 1982). Recent studies indicate an increased prevalence: A national survey concluded that a minimum of 25% of all inpatients have significant alcohol problems; a New York City metropolitan area survey showed that, on average, 21% of all hospitalized patients were unrecognized or undiagnosed alcoholics (New York State Division of Alcoholism and Alcohol Abuse [NYSDAA], 1990).

Despite the high incidence of drug and/or alcohol abusers in the general hospital population, these patients are frequently not identified by clinicians as substance abusers, thereby causing unintended negative consequences for the patient, the institution, and the social worker.

This chapter describes common barriers to the identification and effective management of substance abusers a well as suggesting various assessment and interventive strategies for hospital social workers as they face a difficult patient population in a demanding and stressful hospital environment.

IMPACT OF DRUG- AND ALCOHOL-ABUSING PATIENTS ON HOSPITALS

While substance abuse is not the primary reason for most hospital admissions, there are many medical conditions that result from it and that frequently complicate medical problems and adjustment to hospitalization (Coulehan et al., 1987).

Comorbidity is frequently evidenced in specialty areas of the hospital. Within orthopedic services, approximately 18% of the patients screen positive for substance abuse (Sherin et al., 1982); in obstetrics/gynecology, the figure is 12.5% and rising; in neurology, 19%; and 23% of surgical patients were found to abuse drugs or alcohol (Moore et al., 1989).

Generally the lifestyle of a drug or alcohol abuser makes medical care a low priority. Frequently the patient's substance abuse is a "secret," and seeking medical attention threatens to expose it. The emergency room may be the primary point of entry into the health care system as the patient's condition reaches crisis proportions (Richter & Stanitis, 1987). However, even at this point the patient's substance abuse frequently goes unnoticed and undiagnosed.

Therefore substance abusers have high rates of readmission and continue to overuse emergency rooms. The hospitals incur excessive costs, since treatment in the emergency room is highly labor- and resource-intensive. Further, if these patients continue to utilize emergency rooms in record numbers and are subsequently readmitted (often with increasingly longer hospital stays), the continual drain of resources and staff ultimately decreases revenue potential and effective staff functioning.

While hospital social workers' caseloads have been steadily increasing in general, substance-abusing patients in particular intensify the workload in that they seem never to get better or they do not cooperate with the social workers' best-laid plans and intentions (Lerner, 1978). Further, the social and behavioral problems exhibited by many substance abusers—which must be addressed by the social worker—are time-consuming and frustrating.

Hospitals require that discharges be implemented in an efficient and safe manner, and it is the social worker who is responsible for this extremely critical clinical and financial aspect of care. Patients and their families will often thwart discharge plans due to the behavioral and familial sequelae of substance abuse. If the patient's substance abuse goes undiagnosed, a vicious cycle is created. Discharges are not executed in a timely manner, length of stay is increased, hospital staff and resources are not being maximized, and the worker may feel less effective. The worker, although not treating the substance abuse problem, nonetheless is continually confronted with the negative consequences of the abuse.

The failure to identify and treat the substance abuser adequately also has unintended consequences for the patients themselves. Patients have increased mortality and morbidity; they also suffer economic, social, and legal problems due to hospital bills, loss of employment, loss of entitlements, family disruption, and run-ins with the law (Moore et al., 1989; Westermeyer, 1986). Patients whose substance abuse continues to go unnoticed and untreated are vulnerable to a future of repeated hospitalizations and deteriorating health. Each hospitalization is therefore more difficult and complex and less responsive to intervention. The vicious cycle continues for patient, worker, and institution.

BARRIERS TO PROPER ASSESSMENT AND INTERVENTION

Considering all the highly trained and skilled professionals involved in the health care system, why do we continue to fail in proper assessment of and intervention with these high-risk patients? Lack of knowledge, stereotyping, and the "invisible" nature of these problems appear to be the most common barriers to effective work with substance abusers in medical settings.

Lack of Knowledge

Social workers as well as other health care providers are frequently unaware of the enormous variety of symptoms and comorbid conditions that are associated with drug and/or alcohol abuse (Clark, 1981), in large part because they lack an understanding of alcoholism and other substance abuse as a disease. They therefore fail to realize that addiction is multidetermined, that it can be diagnosed, and that it is therefore amenable to treatment (Clark, 1981). Further, those who work in inner cities see a disproportionate number of indigent, multiproblemed patients, providing them a dismal view of the addiction and the value of treatment. Professionals feel inadequate confronting these patients, perceiving a lack of skill in themselves and believing that only those trained to treat substance abusers can do so (Clark, 1981; Moore et al., 1989; NYSDAA, 1990).

Stereotypes

Stereotypic ideas of substance abusers accompanied by negative or value-laden attitudes tend to obscure the clinician's objective ability to recognize the problem and thus deal effectively with the illness. It is believed that substance abuse is predominantly found among the young, minority groups, poor people, and men (Moore et al., 1989). However, substance abuse is present across all socioeconomic lines, across all ethnic and cultural groups, and across gender and age lines (National Institute on Drug Abuse, 1989).

Workers must assess the possibility of substance abuse in all patients, since it is a potential problem for all. If they do not do so, they will fail to adequately address the true nature of the problem, missing the underlying or comorbid condition of substance abuse as exemplified in the case below:

> A 70-year-old Caucasian wife of a physician was hospitalized for repeated dizzy spells and falling. An intensive medical workup showed no abnormal findings. The etiology of her dizziness remained a mystery until it was discovered that she was abusing sleeping pills and tranquilizers "left around the house" by her physician husband. The medical team had not suspected substance abuse as a possible cause for her dizzy spells, since she did not fit their preconceived ideas as to who abuses drugs.

Health care professionals do not understand that patients may be predisposed toward addiction by genetic factors and familial patterns rather than driven by moral deficiency and willful self-destruction (Clark, 1981). Certainly the addicted are not necessarily more culpable than individuals incapacitated by other chronic and debilitating diseases.

Further, diminution of the ability to identify and treat the substance abuser is related to social workers' and other health care providers' frequent attitude that these patients cannot or do not want to get better. These patients' recidivism can make professionals feel inadequate and hopeless about any possible positive outcome of their intervention. They feel power-less to have an impact on relapses, not understanding that relapse is often part of the illness and subsequent recovery (Vaillant, 1983; Westermeyer, 1986).

It is not uncommon to hear a worker say that she has seen this patient before and that as soon as he is discharged he will go back to using drugs. Since, in many workers' minds, patients' return to substance use is a foregone conclusion, they do not attempt to discuss patients' abuse or suggest avenues toward recovery. As a result, patients will indeed continue using drugs or alcohol and be rehospitalized with similar, if not worse, medical problems.

Any of these attitudes, perceptions, or feelings about the substance abuser can inhibit or destroy the potential for establishing a meaningful therapeutic relationship, the basis of social work practice.

Not My Job—Not My Illness

Compounding the "invisible" nature of this patient population is the fact that the patient's presenting problem is often not substance abuse. The treatment team can therefore legitimize ignoring the abuse and focusing only on the presenting medical condition and/or explain away the manifestations of the abuse by ascribing them to such psychiatric problems as depression.

Patients may deny they have a problem or refuse to discuss issues "unrelated" to their primary admitting diagnosis and illness. Interestingly, they may make their substance abuse visible through the management diffi-culties they present, such as hostility, anger, demanding of staff time, exhibit-ing of emotional lability, and "lying" as they give their histories. Such behaviors, however, alienate professionals and prevent them from develop-ing the positive working relationship that is essential to tackling the difficult problems of substance abuse. Therefore, the patient's invisibility is secure.

INITIAL ASSESSMENT

Proper assessment and early intervention can be achieved only if the worker is open to the possibility that substance abuse is present. Workers must not let the complexity of the diagnosis or the patient's multitude of problems and negative behaviors interfere with the recognition of substance abuse (Vail-lant, 1983).

There are various signs that can alert workers that a more detailed investigation of substance abuse should be undertaken. Special skills are not necessary, since most social workers are trained to begin where the "patient is at" and to gather as much information as possible for a comprehensive biopsychosocial assessment.

Related Medical Problems

The cluster of medical problems and symptoms for which the patient has been admitted can indicate the presence of substance abuse. Alcoholism is highly correlated with certain medical conditions, some of which may be caused by the substance itself: cirrhosis and pancreatitis are illnesses present when a patient's alcohol problem is far advanced; conditions such as hypertension, diabetes, ulcers, and gastritis are exacerbated by the effects of alcohol consumption (Coulehan et al., 1987; Moore et al., 1989; Richter & Stanitis, 1987); increased heart rate, elevated blood pressure, convulsions, ventricular arrhythmia, and delirium can all be secondary to cocaine or barbiturate use. Drug and alcohol abusers are frequently involved in accidents, falls, incidents causing burns, and physical confrontations for which they seek medical attention (Richter & Stanitis, 1987). Abrupt withdrawal of substances such as alcohol or barbiturates can cause such symptoms as tremors, nausea, and headaches. Depression is common in withdrawal. "Crashing" from a cocaine euphoria can cause depression as well as paranoia and restlessness (Richter & Stanitis, 1987).

Some of the symptoms are transient, present upon initial evaluation but remitting through time; others are indications of chronic illnesses or long-standing medical problems. Identification of these symptoms is the beginning step toward breaking the cycle of substance abuse.

The reading and review of the medical chart is a useful beginning tool in the assessment process. Initial admission notes, especially those from the emergency room, contain a wealth of information. The patient may have entered the emergency room smelling of alcohol or in a "high" state that would be indicated in an initial chart note.

During admission the patient may be in a state of crisis and reveal facts that are related to substance abuse. However, when the medical condition has stabilized, the patient may "forget" or deny certain facts and circumstances, supplying "logical" causes for the admitting condition other than substance abuse. Careful fact-finding can reveal that incidents necessitating admission occurred while the patient was under the influence of drugs or alcohol. For example:

> A 28-year-old male was admitted to the hospital for cardiac arrythmia and shortness of breath. When being interviewed on the cardiac unit by the social worker, he was concerned about his heart problem. Earlier in

the emergency room, fearing that he was going to die from a heart attack, he reported that he had snorted "just a little bit of cocaine" prior to the attack. On the unit and no longer in crisis, he failed to mention his cocaine use, focusing only on his supposed heart problem. As the worker had read the emergency room note, she was able to confront the young man about his drug abuse. She told him what was contained in the initial note regarding his cocaine use and explained to him the effects of cocaine on the heart, which can indeed mimic a heart attack, causing palpitations, increased perspiration, and shortness of breath. In this way she helped make sense out of a frightening situation for the patient and paved the way for further discussion of his drug use.

Physical Presentation

In addition to the medical chart and related medical conditions, the worker can also find clues in the patient's physical presentation. Patients who abuse alcohol and/or cocaine can be quite thin, since progressive lifestyle changes and loss of appetite often result from the substance abuse. Patients may have swollen limbs due to alcohol abuse; scratching due to withdrawal from narcotics; red eyes due either to being intoxicated or high at admission or to lack of sleep resulting from use of cocaine or other stimulants.

Physical observation of the patient, therefore, is a critical skill whose importance in the assessment phase should not be underestimated. If physical manifestations are present, it is incumbent upon the worker to further explore other aspects of the patient's presentation and/or functioning in order to further substantiate a substance abuse disorder.

Cognitive Impairments

As the worker interviews the patient, it is crucial to be attuned to additional evidence of substance abuse. Patients may be "fuzzy" in the interview. Facts are forgotten or, due to "blackout" during various incidents, the story does not fit together logically, with important events and dates presented incorrectly. Although the patient's inability to focus or concentrate in the interview may be a clue to substance abuse, it makes it difficult to gather information or form a meaningful therapeutic relationship (Clark, 1981).

Neurological evaluations may show cognitive impairments such as confusion of time sequences, memory deficits such as forgetting the facts or emotional content of recent incidents (Clark, 1981), and impaired ability to reason abstractly that impedes problem-solving skills.

Denial of Abuse

Denial of the problem is a strong component of substance abuse. Patients may want to cover up their drug abuse, since it is not socially acceptable. They may try to delay or to distort the interview process in order to keep the worker at bay and thus prevent detection of the substance abuse.

Frequently patients do not recognize that their pattern of substance use is causing them untold social and medical difficulties. They underestimate how much or how often they use drugs or alcohol. They minimize the negative impact it has had on their life and health, blame others, or project their problems onto the environment. They do not acknowledge their destructive pattern of abuse (Levinson & Straussner, 1978; Vaillant, 1983; Westermeyer, 1986). Denial is so strong a symptom of substance abuse that workers can become frustrated and exasperated by the strength of patients' convictions that they do not have a problem, becoming helpless in the face of this illogical yet strongly held belief.

Behavioral Signs

Concomitant behavioral problems are evident during interviews and in the patient's management on the unit. They may be angry or irritable, show erratic shifts in mood, be depressed, steal from other patients, or be manipulative and demanding (Bartek, Lindeman, Newton, Fitzgerald, & Hawks, 1988).

Workers must keep in mind that the patient is not "doing this to them." This is how the patient is, both in and outside the hospital. Many patients have survived living on the street or living in secret shame and dread that their abuse will be recognized. They have developed behavioral patterns that distance them from people, that intimidate others so that the abusers can get what they want without being challenged.

Substance abusers do not know how to relate to the world without drugs or alcohol. Consequently, when without these substances they become anxious, fearful, or demanding. They exhibit drug-seeking behavior, such as attempts to get sleeping pills, sedatives, or pain medications, in order to calm down, or they request food or cigarettes to fill the void they feel.

Psychosocial Clues

As workers interview and obtain a psychosocial picture of a patient's lifestyle, functional abilities, finances, social supports, and family dynamics, further evidence of substance abuse emerges. Such information can be used in sessions to assist patients in identifying the extent of their addiction and its impact on their health and life.

An erratic work history is a key psychosocial indicator of substance abuse. The alcohol or drug abuser may not be able to sustain gainful employment. They may be frequently late or absent entirely due to late-night binges or hangovers. Cognitive deficits in concentration and memory may make it difficult for them to follow instructions. Arguments on the job can make them too difficult to employ. Frequently they quit before they are "caught" or fired.

Often these patients externalize their problem by supplying other "logical" explanations for their erratic job history or poor work performance. They may blame their boss, their coworkers; the work was boring; the job was too far away to arrive on time. However, workers who recognize these defensive explanations as a way for patients to avoid identifying the problem are better equipped to confront patients about their addiction.

Another key indicator of substance abuse is mismanagement of funds, with subsequent social upheaval. Homelessness is a major social problem of our day and does not necessarily indicate substance abuse. However, a worker must explore why an individual and/or family is homeless. Is it due to an erratic work history and therefore erratic flow of financial support? Is it related to the nonpayment of rent in favor of buying drugs and alcohol? Are bills paid regularly? Does the patient owe money to friends, family, loan sharks? Is there gas, electricity, adequate food in the household? Exploring the patient's ability to maintain him- or herself in the community can point worker and patient toward correctly identifying the problem of substance abuse, which can then be addressed while the patient is under medical care.

A further dimension of the impact of alcohol and drug abuse on the patient's ability to be self-sustaining in the community is exposed when it becomes apparent that social supports, such as friends and family, are absent or erratic. The patient may claim to be a "loner" or treated unfairly by others, again externalizing the problem. Such individuals have difficulty recognizing that they have alienated these important people due to their substance abuse and the manner in which they related to them.

Substance abuse subjects all family members to stress and fear. They may suffer from emotional or physical neglect. To one degree or another all are affected. For this reason addiction may be referred to as a family illness or disease (Ackerman, 1983; Cermak, 1986; McCrady, 1989; Straussner, Weinstein, & Hernandez, 1979).

How the family members relate to one another and the information they reveal or obscure may provide clues pointing to substance abuse. Family members develop certain roles and behavior in adjusting to life with an addicted person, sometimes becoming enablers—"rescuing" the dependent individual, minimizing the unhealthy situation, and thereby indirectly supporting continued substance abuse (McCrady, 1989). A child may perform caretaking responsibilities that the parent is unable to do; a spouse may lie to the abuser's employer, relatives, or friends to hide the substance problem; the family may label the patient's use as social.

Enabling conceals the presence of substance abuse so that its negative consequences are not confronted by family or patient (Ackerman, 1983; Kackson, 1954; Steinglass, 1985). Thus it maintains the family's equilibrium, albeit a dysfunctional one. Enabling also perpetuates a vicious circle of guilt, shame, and deterioration (Levinson & Straussner, 1978) that is similar to the patient's own denial of substance abuse.

Following the various clues presented in the assessment phase, a diagnosis of substance abuse can be made. Attention to this aspect of the patient's condition will aid in successful intervention and ultimately in effective discharge planning.

INTERVENTION AND DISCHARGE PLANNING

Hospital social workers know that discharge planning begins at the time of admission. Thoughts of where patients will be going, what they may need, and who will be necessary to implement the plan in a timely and efficient manner are present in initial contact and assessment. Discharge planning fuels the interventions for the worker. A corollary of discharge is the ability to develop a plan that will diminish the likelihood of readmission to the hospital.

As previously described, many hospitalizations have substance abuse as a comorbid condition to their admitting diagnosis. If planning is to be effective, substance abuse must be addressed in the discharge phase and aftercare plan. Though this appears logical, it is a difficult challenge for the worker, since patients have been hospitalized for reasons other than drug or alcohol abuse; they deny their substance problem and are adept at keeping it secret, making them difficult to engage and ultimately to plan with and for.

The case examples below illustrate both the importance of assessing the presence of a substance problem and the application of social work interventions on various hospital units. Each unit type has its own set of difficulties; however, the generic skills employed to effect discharge in each example can be applied to all units.

Begin Where the Patient Is

Despite all evidence presented to patients regarding their substance abuse, frequently they will continue to deny or minimize the extent of their alcohol or drug problem. Workers must accept that patients cannot give up their defenses and that the task at hand is not to convince them they are addicted. However, as a hospital social worker one can help patients recognize how their patterns of substance use have contributed to their current medical problems as well as family disruption, social crises, job jeopardy, and overall distress (Vaillant, 1983). Relating their substance use to the hospitalization and various sequelae assists in the development of a meaningful contract and plants the seed for one aspect of the discharge plan.

In units such as obstetrics/gynecology, labor and delivery, and neonatal intensive care, workers frequently confront substance-abusing patients. Drug- or alcohol-abusing mothers give birth to infants who are passively addicted to drugs or who suffer from fetal alcohol syndrome. As the following case illustrates, the worker joined the parents/patients and "began where they were" in order to develop a working treatment plan and effective discharge plan.

A newborn was transferred to the neonatal intensive care unit after a premature delivery. A routine urine toxicology indicated that the infant was passively addicted to barbiturates, thus implying that the mother had been abusing drugs while pregnant. Nonetheless, the mother denied abuse; the father equally denied his partner's and his own abuse. He was thought to be a drug user, since he appeared to be high when visiting, frequently was demanding and argumentative with the staff, and physically was quite thin and somewhat disheveled.

Due to the physical findings and the mandated responsibility of a hospital social worker to report suspicions of child abuse and neglect, the worker called the child protection agency, which in turn authorized the hospital to retain the infant pending placement. The worker then called a conference with the parents to inform them that they would not be allowed to take their infant home when medically ready. The parents became enraged. The father threatened to "get" the social worker after she left the hospital for the day, implying that he would attack her once she was off hospital grounds. The worker felt genuinely at risk for being physically confronted and harmed.

In the past, the worker's typical response would have been that these parents were lying about their obvious abuse, taking her for a fool, and that they were being threatening and intimidating in order to get their way. She would have called security to remove them from the unit in order to restore peace and safety. Peace would have been restored, but the worker would have failed to address the family's needs related to their newborn and further would have avoided the substance abuse problem. In essence, the worker would have enabled these parents to continue their denial of their substance abuse problem and forestalled planning for the future of the child and parents.

However, due to the extensive staff training on assessment of and intervention in substance abuse disorders that all hospital social workers had received recently, this worker realized that denial and intimidation are symptoms of a substance abuse disorder and therefore developed a more effective intervention to help this family with their crisis. By engaging the parents in a sensitive discussion related to their concern over the health of their infant, and their upset that the infant was temporarily being removed from their care, the worker stayed with what they felt was important and showed them that she could understand what they were going through.

Once the parents felt the worker's genuine concern for them and her ability to empathize with their pain, they were more receptive to her introducing substance abuse as a factor contributing to this crisis. The worker accepted that they did not agree with the authorities regarding their substance use. However, she explicitly pointed out that the authorities had found the child to be affected by substance abuse; the parents therefore had to show efforts at addressing this problem if they were ever to regain custody of their baby. The couple, though substance abusers in denial of their problem, were also concerned parents who engaged in a discussion of what they could do to win custody. The worker encouraged them to enter drug treatment as a means of addressing the crisis at hand.

This worker neither avoided the issue of substance abuse nor confronted it head on, breaking down defenses. The parents still minimized or denied the severity of their problem, yet both the worker and the parents "won" in that each of them had their agenda met. The worker diffused a volatile situation and expedited an effective discharge and aftercare plan for the mother. The parents were able to keep their defenses intact as, paradoxically, they addressed their substance abuse problem.

Confrontation

There are times when a more direct confrontation of the patient's substance abuse is necessary in order to effect a discharge plan. Due to the patient's vague presentation, attempts to deny or obscure the problem, and real cognitive deficits, confrontation becomes a critical skill. Specific and direct questions elicit specific and direct answers. Repeated attempts to get answers through supportive confrontation are effective in combating the patient's denial and continued self-destruction (Westermeyer, 1986).

A 62-year-old widowed male was brought to the emergency room by the police because he was wandering about, exhibiting inappropriate and psychotic thinking. Though admitted to the psychiatric unit, he was given a medical workup that revealed that his blood sugar level was very high, accounting for his symptomology. Once his mental state was stabilized, he was transferred to a medical unit.

The social worker, in reviewing the patient's medical history, noted that this was the fifth time in a year that the patient had been hospitalized for uncontrolled diabetes. In sessions with the social worker, he seemed not to understand how his sugar level could have been so high, since he took his insulin according to the doctor's orders. He did admit to eating sweets on occasion and "promised" the worker not to do that anymore. During his previous four hospitalizations, social workers had emphasized the importance of complying with a diet that is low in sugar, supported the patient's efforts in taking the insulin as prescribed, and recommended visiting his physician on a regular basis to monitor his medical condition. Further, the discharge plan included a visiting nurse service to supervise the patient's compliance with his medication regime. The patient was discharged quickly each time, having received supportive education on diabetes and with all appointments and services planned for.

This time the worker confronted the patient with the fact that he had had several admissions in the past year and that there must be other reasons for his inability to control his diabetes. The worker pointed out that eating sweets on occasion would not account for the dangerously high sugar levels that had required his hospitalization. The worker then specifically asked the patient to recount how he spends his time, going over the activities he is involved in and with whom. A pattern of frequent socializing with "drinking buddies" emerged. Once this pattern was pointed out, the worker was then able to identify the patient's fears that if he did not drink with his old friends he would be without friends. The worker's confrontation complemented by empathic understanding led the patient to a point where a more open and honest discussion of his alcohol abuse could take place. Referral to an alcohol program with a recommendation to go to Alcoholics Anonymous (AA) was met with receptivity.

The worker's focus on the patient's alcohol problem rather than his diabetes was the key to the case. Had the worker not entertained the possibility that there could be a comorbid condition of alcohol abuse present, it was conceivable that the patient would have been rehospitalized and risked serious medical repercussions and perhaps death. By exploring specific avenues that amplified the substance abuse diagnosis, the worker was able to uncover what the patient could not or did not recognize. The referrals offered the patient opportunities to grapple with his substance problem in more depth upon discharge; put him in contact with others going through similar struggles; and attempted to alter his social network to include a more healthy circle of people and activities (Alcoholics Anonymous, 1976, 1985).

Family Intervention

Medical social workers have increasingly viewed illness as a crisis impacting the entire family as a system, not just the designated patient (Dillon, 1985). As previously described, substance abuse not only affects all family members but also may be perpetuated by them. The worker's attempts at engaging families in the management of the illness and discharge planning are, therefore, extremely important.

Families are essential to the patient's recovery. They can be conceptualized as a context in which to view the illness as well as a resource for the patient (Caroff & Mailick, 1985). Family members can provide valuable information that substantiates the existence of a substance abuse problem. They have intimate knowledge of the patient's functioning and can help break through the denial the patient may present.

Individual substance abusers cannot tackle their problem alone. The family must be enlisted to support discharge and aftercare plans (Westermeyer, 1986). Otherwise they can sabotage the treatment, since it can jeopardize stabilized roles they have had for years, perhaps generations (Clark, 1981; Vaillant, 1983). Bringing the family into the assessment and planning plants a seed for change for the patient and family system alike. This is exemplified in the following case vignette.

> A 48-year-old divorced female was admitted to the hospital after being hit by a car. Her injuries were so severe that she would require extensive rehabilitation after numerous surgical procedures and would be wheelchair-bound for some time. She reported being in tremendous pain from her bruises and operations. She complained of stomachaches, headaches, and hot and cold flashes for which all routine medical treatments had failed. She was angry and dissatisfied with the medical and nursing care she received. She stated that the staff, though administering pain medications, were not taking her complaints seriously enough, as they were not alleviating her distress.
>
> The social worker consulted with members of the treatment staff about why the patient appeared to be in such distress. Although she had suffered a severe trauma, her pain and somatic symptoms seemed unusual. Based on the nature of her physical complaints, her negative drug-seeking behavior, and the fact that she had been so intoxicated on the night of the accident that she did not see the car coming, the treatment team concluded that she might be a substance abuser who was experiencing withdrawal symptoms. Having diagnosed a substance abuse disorder, the treatment team initiated an appropriate medical regime. A detoxification schedule of phenobarbital, used for barbiturate and alcohol abuse disorders, was prescribed.

Since the patient lived with her sister, the sister was asked to meet with the social worker to participate in discharge planning. The worker explored with the sister the patient's functioning prior to hospitalization and her reliance on medications to ease her distress and discomfort. Further, the patient's living condition was assessed. Why was she living with her sister? What was the nature of their relationship? (This was a particularly important question if the sister was to be relied upon to maintain the patient in the community.) The sister characterized the patient as headstrong and independent, yet she frequently "rescued" the patient. When the patient was evicted, the sister allowed her to move in with her because "sisters help each other." She gave the patient an "allowance" because of her difficulties managing money, even though the patient did not contribute to rent or utilities. The sister did not know the reasons for the patient's eviction or financial problems, except that she "never had a head for figures." The sister reported that the patient was "nervous" and took "nerve pills" or had a few drinks to calm down, but that did not make her a "drug addict." The worker recognized that the sister's enabling behaviors, her denial of a substance abuse problem, and her inability to recognize the destructive behavior pattern she was trapped in were clear signs that drug or alcohol abuse was an important factor in this family relationship. It was also a factor that could sabotage the discharge plan and the patient's ability to be maintained safely in the community. Although the sister was prepared to take the patient home and care for her during her recuperation, both she and the patient had to address the substance abuse problem affecting them both. The worker pointed out that the sister was straining herself emotionally and financially. She was under stress to function in her own life while also caring for her sister, and such stress would be exacerbated during the patient's recuperation at home.

Although the patient refused to accept treatment for her alcohol and pill abuse, the sister was open to reading the literature the worker offered her on the impact of substance abuse on the family. She also took the telephone number for Al-Anon.

Referrals of family members to self-help groups, such as Al-Anon or Nar-Anon or Adult Children of Alcoholics, reinforce the knowledge that enabling behaviors are destructive to both the patient and other family members. By providing models for alternative ways to relate to the dependent person, they support the family member's attempts to change (Al-Anon, 1972).

The patient and family are an interdependent system. Better equipping families to withstand the pressures of relating to and "rescuing" a substance abuser by changing longstanding patterns of behavior helps families function better. Further, it moves the substance abuser closer to treatment and recovery, since the family will no longer deny or tolerate the abuse.

CONCLUSION

Studies have shown that even minimal effort on the part of health care team members to address patients' substance abuse can motivate patients to seek out and continue in appropriate aftercare programs. The more intensive worker is in intervention during the hospitalization, the more likely the patient will follow a treatment plan upon discharge (Moore et al., 1989).

As this chapter has pointed out, workers cannot take a narrow view of discharge planning but must take a long view of the patient's functioning both in the hospital and upon discharge. Substance abuse complicates patients' lives and their course of hospitalization. Discharge plans can be affected by the impact the abuse has on both patients and their social supports.

With the skills and repetoire of interventions available to social workers, they can effectively assess and treat patients with drug or alcohol problems. Recommendations for substance abuse treatment must be included in discharge plans in order to increase the likelihood that the plan will succeed and that hospital resources will be maximized rather than drained by rehospitalizations. Further, appropriate referrals decrease the likelihood of future medical problems, unstable functioning, and destructive and unsatisfying family relationships for patients.

Acknowledgment. Thanks are extended to Deborah Little, MSW, for her support and sharing of her ideas that helped crystallize my own.

REFERENCES

Ackerman, R. J. (1983). *Children of alcoholics.* Holmes Beach, FL: Learning Publications.

Al-Anon. (1972). *Alcoholism, the family disease.* New York: Al-Anon Family Group Headquarters.

Alcoholics Anonymous. (1976). *Alcoholics Anonymous* (3rd ed.). New York: Alcoholics Anonymous World Services.

Alcoholics Anonymous. (1985). *Twelve steps, twelve traditions* (30th printing). New York: Alcoholics Anonymous World Services.

Bartek, J. K., Lindeman, M., Newton, M., Fitzgerald, A. P., & Hawks, J. H. (1988). Nurse identified problems in the management of alcoholic patients. *Journal of Studies on Alcohol, 49*(1), 62–70.

Caroff, P., Mailick, M. D. (1985). The patient has a family: Reaffirming social work's domain. *Social Work in Health Care, 10*(4), 35–44.

Cermak, T. (1986). *Diagnosing and treating co-dependence.* Minneapolis, MN: Johnson Institute Books.

Clark, W. D. (1981). Alcoholism: blocks to diagnosis and treatment. *American Journal of Medicine, 71,* 275-286.

Coulehan, J. L., Zettler-Segal, M., Block, M., McClelland, M., & Schulberg, H. C. (1987). Recognition of alcoholism and substance abuse in primary care patients. *Archives of Internal Medicine, 147*(2), 349-352.

Dillon, C. (1985). Families, transitions, and health: Another look. *Social Work in Health Care, 10*(4), 35-44.

Greater New York Hospital Association. (1988, November 14). *Skyline News, 88-23.*

Greater New York Hospital Association. (1990, January 22). *Skyline News, 90-2.*

Kackson, J. K. (1954). The adjustment of family to the crisis of alcoholism. *Quarterly Journal on the Study of Alcoholism, 15,* 562-586.

Lerner, D. (1978). Consultation of alcoholism in a general hospital. *Health and Social Work, 3*(1), 103-125.

Levinson, V. R., & Straussner, S. L. A. (1978). Social workers as "enablers" in the treatment of alcoholics. *Social Casework, 59*(1), 14-20.

McCrady, B. S. (1989). Outcomes of family-involved alcoholism treatment. *Recent Developments in Alcoholism, 7,* 165-182.

Moore, D., Bone, L. R., Geller, G., Mamon, J. A., Stokes, E. J., & Levine, D. M. (1989). Prevalence, detection and treatment of alcoholism in hospitalized patients. *Journal of the American Medical Association, 261*(3), 403-407.

National Institute on Drug Abuse. (1989). *National household survey on drug abuse— Population estimates: 1988* (DHHS Pub. No. (ADM)89-1636). Washington, DC: U.S. Government Printing Office.

New York State Division of Alcoholism and Alcohol Abuse. (1990). *The second formative hospital intervention service report.* Albany, NY: Author.

Pattison, E. M. (1981). Introduction: The social network paradigm. *International Journal of Family Therapy, 3*(4), 241-245.

Richter, R. W. & Stanitis, T. (1987). The neurologist's approach to alcoholism and drug abuse: Out-patient care. *Seminars in Neurology, 7*(4), 336-343.

Sherin, K. M., Piotrowski, Z. H., Panek, S. M., & Doot, M. C. (1982). Screening for alcoholism in a community hospital. *Journal of Family Practice, 15*(6), 1091-1095.

Steinglass, P. (1985). Family systems approaches to alcoholism. *Journal of Substance Abuse Treatment, 2,* 161-167.

Straussner, S. L. A., Weinstein, D., & Hernandez, R. (1979). Effects of alcoholism on the family system. *Health and Social Work, 4*(4), 111-127.

Vaillant, G. (1983). *The natural history of alcoholism.* Cambridge, MA: Harvard University Press.

Westermeyer, J. (1986). *A clinical guide to alcohol and drug problems.* New York: Praeger.

3

Assessment and Intervention with Drug and Alcohol Abusers in Psychiatric Settings

Lois Orlin and Jennifer Davis

In the past decade, the coexistence of substance abuse and mental illness has been well documented in psychiatric treatment facilities. Hall (1979) found that 58% of 57 consecutive patients admitted to a psychiatric unit reported a history of drug abuse, while a study of young chronic mentally ill patients by Pepper, Kirshner, and Ryglewicz (1981) found that 37% abused alcohol and another 37% abused drugs. McKelvy, Kane, and Kellison (1987), in a study of patients in a state psychiatric hospital, learned that the 10% to 15% estimate of dual diagnosis patients on their arrival was vastly underestimated, and, in fact, 60% of those admitted met the criteria for dual diagnosis.

Given the decrease in state hospital beds and the limited number of supervised psychiatric residential facilities and single-room-occupancy dwellings (SROs) staffed with mental health teams, more mentally ill patients find themselves homeless and vulnerable to alcohol and drug use.

Many of the same patients may be seen on separate occasions in drug detoxification, alcohol detoxification, and psychiatric units within the same hospital. How a patient presents him- or herself in the emergency room frequently determines the treatment disposition. Some patients become acquainted with the distinct admission criteria of each unit and spare the staff diagnostic uncertainty by delineating the symptoms that would most likely gain admission to the unit of their choice. If they are successful, this results in treatment for only one illness and inadequate discharge planning.

The purpose of this chapter is to discuss assessment and treatment issues for dually diagnosed patients and to descibe how existing psychiatric and substance abuse treatment models can be utilized to effectively work with this population.

DEFINITION OF DUAL DIAGNOSIS

Any person suffering from two diseases can be considered a dually diagnosed patient. For the purpose of this chapter, the dual diagnosis patient is one having both a major (Axis I) psychiatric disorder, such as schizophrenia, and a psychoactive substance use disorder (Attia, 1988; Wallen & Weiner, 1989).

Mental health providers frequently experience diagnostic dilemmas when a potential patient presents with a myriad of symptoms—mania, depression, anxiety, paranoia, hallucinations, and incoherence. Even if the patient is able and willing to document current and past chemical use, there is still a question as to which triggered off which: Did the painful symptoms lead to drug use or did the drug use precipitate the symptoms? It is even more difficult for emergency room staff and intake workers to make a primary diagnosis, since the symptoms of crack use and schizophrenia are similar. Given the pressures of time, patients can easily be misdiagnosed and given improper treatment. Persons with major psychiatric illnesses can be dismissed from a psychiatric facility with the suggestion that they seek help with their chemical abuse, and substance abusers can be medicated, labeled, and discharged as psychiatric patients. In neither case will the patients be accepted at a drug or alcohol facility once they display or relate their psychiatric symptoms. As a result, these patients consistently receive one basic treatment—that of "referral therapy."

DIFFERENTIAL ASSESSMENT

Many patients enter psychiatric settings with suspected or documented substance abuse. To assess and treat all patients as one diagnostic category is to miss the important distinction that there are two types of dual diagnosis clients: the primary psychiatric patient and the primary chemical abuser.

The primary psychiatric patient, currently referred to as the MICA (mentally ill chemical abuser), uses drugs and/or alcohol in response to the discomfort of mental illness. Such patients self-medicate to relieve the nagging voices in their heads, to feel less frightened of the imagined forces tormenting them, and to experience a high and a sense of control that prescribed antipsychotic medications do not provide. Many patients have reported that the only time they feel safe on the street, free from symptoms of paranoia, is when they are high or stoned. Drug use has a secondary advantage for the mentally ill: In addition to numbing the disease symptoms, it gives them an opportunity to interact with individuals and groups outside the mental health system, to be in the mainstream. The purchase of the drugs, the communal use, "makes me feel like a big shot," reported Ray, a previously shy and isolated schizophrenic.

Thus the primary psychiatric patient who has suffered the pain, stigma, and social limitations conferred by the disease is extraordinarily vulnerable to the seeming benefits of drug and/or alcohol abuse. Unfortunately, the pleasures are short-lived and lead to decompensation and rehospitalization, and, if the patient is not treated for both disorders, the cycle of abuse, decompensation, and rehospitalization is repeated.

The second category of dual diagnosis is the primary substance abuser, known also as CAMI (chemically addicted mentally ill). Such clients may have long histories of depression, anxiety, and poor psychosocial adjustment, but it can be documented that when they experience more florid symptoms, such as hallucinations, delusions, or thought disorder, these symptoms are secondary to substance abuse.

Ideally, when a psychiatric patient presents in an acute phase of illness, a urine toxicology is done immediately whether or not there is evidence or history of substance use. Further, little or no antipsychotic medication is instituted until staff have the opportunity to observe the patient in a drug-free state.

Symptoms of psychosis will persist if unmedicated; symptoms due to chemical use will abate with abstinence (Wanck, 1987). The following case illustrates this.

Marsha, a 25-year-old single, white female, was brought to a psychiatric emergency room by her parents. She was delusional, disoriented, and paranoid. According to her parents, Mr. and Mrs. A., she had a 9-year history of treatment in a variety of psychiatric outpatient settings. Most recently, she had stopped treatment when she moved away from home to live with a man, whom Mr. and Mrs. A. suspected of substance abuse. When asked by the emergency room psychiatrist if Marsha used drugs, her parents assured him "that is not her problem." They continued to document a pattern of Marsha's condition improving for a brief period and then again deteriorating. They were disheartened to once again be seeking help and were greatly relieved when admission to the hospital's psychiatric inpatient unit was offered.

Marsha's mental status on admission and the history given by her parents supported a diagnosis of schizophrenia, and she was promptly treated with antipsychotic medication. Her rapid improvement in the first two days of hospitalization seemed further to confirm this diagnosis. Marsha avoided lengthy sessions with her therapist, but she was oriented and willing to participate in ward activities. On the third day of hospitalization, she developed a dystonic reaction to medication—painful stiffening of her neck, eyes rolling back—and it was necessary to discontinue it. The staff were concerned that her symptoms might not be manageable without medication, but Marsha continued to improve. At this point, her therapist was able to get a more extensive psychiatric history. He learned that she had drunk and smoked marijuana through-out high school and at age 18, prior to her first "breakdown," had begun to broaden her use to include LSD, Quaaludes, and cocaine. She knew that her family would disapprove and, since they paid for her treatment, she did not confide her substance abuse to any of her therapists. It had never occurred to her that her substance abuse and psychiatric illness might be related.

Marsha was discharged with a diagnosis of substance abuse dis-order and a referral to a drug program.

Had Marsha not developed the dystonic reaction to the prescribed medica-tion, she would have left the hospital without the help she needed. Marsha is an example of the dual diagnosis client who is a primary substance abuser but who, once drug use is initiated, presents with symptoms resembling an acute psychiatric disorder.

ASSESSMENT TOOLS

While time is the most reliable assessment tool, taking a history that reflects the course of both diseases and their possible interaction is helpful to both clinician and patient. One tool for obtaining such history is the Dual Diagno-sis Assessment Form that we have developed. This form (see Figure 3.1) includes a chronicle of the diseases, treatment, and periods of remission; it focuses on triggers for both; and it provides for understanding how the patient experiences any positive or negative consequences resulting from the illnesses. It is equally useful in helping to identify the patient's perception of the two disorders and in determining whether any connections between the two can be made. Figure 3.1 shows the use of the Dual Diagnosis Assessment Form in the following case.

Orlando, a 24-year-old Hispanic male, was referred to an outpatient psychiatric clinic on the day of his discharge from the hospital's inpa-tient psychiatry unit. The referral stated that he was schizophrenic, had had three acute hospitalizations in 14 months, and had had very poor follow-up with outpatient treatment recommendations.

The intake social worker discovered how frustrated Orlando was by his frequent hospitalizations and how hopeless he was feeling already. This prompted her to examine with him the triggers of relapse. He acknowledged that he didn't think he needed medication, so he never took it for very long: "I feel better on my own." He was asked, "How do you handle any problems?" He replied, "I have a few drinks and I feel good." As she explored further, it became evident that Orlando's alcohol consumption increased rapidly and that this heightened his paranoia

Patient: 24-year-old Hispanic male
Date: 9/26/90

	PSYCHIATRIC	SUBSTANCE USE/ABUSE
HISTORY		
1. *Age of onset and circumstances*	At age of 18, paranoid symptoms delusional about family members. Hospitalized for 1 month.	At age 17, used cocaine and alcohol with friends.
2. *Treatment history*		
a. Hospitalizations/detoxifications	a. Total of five hospitalizations (age 18 and 20, and three in past 14 months). b. Attended clinic sporadically past 2 years.	No drug/alcohol treatment.
b. Outpatient treatment involvement (include rehabilitation or residential programs) Helpful/not helpful to patient		
c. Medications prescribed (include compliance, length of time) Helpful/not helpful to patient	c. Thorazine, Klonopin. Poor compliance. Does not like effects. Feels "lifeless." Has not found any treatment helpful in past.	
3. *Periods of remission* Length of time and circumstances	Never symptom-free outside of hospital.	Other than hospitalizations, 2 months in 1985 when in summer work program.
4. *Triggers* for return of symptoms/use of substances	With help can identify drinking and stopping medication.	"Boredom, frustration, loneliness."
5. *Positive consequences of illness/es for patient*	Cannot identify.	"Takes away pain."
6. *Negative consequences of illness/es for patient*	a. Fights with mother. b. Loss of faith. c. "Being locked up."	Same.
7. *Patient's understanding of illness/es* Does he/she see connections	Patient believes "I have schizophrenia, but God may cure me someday."	Just beginning to see that alcohol may stimulate psychiatric symptoms.
8. *Family history of illness/es*	Maternal grandmother "depressed" and had many hospitalizations.	Father—alcoholism. Brother—heroin addiction.
9. *Family responses to patient's illness/es*	Mother worries and "wants me to go to clinic."	Drinking minimized and not seen as a disorder by any family members.

FIGURE 3.1. Dual Diagnosis Assessment Form.

and isolation. Given this information, the worker charted with him each relapse—the triggers and the consequences—utilizing the Dual Diagnosis Assessment Form. Orlando was able to see for the first time that there might be some connection between his psychiatric symptoms and his drinking.

The Drug Diary (Figure 3.2), in which a patient records the circumstances of substance use, is another tool that can be helpful in assessing the extent of addiction and psychiatric disorder. The Diary which can be used in either individual or group treatment, helps clients understand the connection between their two disorders and the notion that substance use is triggered by circumstances and feelings of discomfort. For clients who find it helpful, it can also provide concrete evidence of progress. Figure 3.2 shows the use of the Drug Diary in the following case.

Andy, 32, was referred by his psychiatric day treatment program, which described his escalating drug and alcohol use as making him "impossible to treat" in their setting. Andy was pleasant and cooperative in his first appointment, but he had difficulty staying on a subject and appeared to

---

Patient: Andy
Date: 5/17/89

1. DRUGS USED   AMOUNT   TIME
   a. "Crack"   a. "$25"   a. "2–3 PM"
   b.   b.   b.
   c.   c.   c.
   None: _____ Because _____

2. I knew I would use drugs today because "I got my allowance today and had nothing to do."

3. Before I used I felt "I have a pain in my back and my stomach. I want to lighten my head. My head's on fire."

4. When I was using drugs I felt "Not high. Nothing. Is this really power?"

5. Afterwards I felt "I don't know if I want these drug programs to help. Maybe I'm crazy. I want you to arrest me."

FIGURE 3.2. Drug Diary.

be responding to a voice other than the interviewer's. He was able to inform the interviewer that during the past 10 years he had never been drug- and alcohol-free for more than 5 to 7 days but had managed to avoid hospitalization for as long as 3 years.

Since he was totally unaware of what triggered his substance use and could not describe or name his psychiatric symptoms, the intake worker sent him home with copies of the Drug Diary. He was directed to abstain from all chemicals, but if he was unsuccessful in doing so, to record his use on the diary. When Andy returned with his completed diary [see Figure 3.2], it was clear to the intake worker that he was having symptoms due to his psychiatric illness. She explored what it meant to have his "head on fire" and learned "that's my sister's voice telling me I'm a bad person." Getting high was an effort to medicate the symptoms.

Andy's response to question 5 about how he felt afterwards illustrated his ambivalence about wanting and not wanting treatment. In reviewing the diary with him, the intake worker was able to help him express his mixed feelings.

Andy realized the relief obtained from crack was temporary and was willing to see the program psychiatrist to get better stabilized on his medication. Andy has continued to use the Drug Diary in his individual appointments. He is very pleased to bring it in with notations of "clean, clean, clean."

ASSESSMENT OF MOTIVATION FOR TREATMENT

In both mental health and substance abuse facilities, a prospective client's motivation for treatment is part of the assessment. Whether one is motivated or unmotivated may determine acceptance or rejection into a treatment program.

In actuality, neither disorder promotes motivation for treatment. The high incidence of patients' leaving both detoxification units and psychiatric wards "against medical advice" demonstrates this. Treatment, whether for singly or dually diagnosed disorders, is associated with powerlessness and stigma; self-medication or taking no medication at all gives the patient options and some sense of control.

If treatment slots are limited, it is more realistic to assess whether treatment leverage exists for a potential dual diagnosis client. Is there a compelling reason to be in treatment? What will the client lose or gain? A job, housing, financial benefits, family support, and custody of one's children are all excellent points of leverage that providers can use to engage patients in treatment. It is important that clinicians appreciate that leverage is a far better indicator than motivation for treatment engagement and that they employ this knowledge in their work. Two cases, those of Belinda and George, illustrate the issue of treatment leverage:

A single mother of 24, Belinda was admitted to the hospital for an acute psychotic episode. Her mother reported that Belinda had had three similar admissions in the past 2 years but, when discharged, always refused to continue in treatment.

As Belinda became less psychotic and more trusting of staff, it was learned that she had been using crack to treat her paranoia, anxiety, and mood swings. She had never taken medication outside the hospital because she was convinced it would harm her and hamper her ability to care for her 4-year-old son. She had temporarily lost custody of her son, and she was willing to do anything to get him back.

Staff worked to educate Belinda about the nature of her two disorders and the benefit of treatment. It was made clear that only through participation in treatment could she hope to regain custody of her son. This realization helped Belinda to follow-up in the hospital's dual diagnosis treatment program upon discharge.

George, a 54-year-old single male with a documented history of manic depression and alcoholism, was referred from the inpatient unit to the outpatient dual diagnosis program at the same time as Belinda. George, like Belinda, met the dual diagnosis criteria for admission—diagnosis of a major psychiatric disorder and a substance abuse disorder. Program staff worked to engage him, making home visits when he did not attend. Unfortunately, they could find no point of leverage. His housing and benefits were intact. He had no family or friends affected by his disorders. His health was good despite his years of drinking. When he did attend groups, he was unresponsive to the concern of his fellow members. Within 3 months, he dropped out.

ASSESSMENT OF FAMILY

How a family has responded to mental illness and substance abuse in the past and is responding in the present is essential to assessment. Are these disorders minimized or acknowledged? And if acknowledged, with concern and support or with feelings of frustration and helplessness?

It should be highlighted that denial on the part of dual diagnosis patients and their families is an important consideration in assessment. Given the chronicity and painful symptoms involved in either a psychiatric or addictive disorder, it is not surprising that people suffering from both have great difficulty acknowledging them. To compound their own conflicts, they are constantly confronted with the stigmatization that either or both disorders engender in their families, the health care system, and the larger community.

If families can support the need for medication but not for abstinence, or for abstinence but not for medication, this will create a tremendous dilemma for the dually diagnosed client and must be addressed in treatment.

In dual diagnosis treatment, the families need the same education and support as the primary patients. Their reactions have a profound influence on treatment outcome.

TREATMENT OF DUAL DIAGNOSIS CLIENTS

For all working in the helping professions, there must be a secure sense that the treatment skills used are congruent with the needs of the client population. To work effectively with chronically ill psychiatric patients, mental health professionals learn to understand the biopsychosocial aspects of schizophrenia and affective disorders and to set realistic expectations for their patients as well as for themselves. When these same skilled clinicians are confronted with a dual diagnosis client, instead of applying this body of knowledge to the second disorder, they feel inadequate in the face of addictive illness. The addiction is mistakenly viewed as a negative behavior that can be extinguished if the patient is "motivated" or has "the will power."

On the other hand, the skilled addiction or alcoholism counselor understands that drug and alcohol abuse is a disease and that to engage a client in the struggle to gain sobriety or achieve a substance-free state is a tremendous undertaking, not just a matter of motivation. Yet once mental illness is diagnosed, they, too, react with concern that their skills are not adequate to provide successful treatment.

In reality, mental health and chemical dependency practitioners share a common knowledge base and need only support and education to reaffirm this and expand their perceptions. Mental health program administrators have been slow to recognize that they have staff that can effectively treat dual diagnosis patients. Instead, they create policies that exclude these clients or, in some instances, accept them with the provision that they receive concurrent treatment at a substance abuse facility. However, this population is the least likely to follow up in two distinct programs; to expect such patients to do so is unrealistic and a disservice to them. Such practices frustrate staff and perpetuate the feeling that dual diagnosis is untreatable in their setting.

Before discussing treatment similarities, it is helpful to identify those aspects of the two disorders that are alike and must be considered in treatment planning.

SIMILARITIES OF THE DISORDERS

It is essential that service providers understand how similar the disorders are in order to appreciate that the skills they have and the treatment they offer can be of immense benefit to the dually diagnosed.

Both mental illness and substance use disorders, singly or in combination, produce the following:

1. *Impairment in many or all areas of functioning.* Family relationships, school or job performance, financial stability, health, and ability to socialize can be negatively affected by either disorder.

2. *Loss of control.* When an acute episode begins, both the use of substances and the psychiatric symptoms render the patient powerless to manage his or her life.

3. *Chronicity and relapse.* Treatment brings remission, but to remain free of psychotic symptoms and substance abuse requires constant vigilance on the part of the patient, the family, and the treatment providers.

4. *Denial as a primary defense.* For the psychotic and drug- or alcohol-abusing person, coming to terms with either illness is painful and anxiety-provoking.

5. *Social isolation.* When either disorder is untreated, the patient is severely limited in his or her interactions with others. The patient is fearful and secretive, and relationships at best are superficial.

6. *Inattention to physical health.* Untreated mental illness and substance abuse prevent conscious attention to one's health. Minor and serious health problems go unattended.

7. *Extremes in behavior.* There is no consistency in the patient's behavior for either disorder. The disorders can produce passivity, aggression, impulsivity, and, in the extreme, suicidal and homicidal behavior.

8. *Family impact.* Both disorders have a profound impact on family members. Feelings of anger, shame, depression, and helplessness are common and can promote enabling and/or blaming behavior.

SIMILARITIES IN TREATMENT

Given the similarities in the impact of the disorders on patient and family, effective dual diagnosis treatment closely resembles the services offered by both psychiatric facilities and by drug and alcohol treatment programs.

Psychoeducation

Education regarding every aspect of each disease is fundamental to recovering dually diagnosed patients. The nonjudgmental, didactic group format—which confirms that the illnesses are diseases, not moral or behavior issues, with documented symptoms, progressions, and side effects—arms patients with information that they can use to understand and protect themselves. The learning is enhanced in the group setting as members give examples and identify together the common threads of the diseases' impact. The therapist offers information and facilitates discussion and mutual aid. The following is a list of psychoeducation topics for dual diagnosis patients:

1. *Defining mental illness and addiction*
   Purpose: To identify characteristics of each disorder, their similarities and differences, and how they interact.
2. *Theories of mental illness and addiction*
   Purpose: To explore environmental, genetic, and moral models of etiology.
3. *Triggers for relapse: Mental illness and addiction*
   Purpose: To identify triggers (people, places, and things) that precipitate relapse in either or both disorders and to highlight similarities.
4. *Symptoms of illness(es): Mental illness and addiction*
   Purpose: To identify symptoms of both disorders and their similarities and differences.
5. *Tracing the progression and patterns of mental illness and addiction*
   Purpose: To understand how the disorders progress and distinguish between acute stages and remission.
6. *Family role and involvement in mental illness and addiction*
   Purpose: To understand the impact on families when a member suffers from two disorders and the various responses patients can expect.
7. *Good drugs and bad drugs*
   Purpose: To explore the effects of street drugs, alcohol, and medications.
8. *Social and political issues in mental illness and addiction*
   Purpose: To review sociopolitical views of the disorders and their impact on patients.
9. *Treatment planning for mental illness and addiction*
   Purpose: To learn the variety of treatments available and identify what works and what does not.

Supportive Counseling

A one-to-one relationship with a caring professional provides structure and safety, positive feedback on strengths and progress, hope, and validation that the patient can get better and has the ability to control his or her illness and his or her life. The counselor's focus is not on personality change but on helping the patient make gradual behavioral changes. Interventions are geared to presenting the patient with options and creating self-esteem and empowerment. Confrontation, the pointing out of discrepancies between words and actions, and reality testing are all employed.

Crisis Intervention

With either disorder, the patient is always at risk. Patients often handle stress poorly, and they can abruptly stop medications and/or return to substance abuse. Any missed appointment is a signal to the treatment staff that the patient is having difficulties. A "slip" in substance use or the cessation of medication can herald a downward spiral. Follow-up with a phone call or a home visit by staff can help the patient return to treatment before the disorder reaches an acute phase.

Relapse Prevention

Both psychiatric and drug- or alcohol-dependent patients are prone to relapse. To prevent repeated suffering and hospitalizations, patients must learn what circumstances—people, places, or things—trigger an acute episode. Individual, group, and family treatment must stimulate the patient to identify past patterns and ways in which future vulnerability can be diminished. The discovery and rapid arrest of early relapses may help to prevent later ones (Osher & Kofoed, 1989).

The following excerpt from a dual diagnosis education group illustrates the helpfulness of the psychoeducation model and the importance of relapse prevention training.

> At the weekly education workshop led by a social worker, the leader announced the day's topic: identifying triggers. On the board she wrote headings for two lists to be made by the group: "Addiction" and "Emotional Illness."
>
> "Let's get started by remembering the situations and feelings that have led to the relapse of people's illnesses." Mark said, "nerves," elaborating that when he feels anxious he smokes marijuana. Putting "anxiety" under the heading of "Addiction," the leader asked if anyone had also experienced anxiety as a possible trigger of their emotional illness? Mary raised her hand to say "yes." Once when she had started a volunteer job it made her very nervous, and her voices became "noticeable, like when I was in the hospital." Offering the next trigger, Julia said, "when I forget, I have a sickness." She related how she had become so involved in an art project last winter that she stopped going to Narcotics Anonymous and the dual diagnosis program. She figured she was "cured." After the project was completed, Julia, diagnosed with schizoaffective disorder

and crack addiction, found herself celebrating her accomplishments with what she thought would only be "one or two hits" off the crack pipe. Julia described a rapid return to daily use.

Julia's poignant tale prompted the leader to ask if members knew the term used to describe this "forgetting" or ignoring phenomenon. "Denial," chimed in several members. Writing "denial" under the "Addiction" heading, the leader wondered if denial of emotional illness could potentially trigger the same? Tracy said, "Yeah, like when I stop my meds because I've been feeling good." Tracy explained that he had discontinued his antidepressants in the past when he felt good, figuring he had his disease "licked." The members continued to construct their list of triggers, finding that most triggers belonged under both headings.

Emotional Illness	Addiction
Anxiety	Anxiety
Denial (forgetting)	Denial (forgetting)
Depression	Depression
Family and peer pressures	Family and peer pressures
Feeling paranoid	Feeling paranoid
Loneliness	Loneliness
Anger	Anger
Holidays and anniversaries	Holidays and anniversaries
	Physical craving for substance
	Too much money

Group Treatment

Denial, isolation, lack of socialization skills, and absence of pleasurable activities can best be remedied in structured groups. Mutual aid, as well as learning to listen, to articulate one's thoughts and feelings, to be understood, and to have fun are some of the goals of group treatment. Assertiveness training, psychodrama, art, music, and recreational therapy are effective in achieving these goals.

The following vignette demonstrates how group treatment is effective for dual diagnosis patients, providing both mutual aid and an increased understanding of the diseases:

Edward complained that "recovery is boring." There is "no zing" without drugs. He reminded the group that he had now been clean for 40 days, "my longest time ever," and asked "when will anything be fun again, will there ever again be any zing?" He added that "it is hard to feel feelings now," that without cocaine all feelings are dulled and interactions with others are difficult and awkward without a high to help. The leader normalized what Edward described as a commonly experienced stage of early recovery and wondered if others had had similar experiences and/or ideas for how Edward might cope and maintain his psychiatric stability and clean time.

Another member, Tina, agreed wholeheartedly and discussed ways in which she allows herself to use drugs occasionally, at least once or twice a month, "to have something to look forward to, to have some fun." Margie, recently recovering from a third relapse, responded that she understood, but that just this week she had surprised herself. She had gone to a neighborhood flea market and found herself spending several pleasurable hours just browsing.

Jack, 6 months substance-free and psychiatrically stable, turned to Edward to say, "Oh, you'll just get used to it." "How?" queried Edward. Jack, a recovering amphetamine addict with schizophrenia, described how, after a while, he had realized that having "average days" is what everyone, even people without dual diagnosis, have. Jack said it took time to get used to talking to people without a "high on" and, smiling, added that he had just made a comedy video with other members of his residence, an activity he would never have been able to do when he was abusing.

Carla, diagnosed with bipolar disorder and alcoholism, remembered how, before her last relapse, she had been missing that zing, or high-energy feeling, she gets when she goes off her lithium. Asked by the leader to name that symptom, Carla replied, "my mania." Carla then told Edward and the group how her mother tells her she "makes sense" now that she is back on her medicines and off alcohol. She added, "Edward, you make sense to me."

Case Management

Recovering persons, whether they have psychiatric disorders or are substance abusers, have a host of concrete problems directly related to the chaos precipitated by an acute phase of their illness. They need help to partialize and prioritize the issues that need attention, such as securing benefits, housing, education, or job training; following up on medical concerns; and coordinating the prescribed treatment plan.

Family Involvement

Both mental illness and substance use have a major impact on family members. All family members should be involved in treatment in order to better understand the disorders, to support the patient's progress, and to get the support they need for themselves.

Jane, a 21-year-old suffering from a schizoaffective disorder and cocaine addiction, was living with her older sister, Nora, and had frequent contact by phone with her parents. When she relapsed after 4 months of drug-free time, her social worker invited the family to come in and discuss what was happening and elicit their ideas on how best to help Jane.

What emerged early in the family meeting was how differently each family member perceived what would be helpful to Jane. Nora, who in earlier meetings with the social worker had had great difficulty acknowledging the psychiatric illness, was consistent in this thinking: "All Jane needs is a job. The real problem is the drugs, and if she is working, she'll be busy and won't have time to think about them." Jane's mother, Mrs. S., believed that the most helpful thing everyone in the family could do is "detach." Mr. S. had another view: He did not think either work or "detaching" were good ideas; rather, "Jane just needs all the treatment she can get; from early in the morning to late at night, she should be going to groups and attending the program."

The social worker was made aware of how difficult these conflicting family views were for Jane, increasing her stress rather than alleviating it. She acknowledged the caring of each family member and the pain Jane's two illnesses had created for them. She took this opportunity to educate them about the complexity of the two diseases. With this information, Nora realized that her thoughts about getting a job might have felt more like a demand to Jane at this point in her illness. Her genuine concern was evident when she asked, "Can my sister ever get better?"

Mrs. S. began to understand that her daughter still needed her support and that, perhaps out of her own pain for Jane, "I have detached too much." Mrs. S. agreed that it would be helpful to Jane if she became reinvolved to support Jane's taking medication and continuing treatment for her addiction. Mr. S. was able to understand that while treatment was essential, too much would create additional stress.

This session gave the family members an opportunity to learn more about Jane's illnesses and to plan support in a more consistent and realistic manner. It also further engaged them in working with the treatment staff to get the information and support they needed for themselves.

MODIFICATIONS IN TREATMENT REQUIRED TO TREAT DUAL DIAGNOSIS PATIENTS

Certain modifications in expectations and treatment must be made to provide comprehensive dual diagnosis treatment by either psychiatric or alcohol and drug abuse workers.

Modifications for Drug and Alcohol Treatment Providers

1. *A longer time frame to achieve abstinence.* Unlike the case of the singly diagnosed substance abuser, acceptance for treatment cannot carry the expectation that the patient immediately become free of alcohol or drugs. More slips and relapses can be anticipated and should not be viewed as failure on the part of either the patient or the staff. There are two illnesses from which the patient must recover. Any period of abstinence within the first year of treatment is promising.

2. *The value of psychotropic medication.* Traditionally, the treatment approach has been to require abstention from all chemicals, prescribed as well as nonprescribed. Most patients suffering from major psychiatric disorders that have significant biological components, however, must be maintained on medication to prevent relapse and to enable them to participate fully in the treatment offered. Stopping psychiatric medication is a trigger for relapse in both diseases.

3. *Modification of confrontation techniques.* While dual diagnosis patients must be taught that they frequently exhibit behavior that is in direct opposition to their well-being, they will not benefit from the traditional confrontation techniques used in drug therapeutic communities. Confrontation must be gentler and directed only at behaviors, never the patients themselves.

4. *The concept of enabling.* The concept of enabling, which is viewed as a negative enforcer of illness by drug and alcoholism specialists—that is, as protecting patients from the consequences of their behavior (Levinson & Straussner, 1978)—must be considered in a different light with dual diagnosis patients. If a patient appears to be at risk for relapse, staff must respond promptly with appropriate interventions, such as daily appointments, accompanying the client to an appointment, or facilitating negotiations of difficult systems.

5. *Psychiatric availability.* The availability of a psychiatrist to evaluate and monitor mental status and to prescribe and follow patients taking medication is essential. Further, many dual diagnosis patients have fewer relapses when on injectable medication.

Modifications for Mental Health Providers

1. *Assess and monitor substance abuse.* Mental health staff have to fully assess and monitor substance abuse. Psychiatric programs treating dual diagnosis clients must help them understand the effects and consequences of chemical dependency and offer ongoing individual and group education and support.

2. *Urine monitoring and breathalizers.* Such monitoring devices need to be used regularly when patients are not able to openly discuss their current chemical use.

3. *Participation in 12-step program.* Patients need active encouragement to participate in 12-step self-help groups such as Alcoholics Anonymous (AA), Narcotics Anonymous (NA), or Cocaine Anonymous (CA), while family members should be referred to Al-Anon, Nar-Anon, or Co-Anon.

4. *Policy on attendance.* A clear policy should prohibit any patient from being seen in outpatient treatment who "appears" to be high or intoxicated to staff. Since it is impossible for staff to convince a patient that he or she is high when the patient denies this, basing the rules on appearance rather than factual evidence eliminates arguments and helps to stress the importance of a drug-free environment for all patients participating in recovery.

TREATMENT MODEL FOR DUAL DIAGNOSIS PATIENTS

The ideal treatment progression for the dual diagnosis patient consists of three steps:

1. Brief psychiatric hospitalization to assess, stabilize, and, when necessary, provide supervised detoxification
2. Rehabilitation treatment in a residential setting targeted to both disorders for 6 to 12 months
3. Psychiatric outpatient services and 12-step program attendance

Given the limited number of residential treatment facilities for the dual diagnosis client, a more realistic model is one consisting of outpatient day treatment with brief hospitalization when needed. The mental health staff should include a counselor who is him- or herself recovering from an addiction; such a person brings a very special dimension to the treatment of patients by leading 12-step groups and providing a tangible example that recovery is a hope that can be fulfilled. All members of the treatment team need to utilize the following guidelines:

1. In every patient contact, both illnesses are acknowledged and discussed.
2. Abstinence is a goal of, not a precondition to, treatment.
3. Patient admissions of substance abuse are treated as a health concern, not grounds for discharge from treatment.
4. Despite the nonpunitive climate of dual diagnosis treatment, breathalizers are used and urine testing is done. These are objective instruments that allow clinician and patient to monitor progress.

5. Participation in self-help (AA, NA, CA) groups is strongly encouraged, with both on-site meetings and staff accompaniment of patients to outside meetings until the patients are connected.

6. Patients sign a contract that clearly prohibits treatment attendance when they appear to be intoxicated or high and indicates their agreement to be hospitalized when either disease appears acute to staff.

7. Treatment of dual diagnosis is a team effort. A single practitioner cannot provide all the supports essential to recovery; team members bring different subspecialty skills to the many patient crises that are inherent to both disorders.

CONCLUSION

The dual diagnosis (MICA) patient suffers from a major psychiatric disorder as well as a substance use disorder: Both are primary and require specific treatment concomitantly. Treatment that targets only one will not be successful. Given the many similarities in the two disorders and their impact on patients and their families, it is not surprising that well-established treatment models have much in common. The difficulty in integrating psychiatric and substance abuse treatment is rooted in different philosophies and a history of distinctions. These differences, exemplified by self-help versus professional treatment and total abstinence versus psychopharmacological intervention can be resolved if practitioners are willing to expand their thinking.

Mental health service providers can work effectively with this population with only a few modifications in their existing treatment skills. The similarities of the disorders must be highlighted, instead of the differences, to encourage the expansion of comprehensive dual diagnosis treatment in psychiatric facilities. Given the enormity of the needs and numbers of dual diagnosis patients, there is no alternative.

REFERENCES

Attia, P. R. (1988). Dual diagnosis: Definition and treatment. *Alcoholism Treatment Quarterly, 5*(3/4), 53–57.

Hall, R. C. (1979). Relationship of psychiatric illness to drug abuse. *Journal of Psychedelic Drugs, 11,* 337–342.

Levinson, V. R., & Straussner, S. L. A. (1978). Social workers as "enablers" in the treatment of alcoholism. *Social Casework, 59*(1), 14–20.

McKelvy, M. J., Kane, J. S., & Kellison, K. (1987). Substance abuse and mental illness double trouble. *Journal of Psychosocial Nursing, 25,* 20–25.

Osher, F. C., & Kofoed, L. L. (1989). Treatment of patients with psychiatric and psychoactive substance abuse disorders. *Hospital and Community Psychiatry*, 40(100), 1025–1029.

Pepper, B., Kirshner, M. C., & Ryglewicz, H. (1981). The young adult chronic patient: Overview of a population. *Hospital and Community Psychiatry*, 32(7), 463–469.

Wallen, M. D., & Weiner, H. (1989). Impediments to effective treatment of the dually diagnosed patient. *Journal of Psychoactive Drugs*, 21, 161–168.

Wanck, B. (1987). Addiction and mental illness: Assessing the difference. *Mediplex Medical Update*, 3(1), 1-4.

4

Alcohol and Drugs in the Workplace

CAROLE S. BARABANDER

Alcohol abuse has received attention in the workplace since the early occupational alcoholism programs of the 1930s. Only recently, however, has corporate America declared a "war on drugs." Employers are aggressively attacking
the drug problem and demanding a drug-free work environment. In the
process, attention has shifted from alcohol to drugs as the critical issue.
Those involved with addictions in the workplace—managers, supervisors,
unions, employee assistance programs (EAPs), treatment professionals, and
employees themselves—are facing new challenges and dilemmas. The purpose of this chapter is to explore the problem of drug and alcohol abuse in
the workplace, to review the methods being utilized by corporations to
manage the problem, and to discuss the roles of social workers in the
treatment of drug- and alcohol-abusing employees.

PREVALENCE OF ALCOHOL AND DRUGS
IN THE WORKPLACE

According to the Employee Assistance Professionals Association (EAPA), the
cost of alcohol abuse in the workplace has been estimated to be $86 billion
annually, with $71 billion due to lost employment and reduced productivity
and $15 billion due to health costs and treatment (National Institute on
Alcohol Abuse and Alcoholism, 1990). The National Household Survey on
Drug Abuse (National Institute on Drug Abuse [NIDA], 1991) found that 68%
of those who reported using drugs were employed, 55% of them full-time and
13% part-time. Among the 23 million adults who have used illicit drugs
within the past year, an overall 13.5% were employed (NIDA, 1991).

Federal experts estimate that between 10% and 23% of all workers use
illicit drugs on the job and that regular users of drugs often come to work
impaired but do not use on the job. A 1986 survey conducted by the 800-
COCAINE hotline found that 75% of the callers had used drugs on the job;

69% worked regularly while under the influence of cocaine and 25% used cocaine regularly (DeCresce, Lifshitz, Mazura, & Tilson, 1989).

Drug and alcohol abuse cuts across all industries and occupational strata. The prevalence of the drug of choice in the workplace does not appear to be related to the type of business or industry. According to a June 1987 survey of 1,974 employers in manufacturing, insurance, financial services, civil services, transportation, health care, education, retailing, and other businesses, alcohol was identified as the number-one problem by 86% of all the employers responding to the survey. Marijuana was identified as the number-two problem (64%), followed by cocaine (38%) and amphetamines/ barbiturates (23%) (Business and Legal Reports, 1989).

Moreover, the effects of alcohol and drugs are even more pervasive, given the level of compromised performance of "codependents"—employed family members or friends who live with the alcohol or drug abuser.

Notwithstanding extensive media coverage and alarm, employers disagree about the severity of the problem in their companies. Many fear that publicity about the prevalence of drugs may be misinterpreted by outsiders as a reflection on their quality and moral character. However, most agree that cocaine and marijuana are growing problems in industry.

Because alcohol is legal, management often downplays its debilitating effects. Corporate denial of the consequences of alcohol abuse parallels the denial defense mechanism often employed by alcoholics and codependents. However, often overlooked are the enabling aspects of denial by those who are involved in significant workplace relationships with alcohol abusers, including supervisors and upper-level managers (Barger, 1985/1986). Managers, who often drink at company parties and business lunches, view drinking as an adult right and refuse to acknowledge alcohol abuse as a disease in their ranks (Barger, 1985/1986). Some of the corporate executives who deny the problem in their companies may be addicted and denying the problem in themselves.

Lastly, the underestimation of the prevalence of workplace alcohol and drug use stems from managers' and supervisors' ignorance of the signs and symptoms of alcohol and drug use and their effect on job performance. Underreporting of abuse by employees themselves is prevalent because some employees anticipate punishment, including social stigma, legal complications, and disciplinary action (Browne, 1986).

IMPACT OF ALCOHOL AND DRUG ABUSE IN THE WORKPLACE

Alcohol and drug abuse share a common thread in industry in their destructive impact on job performance. Absenteeism and tardiness appear to be the most significant workplace performance problems associated with drug and alcohol use. Other problems, identified in descending order of perceived significant association, include accidents, poor quality of work, conflicts with supervisors, conflicts with peers, low quantity of work, and missed deadlines on assignments (Wilkinson, cited in Backer, 1987). Those harmfully involved with alcohol or other drugs are less productive, more likely to injure themselves or others, absent significantly more often, prone to arrive late or leave early more often, and habitual users of company sickness benefits, including health insurance claims. In analyzing the effects of alcohol and other drugs, it is evident that these substances pose particular risks for the user and nonuser alike in the work environment (DeCresce et al., 1989).

Alcohol

Acknowledged to be the most prevalent and destructive drug of abuse in America today, alcohol has the most destructive impact in the workplace. It is well documented that the productivity of alcohol-impaired workers is significantly compromised (Bureau of National Affairs, 1986). Up to 40% of industrial fatalities and 47% of industrial injuries can be linked to alcohol consumption and alcoholism (Bernstein & Mahoney, 1989).

The physical signs of alcohol abuse observable by supervisory personnel include the odor of alcohol on the breath, slurred speech, unstable gait, and lessening of inhibitions. Employees who are intoxicated or even "under the influence" can be impaired on the job through loss of motor coordination, memory deficits, confusion in following instructions, poor judgment caused by loosened inhibitions, and lack of awareness of the consequences of their behavior while intoxicated. Thus alcohol use can pose serious risk to the employee and others in a potentially hazardous work environment, for example, an automobile manufacturing plant.

Marijuana

Commonly used by employees today, marijuana is a mood-altering substance that produces a pronounced distortion of perceptions. Physical signs of abuse include redness of eyes, loss of motor coordination, and obvious sedation.

Experts disagree about the extent to which job performance can be impaired by marijuana use. However, as a fat-soluble drug, delta-9-tetrahydrocannabinol (THC) is stored in the fatty tissues of the body. Regular users of marijuana are never completely free of THC, since it accumulates in the brain and other organs. Although employees who are weekend and evening users of marijuana claim that use does not impair on-the-job performance, medical experts have discovered that marijuana builds up and remains in the body for up to 3 weeks after use; thus it can impair on-the-job functioning.

This, of course, depends on the frequency and quantity of marijuana consumed.

In the work environment, marijuana use on or off the job can cause decreased work motivation and, thus, lowered performance. Moreover, short-term memory is impaired by marijuana; thus a habitual smoker may be unable to recall important information on the job. Through sedation, sensori-motor function is also impaired, causing slowed reaction times and mis-judged distances when operating mechanical equipment (automobiles, trucks, airplanes, fork lifts, and even typewriters); thus employers may be legally liable if marijuana use has been disclosed and an accident is caused by a marijuana user.

Cocaine

Cocaine is one of the most frequently abused drugs in the United States today. In 1985 it was estimated that 30 million people used cocaine at least once, with 5 million individuals using regularly. Approximately 5,000 people try cocaine every day (Abelson & Miller, 1985).

According to many experts, abuse of cocaine has been increasing rapidly in the inner-city populations, in part because of the popularity of crack. It is thought that the relative inexpensiveness of crack, the "rock" form of cocaine, has been instrumental in its mass marketability (Ferrandino, 1986). However, recent trends suggest that cocaine use is declining somewhat among the middle class, probably in response to the public's awareness of the dangers of cocaine despite its reputation for enhancing social interaction and the euphoric high it induces.

Before the drug takes its toll, cocaine-using employees often believe they are performing well, whereas in reality performance is inadequate, inaccurate, and of poor quality (Browne, 1986). Signs of cocaine use include erratic behavior, dramatic weight loss, untidy appearance and poor personal hygiene, irritability and short temperedness with coworkers, mood swings, fatigue, a lowered sense of self-esteem, and borrowing money from co-workers. As the cocaine user becomes more addicted, the desire for workplace advancement, work quality, and reliability diminishes. As a person becomes increasingly dependent on the drug, frantic efforts to support the habit may include selling cocaine to coworkers, selling company possessions, and embezzling money (Browne, 1986).

Sedatives

Quaalude and other sedatives can produce slurred speech, loss of motor coordination, decreased reaction time, and impaired judgment. On-the-job use of sedatives poses a serious risk of injury to self or others, as demonstrated by the fact that the accident rate for users of sedatives and other central nervous system depressants like alcohol is disproportionately higher than for nonusers (DeCresce et al., 1989). Other drugs or alcohol potentiate their sedative and motor effects.

Heroin

Heroin is used by 1% to 3% of all employees. Heroin produces a feeling of well-being followed by a craving or withdrawal. Therefore use inhibits job performance via distraction (Browne, 1986).

One reason that heroin is not as problematic in the workplace as other drugs is because heroin addicts often cannot maintain normal functioning sufficient to remain employed. Due to the drug's addictive properties, heroin users report "stopping at nothing" to secure the drug, including theft and violence. Thus it is clear how unmanageable a heroin habit is in the work environment, where employees are surrounded by such "distractions" from the heroin habit as schedules, deadlines, and myriad other responsibilities.

Methadone

Methadone was initially used in Germany as Dolophine, a drug to replace the painkiller morphine, during World War II. Early in the 1960s, methadone was imported to the United States to be used as a legally controlled alternative to heroin. Although methadone possesses analgesic qualities, methadone users report none of the euphoric feelings associated with heroin. Experts believe methadone users can function in the work setting as long as they are maintained on a regular dose. Yet since it has analgesic and sedative effects, risks exist in some occupations. For example, a security guard who is using methadone may be less alert than a nonusing coworker.

EMPLOYERS' RESPONSE

Faced with one of the biggest employment issues of the decade, employers are using proactive methods to counter the threat posed by drug and alcohol use by employees. In addition to drug testing, companies are beginning to see the value of rehabilitating addicted employees through implementing EAPs rather than summarily discharging them and hiring replacements. In addition to creating bottom-line cost savings (by eliminating the expense of hiring and retraining), EAPs positively impact employee morale by demonstrating genuine concern on the part of management. Increasing legal challenges by discharged employees also make employers reluctant to terminate employment unless they have tried to rehabilitate the troubled employee. Clearly the best defense for a company sued by a discharged substance-abusing employee is to appear before judicial authority having demonstrated rehabilitative efforts, that is, referral to an EAP.

Drug Testing

Aside from the major motivation of reducing productivity losses, personnel turnover, and health insurance costs, why are employers testing in such great numbers? The first reason is public pressure. Whether due to national media bombardment or local community publicity about the dangers of drugs, our society is more frightened of drug use than ever before. Politicians and the public are demanding a solution that is both inexpensive and immediate (Greenblatt, 1987). Employers are responding to this anxiety by taking control within their corporate limits in the form of drug-testing programs. Second, laboratories and drug-testing companies have placed tremendous pressure on corporate America in their sales presentations, generating competition to test employees; thus, as one employer chooses this method, others follow. Finally, testing technology has only in recent years produced a relatively inexpensive testing procedure that offers an objective, although not always reliable, method of screening and detection.

According to the American Management Association, 63% of industrial firms that responded to a 1991 survey were engaged in some type of drug testing, representing a 20% increase since 1987 (Greenberg, 1991). In 1986, 30% of all Fortune 500 companies were employing some type of drug testing, with more planning such strategies in the future (DeCresce et al., 1989). The College Placement Council, Inc., surveyed 1,200 employers on their use of drug testing. Of the 497 companies that responded to the survey, 30% said they screen new college graduates for drugs; another 20% said they would begin testing soon. Of the companies that do test, 88% said they would not hire a graduate who tested positive, while 38% said they would retest a graduate who tested positive on the first test (DeCresce et al., 1989). Testing programs vary greatly across companies and occur in both public and private work settings.

Numerous court challenges to drug testing—particularly random, unannounced testing—have been generated. These more aggressive methods invoke loud cries from employees, civil liberties groups, and others who have begun to seek legal remedies for what they consider to be, among other things, (1) invasion of privacy, (2) defamation, (3) intentional infliction of emotional distress, and (4) discrimination against those "handicapped" by alcoholism or drug addiction. The Fourth Amendment of the Constitution protects individuals from unreasonable search and seizure by the government. Since private-sector employers are not controlled by the Fourth Amendment, private-sector employees have no federal constitutional protection from drug testing by their employers. Conversely, public-sector employees *are* protected; thus legal challenges to the testing of public employees without probable cause have been relatively successful.

In considering testing procedures, companies must carefully weigh the positive value of maintaining employee health and safety through a drug-free environment against the potentially adverse impact of testing on employee relations.

Types of Procedures

Drug-testing methods are procedures designed to detect metabolites that are formed in the liver after the body metabolizes or removes foreign chemicals from its system. Drug tests are used to provide evidence that drugs have been used (Greenblatt, 1987).

Drug testing can occur in four contexts: (1) preemployment drug screening; (2) testing for reasonable suspicion; (3) randomly; and (4) as part of an annual physical examination.

Preemployment Drug Screening. This involves testing employee candidates during a medical preemployment physcial prior. In general, the purpose of the medical examination is to rule out the existence of any physical condition that might impair the candidate's ability to perform the position being filled. Thus the preemployment drug test is an effective way to screen out addicted workers (Masi & Burns, 1986).

Reasonable Suspicion. This method involves testing employees when supervisory or managerial personnel have a reasonable belief or suspicion that an employee is under the influence of alcohol or drugs.

Random Testing. This method involves choosing a sample of employees randomly for screening. Testing occurs intermittently, with all employees in specific areas eligible for testing during these trials. This method is used to catch the truly addicted worker as well as to deter drug use, since employees never know when testing will occur. This method stimulates heated debates because of privacy concerns and the lack of notice (Masi & Burns, 1986).

Testing as Part of an Annual Physical Examination. As in preemployment physicals, drug testing is part of an annual physical examination. This method, often used to avoid the legal pitfalls associated with random testing, appears, however, to target the more severely addicted or ignorant user.

Obviously, companies cannot ignore the need to control workplace drug use. Regardless of its negative effects on employer–employee relations, drug testing, even random drug testing, will likely be required of those performing jobs that involve the potential of harm arising from drug use, for example, bus drivers, train conductors, and pilots. Here, the cost of an accident outweighs the cost of individual inconvenience or infringement of the right to privacy.

Drug-Testing Methods

Drug-screening methods are unfortunately not completely accurate. The most popular urine test, EMIT (enzyme multiplied immunoassay test), is the cheapest but least reliable one. Since the consequences of a false positive can be grave, more expensive confirmatory tests, including gas chromatography, gas chromatography combined with mass spectrometry, and high-performance liquid chromatography, are utilized. The chromatographic techniques detect a variety of drugs in the body fluids (reliably distinguishing among drugs), whereas mass spectrometry is a quantitative measure (detecting even small amounts). These tests are often more intrusive and more expensive, but they are clearly more accurate.

A major problem with these tests is their sensitivity; drugs may remain in the body long after exposure to them. The EMIT technique produces many false positives, indicating the presence of metabolites when none exist. In some cases, the false positive rate for some drugs, like marijuana, has exceeded 20% (Greenblatt, 1987). Testing indicates only that drugs have been used, not when. Marijuana can be detected up to 3 weeks after use. Smoking a single joint can be detected for up to 5 days. If marijuana intoxication lasts a few hours, how descriptive is a positive urine test for marijuana if it can be excreted even weeks after exposure? A cocaine positive test is more telling, signaling use only within 1 to 3 days after use (Bickerton, 1986).

Moreover, use of such substances as caffeine, cough syrups, and antihistamines can confound test results. Medical literature suggests that false positive results can occur in from 1% to 35% of all tests. Tests positive for amphetamines may be caused by some over-the-counter nasal decongestants; tests positive for cocaine may be caused by certain teas, Advil, or Nuprin; some over-the-counter drugs can show positive for phenobarbital. Since cocaine is sometimes cut with quinine, is a test positive for quinine indicative of cocaine use or simply a preference for tonic water? In addition, urine tests positive for marijuana may be produced by inhalation of someone else's smoke. Thus it is incumbent upon the company to send the positive urine sample for a confirmatory test.

The National Association of Social Workers (NASW), New York City Chapter (1989), has developed written policy guidelines to address the issue of drug testing in the workplace. Basically, NASW believes that substance abuse at the worksite should be approached through education, treatment, and prevention, ideally through an EAP. The NASW opposes the random drug testing of individuals. However, if an organization choses to institute drug-testing procedures, the NASW recommends the following:

1. A written policy outlining the company's drug testing procedures should be developed and distributed to all employees. This policy should specify the circumstances under which testing will occur as well as what will happen if a test result is positive.
2. A licensed laboratory that ensures chain-of-custody and uses split samples and confirmatory testing should be used in order to minimize sampling errors.
3. Disciplinary action against the employee who tests positive should be instituted only after the employee is offered a referral to an EAP. Job termination should be based solely on job performance, not on a positive drug test per se.
4. Employers instituting preemployment drug testing should inform applicants in writing of their policies with regard to testing and the consequences of a positive test. Results should be communicated to the applicants confidentially. Referrals for treatment should be offered to applicants denied employment on the basis of a positive test result (NASW, 1989).

In summary, if a company desires to institute a drug-testing program, it is recommended that the following criteria be followed:

1. Use a high-quality, reliable screen to reduce false positives.
2. Use a reputable laboratory that will do retesting.
3. Use a laboratory that will confirm positive tests with a different method (95% to 99% accurate).
4. Use a laboratory whose procedures for collecting samples minimize dilution and sample switching. Given the frequency and ingenuity with which some addicted individuals substitute another's urine sample, samples should be collected in plain view of a person of the same sex. (This eliminates false negatives but heightens privacy invasion concerns.)

Drug testing should be performed to identify "troubled employees" with a drug or alcohol problem and to provide rehabilitative assistance. One positive test should never be the sole reason for disciplining an employee. The urine sample should be retested by a more accurate confirmatory test and the employee referred to an EAP for evaluation.

Employee Assistance Programs

Despite some companies' reluctance to admit their need for EAPs, the number of companies instituting such programs has grown dramatically in the last decade. According to a survey conducted by the New York State Division of Alcoholism and Alcohol Abuse, 47.5% of companies with more than 2,000 employees had EAPs (Trager, 1992). In 1989 over 90% of the Fortune 500 companies had EAPs (Burke, 1988). Smaller businesses appear to be developing EAPs, both independently and as part of consortiums; however, the rate of growth in general for EAPs in smaller companies is slower than that for larger ones (Trager, 1992).

The increased demand for EAP services over the past two decades is a result of companies' heightened concern about drug use and the proven record of EAPs in helping substance-abusing employees to recover. It costs companies less to treat and rehabilitate a valued employee than to recruit, hire, and train a replacement. According to some experts, it can cost over $7,000 to replace a salaried worker, over $10,000 to replace a midlevel employee, and over $40,000 to replace a senior executive ("Recruiting Trends," 1987). While figures on cost-effectiveness vary widely, employers generally find that they save between $5 and $16 for every dollar invested in EAPs (U.S. Department of Labor, 1989).

Drug Testing versus EAPs

Whereas many companies have responded to the drug crisis by instituting drug testing in concert with EAPs, others have instituted *only* drug testing and other more aggressive methods, including drug-sniffing dogs, locker searches, and undercover agents (Masi & Burns, 1986). If the employer refers employees for drug tests based on performance and does not have an EAP for rehabilitation, the goal of assisting employees with abuse problems is left unrealized. Drug testing solely for the purpose of labeling abusing employees and terminating them is clearly not in the best interests of employees and the company as a whole.

IMPACT OF FEDERAL LEGISLATION ON ALCOHOL AND DRUG USE IN THE WORKPLACE

Both the Americans with Disabilities Act (ADA) of 1990 and the Drug Free Workplace Act (DFWA) of 1988 represent positive steps in the way employees with alcohol or drug abuse problems are managed in the workplace. Under the ADA, employers must accommodate their employees' or job applicants' known disabilities unless doing so would impose an "undue hardship" on the business. The ADA allows for testing of illegal drug use. Employees who show positive on the drug test are not protected by the ADA and thus do not have to be reasonably accommodated. Job applicants who presently use illegal drugs are not considered disabled; thus an employer does not have to accommodate those individuals. However, former drug users who no longer use illegal drugs and are undergoing or have completed treatment are protected by the ADA.

The ADA does, however, prohibit firing and other disciplinary actions against employees recovering from alcoholism through treatment programs. Thus proof of alcoholism may be an individual's protection against termination—as long as the individual agrees to enter a treatment program.

The DFWA specifies that employers with any federal contract or grant in excess of $25,000 must provide a drug-free environment. The requirements to provide a drug-free workplace include the following:

1. Developing and distributing to all employees a written drug policy that specifies what actions will be taken if a controlled substance is used, distributed, or possessed in the workplace
2. Providing an education program to inform employees about the dangers of workplace drug abuse and the availability of drug counseling, rehabilitation, and employee assistance programs
3. Notifying the federal contracting agency of any criminal drug statute conviction occurring in the workplace

The company, however, is not required to establish an employee assistance program, although it must inform their employees about help available in the community. Thus social workers must educate organizations and the community at large about the need for EAPs.

ROLE OF SOCIAL WORKER IN HELPING ALCOHOL- AND DRUG-ABUSING EMPLOYEES

The multifaceted role of the social worker in industry is critical to identifying and treating drug- and alcohol-abusing employees. The social worker is ideally suited to practice in the work setting by virtue of the applicability of a systems approach. Systems theory, the foundation of case management practice, focuses on the environment within which the employee must function rather than on his or her intrapsychic conflicts. The industrial social worker's role is to assist the client and effect change for both the employer and employee by prescribing a treatment plan that, if followed, will enable the employee to perform the job satisfactorily (Roberts-DeGennaro, 1986).

Although the EAP clinician can perform therapeutic tasks, his or her role with substance-abusing employees should be restricted to motivating the employee to seek help and coordinating the rehabilitative treatment by outside resources. This is necessary because clinical practice in labor and business requires brief and effective models of intervention (Kurzman & Akabas, 1981). Social workers have a distinct advantage over others in the EAP field because of their level of understanding of emotional illness, separate and apart from drug and alcohol use, while EAP counselors who are trained solely in alcohol abuse and have no clinical background can be legally liable for either misdiagnosing or failing to diagnose underlying emotional illness (Diesenhaus, 1985/1986).

The social worker has a complex role and must be skilled as (1) a *trainer* who educates supervisors and managers to become aware of performance-based indicators of alcohol or drug use; (2) a *consultant* who collaborates with management to formulate policy and procedures regarding substance-abusing employees, including drug-testing procedures; and (3) a knowledgeable *clinician* who is adept at making quick and accurate assessments of addictive disorders and referring for ongoing treatment.

Role as Trainer

The greatest roadblock to providing treatment for the alcohol or drug abuser is the difficulty of motivating the abuser to seek help. Employers can play a critical role in this process. Simply put, the boss wields the authority to both hire—and fire. The fear of job loss is usually the catalyst that motivates the alcohol- or drug-abusing employee to seek and complete rehabilitation.

Giving supervisors the knowledge and skills to effectively refer employees to the EAP is a critical task of the industrial social worker. The social worker must develop and conduct a comprehensive training program for supervisors and managers based on a performance model for evaluating the work-related effects of alcohol or drug use. In some settings, however, supervisors are trained to spot signs and symptoms of alcohol or drug use. Most EAP training concentrates on observing deterioration in job performance, confronting employees with their compromised performance or conduct, and referring them to the EAP.

Supervisory referrals are especially significant because addicted individuals often use denial; few employees with drug or alcohol problems will self-refer for treatment. Experience shows that supervisor-referred addicted employees often show a high degree of motivation; in such cases, the employee has "hit bottom" and usually cooperates with treatment recommendations. It is well established in the EAP field that the success rate for addicted employees is greater when threat of job loss looms. It is this bold coercion with which some social workers have philosophical difficulty.

Role as Consultant

The consultant role is particularly critical in regard to urinalysis testing. While an EAP should never itself administer drug tests, it should assert its role in this area because of the pervasiveness of drug testing. Remaining aloof from voicing concerns about testing may encourage companies to choose drug testing as a cheaper, expedient way to weed out drug users, rather than as a means of targeting employees with problems who need referral to the EAP. As consultant, the social worker assists management with developing a policy and procedural statement to address alcohol and drug use in the workplace, including drug testing. Will employees who test positive be terminated, suspended, or offered rehabilitation? The consultant should advocate for supervisory referrals to the EAP for all employees who test positive on a urinalysis. EAPs should avoid direct involvement with actual urine testing, since such involvement would compromise its image in the eyes of employees. Although assessment and referral of employees who have tested positive for drugs or alcohol should be done through the EAP, urine testing itself should be monitored by the treatment center, not the EAP (Masi & Burns, 1986).

Industrial social workers often act as consultants to supervisors on how to manage the addicted employee on the job (Straussner, 1990). Frequently, the confrontation process of treatment actually begins on the job during the supervisory corrective interview. The purpose of such an interview is to develop an understanding in the employee of his or her performance, including specific areas of impairment and need for change (Groenveld & Shain, 1985). The effectiveness of the corrective interview depends on the supervisor's communications skill and on the ability of the alcohol- or drug-dependent employee to squarely confront his or her difficulties (Groenveld & Shain, 1985). The social worker often counsels the supervisor on how best to communicate performance expectations to the employee and provides guidelines and suggestions for the supervisor regarding the substance-abusing employee's return to work (Owen & Spicer, 1986).

Role of Clinician

Many social workers are relatively untrained in dealing with addictive disorders, since schools of social work give short shrift to the addictions. Consequently, the effectiveness of confrontation as a clinical tool in addictions treatment is poorly understood by most social workers. Social workers are not trained to "threaten" individuals into accepting help. Although coercion has proved exceedingly successful in the work with substance abusers, the philosophical merit of this approach is questioned by some traditionally trained clinicians. The treatment of addictions in the workplace is externally imposed, not self-directed. The social worker must accept this philosophy prima facie (Levinson & Straussner, 1978).

Still, some traditionally trained clinicians continue to see drug dependence as a symptom of a deep-seated neurosis that must be treated if the addiction is to be cured. This view is contradicted, however, by the success of current rehabilitation programs, which approach chemical dependence as a unique, progressive illness that requires detoxification and structured group treatment (Gold, 1984).

Clinicians need to confront their misconceptions. EAP practitioners cannot assume that adolescents smoke pot, executives snort cocaine, and middle-aged individuals abuse alcohol. These assumptions lead to misdiagnoses or missed diagnoses. Alcohol and drug use cross all socioeconomic strata and job classifications (Browne, 1986).

Industrial social workers in EAPs should consider all employees, whether self- or supervisor-referred, as possible substance abusers. The skilled clinician must provide a thorough assessment, usually including use of a structured questionnaire focusing on alcohol or drug use.

Often the substance-abusing employee comes to the EAP grudgingly, with much hostility and little faith in the ability of the counselor to provide assistance. Ruben (1986) identified a six-step model for effective clinical intervention: (1) introduction, (2) identification, (3) clarification, (4) recognition, (5) empathy, and (6) recommendation.

In the *introduction step*, the clinician presents his or her credentials, explains the EAP's role, and describes the company's policy on employees with personal difficulties. Employees are assured confidentiality in order to facilitate the therapeutic alliance necessary for an honest appraisal of alcohol or drug use. Assurances of confidentiality are further strengthened through use of a written consent form for release of information. This form is often signed by supervisor-referred employees, since EAP intervention is usually considered positively in the supervisor's decision about discipline. When the client has *not* signed such a form, federal regulations, where applicable, clearly delineate the guidelines for the confidentiality of alcohol and drug abuse records. As Hofmann (1981) points out, the problem for EAP practitioners becomes the extent of confidentiality: Is it absolute or are there exceptions when the need to reveal information to supervisory personnel without client consent overrides privacy concerns?

With employees in sensitive positions—such as air traffic controllers, pilots, railroad engineers—the clinician elicits information that may have consequences for the public at large. For example, the EAP clinician finds that an employee in a sensitive or potentially hazardous position is using drugs only occasionally and that true addiction is absent. Should the supervisor or manager be informed, given that even off-the-job, occasional use can cause sufficient distraction to alter judgment and reaction time? Besides the concern that some new industrial social workers may have about disclosure to managerial personnel, the seasoned EAP clinician continues to experience conflict about confidentiality and the extent of information that should be provided to supervisory personnel. Confidentiality and privileged communication are not identical. Confidentiality is governed by rules of ethics; privileged communication, by rules of law (Hofmann, 1981). EAP staff must be careful never to respond to rumors or requests in such a way that they unintentionally reveal confidential information. Generally, only information pertinent to the motivation and cooperation of the referred employee is disclosed, for example, the referred employee has (has not) kept appointments and has (has not) been cooperative with EAP recommendations. Information about the problem itself is not routinely released unless alcohol and drug use would present a clear and present danger to the employee or others if left untreated. If an employee holds a sensitive or potentially hazardous position, the EAP clinician has a duty to society and *the company* to warn management of the potential harm of continued alcohol or drug use.

Also, since the confidentiality is one-sided, employees themselves may disclose any information they choose to anyone. In fact, many alleged violations of confidentiality presumed to be the EAP clinician's fault actually result from careless or deliberate revelations by the clients themselves (Hofmann, 1981).

In the *identification* and *clarification steps*, the clinician takes a general history, listens actively, and asks probing questions. The EAP clinician reflects genuine interest and concern by suspending judgment and expressing a readiness to assist the employee with his or her problem. Besides demographic data, information is gathered about how the individual came to the EAP (supervisor-referred, self-referred, etc.) and about the employee's overall level of job satisfaction. The supervisory referral creates added responsibility for the social worker because this often indicates that the employee's job is in jeopardy and that the supervisor is relying on the professional expertise of EAP staff to evaluate the employee's personnel and occupational conflicts. The client's level of insight regarding the threat of job loss is analyzed in order to assess the degree of denial. Is communication between the supervisor and the employee flawed, or is the employee using denial? The employee must appreciate the consequences of his or her behavior—that discipline or even termination will result from noncompliance. Some supervisors mandate and others simply recommend substance-abusing employees to the EAP.

A thorough history begins with gathering information on past substance use, including age of onset, quantity and frequency of substance use, previous treatment, past employment situations (for evidence of termination for either drinking or taking drugs), and any suspensions of a driver's license for driving while intoxicated. It is important to know if the client has suffered the loss of a major relationship through death or separation, since this may be a reason and an excuse for chemical abuse. A complete assessment includes consideration of self-esteem and level of functioning (Roberts-DeGennaro, 1986), particularly whether the employee is hopeful or depressed to the point of despair.

Through skillful intervention in the *recognition* and *empathy steps*, the employee's denial of abuse is systematically confronted. Confrontation is a necessary and accepted approach in EAP intervention and addictions treatment. The addicted employee often externalizes blame, including blaming the work situation itself, "blind" to his or her own role in the job conflict.

At the end of the clinical intervention, the *recommendation step*, the clinician prescribes a treatment plan for amelioration of the work crisis. The clinician should recommend a treatment plan and inform the employee of the consequences of continued deterioration in job performance if the problem is left untreated. Three basic types of treatment are available for varying degrees of dependence: (1) self-help groups (e.g., Alcoholics Anonymous, Narcotics Anonymous, and Cocaine Anonymous), (2) structured, intensive outpatient treatment, and (3) inpatient detoxification and/or rehabilitation. Common to all these methods is the proviso of permanent abstinence from the abused chemical.

Another possibility is to allow the employee to "go it alone," without outside professional intervention; this is an approach that creates dissension among substance-abuse experts, some of whom believe that a small percentage of addicted individuals can arrest abuse of alcohol or drugs without professional intervention. For example, the employee together with a supportive family member may "contract" with the EAP that if alcohol or drugs are used once again, a structured treatment program will be commenced (Gold, 1984). Unless, however, there are serious assurances (1) that an individual is an infrequent user of a drug, as substantiated by repeated random urine testing, and (2) that the employee is performing work that presents no apparent danger to self or others, the EAP clinician assumes grave risk in sanctioning the client to "go it alone."

Frequently a second evaluation by an outside expert in substance-abuse treatment is useful in adding credence to an EAP diagnosis of addictive or nonaddictive (recreational/social) use of drugs or alcohol. For the addicted, the second opinion can underscore the seriousness of the disease. For the nonaddicted, this evaluation emphasizes the dangers of substance use.

Self-help groups are successful in treating addictions and may comprise the total therapeutic regimen for some employees. Usually they prove most beneficial to the short-term drug or alcohol user or the regular user who is highly motivated (Gold, 1984). Since the EAP is responsible for assuring management that the substance-abusing employee is receiving appropriate help, referring employees to self-help groups carries some risk, since the EAP professional cannot monitor the client's attendance at required meetings. The success of these groups is based solely on self-motivation for change.

Therefore referral to either an inpatient or outpatient treatment program is frequently warranted. Generally, if an addicted individual (1) is cooperative during the assessment, (2) recognizes the problem, (3) agrees to attend outpatient alcohol or drug treatment, including self-help group meetings on no-treatment "free days," and (4) has a supportive network of family or friends, intensive outpatient treatment is the least restrictive method and is frequently successful. During referral, the employee must agree that compliance with the treatment plan is required; otherwise the more restrictive inpatient option will be recommended. The critical factor in recommending outpatient treatment is the support from a system of significant others.

Conversely, if an employee (1) is a high-dose user, (2) has few support systems, (3) has little recognition of the destructiveness of the addictive behavior, or (4) has been unsuccessful in previous outpatient treatment, a referral for inpatient rehabilitation is a safer and potentially more effective referral.

Rehabilitation begins what is an ongoing recovery process—no "cure" for alcohol or drug use exists. Self-help group involvement as an adjunct to primary rehabilitation is frequently a necessity for all forms of addictions treatment.

The EAP clinician locates and screens appropriate treatment facilities near the worksite or residence. A defined policy and referral procedures between the EAP and treatment providers are necessary and should include both criteria for acceptance into the treatment program and the types of information required by the EAP in follow-up on the case.

CONCLUSION

Helping employees with alcohol and drug problems in the workplace challenges social workers, moving them to the forefront in addressing one of the most significant employment issues of the decade. Although substance abuse in industry offers opportunities for social work practice, it also imposes added responsibilities. The challenge becomes whether the clinician can balance the traditional role of assisting the individual, in this case the employee, with serving the needs of the business. Although many clinicians frown on the use of drug testing as an invasion of privacy, these procedures are here to stay. Incorporating their complex roles as trainer, consultant, and clinician, social workers are well suited to providing help to the substance-abusing employee and, thus, to assisting companies in their objective of maintaining a drug- and alcohol-free environment.

REFERENCES

Abelson, H. I., & Miller, J. D. (1985). *A decade of trends in cocaine use in the household population* (National Institute on Drug Abuse Research Monograph No. 61). Washington, DC: U.S. Government Printing Office.

Backer, T. E. (1987). *Strategic planning for workplace drug abuse programs.* Washington, DC: National Institute on Drug Abuse.

Barger, M. D. (1985/1986). Is there a "conspiracy" to deny alcohol? *Employee Assistance Quarterly, 1*(2), 101-104

Bernstein, M., & Mahoney, J. J. (1989). Management perspectives on alcoholism: The employees' stake in alcoholism treatment. *Occupational Medicine, 4*(2), 223-232.

Bickerton, R. (1986, September/October). Urinalysis: Dilemma of the 80's. *EAP Digest,* pp. 27-35.

Browne, A. C. (1986). Drug and alcohol abuse among employees: Critical issues. *Employee Assistance Quarterly, 2*(1), 13-22.

Bureau of National Affairs. (1986). *Alcohol and drugs in the workplace: Costs, controls, and controversies.* Washington, DC: Author.

Burke, T. R. (1988). The economic impact of alcohol abuse and alcoholism. *Public Health Reports, 103*(6), 564-568.

Business and Legal Reports. (1989). 1987 survey presented to the American Society of Personnel Administrators. In *How to comply with the Drug Free Workplace Act.* Madison, CT: Author.

DeCresce, R. P., Lifshitz, M. S., Mazura, A. C., & Tilson, J. E. (1989). *Drug testing in the workplace.* Chicago: American Society of Clinical Pathologists Press.

Diesenhaus, H. I. (1985/1986). Program standards: Can we ever agree? *Employee Assistance Quarterly, 1*(2), 1-17.

Ferrandino, J. (1986, November/December). Crack: A $20 rock, billion dollar problem. *EAP Digest,* pp. 41-45.

Gold, M. (1984). *800-cocaine.* New York: Bantam.

Greenberg, E. (1991). *AMA survey of workplace drug testing and drug abuse policies* (American Management Association Research Reports). New York: American Management Association.

Greenblatt, D. J. (1987). Urine testing and drug abuse. *Harvard Mental Health Letter, 4*(2), 8.

Groenveld, J., & Shain, M. (1985). The effect of corrective interviews with alcohol dependent employees: A study of 37 supervisor-subordinate dyads. *Employee Assistance Quarterly, 1*(1), 63-73.

Hofmann, J. J. (1981). The duty to warn: The flipside of the confidentiality coin. *Labor–Management Alcoholism Journal, 10*(5), 198–203.

Kurzman, P., & Akabas, S. (1981). Industrial social work as an arena for practice. *Social Work, 26*(1), 52–60.

Levinson, V. R., & Straussner, S. L. A. (1978). Social workers as "enablers" in the treatment of alcoholism. *Social Casework, 59*(1) 14–20.

Masi, D. A., & Burns, L. E. (1986, September/October). Urinalysis testing and EAPs. *EAP Digest,* pp. 37–43.

National Association of Social Workers, New York City Chapter. (1989, February). *Drug-testing in the workplace: Guidelines for the profession* (Task Force Report). New York: Author.

National Institute on Alcohol Abuse and Alcoholism. (1990). *Alcohol and health: Seventh special report to Congress, 1990.* Washington, DC: U.S. Department of Health and Human Services.

National Institute on Drug Abuse. (1991). *National household survey on drug abuse: Main findings, 1991.* Washington, DC: U.S. Department of Health and Human Services.

Owen, P., & Spicer, J. (1986). When an alcoholic employee returns to work: The problems for supervisors and employees. *Employee Assistance Quarterly, 1*(4), 67–74.

Recruiting trends. (1987, October). *Enterprise,* p. 1.

Roberts-DeGennaro, M. (1986). The case management model in employee assistance programs. *Employee Assistance Quarterly, 1*(3), 63–74.

Ruben, D. H. (1986). Alcoholism/drug abuse counselors in industry: Do they need interpersonal skills? *Employee Assistance Quarterly, 1*(3), 57–62.

Straussner, S. L. A. (1990). Occupational social work today: An overview. In S. L. A. Straussner (Ed.), *Occupational social work today.* New York: Haworth.

Trager, C. S. (1992, June 8). Counseling plans grow with workplace stresses. *Crain's New York Business,* p. 30.

U.S. Department of Labor. (1989). *What works: Workplace without drugs.* Washington, DC: Author.

5

The Treatment of Addictive Disorders in a Private Clinical Setting

Kathy B. Gordon

Many clinicians consider addiction to be one of the most difficult disorders to treat and have questioned the individual practitioner's ability to have an impact. It is the premise of this chapter, however, that people with addictive disorders can be successfully treated in private practice using individual psychotherapy. While the private practitioner can expect to encounter many obstacles along the road to recovery, it is nonetheless a rich and rewarding work. It will also challenge and "stretch" even the most experienced practitioner.

This chapter focuses on individual treatment of the compulsive use of drugs and alcohol. First it provides a theoretical framework for psychotherapeutic treatment. Next, an outline for treatment is provided, including how to assess the problem, engage the patient in treatment, and help him or her achieve abstinence from all substances. This chapter also explores commonly encountered treatment issues, such as countertransference, the use of prescribed medication, treatment impasses, and the role of 12-step recovery programs.

THEORETICAL FRAMEWORK

There is certainly no shortage of theories on why people use and abuse drugs. Modern psychodynamic theorists have suggested that the addicted individual has major deficits in psychic structure that leave him or her unable to access, tolerate, and regulate affective states. The drug user's compulsive use of mood-altering substances is seen as an attempt to manage painful affects, such as anxiety and depression. The use of substances is the person's attempt to shore up a fragile and vulnerable self.

Krystal and Kaskin (1970) see the alcohol- or drug-dependent person as someone who has experienced trauma early in life. Mood-altering substances are used because the person anticipates, and dreads, being traumatized once again. The drug user is attempting to modify his or her state of consciousness and, in so doing, modify painful affects, such as depression and anxiety, as well as the experience of no affect—the feeling of nothingness. This modification of consciousness through the use of mood-altering substances can take three forms. The first is a form of anesthesia, where the result is a reduction of anxiety. A second takes the form of reinterpretation of the person's psychic reality. By altering affect, there is a basic modification in the person's sense of self. The third change in consciousness is the experience of disorientation and dissociation. This state of consciousness allows the drug user to disavow the painful affect.

Edward Khantzian (1981; Khantzian, Halliday, & McAuliffe, 1990) also writes about the chemically dependent person as someone with developmental and structural deficits. Like Krystal, he sees major problems in affect tolerance and self-regulation, as well problems in self-esteem and the ability to manage relationships. He also identifies impairment in what he calls "self-care" functions. Khantzian argues that the self-destructive behavior so commonly visible among substance abusers is not in fact a deliberate attempt at hurting the self. On the contrary, he feels that due to early deprivation in the mother–child relationship, the addicted person did not develop the ego functions that help a person take care of or protect him- or herself. As a result, the chemically dependent adult lacks a basic self-protective instinct and engages in various behaviors that put him or her at risk for harm. Such a person often lacks the ability to think about or anticipate the consequences of these behaviors.

Leon Wurmser (1980) views drug use as a defense against dysphoric, overwhelming affects. He sees overwhelming anxiety and feelings of "pain, injury, woundedness, and vulnerability" as common to all compulsive drug users (p. 71). Wurmser writes of the addict's "false self," a personality split between compliance and conformity on the one hand, and rebellion and injury on the other.

Richard Ulman and Harry Paul (1988) also view the addict's use of a psychoactive substance as an attempt to modify affects by changing one's state of consciousness. They see the use of the substance as triggering certain early childhood fantasies that, in essence, alter one's state of consciousness. These fantasies are either of being merged with a strong, protective, idealized parental figure who calms and soothes, or of having one's specialness and power recognized, admired, and validated.

Common to all of these theorists is the belief in the significance of which particular substance a person chooses to use. As different substances affect mood in different ways, they are used to provide specific psychological functions. Khantzian (Khantzian & Schneider, 1985) speaks of the "drug of choice" phenomenon, whereby the addict uses a particular drug to medicate a particular affect. He breaks this down into drugs that energize, such as cocaine; drugs that provide a sense of release from inhibitions and anxiety, such as alcohol and barbiturates; and drugs that stabilize, such as narcotics. Wurmser (1980) writes that narcotics and hypnotic drugs are used to defend against feelings of rage and anxiety, stimulants against depression and weakness, and alcohol against anxiety and loneliness. Ulman and Paul (1989) write about "manic" or "rageful" addicts who sedate and tranquilize themselves with depressants, "depressive" or "lonely" addicts who stimulate and inflate themselves with stimulants, and "manic–depressive" addicts who use a combination of depressants and stimulants to regulate their vacillating moods.

Thus, for chemically dependent persons, mood-altering substances are a crucial part of their psychic lifelines. Psychotherapy provides addicts with the unique opportunity not only to relinquish the compulsive use of drugs but also to make significant changes in their basic sense of themselves in the world. Through the therapeutic relationship, addicts' vulnerable selves are strengthened and their self-esteem increased and stabilized; they also develop an ability to access, tolerate and regulate dysphoric affective states. Such individuals are no longer dependent on altered states of consciousness to make their way in the world.

THE THERAPEUTIC STANCE

Heinz Kohut (1971, 1977), who developed self psychology, and others (Stolorow, Brandchaft, & Atwood, 1987) have identified the optimal therapeutic stance as one that is an empathic and attuned inquiry into patients' subjective sense of themselves and their world. Nowhere is this more true and necessary than when treating the addicted patient. The clinician must create a therapeutic environment that invites the patient to open up and share his or her personal world. To create such an environment the therapist must sustain a supportive, involved, and empathic stance.

The challenge before the clinician is to remain empathic while systematically addressing the patient's current substance use. Before abstinence has been achieved, it is important to keep the focus of treatment on the patient's active substance use, while continuing to express interest in other areas of the patient's life. Many active addicts will be more comfortable talking about their other life problems than talking about their overarching problem of drug or alcohol abuse. There is always ambivalence about stopping drug use, even if this is explicitly why the person has entered treatment. This is understandable, given the powerful psychic function the substance serves. This ambivalence will often take the form of denial—denial of use, denial of how much of or how often an addictive substance is being used, or denial of the negative consequences of use. The patient thinks, "If we don't talk about it, maybe I won't have to do anything about it and the problem will go away." It is imperative that the therapist not collude with the patient in side-stepping the issue (Levinson & Straussner, 1978).

Some therapists might be reluctant to redirect attention on the patient's drug use for fear that this will threaten the patient and drive him or her out of treatment. Other therapists might feel that the drug use is merely a symptom of an underlying psychological problem, and when this problem is uncovered and resolved, the substance abuse will recede. While both of these positions are understandable, they are nonetheless countertherapeutic.

While the patient may indeed be threatened or angered by the therapist's persistent focus on the addiction, he or she will have little respect for the therapist who does not do so. The anger the patient will feel at the therapist for trying to take away what is perceived as a lifeline is inevitable and should be directly addressed. On the other extreme, the therapist who confronts the patient's denial or ambivalence in a vengeful and hostile way will very likely end up without a patient. The therapist must talk with the patient about active substance use in a direct and firm manner without becoming accusatory or attacking.

The therapist who treats the addiction as a symptom also colludes with the patient's resistance to stopping drug use by providing a convenient rationale: "I don't have to stop using until I really understand why I started using." This rationale can allow the patient to keep using a life-threatening substance indefinitely. Cognitive understanding of why one began using drugs does not magically remove the compulsion to use them.

Working through a patient's denial of addiction is a critical part of the treatment process (Bean, 1981). The therapist must understand that for the addicted patient, the thought of life without mood-altering substances is terrifying. How, he wonders, will he possibly be able to tolerate the bad feelings, the loneliness? How can she manage without her constant companion? Denial of the label of "alcoholic" or "addict" is often also related to a sense of shame about what the person feels the label implies. Usually the concern is that if one is an "addict," one is therefore "sick," "defective," and so forth. The therapist must empathically help the patient understand and sort through these various feelings.

If the patient comes to a session under the influence of a mind- and mood-altering substance, this naturally must be addressed. The therapist must ascertain why the patient got high. For example, is the patient self-medicating prior to a session in anticipation of experiencing painful affects? In the end, the therapist must point out that no real work can go on while the patient is high. If the patient continues to come to sessions high, the therapist will have to make it clear that the therapeutic relationship cannot continue under these circumstances. At this point hospitalization or a rehabilitation center should be considered.

Once drug or alcohol use has stopped, there will be an intensified need for the therapist. Krystal and Raskin (1970) emphasize that in the initial stages of treatment there is often a need for the therapist to be considerably active in the patient's life in order to help with affect regulation. The patient, stripped of his or her one means of coping, will look to the therapist for help in managing feelings of anxiety, depression, and emptiness.

This need should not be viewed as pathological. It is a legitimate developmental need that patient and therapist need to understand together. Just as substance use was once the focus of the patient's life, therapy and the therapist must now assume a central position.

It is particularly important that the therapist take this into consideration when planning with the patient for times, such as vacations, when the therapist will be away. The newly sober patient will need some support to take the place of the missing therapist. This may take the form of a backup therapist, increased attendance at Alcoholics Anonymous (AA) or Narcotics Anonymous (NA) meetings, or telephone contact with the therapist.

Thus the clinician who chooses to work with addicted patients must be active, flexible, and creative. A case example will illustrate the therapist's use of self in an active and flexible way in an effort to meet the needs of the newly sober patient:

> Linda was a 21-year-old woman of Italian descent, addicted to alcohol, cocaine, and marijuana. She presented herself to the therapist simultaneously as an insecure, anxious lost kid and as a pseudo-tough, wise-cracking, life-of-the-party teenager, always looking for the angle and the way to slide by with a minimal amount of effort. Linda was physically abused by both her mother and her alcoholic father and described feeling lonely and abandoned as a child. As an adult, Linda's entire life revolved around getting high, and all her friends were active users. She had not been sober since she was 13 years old and had no idea how to relate to another person without the use of some mind- and mood-altering substance.
>
> During the early period of her treatment, Linda was considerably more eager to talk about her dysfunctional family or her dislike of her job than about her drinking and drug use. The therapist's stance was to express interest and concern over the difficulties she was having in other areas of her life but to consistently bring the focus of their discussions back to her addictions.
>
> The therapist took an active role in helping Linda create a life for herself without drugs. Together they worked out a schedule of weekly AA meetings for Linda to attend, and Linda made her first call to AA

Intergroup from the therapist's office. They role-played job interviews, planned weekly activities, and discussed how to talk to a potential friend without being high. The therapist's directness—refusal to "ignore" the drug use and talk about anything else—helped Linda to experience the therapist as someone she could not con, as someone who might give her the direction and structure she needed.

INITIAL ASSESSMENT

How does one determine whether a substance abuser is an appropriate candidate for outpatient psychotherapy? Assuming the therapist knows of active use, a full history must be taken of the types of substances currently being used, the frequency of use, whether physical dependency exists, what kind of support systems are in place, and what, if any, previous treatment experiences were like. While most people can be treated in long-term outpatient psychotherapy, some patients will need to be hospitalized before they are able to stop actively using the addictive substance.

The therapist can determine whether physical dependence exists by asking the person how he or she feels physically when not using the substance. If the patient experiences symptoms that are characteristic of withdrawal from a particular substance, some degree of physical dependence exists. The type of drug and degree of dependence will dictate whether hospitalization is necessary. For example, a narcotic user who is just beginning to become physically dependent.may experience withdrawal symptoms such as minor aches in the joints or a runny nose for a day or two. This person is physically dependent and will feel uncomfortable but is manageable on an outpatient basis. However, someone who is heavily addicted to narcotics would experience a full-blown withdrawal syndrome and would require hospitalization. In addition, the withdrawal syndrome from certain drugs, such as barbiturates, can be life-threatening and absolutely necessitate hospitalization. Different classes of drugs have different withdrawal syndromes, and it is important that the therapist be familiar with these differences.

With some patients, it will be clear from the beginning that a rehabilitation center is a necessary first step. For instance, for patients who have long histories of addiction coupled with repeated relapse and little social support, a residential rehabilitation program that provides necessary structure and daily support may be necessary. With other patients, this need for a "rehab" will become clear only within the course of treatment. For example, a patient who is seen in outpatient psychotherapy for 6 months to a year and is unable to achieve abstinence may require a more intensive treatment setting. In either case, there will be instances in which the therapist feels a rehabilitation program is indicated while the patient will not want to enter one for a variety of reasons. This resistance to entering the rehab must then become the focus of treatment.

From the initial gathering of all the particulars on the patient's pattern of drug use, lifestyle, and social supports, a picture begins to emerge of treatment needs. The therapist must determine how often the patient should be seen, whether individually and/or in group, whether adjunct support systems such as self-help groups are called for, and so forth. Most patients with active substance-abuse problems will need to be seen more frequently than once a week if a dent is to be made in their addiction.

As a rule, it is best to wait until a stable therapeutic relationship has been established in individual treatment before the patient is put into a psychotherapy group. However, Khantzian et al. (1990) make a strong case for using a modified dynamic group therapy (MDGT) approach with newly recovering substance abusers. MDGT, a time-limited group with open membership, provides support as well as opportunities for self-reflection and characterological change.

BEGINNING TREATMENT

Many substance abusers come into treatment for a stated problem other than their addiction, such as depression, a relationship problem, or loneliness. Many others may acknowledge that there may be a drug problem, but it is one they can handle by "cutting back." Still others come into treatment because of external pressure from family, spouse, or work. Few come in ready to acknowledge their addiction and their destroyed personal lives and eager to begin treatment.

While the road ahead looks smoother when one has a patient who openly acknowledges a problem, the therapist must be prepared for a degree of ambivalence about treatment in even the most forthcoming and motivated of patients.

Consequently, the therapist must understand what psychic function drug use serves for the patient in order to have a fighting chance of keeping the patient in treatment. Is the patient using alcohol or heroin to calm and soothe unbearable anxiety? Is the patient using cocaine to relieve feelings of empty depression and worthlessness? In either case, once the substance is removed, the intolerable feelings remain and with them the urge to get high. The therapist and patient need to work together to understand which feelings the drug use dulls or activates. Most importantly, the therapist must have a genuinely empathic understanding of how frightening—and perhaps unimaginable—it is for the patient to think of giving up the substance, to think of living life "straight."

To help the patient give up the substance, the therapist needs to provide within the therapeutic relationship the same kinds of self-regulatory functions the substance once served. For example, the person who self-medicates with central nervous system depressants for feelings of anxiety will need to have the experience of being calmed and soothed in the therapeutic relationship. Such a patient may need the therapist to be more active, to give direction, to provide structure. The person who self-medicates with stimulates for feelings of depression and inadequacy must have the experience of feeling admired and special in the therapeutic relationship. Such a patient often requires less direction and more reflection. The case of Jane exemplifies this process.

> Jane was a waifish young woman in her mid-20s who dressed in full black leather punk regalia, replete with chains and padlock. She stood under 5-feet tall, was frighteningly thin with pale white skin and strawberry blond hair worn short and spiky. When Jane entered treatment she had been using heroin intravenously on a daily basis for approximately 2 years.
>
> Jane grew up in a chaotic, violent household, terrorized by her alcoholic father and left to fend for herself by her mother. As an adult, Jane was prone to states of severe anxiety and fragmentation, was agoraphobic, and lived in isolation. Heroin had acted as a protective shield from inside and outside stimulation. It tranquilized and cradled her in a warm, soft cocoon of bliss. Without heroin, Jane found negotiating the outside world overwhelming, frightening, and disorganizing.
>
> Early on in her treatment, Jane began to express her feeling that the therapist was an expert in the field of addiction and someone she could thus depend on for help. In seeing the therapist as capable and dependable, Jane could feel reassured and taken care of by her. The therapist read this as the unfolding of a positive transference and began to provide for Jane within the therapeutic relationship the soothing and organizing function that heroin had served.

Does this mean that the therapist has to, in essence, become exactly the kind of person the patient needs? The answer is "no," the therapist does not have to assume a costume and enact a role. The patient will have a need to see the therapist in a certain way and generally will experience the therapist that way unless the therapeutic relationship is prematurely disrupted by the clinician. Jane's therapist, for example, understood that Jane had a need to experience her as a protector. While she did not go out of her way to act as a protector, she also did not disrupt Jane's fantasy of her and did not interpret the transference.

Still, there are times when the patient is somehow blocked in the ability to consistently experience the therapist in the way he or she needs to in order to be able to relinquish drugs and maintain abstinence. In these instances, the block usually results from a fear of being severely disappointed by the therapist—a fear that the therapist will not be sufficiently emotionally supportive and that one will once again be failed by a significant figure in one's life. In these cases, it is critical to discuss both this fear that the therapist will fail the patient like all the others, and the hope that the therapist will perhaps be different. The case of Michael illustrates this point.

A tall, handsome, 25-year-old black man with a biting sense of humor and a disarming smile, Michael was an alcoholic who came into treatment on his own, following an arrest for disorderly conduct. Michael grew up in a single-parent household with a highly dysfunctional mother who was addicted to pills, histrionic, and totally uninterested in him. She belittled and humiliated him as a child. As a result, Michael expressed tremendous anger and contempt for women's intrusiveness and stupidity. Most of all, he was angry at women for the power he felt they had over him, and angry at himself for needing their approval.

For Michael, alcohol served an antidepressant function. When intoxicated, Michael was center-stage—he felt powerful, virile, and expansive. In order for Michael to give up alcohol and remain abstinent, he would have to experience himself as "grand" within the therapeutic relationship. Recognizing this psychological need of Michael's, the therapist made sure her interventions were primarily reflective. In addition, she did genuinely appreciate Michael's humor, and this appreciation was not lost on him. Indeed, Michael did begin to experience the therapist as providing the same kind of antidepressant functions that the alcohol had served. He asked to double his time from two 45-minute sessions per week to two 90-minute sessions. By increasing his amount of time in therapy, it was as if he were increasing his "dose" to a required therapeutic level.

However, because of the malignant relationship he had experienced with his narcissistic mother, he feared that the therapist—a woman—would disappoint and injure him as his mother had. Within 2 months after this request for longer sessions, Michael began to cancel his appointments. The therapist told Michael she felt there was a connection between his feeling that women were intrusive and smothering and his canceling his sessions with her. She pointed out that he was afraid of the closeness he felt and of needing her and that he experienced need and dependence as weak, flawed, and dangerous. He was afraid that the therapist might turn out to be self-involved and cruel like his mother. Michael quickly admitted that "if I thought I needed you, I'd quit coming tomorrow."

Thus, while in most instances the therapist should not offer observations about the therapeutic relationship early on in treatment, cases such as

Michael are the exception. In order to engage Michael fully and keep him from leaving treatment prematurely, it was necessary for the therapist to confront his attempts at distancing and control.

INVOLVING THE FAMILY

There are instances in which it may be beneficial to involve family members and significant others in treatment. One circumstance where this involvement is useful is when treating the young adult who is still highly involved with his or her nuclear family. In the case of Linda, discussed earlier, the therapist had ongoing telephone contact with Linda's mother—whose behavior was enabling Linda's continued alcohol use. The therapist instructed the mother to set limits with Linda and stop rescuing her from the consequences of her addiction. The mother was also urged to attend Al-Anon meetings.

Another time when family involvement may be useful is when the newly sober person is having difficulty communicating with a spouse. Frankie, a recovering cocaine addict discussed in more detail later, had relied on a cocaine high to stimulate him sexually. Without cocaine he felt depressed and withdrew from his wife into books and music. His wife found Frankie's aloofness intolerable and threatened to leave him unless things improved. Frankie's therapist saw Frankie and his wife for several sessions and helped them begin to understand and communicate with each other. She then referred them to another therapist for ongoing couples therapy.

Family involvement should thus be seen as an adjunct to the patient's treatment with the goal of solidifying the patient's sobriety and preventing relapse. If the therapist feels that any family members need ongoing help for themselves, they should be referred to another therapist as well as to Al-Anon or Nar-Anon.

COUNTERTHERAPEUTIC REACTIONS

At times, despite the therapist's best efforts, roadblocks appear in the treatment process. These may take the form of the therapist's own countertransferential reaction taking center-stage in the therapeutic relationship. It is inevitable that the therapist will have feelings about the patient, positive and negative, which will impact on the process. While all patients evoke feelings in us as therapists or helpers, substance abusers—with their denial, rage, demands, lies—can call forth some particularly powerful ones.

For example, the therapist might experience the patient's continued drug use as a challenge to his or her competence and therefore become angry. Or the therapist might feel that it confirms his or her inadequacy and therefore feel depressed and defeated. A patient's neediness might make one therapist feel important and useful, while another therapist might feel resentful or overwhelmed. In any case, it is crucial that the therapist try to be aware of the kinds of feelings a particular patient evokes and how these feelings impact on the relationship. The case of Carol provides an example of a situation in which the therapist's countertherapeutic reaction prevented him from acknowledging to himself that a relapse had occurred.

> Carol had been in treatment for 6 months on a twice-a-week basis and had achieved abstinence from alcohol. When she got a new job, she called to cancel two appointments, blaming it on her new work schedule and adjustment to her new sleeping routine. She then began simply not showing up for sessions and not returning the therapist's phone calls. The therapist felt both angry at Carol and frantic to get her back. When he finally talked with her on the phone, Carol acknowledged that she had begun drinking again and had been too ashamed to see the therapist. Several more appointments were missed and rescheduled before Carol did come in and express a renewed desire to continue therapy. The therapist then "got tough" and outlined some parameters Carol would have to follow in order to continue in therapy: Carol would have to promise to keep all of her appointments and regularly attend AA meetings.
> For the next 2 months Carol came to sessions and told the therapist she was not drinking and was going to meetings. After being so hardline, so afraid of losing Carol, and so relieved to have her back in treatment, the therapist believed her despite the evidence to the contrary. He did not talk to Carol about her deteriorating physical appearance and her lateness for sessions. Carol again began to miss sessions and then later acknowledged that she had been lying to the therapist for months about her drinking. She also admitted that she was disappointed in the therapist for not picking up on the obvious signs.

ONCE ABSTINENCE IS ACHIEVED:
OTHER SUBSTANCE USE

It is often hard for patients who have achieved abstinence from their drug of choice to understand why they must also stop using substances that they do not feel they were dependent on. This issue of abstinence can easily turn into a tug of war or a battle of wills between therapist and patient. It is important that the therapist not express belief in the necessity of abstinence as an ultimatum. Instead, the discussion should focus on understanding why the patient feels it is so important to be able to continue getting high. A return to the case of Michael, introduced earlier, illustrates this.

> After about the fourth week of treatment, Michael casually mentioned that he had smoked a joint the previous night with his friends. The therapist reacted with some concern and wanted to talk about how he had been feeling and what had prompted him to get high. Michael angrily said he knew the therapist would react this way and that it was no big deal. He did not get high because he was unhappy or upset; he just "felt like getting high." Michael said he did not understand why he couldn't smoke a joint now and then—he was an alcoholic, not a "pothead." The therapist expressed her feeling that that once high on pot, it was much easier to pick up a drink. She also said that he was still relying on a drug to change the way he felt. She suggested that they keep the dialogue on his use of pot open and he reluctantly agreed, stating that she would be responsible for bringing the topic up.
>
> Michael brought the subject of pot up again several weeks later when he again angrily admitted that he had been smoking a joint before bed each night that week to help him sleep. After expressing his initial resentment at the therapist for making him feel guilty about his pot use, he acknowledged that it was time to "cut it loose." He agreed that using it was limiting his growth.

In general, when exploring the issue of so-called recreational drug use, the therapist should explain to the patient that the experience of being high on any substance can easily trigger the desire to use the drug of choice. And when one's judgment is in an impaired state, there is more likelihood of relapse.

Although recreational drug use of any kind should be strongly discouraged by the therapist, there are times when prescribed medication may be indicated. There are some patients, for example, who will experience serious and prolonged sleep disturbance once they stop drinking or using drugs. If this sleep disorder goes untreated, there is a strong likelihood that it will result in a relapse. Medication may be in order for a limited period of time to get the person over the hump. Clearly, where there is profound psychiatric disturbance in addition to addiction, other kinds of psychotropic medication will be needed. The use of these medications in no way interferes with the effective use of psychotherapy. Medication is simply an adjunct to therapy, a way of making the patient more available for help. However, it is important for the therapist and patient to understand the subjective meaning of the medication to the patient.

Methadone is an example of a prescribed medication that enables many narcotics addicts to lead productive lives. It is, in fact, quite possible to treat a methadone-maintained patient successfully in outpatient psychotherapy, as the following vignette illustrates.

> Frankie was a 35-year-old Irish Catholic man who had been maintained on methadone for the past 7 months. He was a very bright and articulate young man who had gotten caught in the web of inner-city drug use as a teenager. Despite his addiction, he had managed to graduate from college and maintain steady employment. Frankie entered psychotherapy in a state of crisis, in the midst of a cocaine binge that he felt was about to cost him his wife, his job, and possibly his life. In taking a history it became clear to the therapist that prior to his cocaine use, Frankie had been feeling depressed and depleted. He described himself as feeling "bored" with straight life, having little energy and no interest in sex with his wife. He felt that his wife did not fully understand or appreciate his thoughts or feelings, and so he kept them to himself. Frankie's use of cocaine was an attempt to manage these painful feelings of depression and emptyness.
>
> In his early sessions Frankie seemed starved for attention and eager for a relationship with a person he felt had the intelligence and depth to understand him. He quickly developed a positive attachment to the therapist, experiencing himself as understood and admired by her. Thus the therapeutic relationship began to serve the same kinds of antidepressant functions that the cocaine had provided, and within 1 month Frankie stopped all drug use, while continuing on methadone maintenance.
>
> During the 3 years he was in therapy, Frankie maintained his complete abstinence, and his family relationships improved immeasurably. Frankie expressed ambivalence about staying on methadone, mostly because of the stigmatization that goes along with the status of methadone patient. The therapist maintained a neutral posture in this decision, expressing her honest feeling that methadone had provided a solid foundation on which Frankie had been able to build. She would support whatever choice he made.

In sum, although complete abstinence from all nonprescribed substances is the goal of treatment, the therapist must differentiate this from the use of medication prescribed and taken under the supervision of a physician.

12-STEP RECOVERY: IS IT FOR EVERYONE?

Twelve-step recovery programs, such as AA and NA, can be a wonderful complement to psychotherapy. These programs provide daily—and if need be, hourly—support for the recovering person. In the 12-step program the patient can hear other recovering addicts' experiences, learn tools for getting through each day sober, and begin to build a new drug-free social circle. Mack (1981) has written about the powerful psychosocial functions that AA serves. AA's philosophies and structure help the alcoholic with problems in "self-governance" as well as with narcissistic vulnerabilities.

Some patients will take to the program immediately, others with time and effort, and still others not at all. As with all aspects of treatment, what works for one patient will not necessarily work for another. The therapist should encourage the patient to explore such a group, and then the two of them should discuss the patient's reactions—both positive and negative. If the patient is able to achieve abstinence through psychotherapy and is not amenable to attending a 12-step group, the therapist should not push the issue. However, if the patient is not able to stop using and/or create a new life via psychotherapy, the therapist should strongly urge the use of a 12-step recovery group. Naturally, it is important for the therapist to be familiar with any group he or she is encouraging the patient to attend. It is therefore strongly suggested that the therapist who works with substance abusers attend at least one open meeting of a program such as AA.

ENDINGS: HAPPY AND UNRESOLVED

The scenario of a happy treatment ending will include stable sobriety and an improved quality of life. The person should have a clear understanding of the psychological function drugs or alcohol served in his or her life and how the therapeutic relationship fulfilled these functions. By the time the patient leaves treatment, there should have been an analysis and working-through of the relationship with the therapist and a takeover of the psychological and emotional functions the therapist provided. A successful treatment outcome does not mean the patient will never again have thoughts about drugs or alcohol or a desire to use. These will likely surface during times of particular stress for the person, times that are good as well as bad. However, the person should now have the tools to deal with these cravings without getting high.

Although relapse is hardly an inevitable part of a patient's life—either while still in treatment or once it is over—it is unfortunately not an uncommon occurance. The therapist must view a relapse or "slip" seriously without turning it into a failure for either the patient or the therapist. Both patient and therapist can use a relapse to understand what went wrong and to plan how they can prevent it from happening again.

There are patients who may require more than one treatment experience before they are willing to attain or maintain abstinence. The therapist should not regard a treatment impasse as a failure. Many of these patients will come away from their experience in therapy with that glimmer of awareness that will make old ways of doing and thinking harder to sustain. This awareness may ultimately lead them back into treatment.

REFERENCES

Bean, M. H. (1981). Denial and the psychological complications of alcoholism. In M. H. Bean & N. E. Zinberg (Eds.), *Dynamic approaches to the understanding and treatment of alcoholism* (pp. 55-96). New York: Free Press.

Khantzian, E. (1981). Some treatment implications of the ego and self disturbances in alcoholism. In M. H. Bean & N. E. Zinberg (Eds.), *Dynamic approaches to the understanding and treatment of alcoholism* (pp. 163-188). New York: Free Press.

Khantzian, E., Halliday, K., & McAuliffe, W. (1990). *Addiction and the vulnerable self: Modified dynamic group therapy for substance abusers.* New York: Guilford.

Khantzian, E., & Schneider, R. J. (1985). Addiction, adaptation, and the "drug-of-choice" phenomenon: Clinical perspectives. In H. B. Milkman & R. J. Schneider (Eds.), *The addictions: Multidisciplinary perspectives and treatments* (pp. 121-130). Lexington, MA: Lexington Books.

Kohut, H. (1971). *The analysis of the self.* New York: International Universities Press.

Kohut, H. (1977). *The restoration of the self.* New York: International Universities Press.

Krystal, H., & Raskin, H. A. (1970). *Drug dependence: Aspects of ego functions.* Detroit: Wayne State University Press.

Levinson, V. R., & Straussner, S. L. A. (1978). Social workers as "enablers" in the treatment of alcoholics. *Social Casework, 59*(1), 14-20.

Mack, J. E. (1981). Alcoholism, A.A., and the governance of the self. In M. H. Bean & N. E. Zinberg (Eds.), *Dynamic approaches to the understanding and treatment of alcoholism* (pp. 128-162). New York: Free Press.

Stolorow, R. D., Brandchaft, B., & Atwood, G. E. (1987). *Psychoanalytic treatment: An interdisciplinary approach.* Hillsdale, NJ: Analytic Press.

Ulman, R., & Paul, H. (1988, October). *The addictive personality disorder and "addictive trigger mechanisms" ("ATM's"): The self psychology of addiction and its treatment.* Revised version of paper (*Critical issues in self psychology*) presented at the 11th annual conference on the psychology of the self, Washington, DC.

Ulman, R., & Paul, H. (1989). A self-psychological theory and approach to treating substance abuse disorders: The "intersubjective absorption" hypothesis. In A. Goldberg (Ed.), *Dimensions of self experience* (pp. 121-141). Hillsdale, NJ: Analytic Press.

Wurmser, L. (1980). Drug use as a protective system. In D. J. Lettieri, M. Sayers, & H. W. Pearson (Eds.), *Theories on drug abuse: Selected contemporary perspectives* (National Institute on Drug Abuse, Research Monograph Series No. 30, pp. 71-74). Washington, DC: U.S. Government Printing Office.

Intervention with Substance Abusers in Specialized Settings

III

6

The Process of Intervention: Getting Alcoholics and Drug Abusers to Treatment

VINCENT CASOLARO AND ROBERT J. SMITH

But man is always capable of growth and change, and
if you don't believe this you are in the process of dying.
—LEO BUSCAGLIA, *Love*

Due to increasing awareness of the relentless pain and destruction that alcohol
and drug dependence cause to an individual and his or her family, as well as to
society as a whole, more people than ever before are getting treatment and are
in recovery for their addiction, and more families are learning how to heal their
pain and move forward with their lives. The archaic notion that the alcoholic or
drug user must "hit bottom" before he or she can be helped has contributed in
the past to prolonged destruction and despair and has resulted in many
avoidable deaths. Through his development of a process called family intervention, Vernon E. Johnson (1973, 1986) helped to change this attitude by offering
a means of help and hope for both alcoholics and addicts and their family
members. Intervention is a process that "brings up the bottom" for the entire
family of a substance abuser by short-circuiting this destructive path toward
progressive physical and mental disintegration.

This chapter explains how and why intervention works and examines
some of the strategies employed and some of the issues that arise and are
resolved in the course of an intervention.

INTERVENTION: ITS ORIGIN, DEFINITION, AND PURPOSE

Webster's dictionary defines *intervene* as "to come between as an influencing
force, as in order to modify, settle or hinder some action, argument, etc." The

task of a professional intervention is twofold: to help family members identify and redirect ineffective and hurtful behavior patterns that have kept them reacting in the same old ways, and to confront alcoholics or addicts with the profound consequences of their behavior and convince them to seek treatment.

The concept and application of intervention with alcoholics and drug abusers were developed in the early 1960s by Vernon E. Johnson, founder of the Johnson Institute in Minneapolis. Johnson's approach was a radical departure from the belief, prevalent at that time, that there was nothing to do but hope an addicted person would eventually "see the light" and change; that only those motivated to seek help on their own could profit from it. Johnson was among the first to recognize that most alcoholics and drug abusers never quit or seek help on their own, because the complex defensive structure of rationalization and denial engendered by their disease inhibit them from recognizing that they had a problem.

In Johnson's method of intervention, the family gathers together and is guided through the process of planning and taking decisive, caring steps to offer help to someone who does not want help. In a carefully prepared and structured confrontation, under the guidance of a trained counselor, those closest to the alcoholic or addict (and consequently most affected by his or her behavior) are able to cut through those defenses by "presenting reality to a person out of touch with it in a receivable way" (Johnson, 1973, p. 11)—doing so without judgment or blame, so as not to provoke the usual arguments and defensiveness. In the process, family members also begin to untangle the complicated net of emotions and reactions in which they themselves have become caught and thus change their own lives.

Because our culture places such a high value on self-determination, autonomy, and individual responsibility, some people might feel uneasy about intervention, seeing it as an act of aggression, a violation of an individual's rights. It may even seem dishonest or sneaky, because the planning sessions are held without the alcoholic's or drug addict's presence or even his or her knowledge of what is happening. But an intervention will be seen as an act of supreme humanitarianism if we remember that we are dealing with "a life threatening illness, not just a chosen lifestyle" (King, 1986, p. 9). In addition to being an expression of concern for the alcoholic or addict, it is also an affirmation of the rights of the family members, whose lives have been severely disrupted by the person's behavior. It is not the individual's right to drink or drug that is being challenged; rather it is the rights of the family members that are being upheld and defended.

In fact, while intervention was originally focused only on the alcoholic, more recent innovations have encompassed the entire family and helped them move toward recovery. Expanding the focus beyond the narrow objective of getting someone to treatment to include the broader objective of helping the family to break their old patterns of behavior and heal their anguish also, in turn, helps the alcoholic or drug abuser by providing the optimum setting in which to recover. Indeed, as King (1986) points out, "the impact on the alcoholic comes from the change in the surrounding system when it declares itself unwilling to continue to suffer harm as a result of the drinking" (p. 12).

The process of intervention begins by helping the family acknowledge that it has been progressively torn to shreds by the destructive effects of this disease; it ends by helping the family not only to survive but also to regain their ability to live to their fullest potential. The ultimate goal of an intervention is to bring about change and growth for the entire family system, achieved through expressing feelings, wants, and needs and by experiencing and sharing love, acceptance, hope, and support. Under the interventionist's guidance, family members begin to communicate, trust, and bond in ways that relieve their isolation, loneliness, and despair. The intervention's objective is to motivate families into treatment, where they can continue to work on these goals.

While originally developed for employed, middle-class alcoholics and their families, intervention has helped individuals of all socioeconomic levels and ethnic groups (since addiction is an equal-opportunity disease) and those addicted to other substances, such as cocaine, heroin, or pills. In over 25 years of application, intervention has been used within a wide variety of settings—the armed forces, employee assistance programs, religious institutions, private practice, and various types of agencies and organizations—offering help to untold numbers of people.

HELPING FAMILIES TO INTERVENE

Usually a family member will contact an interventionist to find out how an intervention works. Often the person calling is the oldest child, who has played the role of "hero" in the family (Wegscheider-Cruse, 1976), or the spouse of the alcoholic or drug abuser. The caller may have seen a newspaper article or a TV program—about Betty Ford's intervention and recovery, for example—or heard about intervention through a friend, the National Council on Alcoholism, or someone in a 12-step program. The interventionist asks the caller to describe the symptoms of the person in question and to give a history of events in order to determine if alcohol or drug abuse is indeed the problem.

The establishment of trust is the first significant factor in the interventionist's working with the family system. Dysfunctional families, especially those in which any kind of addiction is the identified problem, are riddled with inconsistency and unreliability. By the time the family is considering intervention, they have experienced many years of disillusionment, disappointment, and despair. Because of their experiences, these families naturally proceed with caution, pessimism, and distrust. The interventionist must expect this and realize that, even as they make their initial contact, members of dysfunctional families have no real reason to trust him or her or the intervention process itself, since their experience has shown them that nothing they have ever done has worked before. It is important to convey the idea that they have the power to make a difference and that they can be effective in helping their addicted family member. Intervention, like family therapy, is an invitation to bring about change in the here and now.

Family members making contact with an interventionist are struggling with several issues that must be addressed. Among them is the fact that they have lived for so long in a system whose rules have included no talking, no thinking, and no feeling (Black, 1981). They are not only going against these injunctions; they are violating the ultimate taboo against "airing their dirty laundry in public." Members of dysfunctional family also nearly always have difficulty accepting support and consideration of their own needs, since their energies have always been focused on someone else—the addicted family member. In many instances, this is the first time they have come together to talk openly about their shared problem and how it affects them. Willingness to let a professional into the family system must be acknowledged as a sign of courage and strength; it is an honor to be allowed in.

THE PROCESS AND STRUCTURE OF INTERVENTION

When a family begins the intervention process, they are the client (Minuchin, 1974). In the family members' minds, however, the alcoholic or drug addict is the sick one. It is quite often the family's belief that if the addicted member would just get help, the family would be fine. This is why the entire family is encouraged to come to the initial session *without* the chemically dependent person; in order to break through that person's delusion and denial, it is first necessary to work on the delusion and denial of the family members.

Dealing with the family's pain and need also helps to shift the focus, in part, from the addict. Family members begin by addressing their concern for the chemically dependent member; gradually they progress to sharing their concern for one another and eventually for themselves. Emotional strength and empowerment ensue; often the family members' cooperation and spontaneity increase because there is now a safe and accepting arena in which they can share. The interventionist conveys three therapeutic postures: permission ("It's okay to be here"); protection ("Nobody will be blamed or judged"); and potency ("You have the power to make a change and make a difference"). While intervention is not insight-oriented counseling (since that would require years of psychotherapy for each of the people participating), a supportive environment is a must to facilitate movement, creativity, and action in the sessions.

A family usually meets for three to five sessions, each lasting about 2 to 4 hours, before the actual intervention. One of the first sessions for the family involves educating them both about the concept of alcoholism or drug addiction as a disease and about the entanglements of enabling and codependency. Typically, the initial sessions include several films that are viewed and discussed (such as *Enabling: Masking Reality*, produced by the Johnson Institute and narrated by Hugh Downs). Education is a wonderful tool that corrects misconceptions, penetrates delusion and denial, and creates unity by allowing family members to identify patterns and see that they need help too. The family gradually comes to understand that their family member's addictive illness has affected not only him or her but also, to some degree, every single member of the family. At this stage, family members will often tease one another or get involved in a playful competition, with much laughter, about who is the "biggest enabler." This is a hopeful sign of change, indicating a decrease of guilt while facilitating openness and honesty, acceptance and trust. Humor is an invitation to join with one another in a supportive way.

The educational sessions are followed by several planning and role-playing ones. As an assignment after the first session, each family member compiles a list of his or her first-hand observations of the behavior associated with intoxication. This data, which will be presented verbally to the addict during the intervention itself, is written down for two reasons. Often this information is expressed in a blaming or critical manner, so that the interventionist must work with the family members during the next session to rephrase it into a more objective and less judgmental form. These lists are also sent to the treatment facility to be used as a resource by the identified patient's counselor during treatment. Other details worked out during the planning sessions are the order in which family members will speak during the intervention and the seating arrangement (which may include positioning the alcoholic or addict away from the door, making it harder for him or her to bolt when the session begins).

The next-to-last session is a "dress rehearsal" of the intervention, ordinarily conducted the night before. The intervention itself usually takes place in the morning because it is more likely that the alcoholic or addict will be sober or straight at that time.

Because of the nature of addiction, the alcoholic or addict may need inpatient care. Arrangements for this are made during the planning sessions, along with plans for transportation to a detoxification unit or rehabilitation center, clothes for the patient, and handling of his or her scheduled obligations. In some cases, a structured, intensive outpatient setting for detoxification and counseling is sufficient. The participation in Alcoholics Anonymous, Narcotics Anonymous, Al-Anon, Nar-Anon, and other 12-step programs is recommended in all cases to ensure a long-term recovery. These options are always discussed and determined with the help of the family.

Another major consideration is the individual's insurance coverage or the family's ability to pay for treatment, family care, and aftercare. Efforts must be made to tailor appropriate treatment and services to the finances of the family. If any of these details are neglected during the preintervention sessions, there is a much greater likelihood of the whole process falling apart after the intervention has taken place.

After the intervention has taken place, a postintervention session is scheduled, with all who participated coming together again. The atmosphere of this meeting is usually very positive, with a lot of energy evident among the family members. The postintervention session is an important time to assess the family members' commitment to their own recovery, which may include attending Al-Anon, family treatment programs, individual therapy, and so forth. It is also an opportunity to reinforce the family's goal of continued progress and to stress the importance of this goal in the overall recovery of the identified patient.

One last note on planning sessions and structure: At times, a crisis in the family necessitates an accelerated intervention process that involves marathon sessions of 5 or 6 hours. One can imagine the intensity of these sessions and the stress on both the family system and the interventionist, but an extreme situation makes them essential. In one particular instance, an alcoholic in seriously advanced physical deterioration was rushed by ambulance to a hospital detoxification unit. The interventionist spent 5 hours with family members, and an additional 5 hours on the phone with them, preparing the family to do an intervention in the detox unit. In addition to getting the alcoholic into a rehabilitation center, it was crucial to help the family understand the importance of their getting treatment for themselves.

An important element in the success of this kind of case is the cooperation of the staff in the detox unit. The staff members of this particular unit were willing to work with the interventionist (who was required to provide professional credentials and verification of his experience) in supporting the family's attempt to get the alcoholic to accept additional treatment.

As indicated previously, families are engaged during intervention by teaching them what the process consists of, what their participation will involve, and what they might expect. For the interventionist, the process is like painting a picture or producing a play—each one is different. It is important to help the family understand that they themselves will help to construct the process to fit their particular family system. This is not to say that the interventionist relinquishes his or her role to the family—which could be harmful where controlling family members have a need to be in charge—but rather that he or she must take into consideration *their* awareness of how their family is. For example, most families do not believe that, on the day of the intervention, the alcoholic or addict will attend the session. It is important to listen to their suggestions about how he or she might be encouraged to come. In most instances, families know what the alcoholic or addict will tolerate with regard to who should participate and how they will get him or her to cooperate. After all, they have lived with the person most of their lives.

MULTIFAMILY INTERVENTION

Multifamily intervention, in which as many as four families go through the educational and planning sessions together, is an exciting and effective new development in family intervention. One of the most positive aspects is the tremendous support families offer one another during the training sessions. This support carries over into the time between training sessions as well. Another benefit is that it is easier for people to acknowledge their own behavior when they see it reflected in the other family's members, especially during the various role-plays. Yet another benefit is that, because the family secret has already been shared, it is easier for the family to overcome their reluctance to connect with self-help groups such as Al-Anon.

In multifamily work, each family makes their first contact with the interventionist separately. The initial session of evaluation and assessment, which lasts about 1½ to 2 hours, is also conducted separately with each family.

The first training session, revolving around education, is attended by all the families that have indicated an interest. Three or four families may participate, adding up to as many as 25 to 30 individuals. This session can last 3 hours or more.

During the second session, family members begin to share the data they have prepared for use during the intervention: Each family takes its turn sharing data while the other families listen and offer helpful feedback. Next, the families decide on how they intend to get their alcoholic or addict to the intervention site (usually the interventionist's office). The majority decide just to "invite" the person to come for an hour session. This "invitation" is role-played by each of the families in turn; again, they receive feedback from the other families who are observing.

The third session, scheduled a few days after the second, is a rehearsal of the families' interventions. The members of one family role-play their intervention, with a member of one of the other families (a volunteer) taking the part of the patient. The other families observe this role-play and provide valuable feedback.

A different interventionist may lead each of the first three sessions. This gives the families a choice of several interventionists and an opportunity to select the one they feel most comfortable with for their actual interventions.

Most families are ready to proceed with their intervention at this point. If further work is needed by a particular family, they will be seen privately for a final rehearsal with just their interventionist.

As can be seen, multifamily training goes a long way toward breaking down the barriers of isolation and shame that have been erected by these confused and suffering families.

SELECTING THE INTERVENTION TEAM

The intervention team consists of anywhere from 4 to 12 family members or significant others. The most important requirements for team participation are being able to express concern for the alcoholic or addict and being someone who is significant to that person. In addition, participants generally need to have first-hand facts about the person's alcohol or drug use. This may be more difficult in cases involving drug users, since cocaine, heroin, and other drugs, unlike alcohol, are not often used in social situations. In the case of a cocaine, while family members may not have witnessed the addict smoking or snorting it, they usually have seen and experienced many of the symptoms and behaviors associated with its use. These include being agitated, hostile, and paranoid; exhausting a bank account or credit cards; stealing money; missing work; not coming home for days and then negating the family's concern about this. The following example demonstrates these symptoms and behaviors.

> The wife and business partners of Mr. S., a suspected cocaine addict, reported that he was missing for a couple of days, after trying to borrow money from his doorman and garage attendant. When his wife found him later, standing soaking wet in the street, he told her he needed a gun to protect himself because "they're out to get me." When she tried to get him to come home, he got into a cab and drove away. After returning home, he denied that there was anything wrong with him. In the sharing of this and other events during the intervention planning sessions, the family members began to realize that they could not *all* be wrong or crazy; that what they had in fact been witnessing was drug-related behavior.

In most interventions involving alcoholics, first-hand facts are more readily available. Family members are more likely to have observed loss of control and embarrassing social behavior, such as staggering into a Christmas tree directly following alcohol intake. In one case, several children of an alcoholic father recounted that the father had taught each of them the proper way to vomit. Prior to this preintervention session, none of the siblings had shared their common experience or had realized how truly bizarre it was.

It is the sharing of these "family secrets" that diminishes the family members' delusion and denial and lets them acknowledge and begin to accept that there is in fact a problem with their family member's drinking or drugging. As the families express their feelings about these past incidents, they prepare themselves to present reality to the addicted person during the intervention. Sharing experiences and feelings draws the team members together and mobilizes their combined energies as they begin to realize how bad the situation actually is. Shifting from their "us against them (or her)" posture into one of concern and caring for one another gives them the courage to move forward and stimulates the belief that something must be done.

EFFECTING CHANGE

In encouraging and facilitating the healing process, the interventionist helps the family members identify the roles they have played and invites them to change these roles. Commitment to change is ensured by asking team members to contract to behave differently by relinquishing old roles, such as rescuer or enabler. Each family member makes this contract with the other members, agreeing to support one another in this change.

As Salvador Minuchin (1974) points out,

> Family therapy uses techniques that alter the immediate context of people in such a way that their positions change. By changing the relationship between a person and the family context in which he functions, one changes his subjective experience. . . . The therapist joins the family with the goal of changing family organization in such a way that the family members experience change. . . . The changed organization makes possible a continuous reinforcement of the changed experience which provides a validation of the changed sense of self. (p. 13)

The various stages of the intervention process are very powerful emotional experiences. The tension, anticipation, anxiety, and confusion are dealt with by keeping everyone focused in the now. As family members begin to understand and accept on some level that their behaviors are a consequence of the disease and their adaptation to adverse situations, their defensiveness is lowered and their hidden shame can be addressed. Acknowledging the change that has begun as they take risks and relinquish their "don't talk, don't think, don't feel" injunctions furthers their empowerment. This is a stage of the process called reframing.

Reframing involves creating boundaries that allow the family's anger, rage, and frustration to be redirected at the disease of alcoholism or drug abuse as a *thing*, a separate entity from the addicted person. "Beyond empowerment and speed, the most important result of reframing, in terms of family recovery, lies in the release of feelings" (Bratton, 1988, p. 31). Honesty, vulnerability, love, and caring can now be experienced as strengths rather than liabilities. Therapy becomes not the refuge of the weak but a resource for the strong; sharing oneself is a virtue and a way to be heard and understood. Reframing also enables the family members to stop blaming themselves or the chemically dependent person for the problems in their family. Letting go of their isolation and sharing their experiences and feelings create a sense of empowerment.

During this stage, the family also begins to express their doubts, presenting a challenge both to themselves and to the interventionist. (It is important to note that, by now, the interventionist has been incorporated into the family system to such a degree that the family members allow him or her to participate in the decision-making process.) Often families project such fears by saying something like, "He probably won't come or listen, and what if this makes things worse?" The interventionist accepts and validates their concerns, while at the same time asking them to trust that the alcoholic or drug addict will come and that the intervention will work. It is important to remind the family that, due to the nature of the disease and the history of their family member's dependency, things will probably get worse without the intervention.

Although most people do not believe that their alcoholic or addicted family member will attend the intervention, it is the exception, not the rule, when that person refuses to cooperate. In reassuring the family of this, it may be useful for the interventionist to talk about past successes, or even to have a member of another family who has gone through the entire intervention process speak to the potential intervention team.

It is important to help the family understand that intervention is a process, not an event. Both the interventionist and the family must be wary of becoming too invested in the alcoholic's decision to accept help. Even if their alcoholic or addicted family member does not attend or does not get treatment, the intervention has not been a failure; the healing that the family is experiencing and the change in the family's focus is what is most important.

Typically, by the time that a family presents itself for an intervention, both the alcoholic or drug addict and the family members have been severely affected by the disease. In order for the intervention process to be effective, the family members must begin to formulate consequences that they will carry out if the alcoholic or addict does not change his or her behavior. This is one of the most difficult stages for the family. These consequences may include such things as a wife's seeking legal advice for a separation or divorce should her alcoholic husband not be willing to go for help, or a mother's withdrawing financial support from her cocaine-addicted daughter unless she agreed to treatment, or a daughter's not letting her alcoholic father hold his infant granddaughter because he might drop her. It is especially important in cases involving potential physical danger—such as driving under the influence, being physically violent when intoxicated, or having potentially suicidal tendencies—to help family members protect themselves from that imminent danger by creating such consequences as refusing to ride in a car, getting a court order of protection, or taking steps to protect someone's life. These protective steps are difficult to carry out; it is common for the family members to feel that they are betraying or abandoning the alcoholic or drug addict in even considering and expressing them. These painful decisions need to be reframed as gifts of love and concern; they are not trying to hurt the person but rather to regain him or her as a healthy, productive family member.

ACKNOWLEDGING SHAME AND GRIEF

Despite a more educated and understanding social attitude regarding alcohol and drug dependency, families continue to feel tremendous shame brought on by the stigma of this disease. At the core of their being is the feeling that there is something flawed about their character. (Guilt is distinguished from shame in that guilt is feeling "I did something wrong," while shame is feeling "I *am* something wrong.")

Families frequently conceal their shame by trying to be perfect all the time. The entire intervention process involves dealing with the family's shame. Each family member feels that, on some level, he or she is at fault for the chemical dependency and pain in the family. While they blame themselves, they also project their blame onto others, with statements such as, "If it weren't for . . . , this wouldn't be happening." Blame is, of course, a way to cover one's shame by projecting it onto someone else. "Since a shame-based person cannot feel vulnerable or needy without being ashamed, blame becomes an automatic way to avoid one's deepest feelings and true self. Blame maintains the balance in a dysfunctional system when control has broken down" (Bradshaw, 1988, p. 81).

In working through the intervention process with families, a great deal of time is spent helping the family to see that it is not their fault that their loved one is addicted—that, as the principles of Al-Anon state, they did not cause it, cannot control it, and cannot cure it. Such an approach helps to sustain and prepare them for the final stages of the intervention process.

Because intervention brings about so much change and letting go, it incorporates, on some level, the grieving process of denial, anger, bargaining, depression, and acceptance (Kübler-Ross, 1969). Grief becomes a vehicle for expressing the family's unresolved feelings of loss, including the projected loss of their dysfunctional roles and, even worse, fear of a complete loss of the alcoholic or addicted family member. While grief has the ability to bring the family together, to mobilize them, and to create a commitment to saving the chemically dependent member from the ultimate "bottom line" (his or her death), it is often the most difficult thing to acknowledge. Interventionists must be careful not to neglect it in favor of focusing on the drama of the alcoholic's or addict's behavior. Some of the most emotionally potent statements are the ones such as, "Dad, I love you and miss having you as a father," or "Dad, I want you back because we don't go fishing anymore." Statements such as these, while not having the drama of addictive behavior, focus keenly on the value of an individual as a family member and underline how addiction has kept him or her from fulfilling an important and unique role within the family.

Families approach intervention "with not only a substantially abnormal number of significant losses in their lives, but also with those losses largely, if not entirely, unresolved and unfinished" (Nash, 1989, p. 62). They may not feel "finished or completed" and may take their guilt and shame to their graves, unless they have tried to make a positive effort to bring about change for their addicted loved one.

> Even when interventions do not conclude with the alcoholic's accepting treatment . . . [family members] realize they did the best they possibly could. This genuine effort enhances self-esteem and gives participants the confidence to explore further the effects of the disease on their own lives. (Marlin, 1987, p. 227)

The following example of an intervention conducted by an alcoholic doctor's family makes these dynamics apparent:

> Dr. B.'s family had tried to address his drinking problem on their own 5 years earlier, but he ran out of the room when confronted by them. This time, the family called us and worked diligently together for about a month to plan the intervention. The intervention took place in the doctor's home, with his wife, three sons, and two daughters-in-law present. Another son, who was in Alaska, sent a videotaped expression of his concern that was played during the session. The intervention lasted over 4 hours, about 3 hours longer than average.

Dr. B. was in a state of severe denial, intellectualizing his drinking. The family expressed their grief at the loss of his emotional presence and summarized how significant he was in their lives. One son stated that, through the intervention process, despite feelings of anger, helplessness, and powerlessness that he had experienced for 10 years, he had come to realize that he loved his father very much.

At the end of the intervention, Dr. B. agreed to go to a rehabilitation center 3 days later. However, during admission to the center, he decided that the other patients were a lot sicker than he was and left the facility. He stopped drinking on his own and went to Alcoholics Anonymous. Sadly, in spite of his being sober for 1 month, he died from a stroke. During the postintervention session, the family members expressed their gratitude that they did the intervention, which not only helped Dr. B. die in dignity but also allowed them to express their love and concern to him before he died.

THE ROLE AND SKILLS OF THE INTERVENTIONIST

The role of the interventionist is a creative and demanding one. The therapeutic approach is expansive and holistic; the interventionist must frequently depart from conventional models and techniques of counseling in his or her search for effective strategies. Mobilizing the family's strengths through education, role-playing, sculpturing, and modeling different behavior are some of the tools the interventionist draws on to help and support those families in need. Since these are people who have learned not to trust words, the interventionist must in effect "show them the sermon, not tell them the sermon."

Unlike social workers in other settings, interventionists may often need to take greater risks of self-disclosure and share their feelings in order to provide a vision of hope in an arena of hopelessness and despair. This serves as a joining technique, helping the interventionist to function within the family system itself. It is especially meaningful because, in some cases, interventionists are able to draw from their own experiences in families troubled by addiction or alcoholism.

Intervention also differs from many other forms of social work in that it is never a nine-to-five job. Because intervention is frequently precipitated by a crisis and because it involves a number of people, interventionists must fit their own schedules around the needs of their clients. They must be prepared to come into the office on weekends and work late hours to attend to all the details involved in a successful intervention.

The sadness, grief, and pain that is inherent in working with these families can at times seem overwhelming. But the results of saving someone's life and bringing about positive change for each family member is the ultimate reward.

CONCLUSION

Intervention is a powerful tool for getting individuals to treatment and changing the family structure. It is an emotionally potent therapeutic vehicle that helps to bring about change in both the addict and his or her family. Its power arises from the family members' love and concern for one another and their willingness to bring about a change and to set limits to destructive behavior. Intervention offers great hope for addicted individuals, as well as an opportunity for their families to help themselves. Developing strategies, methods, and techniques in helping to facilitate these objectives remains an interventionist's goal and challenge.

REFERENCES

Black, C. (1981). *It will never happen to me.* Denver: M.A.C. Publications.
Bradshaw, J. (1988). *Bradshaw on: The family.* Deerfield, FL: Health Communications.
Bratton, M. (1988, July/August). From denial and delusion to reality and recovery. *Alcoholism and Addiction,* pp. 24-25.
Buscaglia, L. (1972). *Love.* New York: Random House.
Johnson, V. E. (1973). *I'll quit tomorrow.* New York: Harper & Row.
Johnson, V. E. (1986). *Intervention.* Minneapolis, MN: Johnson Institute Books.
King, B. L. (1986). Decision making in the intervention process. *Alcoholism Treatment Quarterly, 3*(3), 5-22.
Kübler-Ross, E. (1969). *On death and dying.* New York: Macmillan.
Marlin, E. (1987). *Hope.* New York: Harper & Row.
Minuchin, S. (1974). *Families and family therapy.* Cambridge, MA: Harvard University Press.
Nash, T. (1989). The psychodrama of grief in chemical dependency treatment. In R. L. Fuhlrodt (Ed.), *Psychodrama, its application to ACOA and substance abuse treatment* (pp. 52-75). East Rutherford, NJ: Perrin & Taeggett.
Wegscheider-Cruse, S. (1981). *Another chance.* Palo Alto, CA: Science and Behavior Books.

7

Alcoholism Treatment Facilities

PHILIP O'DWYER *

Programs designed to treat clients with alcohol problems have enjoyed enormous growth over the past 15 years. Yet despite representing a significant portion of modern health care, chemical dependency treatment remains a little understood industry. Its mixture of philosophy, methods, and jargon often leaves the uninitiated professional confused and feeling like an outsider.

This chapter describes the antecedents of the modern alcoholism treatment industry, provides a general introduction to prevailing practices in specialized alcoholism treatment facilities, and discusses the implications of current trends for the clinician of the future.

HISTORICAL DEVELOPMENT

Throughout history, societies have struggled to reconcile the pleasure of moderate drinking with the problems associated with its abuse. One of the earliest attempts to regulate alcohol use occurred in the Code of Hammurabi, almost 4,000 years ago. The Bible condemns drunkenness (I Corinthians 5:11-13), yet Jesus's first miracle turned water into wine (John 2:1-10).

In the 16th century several religious groups introduced sanctions against those who drank excessively. The Puritans generally perceived alcohol as an instrument of the devil and punished intoxification with flogging. When Thomas Trotter, at the end of the 18th century, presented his dissertation on habitual drunkenness at the University of Edinburgh, he approached it as a public health problem. Trotter believed that habitual drunkenness should be understood as a "disease," not as a sign of "depravity." A few years later Benjamin Rush published a similar paper in the United States in which he insisted that drunkenness should be regarded no differently than any other human condition that might occur naturally or by accident (Rush, 1785/1943).

This "disease" notion was initially opposed on religious grounds, since it seemed to absolve "inebriates" of responsibility for their actions. Medicine, too, reacted negatively to this new theory, which suggested that physicians offer remediation to these "unsavory" clients whom they believed to be beyond the reach of effective treatment. The public perception of the chronic inebriate as a "moral degenerate" prevailed, and the work of Trotter and Rush failed to have a significant impact.

By the second half of the 19th century there was growing public concern with drunkenness. In Boston an "Institution for Inebriates" was opened, and several similar institutions soon followed. Some treatment was attempted with minimal success (Milam & Ketchum, 1981).

Toward the end of the 19th century, public discontent with drunkenness expressed itself in the temperance movement. An early leader of this movement, Justin Edwards, provides insight into their thinking in his proclamation: "Keep the temperate people temperate; the drunkards will soon die, and the land will be free" (quoted in Maxwell, 1950). The temperance movement gained momentum with the assistance of several religious groups and culminated in the Volstead Act in 1919, which ushered in Prohibition. Until its repeal in 1933, interest in treatment dwindled and few researchers considered this issue worthy of study. Physicians tended to confine their work with this population to ameliorating associated medical complications (Milam & Ketchum, 1981; Wilford, 1981).

In 1935, two problem drinkers, Bill Wilson and Dr. Bob Smith, having failed to achieve sobriety on their own and regarded as "hopeless" by the professional community, decided to help each other. The success of their self-help approach led to the founding of Alcoholics Anonymous (AA). Soon a subculture of recovering people emerged and for the next 25 years became the principal source of help for problem drinkers. Their philosophy is crystallized in 12 steps and amplified in what is called the "Big Book" (Alcoholics Anonymous, 1976). The more charismatic among them often took drinking clients into their homes and began to acquaint them with the 12 steps. Others opened residential centers using a similar approach. These were usually referred to as shared recovery centers. They were frequently semireligious in nature and were administered in an authoritarian style (Stuckey & Harrison, 1982). Yet the efforts of these early recovering people became an important component of the modern treatment facility.

Parallel to the growth of AA, the federal government established two hospitals primarily for the treatment of prison inmates with drug problems, although voluntary clients were later admitted. These centers—in Lexington, Kentucky, and Fort Worth, Texas—provided an opportunity for research into addictive disorders. Slowly the professional community began to recognize the potential for recovery through treatment. A pivotal figure in advancing the scientific study of alcohol problems was E. M. Jellinek (1890–1963). He provided one of the earliest reviews of treatment (Bowman & Jellinek, 1941) and was instrumental in establishing the Yale School of Alcohol Studies in 1942. In 1955 the American Medical Association (AMA) endorsed the disease concept of alcoholism. Marty Mann and the National Council on Alcoholism (NCA) were instrumental in influencing this decision. This endorsement elevated the status of working with alcoholics, although the attitude of the bulk of the professional community remained suspicious.

Studies of professional sentiment toward treating clients with alcohol problems show pervasive negative attitudes about treatment and pessimism about treatment outcome (Cook, Straussner, & Fewell, 1985; Dorsch, Talley, & Bynder, 1969; Knox, 1973; Peyton, Chaddick, & Gorsuch, 1980). While social workers, as exemplified in a study of graduate social work students, were more willing to treat these clients than were psychologists, they also showed significant bias against accepting clients with drinking problems (Peyton et al., 1980).

Efforts were made to design clinically effective programs in the 1960s, but it was not until the early 1970s that Congress seemed committed to making treatment widely available for those with alcohol and drug problems. The Hughes Act in 1970 established the National Institute on Alcohol Abuse and Alcoholism (NIAAA) and initiated extensive federal funding for treatment and research. This effort was further expanded when insurance carriers recognized treatment as a reimbursable service.

A network of alcoholism treatment programs arose using diverse characterizations of the problem and offering different treatment regimens. Some mental health workers with specializations in social work, psychology, and counseling saw the treatment programs of the 1980s as opportune places to practice. Their involvement in a field previously driven by paraprofessional recovering persons created tension. By the end of the 1980s, however, their presence and contribution had become essential components of the movement toward the application of more innovative treatment methods. States established divisions of alcoholism services or offices of substance abuse services to organize the delivery of treatment and establish performance standards through the licensing process. Counselor credential organizations sprang up to provide educational opportunities and require certain minimal levels of competence. The Joint Commission for the Accreditation of Healthcare Organizations (JCAHO) finally developed performance standards that required most programs to upgrade and monitor the quality of their services. While JCAHO accreditation was optional, it became the insignia of quality. As prominent citizens acknowledged receiving treatment, public awareness shifted toward greater support for treatment, making the 1980s the golden age of alcoholism treatment.

TREATMENT PHILOSOPHY

As we have seen, the essential nature of the addictive process remains a contentious issue. This set of human problems has been viewed at once as relatively simple and as highly complex. The lack of agreement that occurs at the conceptual level is even more pronounced at the treatment level. Since treatment orientations exist on a continuum from the basic to the highly sophisticated, any attempt to reduce them to discrete categories can be somewhat arbitrary.

Implicit in the notion of "treatment program" is an organized set of internally consistent activities presumed to affect behavioral change in the client. While programs can be distinguished along ideological lines, the preponderance of alcoholism treatment facilities in the United States follow the "Minnesota Model" (Engelmann, 1989). This approach has undergone several refinements since its inception in the early 1950s at Willmar State Hospital. Subsequently, more widely known versions of this model have been established and nationally promoted by the Hazelden Foundation.

The Minnesota Model blends professional services with the 12 steps of AA. In an innovative move at the time, the counselors generally are themselves recovering alcoholics. They give lectures and integrate the principles of AA with individual and group therapy. Initially, they were required to have at least a high school education and to have been sober for at least 5 years (Laundergan, 1982).

The Minnesota Model operates on several assumptions:

1. The client population is homogeneous—all have the same disease.
2. Alcohol problems represent a primary disease that is progressive and to which many of its victims are genetically predisposed.
3. The disease is characterized by loss of control over alcohol and denial of its negative consequences.
4. Recovering alcoholics should be part of the interdisciplinary treatment staff.
5. The 12 steps of AA are the pathway to recovery.
6. Education about the effects of alcohol on the physical, psychological, and spiritual domains is essential.
7. Alcoholism is also a family disease; thus family members also require education and treatment.
8. Individual, group, and family therapy are necessary elements of the recovery process.
9. Clients must attend self-help groups while in treatment and upon discharge continue the practice for life.

From the perspective of this model, all alcohol problems are seen to have a similar cause, generally believed to be a "disease" entity, that is amenable to a singular treatment approach. The current alcoholism treatment facilities seem to reflect an evolved version of this model. Today, strong self-help tenets continue to be emphasized in conjunction with individual, family, and group counseling. Some varieties may add psychological services, such as personality assessment and psychotherapy. The actual mixture in any given program may vary greatly.

THE CONTINUUM OF ALCOHOLISM TREATMENT

As the Minnesota Model evolved, specific components were identified and integrated into a continuum of care (Anderson, 1981). Detoxification was distinguished from rehabilitation, the former ranging from 3 to 7 days and the latter continuing for 60 days. In the 1970s the 28-day inpatient program became standard practice.

The continuum of care falls into three phases: detoxification, rehabilitation, and aftercare. It also can include assistance for the alcoholic's family.

Detoxification

The detoxification process is usually managed in either an acute care hospital, a subacute residential center, or a community setting. Detoxification from alcohol can be life-threatening, often requiring medical management. Laboratory studies that include blood alcohol level are usually conducted to guide the physician's orders. During detoxification the client is generally experiencing significant distress, and Librium or phenobarbital are sometimes prescribed to ease withdrawal discomfort. The medical and nursing staff monitor the client's progress, checking vital signs at regular intervals and attending to concomitant conditions. Disturbed sleep is often relieved with Benadryl or similar-acting medication. Within 72 hours of admission, most clients are "chemical-free."

It is considered important that contact with the counseling or social work staff occur as soon as possible after the crisis that precipitated admission. Counselors initiate the development of a therapeutic relationship and provide supportive and motivational counseling. Psychotherapy is not possible at this time due to the client's medical status.

The following case illustrates this process:

John Jones, a 52-year-old engineer, was brought to a local general hospital by his wife. Mr. Jones had been drinking excessively at a company function, got into a fight, and finally passed out. Mrs. Jones reluctantly disclosed that this was a common occurrence and that she was "tired of taking him home and putting him to bed." Mrs. Jones continued: "The last time he was this bad, I thought he was going to die." A family friend had assisted Mrs. Jones in taking him to the hospital.

In the emergency room the medical staff checked his vital signs, conducted a general physical examination, and ordered laboratory tests. A review of the findings revealed seriously elevated blood pressure, a blood alcohol level of 0.35, and a history of delirium tremens (i.e., confusion, disorientation, increased agitation, tremulousness, hallucinations, and extreme fear) during previous withdrawal. Mr. Jones had an enlarged liver and was 70 pounds overweight. He was admitted for acute detoxification.

The attending physician prescribed Librium and a vitamin regimen. Nurses monitored vital signs, and an alcoholism counselor met with him daily to provide supportive care through education and to motivate him for additional treatment. The counselor reviewed the medical chart and obtained additional information about his drinking from Mrs. Jones. This information was used to dissolve Mr. Jones's minimization of his problem and to motivate him to accept the next phase of treatment.

The unit social worker met with Mrs. Jones to discuss the impact of her husband's drinking, to provide her with basic information regarding alcoholism, and help her encourage her husband to obtain additional treatment. Mr. Jones was discharged after three days.

Rehabilitation

Inpatient Treatment

Rehabilitation on an inpatient basis is designed for those clients who are unable to remain chemical-free without being placed in a structured residential environment. Admission criteria are usually governed by the client's social and emotional stability, his or her history of treatment and sobriety, and the criteria of third-party payers. The average length of stay is usually between 21 and 28 days; however, given present trends as well as improved treatment technology, the period of time is likely to be greatly reduced in the future. Cost-containment efforts in the form of restrictive covenants, managed care systems, gatekeepers, and preauthorization dispensers have substantially reduced the use of this form of treatment in recent years. This trend may make residential treatment unavailable to many who need its level of intensity.

Once in the rehabilitation center, clients are expected to follow a relatively rigid daily schedule. Most facilities are highly structured and include among their daily activities morning meditation, educational films, individual counseling, group counseling, didactic lectures, self-help meetings, recreational activities, family counseling, and occupational therapy.

While this list is intended to convey the flavor of life in the residential program, it is by no means exhaustive.

The case of John Jones will illustrate the rehabilitation experience:

Following detoxification, Mr. Jones agreed to participate in the 21-day inpatient rehabilitation program associated with the hospital. Mr. Jones was oriented to the specific daily regimen he was expected to pursue, and his rights and responsibilities as a recipient of treatment were provided verbally and in writing. A psychosocial history was conducted by a social worker, and an initial treatment plan was established with the concurrence of the medical director. This plan included the chief goals of treatment as well as the objective experiences that were designed to achieve these goals.

The treatment of Mr. Jones began with his assignment to an alcoholism counselor whose task was to manage the treatment and ensure that the goals outlined in the treatment plan were pursued. The counselor was also responsible for monitoring Mr. Jones's progress.

Mr. Jones's daily schedule was highly structured and was comprised of the activities outlined above. The content of the didactics lectures included such topics as: the medical consequences of alcoholism, the signs and symptoms of addiction, the disease concept of alcoholism, alcoholism—the family disease, the philosophy of AA, the 12 steps of AA, the recovery process, and relapse prevention.

The purpose of the daily group counseling sessions, which were usually conducted by a master's-level social worker or the staff psychologist, was to help Mr. Jones apply this didactic material to his life, make lifestyle changes, and relate to and learn from other clients.

Mrs. Jones attended weekly group sessions for family members, which were led by the social worker. These sessions were designed to provide family members with an understanding of the disease of alcoholism and the recovery process. Mrs. Jones was encouraged to attend Al-Anon meetings. Prior to discharge, Mr. and Mrs. Jones attended a joint session to discuss his discharge plans and to open up communication between them.

During the 21 days Mr. Jones spent in the rehabilitation program, he underwent psychological testing and a psychiatric evaluation. The results of both were unremarkable. At discharge Mr. Jones agreed to participate in weekly outpatient group treatment for 15 weeks and to attend AA meetings regularly. Mrs. Jones agreed to continue with her Al-Anon meetings.

Outpatient Treatment

Historically the bulk of treatment took place in residential or inpatient settings. Indeed, it was believed that taking the clients out of their environment and placing them in a structured setting was essential for recovery.

However, many clients with good social stability can be treated effectively on an outpatient basis. It is arguable that these clients are better served when treated in the "real world" rather than in the artificial environment of the inpatient facility. In addition, outpatient treatment has the advantage of being less expensive; thus high-cost, high-intensity treatment can be reserved for those in greater need of it.

Current outpatient treatment for alcohol problems is distinguished in terms of intensity. The usual level of treatment participation in outpatient settings is once or twice each week on either an individual or group basis. It is usual to conduct occasional drug screens in the outpatient setting. Disulfiram (Antabuse) and naltrexone (Trexan) are frequently used in conjunction with therapy, since they temporarily preclude alcohol or heroin use and thus protect a client against a sudden impulse to relapse.

Recently, intensive outpatient programs have gained popularity as an alternative to inpatient care. These programs typically consist of intensive treatment ranging from 4 to 6 hours daily for 2 or more weeks. The content of such programs is similar to that of residential programs. The most notable advantage of intensive outpatient treatment is that clients experience treatment while residing in the "real world" and are able to maintain their work and family responsibilities. Issues arising from the client's living conditions are often more realistically dealt with in this setting.

Aftercare

When "care" was considered to be residential care, it was believed that some contact should be maintained with the client subsequent to discharge. That contact, whether on a monthly basis or less frequently, was called aftercare. It was intended not as intensive therapeutic events but periodic checkups. Many clients regard participation in self-help groups as fulfilling the same function.

In recent years, outcome studies have suggested that clients are vulnerable to relapse in the early months of recovery; in light of that knowledge, standard outpatient care, like residential care, began to include an aftercare component. Currently, general practice perceives aftercare as an important service that occurs subsequent to the conclusion of outpatient treatment. Recent research suggests that aftercare is a critical part of the treatment service and should be planned carefully (Skinner, 1988).

Some variants of aftercare involve monthly group sessions of a didactic nature designed to remind clients of the reality of their addiction to alcohol and the importance of avoiding complacency regarding their recovery. Others add questionnaires and periodic telephone contacts with both the client and a designated family member. The purpose is to reinforce the achievements accomplished in treatment. The case of John Jones illustrates this component.

> Upon his completion of 15 weeks of weekly outpatient group therapy, the clinical staff agreed that Mr. Jones had the essential motivation, ability, and support to render his recovery reasonably secure. Mr. Jones and his case manager worked out an aftercare plan that consisted of attendance at the monthly alumni meeting at the treatment center for the next year. At the conclusion of the year, the case manager conducted an individual session with Mr. Jones to review his progress. It was agreed that Mr. Jones would continue to attend the alumni meetings each month for another year and continue involvement in AA.

Family Treatment

It is commonly believed that alcoholism can have devastating effects on the family (Straussner, Weinstein, & Hernandez, 1979). Spouse and children are likely to develop dysfunctional patterns of behavior in attempting to cope with the strain of living with an alcoholic. The term "codependency" has been used to describe this phenomenon. While definitions of codependency vary greatly in the literature, it is generally regarded as a "primary disease and a disease within every member of the alcoholic family" (Wegscheider, 1984, p. 45). The recent flurry of literature on adult children of alcoholics (ACOAs) emanates from the belief that untreated children develop predictable problems in adult life. Concern for this population blossomed into a self-help movement for ACOAs, which is generally available throughout the country.

The treatment community has embraced this model of the alcoholic family and its jargon. It is considered axiomatic that dysfunctional roles occur in the alcoholic family and that adequate treatment programs should address them. Some treatment facilities require family participation in treatment as a condition of client admission. While great emphasis has been placed on the treatment of the entire family, in practice it seems to amount to little more than didactic presentations of a variety of dysfunctional roles—the enabler, the hero, the scapegoat, and so forth. Yet despite the popular use of these terms, they seem "rather simple-minded conceptualizations" (Gomberg, 1989, p. 114) that not only lack clarity of definition but also unfortunately tend to distract from a growing literature in the field of family therapy. It seems unwise to replace careful family assessment with the assumption that these roles necessarily occur or that they are the only aspect of the disease.

LIMITATIONS OF CURRENT TREATMENT APPROACHES

General dissatisfaction with the traditional treatment approach arises from several areas to cast doubt on the wisdom of the present delivery of alcoholism treatment services. Research findings call into question the unitary notion of addiction (Pattison, 1982; Skinner, 1988). The universal application of any method of treatment or combination of methods, including the so-called Minnesota Model, is unlikely to benefit all clients. Indeed, the growing body of data argues persuasively that the population of persons with alcohol (and drug) problems is multivariant (Pattison, 1982). This would suggest that different kinds of clients may require different kinds of treatment. The entry of more highly trained mental health workers into the field coupled with research-based demonstration projects facilitates a shift to the systems paradigm that has been implemented in a few centers (Institute of Medicine [IOM], 1990).

The assumptions that support the emerging systems paradigm include the following:

1. The client population is vastly heterogeneous, and therefore an objective assessment of each client is required.
2. Treatment methods can be distinguished and variously applied.
3. When clients are matched to the most appropriate treatment method, a more favorable outcome can be expected.

The systems paradigm applies the principle of differential diagnosis leading to differential treatment assignment. This paradigm envisions certain key functions that must occur in a treatment program (Glaser et al., 1984; IOM, 1990; O'Dwyer 1984). These include assessment, differential treatments, and matching.

Assessment

Prior to admission to rehabilitation, a client must be safely detoxified and stabilized. When this stage has been reached, each client is carefully assessed by a therapist skilled in psychometrics, using objective, standardized instruments. While there is still debate about the client characteristics to be measured, the following have been suggested: level of addiction, level of social stability, level of personality functioning, level of cognitive functioning, and level of field dependence/independence (O'Dwyer, 1988). The instruments selected are subject to discussion among the clinical staff until a satisfactory roster is established. Such an assessment will be sequential in nature: The problem is assessed first and then the client in whom this problem arises. A client profile is generated that can be used to assign the client to treatment. For example, a client with a moderate level of addiction, high social stability, unremarkable personality functioning, low cognitive functioning, and high level of field independence might be a prime candidate for individual behavior therapy on an outpatient basis; while a client with a high level of addiction, low social stability, unremarkable personality functioning, high cognitive functioning, and high level of field dependence might be a candidate for insight-oriented group therapy in a residential setting in conjunction with AA involvement.

Differential Treatments

The systems paradigm requires clear differentiation between all treatment services offered irrespective of the setting in which they are delivered. In this context a treatment is considered to be any activity or set of strategies directed toward altering a client's drinking behavior or related problem. Each treatment design is a written module of care articulated by a clinician and usually consistent with existing psychological or social work theoretical frameworks. Innovative treatment modules can be designed for specific populations.

Each written treatment design includes the following (O'Dwyer, 1988):

1. *Rationale*: a brief summary of the theoretical basis for the specific treatment
2. *Admission criteria*: the client characteristics that would qualify a client for this treatment
3. *General objectives*: the overarching focus of the treatment, for example, relapse prevention
4. *Session outlines*: descriptions of the strategies and techniques to be used in each session or group of sessions
5. *Outcome measures*: some simple measure given at the end of the treatment to evaluate outcome and guide treatment matching.

By using this format, a treatment facility is not limited to one model of treatment—the Minnesota Model—but can design a range of highly focused treatments for different subsets of the client population. Since the treatment process is specified in objective terms, each design can be replicated exactly and its effectiveness tested. Over time this matching can be refined and clients can ultimately be directed to a treatment design known to have been successful with similar clients.

Matching

Meticulous assessment will provide the clinician with objective measures of several client characteristics, and given the development of a range of described treatments, the process of matching can begin. Initially the matching may be based on subjective clinical judgment, but with experience gathered over time the matching can be based on outcome data. By building in simple outcome measures—such as generalized contentment scales and marriage satisfaction scales—coupled with measures of goal attainment, the efficiency of the matching process is refined. This model advances treatment to more objective terms and allows a rational basis for treatment selection. While this approach is appealing, it does initially awaken anxiety in clinicians, who are often reluctant to provide definitive descriptions of discrete treatments. Implementation of this model across the treatment network would significantly enhance the existing service delivery arrangements: It would improve outcome and increase the credibility of the field.

The process of matching can be illustrated by the case of John Smith:

Following inpatient detoxification, Mr. Smith was referred to an outpatient chemical dependency clinic for assessment and treatment of alcohol problems. Initially a standard psychosocial history was taken by an alcoholism counselor. Mr. Smith's use of alcohol was carefully evaluated by history and through the use of the Michigan Alcoholism Screening Test. Several characteristics of Mr. Smith were then assessed using a battery of instruments selected from an available roster. The instruments included (1) Social Stability Index, (2) Wechsler Memory Scale, (3) Basic Personality Inventory, (4) Hooper Visual Organization Test, (5) Trail Making Test, (6) Embedded Figures Test, and (7) Treatment Goal Inventory.

These instruments were scored by the psychologist, and a crisp profile of Mr. Smith emerged to guide treatment selection. He was assigned to insight-oriented outpatient group therapy in conjunction with AA involvement and was seen in an individual orientation session by the social worker who ran this group. The social worker used the session to outline this treatment module and familiarize Mr. Smith with the general objectives of the group and how his specific treatment goals should be met through this treatment experience. Mr. Smith began the group aware of the expectations and duration of the treatment.

FUNDAMENTAL KNOWLEDGE BASE
FOR ALCOHOLISM TREATMENT STAFF

The development of specialty treatment services for alcohol problems parallel to a growing mental health field has led to issues of "turf." Traditionally addiction counselors tended to attribute all emotional and behavioral problems of a client to the use of alcohol and drugs, often ignoring coexisting mental health problems. Likewise, the mental health professional sought to explain the client's emotional difficulty without referencing the use of alcohol or drugs. Indeed, some mental health professionals were reluctant to investigate a client's use of alcohol or drugs, and when they did, they were easily overwhelmed.

By the latter part of the 1980s, graduate programs in psychology, social work, and counseling had introduced curricular components that provided the students knowledge of ways to identify alcoholic clients early on. Specialized training is generally available for those who directly provide treatment. A model of professional standards of knowledge, functions, and clinical skills has been developed by the National Association of Alcoholism and Drug Abuse Counselors (1986). The model serves as a basis for counselor credentialing.

Whatever the mix of clinical staff in a specialized treatment center, the following specific functions must be performed:

- Intake and assessment
- Initial and subsequent treatment planning
- History and physical examination
- Design and delivery of psychoeducation as well as individual, group, and family therapy
- Crisis intervention
- Discharge planning
- Aftercare planning
- Referral networking
- Clinical supervision
- Quality assurance, client care monitoring, and utilization review

These and many other tasks are performed in accord with the philosophy of the treatment center. Since most of these duties arise in any clinical setting, every graduate-level clinician can be expected to be familiar with them.

In order to adequately execute these tasks in a specialized treatment center, specific knowledge is necessary. Minimally, the clinician should have substantial knowledge of the following:

- Withdrawal signs and symptoms
- The effects of alcohol and drugs on the client
- The models and techniques of treatment
- The pharmacology of alcohol and psychoactive drugs
- The role of denial in a client's evaluation of the problem

- Diagnostic laboratory studies
- Confidentiality regulations and ethical standards
- Alcohol problem and client assessment instruments
- Crisis counseling, both in theory and in practice
- The history and steps of self-help
- The signs and symptoms of mental illness and emotional disturbance
- Transference and countertransference
- Relapse prevention
- Research

With competency in these areas, the effective clinician develops skills by which this knowledge is expressed. Beyond the usual counseling skills the following are indispensable:

- Displaying unconditional positive regard for the client
- Communicating a nonjudgmental disposition
- Facilitating the client's self-diagnosis
- Designing and articulating treatment strategies
- Practicing in interdisciplinary teams
- Motivating clients for treatment
- Matching clients to the most effective treatment

Just as there are different levels of academic knowledge, so there are different levels of skill sophistication. The clinical privileging process is designed to ensure that those who perform specified tasks or treatments have the knowledge and skills to do so.

Greater emphasis is being placed on the delivery of high-quality care. Regulatory agencies and third-party payers using the clinical privileging system and utilization review mechanisms can be expected to enforce adherence to high standards. The clinician of the future will be required to articulate the goals, strategies, and duration of treatment in advance. The treatment plan itself is likely to be negotiated between the clinician, client, and payer.

CONCLUSION

The field of alcoholism treatment has made remarkable progress in a relatively short time. Teams of dedicated clinicians in hundreds of treatment facilities bring hope and healing to countless clients and their families. However, not all treatment is effective. Neither is there a treatment that is superior to all others. Indeed, the challenge to the growing cadre of researchers now working in the field is to determine which treatment works for which type of client in which setting. Alcoholism treatment in the years ahead is more likely to reflect greater influence from research as more randomized clinical trials are conducted. The challenge to the field is to participate actively in the process of developing more effective treatment strategies while resisting the appeal of simple solutions for complex human problems.

REFERENCES

Alcoholics Anonymous. (1976). *Alcoholics Anonymous* (3rd ed.). New York: Alcoholics Anonymous World Services.

Anderson, D. (1981). *Perspectives on treatment: The Minnesota experience.* Center City, MN: Hazelden Foundation.

Bowman, K., & Jellinek, E. M. (1941). Alcohol addiction and its treatment. *Quarterly Journal of Studies on Alcohol, 2,* 18-176.

Cook, D, Straussner, S., & Fewell, C. (Eds.). (1985). *Psychosocial issues in the treatment of alcoholism.* New York: Haworth.

Dorsch, G., Talley, R., & Bynder, H. (1969). Response to alcoholics by the helping professions and community agencies in Denver. *Quarterly Journal of Studies on Alcohol, 30,* 905-919.

Engelmann, J. (1989). Minnesota treatment revolution. *Hazelden Update, 7,* 3-5.

Glaser, F. B., Annis, H., Skinner, H., Pearlman, S., Segal, R., Ogborne, A., Bohman, E., Gazda, P., & Zimmerman, T. (1984). *System of health care delivery* (Vols. 1-3). Toronto: Addiction Research Foundation.

Gomberg, E. L. (1989). On terms used and abused: The concept of co-dependency. *Current Issues in Alcohol-Drug Studies, Drugs and Society, 3*(3-4), 113-132.

Institute of Medicine. (1990). *Broadening the base of treatment for alcohol problems.* Washington DC: National Academy Press.

Knox, W. J. (1973). Attitudes of social workers and other professional groups towards alcoholism. *Quarterly Journal of Studies on Alcohol, 34,* 1270-1278.

Laundergan, J. (1982) *Easy does it: Alcohol treatment outcomes, Hazelden and the Minnesota Model.* Minneapolis, MN: Hazelden Foundation.

Maxwell, M. (1950). The Washington movement. *Quarterly Journal of Studies on Alcohol, 11,* 410-451.

Milam, J. R., & Ketchum, K. (1981). *Under the influence.* New York: Bantam.

National Association of Alcoholism and Drug Abuse Counselors. (1986). *Development of model professional standards for counselor.* Dubuque, IA: Kendall/Hunt.

O'Dwyer, P. (1984). Cost-effective rehabilitation: A process of matching. *EAP Digest, 4*(2), 33-34.

O'Dwyer, P. (1988). *From research to application: Practical consideration.* Paper prepared for the Institute of Medicine Committee for the Study of Treatment and Rehabilitation Services for Alcoholism and Alcohol Abuse, Washington, DC.

Pattison, E. M. (1982). A systems approach to alcoholism treatment. In E. M. Pattison & E. Kaufman (Eds.), *Encyclopedic handbook of alcoholism* (pp. 1089-1108). New York: Gardner.

Peyton, S., Chaddick, J., & Gorsuch, R. (1980). Willingness to treat alcoholics: A study of graduate social work students. *Journal of Studies on Alcohol, 41*, 935–940.

Rush, B. (1943). An inquiry into the effects of ardent spirits upon the human body and mind, with an account of the means of preventing and remedies for curing them. *Quarterly Journal of Studies on Alcohol, 4*, 325–341. (Original work published 1785)

Skinner, H. A. (1988). *Toward a multiaxial framework for the classification of alcohol problems* (Position Paper). Washington, DC: Institute of Medicine.

Straussner, S. L. A., Weinstein, D., & Hernandez, R. (1979). Effects of alcoholism on the family system. *Health and Social Work, 4*(4), 112–127.

Stuckey, R., & Harrison, J. (1982). The alcoholism rehabilitation center. In E. M. Pattison & E. Kaufman (Eds.), *Encyclopedic handbook of alcoholism* (pp. 865–873). New York: Gardner.

Wegscheider, S. (1984). Co-dependency—The therapeutic void. In R. Subby, J. Friel, S. Wegscheider, C. Whitfield, K. Cappel-Sowder, et al. (Eds.), *Co-dependency, an emerging issue* (pp. 43–62). Pompano Beach, FL: Health Communications.

Wilford, B. B. (1981). *Drug abuse, a guide for the primary care physician.* Chicago: American Medical Association.

8

Methadone Maintenance in the Treatment of Addiction

Ellen Grace Friedman

This chapter discusses methadone maintenance treatment, a widely used treatment for narcotics abuse in the United States. It provides a brief history of narcotics use and treatment, addresses the treatment offered to narcotics addicts enrolled in methadone maintenance treatment programs, and examines the roles of social workers in these programs.

BRIEF HISTORY OF NARCOTICS ADDICTION

Narcotics is a classification of drugs that includes opium, morphine, heroin, codeine, and the synthetic narcotics such as methadone. Narcotics are widely known for their addictive potential and have been used throughout history for therapeutic reasons, such as the alleviation of physical pain, as well as for pleasure.

Narcotics were used for medical purposes in the American colonies as early as the 1700s. In the early 1800s, two opium alkaloids, morphine (1805) and codeine (1832), were isolated from the opium poppy, increasing the number of available narcotics (Winn, Chester, May, & Sutton, 1967). Radical changes in the extent of narcotics use resulted from two events in the 1800s: the invention of the hypodermic needle and the Civil War. The hypodermic needle, invented in 1843, was brought to the United States in 1856. The needle allowed opiates, notably morphine, to be injected directly into the veins, increasing the strength and speed of the drug. It was during the Civil War that narcotics began to be widely administered to soldiers either wounded in battle or suffering from dysentery. After the Civil War ended, there were many medically addicted soldiers. "A term prevalent at the time, 'soldiers' illness,' actually meant narcotic addiction" (Winn et al., 1967, p. 18).

During the 1800s, the use of narcotics was "not generally offensive to public morals" (Winn et al., 1967, p. 21). Opium, the most widely used narcotic, was taken orally, smoked, and used in suppository form, while morphine was taken orally, rectally, and hypodermically. In 1898, heroin was first synthesized, and because its addictive potential was not fully understood, it was used to detoxify addicts from morphine (Winn et al., 1967).

Medical and public opinion of narcotics use began to shift around 1900. Physicians recognized narcotics use as a problem, and legislation was enacted to control narcotics in the United States. The first federal attempt to control narcotics use came in 1909, "with an act that prohibited the importation of opium, its preparations and derivatives except for medical purposes" (Winn et al., 1967, p. 22). The Harrison Act of 1914 further attempted to control the production and distribution of narcotics through the requirement of registration and payment of an occupational tax by all persons dealing with narcotic drugs. While prior to the Harrison Act, physicians were allowed to distribute narcotics to maintain addicts, court decisions following the act prohibited the maintenance of addicts by physicians. Many doctors were arrested for prescribing narcotics (Brecher & the Editors of Consumer Reports, 1972), and soon most doctors stopped treating addiction. Although passage of the Harrison Act did not stop narcotics use, it did change the nature of the users. Before the Harrison Act, women represented the majority of heroin and morphine users; afterwords, the sex ratio changed such that estimates "during the 1960's indicated that males outnumbered females among known addicts by five to one or more" (Brecher et al., 1972, p. 17).

By 1920, it was reported that there were more than 1.5 million "victims of the drug habit" (Newman, 1971, p. xvii). "Cut off from both legal drugs and clinic assistance [and] unable to break their habits addicts turned to an underworld market that had been only a minor source of supply previously" (Winn et al., 1967, p. 23). As pointed out by Brecher, "as a result, the door was opened wide to adulterated, contaminated, and misbranded black-market narcotics of all kinds (Brecher et al., 1972, p. 47)."

In the early 1950s, the American Medical Association and the American Bar Association issued reports urging that the government reevaluate its narcotics policy. In 1962, the Supreme Court, in *Robinson v. California*, ruled that criminal conviction for being addicted to narcotics violated the Eighth and Fourteenth Amendments (Chavkin, 1990). These events helped bring about the present era in which medical intervention has once again become an accepted treatment for narcotics addiction.

TREATMENT APPROACHES

Narcotics treatment takes various forms: detoxification, residential treatment, therapeutic community treatment, drug-free outpatient and community-based treatment, self-help group treatment, acupuncture, and methadone maintenance.

Detoxification, which is the process of freeing the addict's body from physiological dependence on narcotic drugs, can be done either during inpatient hospitalization or on an outpatient basis. During inpatient detoxification, addicts are admitted to a hospital and undergo a medically supervised withdrawal from narcotics. The time necessary for inpatient detoxification varies. During detoxification, addicts often receive various services such as individual, group, and family counseling in addition to medical treatment.

Another form of narcotics treatment is the therapeutic community. The first therapeutic community in the United States, Synanon, was started in California in 1958. In therapeutic communities, addicts are helped to change in a highly structured residential setting that relies on peer influence (Falco, 1989). Most of the staff members are former addicts. Residents are resocialized to assume responsibility for themselves, and privileges are given according to the resident's willingness to learn and participate. This form of treatment is long-term and either provides for residents gradual reentry into the outside community or incorporates them permanently into its structure (Freilich, 1974).

Drug-free outpatient programs treat addicts using individual and group counseling techniques. Sometimes family treatment is offered, with family members brought in to support the patient and to receive counseling themselves.

The 12-step model of treatment for narcotics addiction is based on the principles and practices of Alcoholics Anonymous. These are leaderless groups with no fees, no professionals, and total anonymity granted to its members. Addicts attending Narcotics Anonymous may participate as much or as little as they choose, with a shared goal of abstinence from narcotics use. Twelve-step programs are also available for family members of narcotics addicts (Nar-Anon).

Additional forms of treatment available to help narcotics addicts include acupuncture treatment, outpatient medically supervised detoxification using drugs such as methadone, individual and group psychotherapy, and the temporary or extended use of medications such as naltrexone.

METHADONE

Methadone is a long-acting synthetic narcotic, developed during World War II as a synthetic painkiller (Rosenbaum, 1982). In the early 1960s, Drs. Vincent Dole and Marie Nyswander of Rockefeller University opened the first methadone maintenance treatment program at Beth Israel Hospital in New York City to research the therapeutic value of methadone maintenance.

Although methadone had been used in the United States since 1948 to detoxify narcotics addicts, the concept of maintaining addicts on it was new (Rosenbaum, 1982).

Dole and Nyswander postulated that methadone maintenance could relieve what they believed was the metabolic disorder created by chronic addiction. Reports of their findings demonstrated that addicts maintained on methadone quickly stopped using narcotics, and methadone was hailed as the "Cinderella drug," which many believed could quickly solve the narcotics problem (Newman, 1971, p. xiv). Methadone was credited with the ability to save lives, eliminate criminal behavior, and totally eliminate drug craving. In 1967 methadone programs became publicly funded, and in 1968 the American Medical Association endorsed the use of methadone for maintenance.

Government funding allowed for a tremendous growth in the number of methadone clients in the 1960s and 1970s. The number of clients enrolled in methadone maintenance treatment programs increased from 25,000 in 1971 (Rosenbaum, 1982) to 135,000 in 1976 (Bourne, 1976). Currently between 110,000 and 120,000 clients are enrolled in methadone programs in the United States (Kleber 1991), with over 27,000 in New York City alone (Blanche Frank, personal communication, May 7, 1991).

THERAPEUTIC USES OF METHADONE

Today methadone is used in several different ways. To begin with, methadone is used to detoxify addicts from heroin by first substituting it for heroin and then gradually lowering the dose until the addict is drug-free. A major criticism of this form of treatment is that detoxification alone without follow-up care is often ineffective and results in a high relapse/readmission rate.

Methadone is also used for prolonged detoxification over a period of years, during which the addict is offered psychosocial rehabilitation. This gradual reduction allows time for the addict's body to adjust and for the client to change his or her lifestyle before complete withdrawal of medication.

The most common use of methadone is as a long-term treatment, that is, methadone maintenance. In this model, clients remain in treatment indefinitely and receive ongoing counseling, medical assistance, and vocational services. Detoxification from methadone is voluntary and neither encouraged nor discouraged.

In spite of the growth of methadone programs, "controversy still exists about the legitimacy of this treatment approach. Some of the antagonism towards this form of treatment results from personal bias and prejudice regarding this patient population, which is perceived by some to be composed largely of antisocial or weak persons unable to give up their self-destructive behavior" (Cooper, 1989, p. 1664). Supporters and critics of methadone maintenance cite various advantages and disadvantages of this model.

Some of the advantages are the following:

1. At sufficient doses, methadone successfully blocks the effects of heroin. Therefore taking additional narcotics will have no euphoric effect.
2. Methadone can be taken orally, modifying or eliminating the risk of getting and transmitting diseases such as cellulitis, hepatitis, thrombophlebitis, HIV infection, and AIDS.
3. Methadone has an extended duration of 24 to 36 hours, while heroin lasts 6 to 8 hours. This means that as long as methadone is taken daily, clients will not experience withdrawal.
4. Methadone is devoid of serious side effects, although, as with other narcotics, constipation and sweating may occur. Impotence, sleep problems, and loss of libido, which have been reported as side effects, can be easily corrected by dose adjustment.
5. Methadone is an inexpensive treatment. Despite variations in program expenses, it regularly costs less than $5,000 to maintain a client on methadone for 1 year (Mark Parrino, personal communication, May 17, 1991).
6. Clients attend methadone clinics according to schedules based on their progress. Clients most in need of supervision and care attend most often. Clinic visits to pick up methadone brings clients into contact with health care professionals and thus provide them access to medical and social services.

Critics of methadone maintenance cite the following disadvantages:

1. Methadone is addictive, and its use substitutes one drug addiction for another.
2. When used by pregnant women, methadone is transmitted to unborn children who are born addicted and may have to be detoxified.
3. Methadone programs do not really treat addicts and help them to change; they only make them more comfortable.
4. Methadone treats only the symptoms of narcotics addiction, leaving people vulnerable to other addictions.

A TYPICAL METHADONE MAINTENANCE TREATMENT PROGRAM

The operations and staffing patterns of methadone maintenance treatment programs are bound by federal and state regulations. Many conditions are placed upon methadone maintenance programs, including maximum allowable dose, duration of treatment, scheduling of client visits, and staffing patterns.

Program admission is based on an interview with a counselor and a program physician, as well as a urine test to determine current drug use. To be admitted for treatment, applicants must demonstrate at least a 1-year history of narcotics addiction. This can be demonstrated by "track marks," the scar tissue that forms after puncturing the skin during drug use, and by hospital or prison records. The urine test demonstrates current narcotics use and reveals other drugs that the applicant is currently using.

Methadone programs are either free-standing or hospital-affiliated. Programs are staffed by a physician, an administrative supervisor, nurses, and counseling staff comprised of both ex-addicts and professionals such as social workers. Some programs also employ physician's assistants, vocational counselors, and HIV specialists.

All clients receive a complete physical examination upon admission and, in some states such as New York, every year thereafter. The methadone dose, which is determined by the physician who is following state law, is adjusted according to medical need.

Progress in rehabilitation is measured by the absence of substance abuse, length of time in treatment, responsibility in handling the methadone, lack of criminal activity, and productive use of time. Drug abuse is measured by client self-report, clinical appearance, analysis of randomly collected urine samples, and physical examinations.

Frequency of individual and group counseling sessions is determined on a case-by-case basis. Individual counseling provides a context for clients to explore personal and vocational concerns that are impacting on their ability to remain drug-free and to assist them in developing productive and fulfilling lives.

Group counseling, based on a rehabilitation model, provides an important context to explore personal and shared concerns. Groups offer support, nondestructive socialization, the development of problem-solving techniques, information, and education. Many methadone maintenance programs also offer parenting classes, on-site vocational and educational services, and support groups targeted at helping with such special problems as cocaine and alcohol abuse and HIV infection.

Consistent with the concept of maintenance, detoxification from methadone is voluntary and most often done on an outpatient basis. After clients detoxify, some programs offer them the opportunity to continue in counseling for support. Another advantage of remaining in treatment after detoxification is that if clients begin abusing narcotics again, they can be immediately restabilized on methadone.

TREATMENT NEEDS OF METHADONE CLIENTS

Despite the fact that methadone clients come from all walks of life and all ethnic groups, their common history of chronic narcotics use, most often beginning during adolescence, creates serious emotional, health, social, and vocational problems. This section will address some of the common treatment needs of methadone clients.

Social and Vocational Issues

Many addicts entering methadone maintenance treatment programs display serious social dysfunction. Many come from emotionally and financially impoverished backgrounds. These addicts have never had the opportunity to develop productive and fulfilling lives. Many narcotics addicts entering methadone maintenance treatment programs, especially in urban areas, are people of color. At the Beth Israel Methadone Maintenance Treatment Program in New York City, which has the largest number of clients in the country, over two-thirds of the almost 8,000 clients in treatment are African-American or Hispanic (Beth Israel, 1989). These clients face racial prejudices as well as society's negative stereotyping of all addicts.

Narcotics addicts often fail to complete high school and to develop the skills necessary for employment or adult socialization. Those who have been able to work during their addictions most often have unstable work histories, having lost jobs because their work adjustments were poor or because their addictions became known to their employers. Clients in methadone maintenance treatment need assistance in developing the skills necessary to make them employable as well as help to learn how to find and keep jobs.

Addicts often have police records, due to arrest either for possession or for committing crimes to support their habits. Once they are involved in criminal lifestyles and have police records, legitimate employment options become very limited. Many clients with both addiction and criminal histories have learned to be tough and street-savvy. They do not understand how to live by the rules of and function successfully in the straight world. Although enrollment in methadone maintenance treatment reduces their criminal activity, these clients need help to establish lifestyles that support drug abstinence, vocational achievement, and healthy ways of relating.

In the process of becoming addicted and maintaining their addictions, many addicts lose family contact and become entrenched in dysfunctional relationships with other addicts. The loss of family and meaningful social ties increases their sense of shame and alienation. A large number of female addicts become involved in relationships fraught with battering and abuse, which further increases their sense of worthlessness.

Studies of the family configurations of adicts have described inconsistent, overindulgent, and rejecting mothers concomitant with passive and absent fathers (Freilich, 1974). Research into the families or origin of methadone clients indicates that many experienced abuse or neglect as children and one-third came from substance-abusing homes (New York State Division of Substance Abuse Services [DSAS], 1987).

It is not surprising that many people with narcotics addiction histories feel hopeless about themselves and about the possibility of changing. Childhood memories of loss and pain and adult experiences of isolation and humiliation are related to their low self-esteem. The veneer of arrogance addicts often present is used defensively to hide their longstanding feelings of worthlessness. Treatment planning in methadone maintenance treatment programs must take into account the self-esteem and cultural issues of clients. Treatment can provide consistency, support, and reassurance as well as opportunities to change attitudes and lifestyles.

Clients are resocialized through the many rules of treament, which offer progressive responsibility and autonomy by learning to play by the rules. Counseling and rewards for abstinence help clients to change. Methadone maintenance programs frequently provide the first successful interaction an addict has with a social service agency. The following vignette portrays a typical client.

George was a 21-year-old male at the time he applied for methadone maintenance treatment. He was fearful that without the stability of methadone treatment his narcotics use would destroy his family life, employment, and health. Two drug-addicted siblings had died from complications of HIV–AIDS.

George was born in Puerto Rico and came to New York City at age 6. His father left home when George was 3 years old, and he was raised by his mother and stepfather. George was the youngest of three siblings. He does not remember his father but states that his stepfather was an alcoholic who physically abused his mother and him. George began using marijuana and alcohol at age 13 and heroin at age 14. He dropped out of school at this time and began hanging out on the streets. George realized that he was addicted at age 15 when he first experienced withdrawal. He had tried to detoxify three times, twice in a hospital and once on his own. Upon admission, George was supporting his addiction by work as a building superintendent and by robbery.

George was living with a nonuser with whom he had two children. His legal history included five convictions, two for robbery and three for loitering and possession. At the time of program admission, George was on probation.

During the first year of methadone maintenance treatment, George sporadically abused cocaine and alcohol. He continued to work, and his family life improved. He was seen by his counselor several times each week for support. Although referred to the cocaine abuse group and Alcoholics Anonymous (AA), George refused to attend. When offered testing for the HIV virus, he agreed and tested negative for the virus. Initially he was guarded and shared little information with program staff. After his counselor repeatedly initiated discussions about the presence of cocaine in his urine, George finally admitted his cocaine problem. With the help of his counselor, George then detoxified from cocaine and alcohol and began to attend cocaine groups at the methadone program. After 3 years in treatment, George requested educational services in order to receive his high school diploma.

George has been in treatment for 5 years and remains on methadone maintenance. He works full-time now and no longer abuses any drugs. He has completed probation and has not been arrested since enrolling in the methadone maintenance treatment program. Individual weekly counseling, once used primarily to support drug abstinence, now focuses on helping him raise his children and improve his relationship with his family and on encouraging him to upgrade his employment. He continues to attend clinic groups to support his abstinence from cocaine and alcohol. George believes that his enrollment in methadone maintenance has provided him with the assistance he needs to keep his family together.

Health Issues

Many methadone patients report minor and major illnesses upon admission and after beginning treatment. Many are related to prior drug use, and many others are due to poor self-care. Regular health screenings and frequent contact with medical staff enable clients to overcome their distrust of health care providers.

Today many methadone clients are infected with the HIV virus. Preliminary studies estimate that between 30% and 50% of all methadone clients are HIV-positive (Nina Peyser, personal communication, May 16, 1991). Of great importance is the fact that the rate of HIV infection is accelerating faster among people of color and women who make up a large percent of methadone clients (National Institute on Drug Abuse [NIDA], 1990). Therefore some methadone maintenance treatment programs now include mandatory HIV education and risk assessment, voluntary HIV testing, and referrals to social services for clients suffering from AIDS. In addition, some methadone maintenance treatment programs provide counseling on safer sex and provide home-based support services for clients who become too ill to attend the program. The following case illustrates the care given to one such client.

Susan was a 37-year-old Jewish female who had been enrolled in methadone maintenance treatment for 6 years. She was married to a man who was also in methadone treatment, and they lived together in a welfare hotel. Her 11-year-old son had been adopted by Susan's brother while Susan was using drugs. After 1 year in methadone treatment, Susan took the HIV test and tested positive for the virus. A year later, Susan developed pneumocystis carinii pneumonia (PCP) and was diagnosed with AIDS. Until this diagnosis, Susan continued to use cocaine and avoided counseling. When Susan became ill, her counselor visited her at the hospital and suggested that she join the women's group and the cocaine group at the clinic once she was better. Susan agreed and became an important and well-liked member of the groups. She was witty, candid, and endearing.

As her condition deteriorated, Susan joined the "People with AIDS" lunch group at the program. She suffered with AIDS for 4 years. When she became too weak to attend the program, she was placed on the caseload of a social worker who met with her at home. Her social worker supported Susan in reaching out to her estranged family, and before her death, Susan was able to resolve her relationship with her brother and son. Staff from the methadone maintenance program and members of the groups that she attended visited Susan every day when she was hospitalized, bringing news, companionship, and hope. When she died, staff were there to provide solace to her husband.

TREATMENT NEEDS OF POLYSUBSTANCE ABUSERS

Polysubstance abusers are those people who use and are often addicted to more than one drug. Frequently polysubstance abuse precedes entry into methadone maintenance treatment. It is not unusual for clients applying for treatment to report that they are addicted to heroin, marijuana, cocaine, and/or alcohol. Another route to polysubstance abuse and addiction is through mixing drugs together to increase the high or to mitigate withdrawal symptoms. For example, clients report the use of Valium (a minor tranquilizer), alcohol, and heroin to decrease the withdrawal symptoms following crack cocaine use or the use of Elavil to feel less depressed.

Since the beginning of the crack cocaine epidemic, there has been a dramatic rise in the number of polysubstance abusers enrolled in methadone maintenance treatment programs. Studies of methadone clients in New York City indicate that between 35% and 50% use cocaine (Beth Israel, 1989, 1990). Many of the clients in methadone programs who use cocaine inject the drug intravenously (Zweben & Payne, 1990), placing them at high risk for HIV infection.

Alcohol abuse is another serious problem for some methadone clients. Studies indicate that between 20% and 53% of all methadone clients are abusing alcohol at the time of intake (Hunt et al., 1986). Clients who have alcohol problems can suffer from "cirrhosis, bleeding varices, pancreatitis, hepatic coma and esophageal bleeding" (Hunt et al., 1986, p. 150). Since methadone can block only narcotics and cannot stop the effects of alcohol, cocaine, or pills, the only remedy for these addictions is detoxification followed by abstinence.

Polysubstance abuse is revealed by history-taking, client appearance, client self-report, urine screenings, and physical examinations. Often polysubstance abuse is vigorously denied by clients who feel ashamed of their multiple addictions, are unwilling to stop using other drugs, and/or fear a loss of program privileges. Individual and group counseling are used as first steps to helping clients overcome denial and use available services.

Clients with polysubstance abuse problems need medical evaluations to determine if inpatient drug detoxification is required. If clients require hospitalization, this can be arranged by the methadone maintenance treatment program. Most hospitals and some long-term residential treatment programs will allow clients to remain on methadone while in their facilities.

If clients do not require or are unwilling to accept inpatient treatment, they are encouraged to attend daily activity or educational groups at the methadone program or in the community, such as Narcotics Anonymous or Cocaine Anonymous. Additional referrals are made to mental health services as needed. Because opiate abuse is recognized as a chronic condition, relapse does not mean failure (Newman, 1989).

The case of Bill provides an example of how methadone maintenance treatment programs work with clients who use other drugs.

Bill is a 53-year-old Italian man who has been in methadone maintenance treatment for 15 years. For 12 years he worked as a doorman. When his mother died 3 years ago, Bill began to drink heavily, and he lost his job 2 years ago. He lives with Gloria, a 38-year-old woman who is also enrolled in methadone treatment. They have been dating for 10 years and living together for 2 years.

Bill had been very dependent on his mother throughout his life. He is an only child whose father was killed in an accident when he was 6 months old. His mother never remarried, and Bill lived with his mother until she died. When his mother died, Bill was grief-stricken and overcome with loneliness. He began to drink for solace, but his drinking quickly got out of control.

Efforts to assist him with his drinking problems and grief were unsuccessful until Bill lost his job and Gloria threatened to leave him. Once Bill was willing to accept assistance, his counselor referred him for inpatient alcohol detoxification followed by daily attendance at AA meetings. During his detoxification from alcohol, Bill's methadone dose remained stable and Gloria began to attend Al-Anon meetings.

FEMALE METHADONE CLIENTS

Female addicts are an underreported and understudied population. The number of female addicts cannot be accurately measured by their entry into the criminal justice system, a typical referral source of males into treatment, because many female drug addicts are financially supported by partners and friends. Furthermore, when females are known to be addicted, it is common for them to be referred to psychiatrists or mental health clinics rather than drug treatment programs.

Research on the characteristics and treatment needs of female narcotics addicts has been hampered by the fact that most studies have used male cohorts. However, existing studies do create a picture of the female addict that is, in some ways, different from her male counterpart (Hser, Anglin, & Booth, 1987).

Female narcotics addicts have been found to have lower self-esteem than both male addicts and women in the general population. They are more anxious and depressed, less assertive and more suspicious, more dependent and more isolated than drug dependent men (NIDA, 1979).

Females entering treatment have fewer emotional and social supports. They are more likely to live alone, to be single parents, or to live with a partner who is abusing drugs or is in treatment (DSAS, 1987). This means that female narcotics addicts in treatment often require more support and social services from their programs than do their male counterparts.

Among the special services needed by women are support groups, gynecological and prenatal care and education, as well as assistance in locating daycare facilities for children. To help female clients, methadone programs must also work to eliminate the sex-role stereotyping in counseling that is detrimental to the rehabilitation process for women (Hser et al., 1987).

The following case illustrates help given to a female client.

Mary is a 42-year-old single Hispanic woman who has been supported by welfare for the past 16 years. Her 26-year-old daughter, married to a policeman, hardly ever speaks with her because she blames Mary for neglecting her as a child. Mary's 10-year-old son lives with Mary.

Mary's mother was a gambler; her father is unknown. She was raised in a convent until age 15, when she became pregnant and ran away to get married. Mary became addicted to heroin at age 17; she explains that her marriage was failing and that she used heroin to get away from her sad life. She entered methadone maintenance treatment when her son was born 10 years ago, since she was determined to create a better life for herself and for him. With the help of her counselor, Mary entered therapy at a local mental health center. However, she remained depressed and lonely.

In 1990 the methadone program that she attended received a grant that allowed stable methadone clients to train to become assistant counselors. With support from her counselor, Mary applied for this training and arranged for after-school care for her son. Mary's sensitivity to others and strong desire to learn quickly became apparent. She studied and embraced the training as an opportunity to use her past to help others.

CHILDREN OF METHADONE CLIENTS

According to one study, the "vast majority of narcotics addicts in treatment are of childbearing ages (16-40)" (Deren, 1986, p. 77), and 69% of methadone clients have at least one child (DSAS, 1987). In 1984 (most recent statistics available), there were approximately 43,000 children of methadone clients in New York State, 27,000 of whom lived with their parents. Twenty-five percent of these children were under 5 years of age (DSAS, 1987).

The physical, social, and mental health needs of the children of methadone-maintained parents are of great concern to methadone programs. During pregnancy, the health of the expectant mothers is monitored by program physicians and social workers. Pregnant clients are given information about drug interactions, encouraged to use prenatal services regularly, and taught what to expect during and after delivery. Women of childbearing age are encouraged to have their HIV statuses checked, since HIV infection can be passed on to their fetuses.

Pregnant women are not encouraged to detoxify from methadone out of concern that they will potentially return to opiate abuse, causing damage to themselves and their unborn children. Pregnant women who remain on methadone are counseled about the likelihood that their infants will be born addicted to methadone and will need to be detoxified at birth. These clients are also given clear information about child protective service laws. Child protective service laws mandate the reporting of children born addicted but clearly indicate that no case is to be reported if the mother is taking a legally prescribed medication, such as methadone (Straussner, 1989).

Studies of women in methadone maintenance treatment programs indicate that these women have better pregnancy outcomes when compared with heroin addicts or addicts taking methadone on the streets (Chavkin, 1990).

Because many women enrolled in the methadone maintenance treatment programs have suffered from inadequate parenting, there is concern about how these women will parent their own children. The parenting competence of women on methadone can be improved through parenting instruction (NIDA, 1981).

When a parent is clearly unable to provide for the well-being of his or her child and is unwilling to accept assistance, the case must be reported to the state child protective service bureau. After the case is reported by the methadone program, help is offered to clients to assist them in making the necessary changes to keep or (re)establish custody of their children.

SOCIAL WORKERS IN METHADONE MAINTENANCE TREATMENT PROGRAMS

The roles social workers play in methadone maintenance treatment programs vary. Because regulations governing methadone program staffing do not specify a particular role for social workers, they may be found working in direct practice, as supervisors, or as administrators. Recently the move toward a greater professional involvement in the field of substance abuse treatment has brought more and more social workers into leadership roles in methadone programs.

Social Workers as Clinicians

Social workers are uniquely able to help treat narcotics abusers. Trained in a biopsychosocial perspective, they are knowledgeable about the impact of the emotional, cultural, and socioeconomic factors influencing drug addicts. The professional value of nonjudgmental service is very important in the treatment of a population of clients who have internalized society's view of addicts as weak, antisocial, and self-destructive people (Cooper, 1989). Commitment to client self-determination allows social workers to understand, remain objective, and display empathic skills in their work with clients who may remain deviant and self-destructive. Social workers are trained to recognize relapse, child neglect, and HIV illness as human problems to be understood and resolved through care and support rather than as signs of moral failure.

Social workers are trained to assess and intervene using a range of techniques useful in working with addicted clients. Individual casework helps clients establish a relationship with a worker through which problems can be addressed and trust developed. Such a relationship enables a client to accept support and develop self-awareness. The worker serves as a positive role model for clients, many of whom have had no such model in their lives.

Training in group work allows social workers to establish and lead groups that provide clients with the opportunity to overcome social isolation, to receive peer support, to develop alternatives to drug and alcohol abuse, and to develop healthier ways of relating to others.

Crisis intervention skills allow social workers to assess situations quickly and to intervene professionally on behalf of clients. Social workers know when and how to enlist community support and how to locate and network with community resources.

Social Workers as Clinical Supervisors

In the role of clinical supervisor, social workers help develop the skills and knowledge base of the counseling staff by providing guidance and direction. Outcome studies have shown that clients improve most when provided with a positive staff attitude and flexible treatment (Cooper, 1989). Social workers are well trained to provide this supervision since, as a profession, they have been supervising since the late 1800s (Kadushin, 1976).

Supervision of counseling staff in methadone maintenance treatment programs is a complex task. Many methadone maintenance treatment programs employ both former addicts and professional counselors. Counselors who are former narcotics addicts require supervision to address their issues of overidentification and countertransference as well as to develop basic counseling skills. Professionals require supervision to overcome their biases toward addicts, their lack of understanding of addict lifestyles, and their countertransference. Since clients present many different problems and require individualized treatment planning, all counselors need training and supervision to develop their assessment and interventive skills, their knowledge of HIV infection as well as cocaine and alcohol abuse, and their ability to help clients with such issues as death and dying, relapse, parenting, and child neglect. Helping staff to increase their knowledge of resources and their skill in using them, as well their knowledge of how to optimally time referrals, is an important part of social work supervision.

The following are two vignettes of how social workers function as clinical supervisors.

Jeffrey was a 43-year-old counselor with a history of narcotics addiction. He came to supervision feeling overwhelmed and angry about the amount of work he had to do. At first, he was angry with his social work supervisor and the system. During many discussions with the social work supervisor, Jeffrey came to understand that he was most upset with his clients for not getting better as he had and for making him feel devalued. He also recognized that his clients' resistance induced feelings of worthlessness in him and aroused fear that his performance as a counselor would be judged by whether his clients recovered quickly. The supervisor helped Jeffrey to recognize the differences between his clients and himself, to reframe his work, to develop more realistic expectations of himself, and to become less angry and more empathic.

Doris was a new social worker assigned to helping patients who were terminally ill with AIDS. She felt frustrated that patients were rejecting her help and discouraged that they refused to speak with her about their feelings and fears. With the help of the social work supervisor, Doris began to understand that her unspoken demand that clients speak about their illness every time they met was the reason some clients avoided her. She redefined her work to allow her clients greater autonomy and began to establish relationships in which clients felt free to talk about their various interests and concerns as well. As Doris learned to be more flexible in her approach to her work, much of her clients' mistrust dissipated and they began to reach out for her help.

Social Workers as Administrators

As administrators, social workers can help create programs that meet federal and state regulations, maximize staff utilization, and improve client care. By assessing the strengths and problems in the agency, social workers are able to create a cooperative, respectful, and creative environment for staff and clients. As administrators, social workers are able to develop new programs for clients, to network successfully with other service providers, and to facilitate methadone clients' access to care in the community by sensitively and skillfully explaining clients' dynamics and needs to other professionals and funding sources. The following is an example of how a social work administrator may function in his or her role.

Since becoming the administrator of a methadone maintenance treatment program 2 years ago, Betty had established a social work student unit at her program. In addition to training students, this unit provided work satisfaction and professional growth for her social work staff and helped to increase the number of professionals who were knowledgeable about drug abuse treatment. She worked to develop inservice group training for line staff and created a group program at the agency. In response to the staff's feeling overwhelmed, Betty worked to eliminate unnecessary paperwork and to streamline existing systems. She was able to allow the clinic to close for 2 hours each week to give staff the opportunity to catch up on paperwork and raise morale.

Because of her training in social work, Betty worked closely with other service providers and was able to explain the treatment needs and dynamics of methadone patients to them and assuage their fears. This process increased the opportunities for clients to receive treatment in the community. Betty also obtained grants to meet the vocational and social service needs of program clients.

CURRENT ISSUES AFFECTING METHADONE MAINTENANCE TREATMENT

At a time of fewer resources, the health and social service needs of clients have become staggering. Methadone maintenance treatment programs serve many clients who are HIV-infected or suffering from AIDS or abusing crack cocaine. Because of budget cuts, methadone maintenance treatment programs now serve an increasing number of people with fewer housing options or vocational opportunities.

This leads to the challenge of providing more comprehensive treatment—at a time of more limited resources. This is also, fortunately, a time of growing professional interest in helping narcotics addicts. More professionals are entering the field of addiction treatment, bringing with them an understanding of psychodynamics, family work, and public health.

Given the large population of narcotics addicts served in methadone maintenance treatment, methadone programs are in a unique position to contribute to the body of knowledge of the care of addicts, to provide high-quality social and vocational services, and to create innovative treatment strategies. New treatment strategies are currently being developed through networking by different groups of drug treatment providers. Methadone programs are incorporating groups used in therapeutic communities as well as self-help (12-step) groups and family support networks.

This is a most challenging and important time for the field of addiction treatment. As more social workers become knowledgeable about this treatment, they will surely contribute to the new directions that unfold.

REFERENCES

Beth Israel Methadone Maintenance Treatment Program. (1989). *Patient statistical report*. Unpublished data.
Beth Israel Methadone Maintenance Treatment Program. (1990). *Patient statistical report*. Unpublished data.
Bourne, P. (1976). Methadone maintenance. In *Overview of substance abuse* (pp. 161–172). New York: Narcotics and Drug Research, Inc.
Brecher, E. M., & the Editors of Consumer Reports. (1972). *Licit and illicit drugs*. Boston: Little, Brown.

Chavkin, W. (1990). Drug addiction and pregnancy: Policy crossroads. *Public Health and the Law, 80*(4), 77–94.

Cooper, J. (1989). Methadone treatment and acquired immunodeficiency syndrome. *Journal of the American Medical Association, 262*(12), 1664–1668.

Deren, S. (1986). The children of substance abusers: A review of the literature. *Journal of Substance Abuse Treatment, 3,* 77–94.

Falco, M. (1989). *The substance abuse crisis in New York City.* Briefing paper prepared for the New York Community Trust, New York.

Freilich, C. (1974). Personality and life history differences of heroin addicts accepted to a drug free and a methadone maintenance program. (Doctoral dissertation, City University of New York). *Dissertation Abstracts International, 35*(5), 2427B.

Hser, Y., Anglin, M., & Booth, M. (1987). Differences in addict careers. *American Journal of Drug and Alcohol Abuse, 13*(4), 253–280.

Hunt, D., Shrug, D., Goldsmith, D., Lipton, D., Robertson, K., & Truitt, L. (1986). Alcohol use and abuse: Heavy drinking among methadone clients. *American Journal of Drug and Alcohol Abuse, 12*(1 & 2), 147–164.

Kadushin, A. (1976). *Supervision in social work.* New York: Columbia University Press.

Kleber, H. (1991, March). *Call for unity.* Speech presented at Inaugural National Methadone Conference, Boston.

Lief, N. (1976). Some measures of parenting behavior for addicted and nonaddicted mothers. In *Symposium on comprehensive health care for addicted families and their children.* Rockville, MD: National Institute on Drug Abuse.

National Institute on Drug Abuse. (1979). *Addicted women, family dynamics, self-perceptions and support systems* (USDHEW Pub. No. 80-762). Washington, DC: U.S. Government Printing Office.

National Institute on Drug Abuse. (1981). *Treatment services for drug dependent women* (DHHS Pub. No. (ADM)81-1177). Washington, DC: U.S. Government Printing Office.

National Institute on Drug Abuse. (1990). *AIDS and intravenous drug use: Future directions for community based prevention research* (DHHS Pub. No. (ADM)90-1627). Washington, DC: U.S. Government Printing Office.

Newman, R. (1971). *Methadone maintenance in the treatment of narcotics addiction.* New York: Academic Press.

Newman, R. (1989, October 31). Unpublished letter to the Editor, *Medical Journal of Australia.*

New York State Division of Substance Abuse Services. (1987). *Parents in methadone treatment and their children.* Albany, NY: Author.

Rosenbaum, M. (1982). Getting on methadone, the experience of the woman addict. *Contemporary Drug Problems, 11*(1), 113–114.

Straussner, L. (1989). Intervention with maltreating parents who are drug and alcohol abusers. In S. Ehrenkranz, E. Goldstein, L. Goodman, & J. Seinfeld (Eds.), *Clinical social work with maltreated children and their families* (pp. 149–177). New York: New York University Press.

Winn, M., Chester, A., May, M., Jr., & Sutton, M. R. (Eds). (1967). *Drug abuse: Escape to nowhere.* Philadelphia: Smith, Kline, & French.

Zweben, J., & Payne, J. T. (1990). Methadone maintenance in the treatment of opioid dependence—A current perspective. *Addiction Medicine, 152,* 588–599.

9

12-Step Programs as a Treatment Modality

For centuries people with similar interests and concerns have banded together and formed what have more recently been termed self-help groups. Thus some of our religious institutions were "self-help" groups before they became institutions. In recent years, according to one source, "perhaps the most rapidly expanding group movement is the self-help group. By the end of the decade of the 1970s, Alcoholics Anonymous had over 30,000 Chapters" (Yalom, 1985). The purpose of this chapter is to describe the various kinds of Anonymous or 12-step programs, such as Alcoholics, Cocaine, Narcotics, and Overeaters Anonymous, as well as groups for family members such as Al-Anon and Adult Children of Alcoholics. How these groups and the 12 steps provide a potent and sophisticated modality of treatment capable of characterological change is the major thrust of the discussion.

THE ANONYMOUS OR 12-STEP PROGRAMS

Anonymous programs are self-help fellowships based on the 12 steps described in *Twelve Steps and Twelve Traditions* (1952). Membership in the 12-step programs was originally focused exclusively on helping alcoholics and their families. It is now open to all who share the common goal of recovery from a variety of other substances and conditions. Such programs have proliferated in the past two decades beyond all expectation; according to the director of the National Self-Help Clearing House, there are more than 200 different groups based on the principles of Alcoholics Anonymous.

Alcoholics Anonymous and the other 12-step programs grew spontaneously; they are based on the principle of attracting participants rather than proselytizing. Any form of publicity is not in keeping with AA's tradition of placing "principles above personalities" (*Twelve Steps and Twelve Traditions*, 1952). The tradition of anonymity is the fulcrum of a 12-step program. It bestows an immediacy and a freedom on the member, who can feel able to share without fear of rejection or betrayal, and creates an atmosphere of trust.

Other facets of 12-step programs include: regularly scheduled meetings, a 24-hour telephone network for immediate intervention, the provision of services such as outreach to others, and sponsorship. Sponsorship is a mutually beneficial relationship in which a long-term member provides ongoing, voluntary guidance to a newcomer. Another tradition is the self-supporting nature of these programs. A 12-step group does not lend its name to other causes or solicit outside funding; it supports itself through voluntary contributions collected during meetings and through the sale of publications that provide information, education, and inspiration.

Alcoholics Anonymous

Alcoholics Anonymous (AA) officially began in May 1935 when Bill Wilson, a formerly hopeless alcoholic then trying to stay sober, met with Dr. Bob Smith, another floundering "drunkard." They found that by supporting each other and helping other alcoholics they were able to attain and maintain sobriety. Bill Wilson had been a member of the Oxford Group, which in the 1920s and 1930s was an international movement based on the spiritual teachings of the early Christians. Some of the ideas and spiritual beliefs of AA, particularly the 12 steps, are derivatives of this movement. Dr. Bob said of Bill W. after that first meeting, ". . . he was the first living human with whom I had ever talked, who knew what he was talking about in regard to alcoholism from actual experience" (quoted in Robertson, 1988, p. 35). In other words, "he talked my language." Both men had social stature, were articulate and educated, and were able to spread their ideas first to Akron, Ohio, and then throughout the rest of the country.

Newcomers at their first AA meeting today encounter many of the same things as did those in the days of Bill W. and Dr. Bob 50 years ago. Many AA meetings take place in church basements because churches opened their doors to AA early in its life. A beginner usually goes down a set of stairs and is greeted by the same old slogans, such as "Easy does it," "First things first," "HALT" (don't get hungry, angry, lonely, or tired), or "Keep it simple."

A beginner is encouraged to attend 90 meetings in 90 days. In other words, almost total immersion is recommended when the person first puts down the bottle and learns to replace booze with people and meetings. The following vignette is the experience of one member, Martha, at her first AA meeting.

Martha is a 37-year-old school teacher who drank periodically for 7 years. She was persuaded by an old friend to call AA after a serious binge resulted in head and leg injuries that she had no recollection of sustaining. Her call was answered by Jim B., an AA volunteer, whose direct and compassionate manner eased her fear and shame. "We alcoholics have a disease," he told her. "We have a disease of loneliness." He arranged for her to be escorted to her first AA meeting by another volunteer, Ramona M., who was a longtime member of the fellowship.

The meeting was held in a church in her community in a large city. As soon as Martha walked in, she saw well-dressed smiling men and women at a table with books and pamphlets. She was greeted by two older women wearing blue badges labeled "Hospitality." Martha was stunned. Where were the bag ladies? Where were the winos? A young woman approached her with a friendly, welcoming "hello" and an offer of a telephone number. Two more women followed suit. Then Martha saw plastic scrolls at the front of the room. One said "Twelve Steps" and the other, "Twelve Traditions." Most of the letters were a blur, but she managed to remember the first words of the first step: "We admitted we were powerless over alcohol."

Martha remembers being both frightened and exhilarated. She was especially relieved to see so many attractive, professional women. It was the speaker's story that finally convinced her that she was in the right place. "I never thought I was any good," he said, "I never felt I belonged until I found alcohol."

Martha does not know if it was the speaker or the heads nodding in agreement, but she began to cry. She recalls feeling safe for the first time in years. She knew she was home.

As Martha discovered, an AA meeting can range from 2 people to 200. For each meeting there is a chairperson, who opens and closes the meeting; a secretary, who makes announcements and asks if there are any anniversaries, visitors, or additional announcements; and a treasurer, who monitors the collection and disbursements of contributions. All contributions to AA are voluntary, and each group is self-supporting. Officers are elected and change every 6 months. *Open* meetings consist of three speakers who have a minimum of 90 days sobriety and who tell the story of their addiction and recovery. These meetings are open to all who are interested. *Closed* meetings are exclusively for the fellowship; the tradition of anonymity is taken very seriously. Most meetings involve a "qualification," which is a speaker's story of drinking, bottoming out, and recovery. The speaker usually presents a topic for discussion. A *step* meeting is one in which one of the 12 steps is read. The speaker's story or qualification is usually focused on this step, as is the discussion from the floor that follows. A *beginners* meeting addresses the tools necessary in early sobriety. Many are embodied in slogans such as "It's the first drink that gets you drunk," "Easy does it," and "First things first." Beginners are encouraged to share their concerns and feelings. Through the process of identification, beginners learn that they are not alone.

The sponsorship relationship is crucial in ending isolation and ensuring recovery. A sponsor is someone of the same sex with sober experience in AA who becomes a mentor or special friend and guides the newcomer on his or her journey of living sober. According to a recent AA membership survey, 85% of AA members have a sponsor (AA, 1990).

The results of the AA membership survey further revealed that as of 1989: AA is composed of 35% women and 65% men. The average length of sobriety is more than 4 years, and the average age of an AA member is 41. Most members attend three meetings per week. Occupationally, 23% of AA members are classified as professional, 17% as labor, and 13% as managerial. In addition to their alcoholism, 42% said they were addicted to other drugs (AA, 1990).

Cocaine and Narcotics Anonymous

Alcoholics Anonymous has had an increasing number of "offspring," which offer programs to treat addictions to everything from narcotics, pills, and cocaine to sex and procrastination.

Cocaine Anonymous (CA), founded in Los Angeles, is now over a decade old. Members of CA tend to be younger than AA members. The format of the CA meeting resembles an AA meeting: The qualification and shared feelings are the same. CA also recommends going to 90 meetings in 90 days and utilizes sponsorship. In CA people share their experiences of the high, the sensation, the thrills associated with cocaine; they talk about their attempts to seek escape from profound feelings of apathy or deadness.

Narcotics Anonymous (NA), for the users of illicit drugs, follows the same format as AA and CA, with small variations. The slogan is "Take people, not a hit," and chips are given out for anniversaries with a quarter taped to one side and a phone number to the other—thus impulsive members can turn to people instead of a "hit."

Al-Anon

Al-Anon is the biggest and oldest group for the families and friends of alcoholics. In the early days of AA most meetings were in people's homes. The spouses were left in the kitchen to take care of the coffee and cake, and it was in these kitchens, with the help of Lois W., wife of Bill Wilson, that Al-Anon was born. According to Al-Anon–Alateen World Services, there are now over

32,000 Al-Anon and Alateen groups worldwide, over 19,500 in the United States alone. Eighty-eight percent of its members are women. Its major slogan is called the Al-Anon "3 C's"—"I didn't cause alcoholism, I can't control it, and I can't cure it." Another slogan, which also tells the essential story is "Keep the focus on yourself." Programs like Nar-Anon and Co-Anon follow the principles of Al-Anon for the families of narcotic users and cocaine addicts.

Adult Children of Alcoholics originated within the Al-Anon program in 1976. In the 1980s it emerged as the fastest growing 12-step program in the country, aimed at the estimated 28 million Americans who have at least one alcoholic parent (Robertson, 1988).

Overeaters Anonymous, Debtors Anonymous, and Other Programs

Overeaters and Debtors Anonymous illustrate how the 12 steps can be applied to substances from which complete abstinence is impossible.

Overeaters Anonymous, founded on January 9, 1960, is a fascinating and effective program utilizing the 12 steps, meetings, and sponsorship to achieve support for weight loss. The newcomer is asked to "turn over," or discuss, the eating plan for each day to the sponsor. While on the surface this may seem an overly dependent relationship, it is based on a quite sophisticated psychodynamic framework. "Turning over" the food takes the isolation, mystery, and willfulness out of overeating. It also gives structure to the daily intake of food and reinforces commitment to sharing feelings about it with another person.

In 1976 a sober alcoholic named John H. founded Debtors Anonymous (DA). There is an informal saying: "In AA you get sober but in DA you grow up." DA is based on the principle of abundance. The premise of DA is that the world is full of abundance and prosperity and that everyone is entitled to his or her share. Incurring debts is considered an act based on feelings of deprivation rather than greed. The notion that there is enough for everyone acts like AA's serenity prayer on frightened debtors, who usually believe they are not entitled to their share and/or covet much more than their share. While continuing to go into debt is viewed in the same way as drinking and overeating, it is the feelings behind the behavior that are addressed by the program. The member is asked to keep a record of the amount and nature of each day's spending, attend meetings, share with a sponsor, and eventually sit down with a man and a woman from the program to develop a spending plan—one which will include debts to others and to the self. A man and a woman are suggested because it was found that each has a different perspective on money. The meeting is called a "pressure group." It is designed to take the pressure off!

Gamblers Anonymous addresses the compulsive gambler. In this program the sponsor often accompanies the newcomer on visits to his or her creditors and helps arrange a schedule of payment.

There are new 12-step programs for compulsive sexuality and compulsive procrastination, as well as for people who are already in 12-step programs and are HIV-positive.

THE THERAPEUTIC VALUE OF ANONYMOUS PROGRAMS

The premise of this chapter is that the Anonymous programs and the 12 steps constitute an opportunity for internal, structural, therapeutic change that addresses characterological issues. The meetings, slogans, literature, sponsor, and the 12 steps themselves all act as therapeutic agents.

The Anonymous programs provide a *holding environment*, a term first used by the British object relations theorist D. W. Winnicott (1975). Winnicott believed that the therapy session, the therapist, the office, and so forth, provide an environment that is safe and nurturing and that set and hold the stage for psychological exploration and development. AA and the other 12-step programs, with their consistency of meetings, literature, qualifications, and sharing, provide such a holding environment.

One way of looking at the recovery process in addiction is to apply Margaret Mahler's conceptualization of early ego development. Mahler and her colleagues studied how infants, toddlers, and preschoolers negotiate the separation–individuation process (Mahler, Pine, & Bergman, 1975). From this theoretical perspective, the process begins with a period of symbiosis in which the early ego (1–5 months) is characterized by lack of differentiation between the child and the mother. Symbiosis is a period necessary to further growth. When the infant begins to develop some language and motor skills, the lifelong journey of individuation begins—a journey of gradual and increasing separation from the mother and investment in the outside world. There are various substages to this stage. The practicing substage is characterized by a toddler's making forays into the outside world and then returning quickly to the mother for "refueling." The period of rapprochement (15–24 months) is concerned with further individuation and the integration of the rewarding and frustrating aspects of the mother. In the last stage, that of object constancy, the "good enough" mother has been internalized, permitting successful coping in most life situations. It should be noted that the process of separation–individuation is in actuality never complete and that no one has perfect object constancy (Goldstein, 1984). Life is like a spiral; one always returns to the same place but at a higher level.

The recovery process in addiction shows some interesting parallels to Mahler's separation–individuation process. Whatever the degree of physical and emotional decompensation, all newcomers to AA, and the other programs modeled after it, share some similar traits. Usually they are desperate, full of pain, and have a low sense of self esteem. The pain and desperation shatters the wall of narcissistic pride and grandiosity that prevents the self-destructive, active alcoholic from asking for help. When the defenses crumble, access to an earlier, more authentic, self facilitates the bonding with others and sometimes a renewed sense of spirituality.

It is possible that the attachment to AA duplicates the early bonding with the mother. Those who do bond can make a very productive and exhilarating connection with the program. Here we see the magic, the grandiosity, and the mystery of the symbiotic stage. In the parlance of Alcoholics Anonymous it is called the "pink cloud." If the recovering alcoholic were to apply words to this stage, it would be something like, "The program is magic, my sponsor is magical, and everything will be all right."

Eventually, during the second or third year of sobriety, the newcomer begins to sense another reality. Like the separating toddler in Mahler's studies, he or she begins to see the world outside and hear the slogan that "AA is a bridge back to life."

To use Winnicott's language, the program is utilized as good enough mother who can be accessed as much or as little as necessary. When the AA member needs "refueling," there are always meetings, sponsors, and friends available. Many members have had childhood nurturing that was flawed at this juncture, and they find in AA an opportunity to pick up the abandoned bricks of self-actualization and begin to build anew.

Thus the growing perception of separateness and responsibility for one's future brings the newcomer out of the symbiosis and into a new relationship with the program. The program and its accoutrements become home base and the world outside, a new challenge. Often there is a real abandonment depression at this juncture, and many people seek and benefit from psychotherapy. The recovering person is able to move back and forth between the "good enough" mother (AA) and the outside world. Thus the program with its varied tools and components offers a kind of an institutional consistency, and the experience of individuation becomes a corrective emotional experience. As the Anonymous program—the people, the principles, the slogans, the literature—is internalized, recovering persons can truly take it with them wherever they go.

The Promises

The result of this internalization is the fulfillment of the "promises" recorded in the book *Alcoholics Anonymous* (1939). Having rigorously adhered to the AA program, the alcoholic will find new paths of being and relating. The promises are statements such as "You will instinctively know how to handle situations that once baffled you" and "Self-seeking will slip away." The words "instinctively" and "slip" indicate that the changes are pervasive. They have become part of the unconscious self.

Sponsorship

The use of the sponsorship relationship is an important tool in the recovery from addiction. Most addicts did not experience an essentially loving relationship with the parent of the same sex. This "dysfunctional" relationship did not permit the idealization necessary for a positive identification that, when internalized, produces a healthy sense of one's gender and roles.

The deficit in same-sex parenting is addressed in the sponsorship relationship. The sponsor can become a confidant(e), mentor, and even "good enough" parent. Old conflicts can surface and be resolved in the light of a compassionate, understanding relationship. Sponsorship is one key that turns the lock in the door of sobriety.

The 12 Steps

The alcoholic or drug addict who is practicing the 12 steps obtains an important structure and a roadmap for recovery. The 12 steps and their tasks are as follows.

1. "We admitted we were powerless over alcohol—that our lives had become unmanageable." This is the admission step, which provides access into the process and acknowledges the pervasiveness of the illness.
2. "We came to believe that a Power greater than ourselves could restore us to sanity." This step instills hope in the recovery process that AA offers.
3. "We made a decision to turn our will and our lives over to the care of God as we understood Him." Here, a commitment is made to accept help from an outside source that is not fully comprehended. This is an extension of the previous step into faith and a surrender of one's own will to a higher order.
4. "We made a searching and fearless moral inventory of ourselves." This step focuses a member upon him- or herself and provides for the listing of personal assets and liabilities.
5. "We admitted to God, to ourselves, and to another human being the

exact nature of our wrongs." The appraisal of the previous step is shared and examined with others.

6. "We were entirely ready to have God remove all these defects of character." Continuing the process begun in steps 4 and 5, one seeks a change in attitude and becomes willing to give up negative aspects of the self.

7. "We humbly asked Him to remove our shortcomings." Going beyond the previous step, one surrenders to a deeper level of change, seeking help from an external source to do so.

8. "We made a list of all persons we had harmed, and became willing to make amends to them all." Here one accepts responsibility for past negative actions and alters one's attitude toward others.

9. "We made direct amends to such people whenever possible, except when to do so would injure them or others." Now active restitution is implemented for any destructive behavior outlined in the previous step.

10. "We continued to take personal inventory and when we were wrong promptly admitted it." This provides for daily appraisal of one's behavior and corrective action.

11. "We sought through prayer and meditation to improve our conscious contact with God as we understood Him, praying only for knowledge of His will for us and the power to carry that out." One now, on a daily basis, commits to the spiritual aspects of the program, seeking an inner state of peace and harmony.

12. "Having had a spiritual awakening as the result of these steps, we tried to carry this message to alcoholics, and to practice these principles in all our affairs." This culmination step integrates the ideals and values of the program and is a commitment to help other alcoholics.

If one takes the steps sequentially, an increasingly stronger and more flexible ego is built. We can use as an example the ego function of reality testing. A major function of the ego is to insure the individual's appropriate relation to reality (Spiegel & Mulder, 1986). Reality testing concerns the adjustment of one's needs and impulses to the world's ever-changing roles and expectations. The relationship between inner and outer world is mediated through firm ego boundaries and a cohesive sense of self. Reality is confronted immediately in step 1 in the statement "We admitted we were powerless over alcohol—that our lives had become unmanageable." To pierce through the denial of active alcoholism and clearly see the turmoil and damage in its wake is a painful awakening. In step 4, where the alcoholic is asked to make a searching and fearless inventory, good reality testing is essential. This step can only be accomplished with better reality testing than is necessary in step 1, since one must review the drinking years and acknowledge how one's sense of reality was distorted. Working the steps also aids in relaxing a harsh and punitive superego. An alcoholic is usually his or her own most severe critic, and the softening of the superego is essential to sobriety. This can be done by listing assets as well as liabilities in step 4. A harsh superego can interfere with accurate reality testing just as much as can a grandiose and infantile ego.

It is interesting how the ego function of object relations is developed through the 12 steps. Early object relations are characterized by striving for self-gratification and preoccupation with one's own survival. Later, as object relations become more cohesive, good and bad aspects of others and the self can be integrated. Eventually the pervasive fear of abandonment subsides. Thus it is significant that the pronoun used in all of the 12 steps is "we." It is likely that the active alcoholic has not thought in terms other than "I" in a long time. The first relationship a newcomer is asked to have is with a "Power greater than ourselves." As seen in step 3 one is asked to turn one's life and one's will over to "God as we understand Him." This entails a transfer of one's grandiosity from the injured self to an external force, the Higher Power. This sets the stage for the breakdown in grandiosity and reconstruction of relationships to both the self and others. If one examines step 8, which suggests making a list of those people one has harmed, one can see that it cannot be done without the capacity for empathic feeling for others. Certainly it cannot be done by the newcomer, who still objects to the "we" in step 1. Empathic feelings lead to compassionate activity. Thus, in step 12, the last step, the member is asked to help other alcoholics and carry the message of AA to all who still suffer. Successful and genuine 12-step work produces mature feelings, boundaries, and solid reality testing.

Defense mechanisms are also admirably handled by working the steps. As with the other ego functions, they are strengthened as one works the steps in sequence. For example, it is the primitive defense mechanism of denial that is addressed in step 1: "We admitted we were powerless." The key word here is not *powerless*, but *admitted*. Projection, another primitive defense, is addressed in steps 4 and 5. These are the steps in which the defects are written down and shared with a trusted person. While the defense of projection permits a person to deny his or her own feelings and displace them onto someone else, making a list of defects destroys this defense; the person can no longer avoid responsibility for his or her own actions. The most sophisticated defense mechanism is sublimation. The recovering alcoholic is asked to sublimate his or her grandiosity and power strivings into providing help to another alcoholic.

What happens in meditation and prayer is best explained by looking at what happens to the ego during the state of creative inspiration. Ernest Kris

(1952) states that "impulses, wishes and fantasies derived from the unconscious are attributed to a supernatural being and the process of their becoming conscious is experienced as an action of this being upon the person" (p. 302). In meditation, unconscious and preconscious aspects of the self are split off, attributed to God or a Higher Power, and then reintegrated by the ego. Meditation and prayer provide the ego with a means of relating to parts of the self that have been outside of ordinary awareness. This may explain the expansive feeling that accompanies the use of step 11.

Perhaps the most sophisticated ego function is that of synthesis and integration. This entails making a cohesive whole out of fragments of self (information and/or feelings). The last words of step 12 are "and to practice these principles in all our affairs." In order to do this, the AA member must have integrated and internalized all the principles of the program and developed an entirely new character structure and, indeed, a new life.

AL-ANON AS A TREATMENT MODALITY
FOR CODEPENDENCY

The pathology in an addictive marriage tends to be equal. While a spouse who is codependent may appear highly competent, continued treatment often reveals levels of developmental arrest and defensive functioning that parallel that of the active addict. When the addict gets clean and/or sober, many spouses decompensate. Why? Many spouses who are codependents buy their emotional health at the expense of the addict. Through the process of projective identification, spouses have been able to split off their own pathology and attempt to cope with it by managing and/or controlling the pathology in their mate and children.

The recovery process for codependents in Al-Anon is similar to that of alcoholics in AA. Both programs function with the same structure: meetings, sharing, sponsorship, literature, and slogans. In some ways the codependent's plight is equally serious. His or her life is filled with catastrophe that must be kept a secret. It is this deception that ultimately destroys the individual as he or she hides behind a rapidly crumbling wall of artifice. Both the identification in meetings with others and the relationship with a sponsor who has suffered similarly decrease the poisonous isolation with its accompanying need for deceit. The sponsorship relationship can also be regenerative as it meets the underlying dependency needs of the codependent. It is not unusual for a husband and wife to have a parallel recovery in a 12-step program. Often each partner evidences similar resistance and similar progress.

An examination of the slogans in Al-Anon can illustrate how the 12-step program acts psychodynamically. "Keep the focus on yourself" is an Al-Anon theme that addresses the destructive tendency to experience life through another person. "Let go, let God" addresses the concomitant need for control as well as the constant fear. "You didn't cause it, you can't control it, and you can't cure it" speaks to overwhelmingly poor ego boundaries and the tendency to merge with the addict.

Al-Anon uses and adapts the 12 steps of AA. For the Al-Anon member the first step of AA—"We admitted we were powerless over alcohol—that our lives had become unmanageable"—becomes "We admitted we were powerless over the alcoholic. . . ." It teaches its members that sobriety is not an end but a beginning.

ADULT CHILDREN OF ALCOHOLICS

The fastest growing 12-step program of the last decade has been the Adult Children of Alcoholics (ACOAs). Perhaps the difficulties faced by this group are universal to all individuals who grew up in dysfunctional families. Certainly the issues addressed by ACOAs are rooted in what the psychoanalytic community would consider pathological narcissism. In other words, ACOAs have been trained to sacrifice internal security (who they really are) for external security (who others want them to be) (Wood, 1987, p. 60).

Unlike Al-Anon, which suggests that members take responsibility for themselves, ACOA encourages assigning appropriate responsibility to others. Why? Because ACOAs have internalized the pathology of the family and live it as if it were their own. Step 4 for ACOAs reads: "We made a searching and fearless moral inventory of our parents because in essence, we had become them" (Tony A. with Dan F., 1991). They also received a covert message not to move out of the family system into the larger society. Thus ACOAs find themselves hopelessly mired in a family system for which they feel responsibility.

Official ACOA literature explains that children in alcoholic families learned early not to trust, feel, or talk about the pain inside them. Unexpressed feelings find an outlet in ACOA meetings, where emotions, especially anger, can reign. Often this expression of feeling is cathartic, leading to a sense of at last being entitled to one's feelings.

The ACOA movement values what is called the "laundry list," which enumerates the 14 characteristics ACOAs take on (Tony A. with Dan F., 1991); for example, "We judge ourselves harshly and have low self-esteem" or "We confuse love and pity." These statements make concrete the heretofore nameless feelings of the member. Identifying and owning feelings is a relief.

A major concern of ACOAs and just about every other recovering person is that of authenticity. Many children in alcoholic households are exploited. Some are exploited emotionally; others, physically or sexually. Because of the severe dysfunction in these households, the parents cannot give empathically, although they do give in narcissistic ways. In other words, the child learns early to do what is necessary to ensure self-esteem in one or both parents. The relationship of exploitation is internalized, as is that of masochism and/or sadism. Thus in adulthood these people repeat the dysfunctional relationship by continuing to exploit either themselves or others. In the ACOA program, freedom to feel and express feelings is paramount. Members are urged to establish boundaries and affirm the healthy aspects of themselves. Freedom to escape from the necessity of living from crisis to crisis is also the subject of intensive scrutiny.

A useful aspect of the ACOA program is the notion of the "inner child." The "inner child" is an aspect of the self that, although usually small, is nonetheless very much alive under a false self that has been developed to protect it and to appease the forces of the world. Naming and focusing on the "inner child" gives the person a kind of psychic permission to experience and express that aspect of the self that often has been in hiding since childhood.

CRITICISMS OF 12-STEP PROGRAMS

Critics of 12-step programs claim that they are not appropriate for everyone. The most common complaint is the involvement with God or a Higher Power. An old-time AAer would respond, "The program is cafeteria-style; take what you like and leave the rest." Today one might hear, "Think of God as Good Orderly Direction" or even "Group Of Drunks."

Other criticisms include a concern that 12-step programs create the same kind of dependence on each other that the members once had on the substance. This is initially true. As discussed earlier, these programs serve a re-parenting function. While most people mature out of the early symbiosis with the program, there are those who remain highly dependent on it. This dependence, however, is rarely life-threatening or permanent.

WOMEN AND THE 12-STEP PROCESS

AA and other 12-step programs grew mainly from the experiences of men. Therefore some of their written and informal suggestions need to be adjusted to meet the needs of women.

Carol Gilligan (1982) describes the psychological development of women, who must ultimately identify with the same person (the mother) who nurtures them. Thus the issue of separation and connection is central for women. While men often enter a 12-step program because of a failure at work or mastery, women may bottom out because the web of attachments has fallen apart and/or someone important has left them. Women often define themselves in terms of their relationships. Therefore the informal "code" or suggestion in the 12-step program of no close emotional and/or sexual relationships during the first year can be a real hardship for them. Moreover, for men, anger can be dangerously overstimulating. For women, however, the first manifestation of anger can be a positive breakthrough from a life of passive-aggressive behavior.

For many addicted women, womanliness is filled with conflict. Confusion around role, gender, and sexuality cannot be resolved with a bottle or with a line of cocaine. One response to this issue has been the increase of separate women's groups in the Anonymous programs. Many women find more freedom to express their authenticity in these groups. Likewise, separate men's groups are now developing to meet similar needs of men.

SOCIAL WORK INTERVENTION AND THE ANONYMOUS PROGRAMS

The *Alcoholics Anonymous 1989 Membership Survey* (1990) indicates that 68% of members received counseling; and 80% of those surveyed stated it played an important part in their coming to AA. Sixty percent of members received treatment after coming to AA, and 85% believed it played an important part in their recovery. Much of this good news is due to the increased knowledge about addiction and the recovery process among social workers and other mental health professions.

While alcoholism and drug counselors—with their more direct, confrontive stance and their capacity for disclosure of their own recovery experiences—may be more effective in connecting people to 12-step programs (King, Bissel, & O'Brien, 1979), eventually the more flexible approach of social workers proves invaluable in dealing with grief, aggression, and sexuality.

Social workers addressing the needs of addicts and codependents greatly increases their effectiveness when they understand the value of the 12-step process and program. In early recovery, when the need for support and the potential for relapse are both massive, the Anonymous program may indeed be the primary "therapist." Some people, however, may need help in using these programs. The following is an example of a social worker's use of psychodynamics in dealing with a patient's resistance to a 12-step program.

John, a rather depressed young man, could not connect with AA. He was being seen in an outpatient clinic by a social worker who encouraged him to go to meetings and to share. John finally said that he was fearful of sharing because if he did he would lose his thoughts and feelings to the people in the room. Understanding his disturbance and boundary difficulties, the social worker replied that he was right. He was in early sobriety—a time to take and not give; therefore he was to attend meetings but not speak until he felt ready to do so. This interpretation enabled John to attend AA and to maintain his fragile sense of self.

This example illustrates how a social worker can utilize both psychodynamics and a knowledge of 12-step programs in the same intervention.

In addition to being sensitive to their substance-abusing clients, social workers must extend awareness to themselves and their colleagues. Special AA meetings for helping professionals have been established in many communities. Moreover, for over a decade an organization called Social Workers Helping Social Workers (with chapters in the Northeast and Midwest and on the West Coast) has focused on helping impaired social workers with workshops, retreats, and meetings.

CONCLUSION

Clearly the 12 steps and the community and spirituality of the Anonymous programs appeal to millions as a solution to the agony of addiction and/or compulsive behavior. The honest sharing, opportunity for identification, and tradition of anonymity provide an alternative to the isolation and loneliness experienced by so many in today's rootless society.

Social workers are on the front line in hospitals, mental health facilities, and educational institutions. The social work profession emphasizes understanding of the environment and working with the community. For those in recovery, the 12-step program may indeed be their community. Understanding the value and function of this community is crucial in helping clients.

In AA there is a saying that "It's a simple program for complicated people." It is indeed simple, as well as prophetic and profound.

REFERENCES

Alcoholics Anonymous. (1939). New York: Alcoholics Anonymous World Services.

Alcoholics Anonymous 1989 membership survey. (1990). New York: Alcoholics Anonymous World Services.

Gilligan, C., (1982). *In a different voice.* Cambridge, MA: Harvard University Press.

Goldstein, E. G. (1984). *Ego psychology and social work practice.* New York: Free Press.

King, B. L., Bissell, L., & O'Brien, P. (1979). Alcoholics Anonymous, alcoholism counseling, and social work treatment. *Health and Social Work, 4*(4), 181–198.

Kris, E. (1952). *Psychoanalytic exploration in art.* New York: International Universities Press.

Mahler, M., Pine, F., & Bergman, H. (1975). *The psychological birth of the human infant.* New York: Basic Books.

Robertson, N. (1988). *Getting better inside Alcoholics Anonymous.* New York: Morrow.

Spiegel, E., & Mulder, E. (1986). The Anonymous program and ego functioning. *Issues in Ego Psychology, 9*(1), 34–42.

Tony A. with Dan F. (1991). *The laundry list.* Deerfield Beach, FL: Health Communications.

Twelve steps and twelve traditions. (1952). New York: Alcoholics Anonymous World Services.

Winnicott, D. W. (1975). *Through paediatrics to psychoanalysis.* London: Hogarth.

Wood, B. L. (1987). *Children of alcoholism.* New York: New York University Press.

Yalom, I. (1985). *The theory and practice of group psychotherapy.* New York: Basic Books.

Assessment and Intervention with Families of Substance Abusers

IV

10

Family Treatment of Substance Abuse

Jeffrey R. McIntyre

It is estimated that 19% of the adult population who use mind- and mood-altering substances abuse them (*Seventh Reports to Congress*, 1990). Using the commonly accepted formula that one person's behavior affects four to six other people, then 92.7 to 139.1 million Americans—37% to 55% of the population—are regularly affected by another's substance abuse.

People develop compulsive attachments to mind- and mood-altering substances for a variety of biophysiological, psychoemotional, and social-interpersonal reasons. As a person forms an attachment to a substance and its effects, the partner/spouse develops complex psychological and behavioral ways to manage him- or herself and expends increasing amounts of time and emotional energy struggling to control the substance abuser. Through this subtle and covert process, codependency and addictive family systems are created (Bepko & Krestan, 1985; Berenson, 1975; Black, 1981; Elkin, 1984; J. Jackson, 1954; Kaufmann, 1985; Stanton, Todd, & Associates, 1982; Steinglass, Bennett, Wolin, & Reiss, 1987; Straussner, Weinstein, & Hernandez, 1979; Treadway, 1989; Wegscheider-Cruse, 1989).

This chapter provides an overview of the role of addictions in the family process, describes how addictions to alcohol and other drugs alter family members' beliefs and behaviors about themselves and their interpersonal functioning, and discusses the factors that are important to include in assessment and treatment of chemically dependent families.

AN OVERVIEW OF THE CHEMICALLY DEPENDENT FAMILY PROCESS

Substance abuse can serve two different functions. It can be a primary problem that is causing difficulties and conflicts for the individual and the family; it can also be a symptom of underlying, unmet needs and undeveloped life skills that the substance abuser and her or his family are attempting to meet through the help of the substance(s). In this systemic view (Lankton, Lankton, & Mathews, 1991) a presenting problem—in this case, addiction— is understood to be an attempt by the family to deal with life's needs and challenges. For example, the use of the substance can help in expressing intimate behaviors, such as tenderness, affection, support, and sexuality; in handling conflict and anger; in relieving anxieties, fears, guilt, or shame; in maintaining interpersonal boundaries; in developing self-esteem, a sense of power, and self-confidence; or, conversely, in managing fear and anxiety about any of these needs or concerns. In conjunction with these psychological and interpersonal issues, the habitual abuse of a substance is also likely to result in a process best described in disease terms as a linear and progressively developing physiological dependence. Drinking or drugging after work may be a way to relieve stress, to mark a boundary between the day's work and going home, to bond a couple through the ritual of drinking together, or to cope with the anxiety evoked by the intimacy of family life. Finally, it may be a way to satisfy a developing psychophysiological dependency that is increasingly regulated by needs of the abuser's brain biochemistry independent of psychological and interpersonal factors. What began as coping behaviors eventually results in a substance-abusing or chemically dependent family system.

It is important to remember that few people set out deliberately to develop an addiction or to be a member of a chemically dependent family system. Although there are some ethnocultural variables that contribute to high and low rates of addiction (e.g., cultures that encourage unrestrained use have higher rates of addiction than cultures that encourage moderate use and heavily sanction intoxication), there is not one type or class of family that is more likely to develop an addiction. The impact of chemical dependency on the family usually develops indirectly and insidiously, and the damages from repeated incidents of substance abuse are profound and long-lasting (Cork, 1969; J. Jackson, 1954; Straussner et al., 1979).

While intoxicated, in a "wet" state (Berenson, 1975), addicted family members may feel permission or become habituated to behave in ways unacceptable to them when sober, or in a "dry" state. Alcohol and other drugs disinhibit cognitive attitudes and beliefs as well as emotional references (learned experiences that control behavior), giving people a false sense of inflated powers. For example, a person might be more assertive, aggressive, or sexual when drunk than otherwise. Alcohol and other drugs will disinhibit people in the family system, contributing to their behaving in new and irresponsible ways. The user and the codependent members use the substances to act out rather than talk out what they want and need from one another. A limited range of learned responses, family role expectations, beliefs, and "rules" that regulate communications develop (Black, 1981; Steinglass et al., 1987; Wegscheider-Cruse, 1989). The family evolves interpersonal processes without responsible negotiation or mutuality in their requests of one another. This behavior is an expression of "power without responsibility" (Elkin, 1984) that confuses emotions and destroys trust. Expectations family members have of one another to behave in certain ways rigidify "under the influence" into emotional overfunctioning (codependent) and underfunctioning (substance abuser), leading to an increasing experience of false, inflated pride that defends against feelings of failure to behave in a "normal" way (Bepko & Krestan, 1985). Substance abuse may be a way a person attempts to escape or find relief from rigid expectations by self and others. Trying to maintain the balance of interactions, codependent family members often become as "intoxicated" in their emotional reactivity as the chemically dependent member is in his or her drinking or drugging (Brown, 1988; Subby & Friel, 1982; Treadway, 1989; Wegscheider-Cruse, 1989).

Recursive communication patterns become established. For example, the communications expressed in intoxicated states, even though they might have some truth in them, are split off from and defined as less valid than the communications of the sober state. Family members do not take the intoxicated communications seriously ("Oh, dad [or mom] has just been drinking again"), a fact that paradoxically reinforces abusers' sense of frustration and powerlessness and insures their turning to drugs or alcohol again to feel powerful enough to deliver their communications (Elkin, 1984; Steinglass et al., 1987).

As a person's addiction progresses from social use to psychological and even physical dependency, and as the codependent partner or parent develops more out-of-control responses (lectures, nagging, etc.) in an attempt to maintain control, the system locks into predictable patterns of mismanaged or ineffective expressions of power and control as well as poor communication of needs and affects. Paradoxically, reactions progressively become both exaggerated and constricted, or else limited to such feelings as sadness, anger, disappointment, frustration, and failure. Contradictions in communication (simple binds and double binds), confusion, and other complicated negative processes take over the cognitive, emotional, interactive, and spiritual life of the family.

THE PROCESS OF RECOVERY

Recovery is a process with somewhat predictable stages for both the substance abuser and the family. However, it is important to view each family's way of handling each stage as unique. Some families will not follow the stages as described here, while others will follow them quite predictably. Some families will pass through them quickly; others, slowly. Often issues that are part of the recovery process, such as developing a new identity as a recovering person (Brown, 1985), may overlap with the developmental issues that are inherent in the family life cycle (Carter & McGoldrick, 1989), such as parents having to redefine their roles as children leave home.

Early recovery, the first year or two, is marked by the restabilization of biological as well as psychological and interpersonal systems that had been disrupted or destroyed over the years. People have to get to know one another all over again without the interference of alcohol or drugs. Former patterns of drinking and drugging, which were once reliable and predictable, disappear. This transition to new ways of relating is painful, in part because of the profound sense of "groundlessness," of not knowing what to expect. It is a period that has been referred to as "the crisis" (Straussner et al., 1979) or "the trauma" (Brown, 1991) of recovery and can be as terrifying as the earlier years when the addictions were developing.

The period of middle recovery usually ranges from the third to the fifth year. During this phase, some will find themselves increasingly focused on issues of family life, work, and the world around them. Yet they still may be experiencing some of the same interpersonal problems that led them to abuse drugs or alcohol or, as a spouse or parent, to be too tolerant, confused, or reactive about their partner or child's substance abuse. Some hope may linger that many underlying problems will just evaporate. If changes do not occur, either spontaneously or with the help of 12-step programs, families often bring their problems to therapists through the formation of symptomatological behavior(s) such as an affair, the development of phobias, eating disorders, or psychosomatic disorders, often thinking that the recovery from the drinking or drugging is not part of the problem. Children may begin to act out or express negative feelings either because they are fed up with their parents' lack of change or because they may now trust the recovering person to handle their feelings. Their acting out may serve a protective function (Madanes, 1984) that brings the family together to address the fears and anxieties that are simmering under the surface.

From the fifth year on, a variety of spiritual and philosophical questions may become important to some recovering families. These often include a desire to find a way to express feelings of gratitude for having a chance to live and enjoy life. During this stage the family will be challenged to create an environment in which further redefinitions of identity and differentiation of individual members must be supported.

BASIC ISSUES IN ASSESSMENT

Individuals or families requesting treatment will present their substance abuse problems either directly or indirectly (Treadway, 1989). The direct approach will take the form of an adult's requesting help with his or her own substance use disorder, codependency, or problems he or she attributes to being raised in a chemically dependent family; or help with the drinking or drugging of a spouse/partner, child, or parent. Indirect requests for help are made by people who do not or only minimally connect their problems to the impact of their own or a family member's substance abuse. These may include problems of depression, emotional unpredictability, phobias, specific and unspecific anxieties, psychosomatic disorders, and marriage/relationship difficulties, or such problems with children as learning disabilities or behavioral misconduct in the community or school. In short, the usual problems that people present to a mental health, family, or social work agency or clinician.

In assessment, a clinician needs to discern how the family is presenting their problems and to begin to create appropriate treatment plans and interventions. To confront an indirect presentation of an addiction problem directly by being either too "educational" or too confrontative is to risk creating an unnecessary conflict with the family. These approaches will either reinforce denial, shame, and failure or drive the family away in a state of disappointment, anger, and feeling misunderstood. Either way the family therapist will have created more work for him- or herself than is necessary for the assessment and treatment process.

Many issues with substance abuse may not be obvious at the beginning of assessment, becoming clear only with time as the therapist explores the extent of the abuse and the family's denial. It is also important to appreciate the capacities, strengths, and resiliencies (Treadway, 1989; Jacobs & Wolin, 1991) the family has developed in response to the chemical dependency.

A clinician usually receives a request for treatment from one member of a family. The first consideration is to involve all family members in the assessment and treatment process. A simple strategy is to suggest that the individual invite other family members to attend the first session in order to help create a more comprehensive picture of the family. This is known as the system-building stage (Treadway, 1980). How the steps of this stage are accomplished—who first requests help and what he or she has to do and say to get other family members join the therapy—provides the therapist with the initial assessment data. As other members of the family come to therapy, the assessment and treatment process focuses on the presenting issues and the interactional and emotional processes of the family that are contributing to the creation of those issues.

Children are profoundly affected by parental addictions because of the unpredictability of the behavior of both parents (Black, 1981; Cork, 1969; Jesse, 1989; Seixas & Youcha, 1985; Wegscheider-Cruse, 1989). Assessment therefore has to include a careful evaluation of the children's experience (Hawley & Brown, 1981; Zilbach, 1986). This can be presented to parents as a routine component of the assessment process.

The assessment needs to focus on the severity and function of the addiction for the substance-abusing person, for other individual family members, and for the family as a whole. In assessing the severity of the impact of the addiction(s), it is important to determine whether the chemically dependent or codependent family members need inpatient/rehab treatment. If the substance abuser experiences physiological withdrawal, managed medical care, either inpatient or outpatient, will be necessary. Some people may want to withdraw themselves "cold turkey." The therapist will have to discuss the risks of such an approach—that is, the possibility of severe shakes, hallucinations, and seizures—with the substance abuser and the family while encouraging withdrawal in the safest way possible. Codependent persons may need inpatient treatment if they are clinically depressed or in such a constant state of rage or anxiety that they cannot function effectively.

Family assessment also needs to explore ideas about what psychological, attitudinal, and behavioral skills the family will need to develop in order to support their substance-free existence. The therapist should examine such areas as life-cycle stages, the self in family system, family of origin, social and community networks, and the family's communication and emotional processes. Such data will aid the therapist in formulating goals and protocols for treatment, in making a differential diagnosis, and in tracking the effects of the addiction(s) to distinguish them from other developmental issues that need attention (Treadway, 1989).

Life-Cycle Stages

The concept of life-cycle stages with inherent goals and tasks that have to be mastered by family members was developed as the basis of family therapy by Milton Erickson (Haley, 1973). Carter and McGoldrick (1989) have taken the concept further, referring to it as a framework for family therapy. They refer to six stages: (1) the launching of the single youth adult; (2) the joining of families through marriage—the couple; (3) becoming parents—families with young children; (4) the transformation of the family system in adolescence; (5) families at midlife—launching children and moving on; and (6) the family in later life. They also encourage therapists to consider such variables as race, class, religion, and ethnicity in each stage. Divorce and remarriage, as well as living in poverty, are also mentioned as special issues with their own inherent goals and tasks.

The theory is that in each of these stages there are behaviors and beliefs that the family as a whole, and family members individually, have to be aware of and deal with in order to handle that stage and to move onto other stages. When they cannot or will not learn how to handle those tasks, or when they have high levels of anxiety about them, then they may substitute fear-based, compulsive behaviors—such as abuse of alcohol, drugs, food, work, money (gambling), and/or sexual activity—in order to experience a sense of power, self-esteem, control, and mastery.

Evaluating the family's life-cycle stages helps to answer such questions as: What are the life tasks, as well as age- and situationally appropriate attitudes and behaviors, they ought to be working on? What is the function of the substances in helping them with this stage and these tasks? Does the substance abuse result from the anxiety evoked in handling a previous stage, or is it connected to the family's inability to handle the tasks of the current stage? The clinician has to decide what emotional, behavioral, interpersonal, and attitudinal skills might be suggested to the family in order for them to handle the emotional and interactional experiences of the stage they are in and allow them to move to the next stage. A therapist may have to suggest that a mother look for meaningful work as her daughter enters high school so she will not be staying home feeling lonely. At the same time, the therapist may have to help the husband and wife communicate in supportive ways to eliminate the unnecessary resentments about the wife's sadness, the husband's distance, or the daughter's anxiety that have built up over the last 3 years since mom became sober or drug-free.

The Self in Family System

It is useful to gather information and develop hypotheses about people's individual self systems: the way they present themselves; what that presentation says about their self-esteem or internal experience of themselves; their self-respect (external presentation of self); their self-image thinking (the flexibility with which they process both internally generated thoughts and feelings and external feedback about the self; Lankton & Lankton, 1986); and their skills in self-care. For example, many overfunctioning adult children of alcoholics experience self-respect about how they handle themselves in the external world (work, PTA, church) and have good self-care skills, but they have a depressed, low sense of self-esteem at home. A cocaine abuser may experience self-respect at work, using this sense of self to defend against the shame and low self-esteem experienced with each episode of drug abuse. Understanding family members' self systems helps the therapist create interventions that may help families develop flexibility and responsiveness to both internal and external feedback.

Family of Origin

It is important to obtain data about the families of origin. This includes information about multigenerational drug and alcohol use and abuse, familial patterns of communication, emotional triangles (Bowen, 1978; D. Jackson, 1967), and cross-generational coalitions (Minuchin, 1974) in which members of the family of origin cross over generational boundaries. Such an assessment helps the clinician understand how active drinking or drugging connects people with their family of origin (Stanton et al., 1982) and how patterns of behavior may express bonds of loyalty to the family. For example, during some of the earliest studies of alcoholic families, Steinglass, Weiner, and Mendelson (1971) observed that the resumption of drinking by one family member would frequently provoke similar behavior in another family member, especially in father–son and brother–brother dyads.

Since the drinking or drugging or codependent behaviors may connect or disengage members of the presenting family from members of the family of origin, the clinician may recommend that other family members be brought into therapy. The presenting family can be helped in their recovery by including extended family members who will support the substance abuser's sobriety and recovery (e.g., an uncle who is active in Alcoholics Anonymous [AA] and will help a niece feel comfortable by accompanying her to her first AA meeting) or, at least, agree to understand it and not interfere with it. It is also important to assess possible tensions or conflicts around important family events, such as weddings, births, graduations, deaths, or anticipated deaths, and the "unfinished emotional business" among members of different generations (e.g., hurts, resentments, and grudges). The therapist can help family members understand the pain of past events and actively prepare them for upcoming events.

Social and Community Network

It is important to assess family members' connectedness to other people in the community, social organizations, and business or professional groups, as well as their skill in making use of human and material resources. If a family is isolated in their community, as happens to many families in the late stages of addictions, they may need a great deal of support and direction about how to get through the door of a 12-step and/or Rational Recovery meeting. This area of assessment also helps the clinician understand how certain behaviors such as drinking or drugging or codependent martyrdom may bond family members to other people. For example, if drinking with "the boys" in the afternoon is the only way a husband has of relaxing, then other ways of relaxing are going to have to be explored during the therapy. A mother who becomes overinvolved with her church to manage feelings of anger and disappointment with her heroin-addicted son, and who receives much praise or solace for her suffering from the priest and other parishioners, is going to need help in finding other ways to meet those needs when her son becomes clean and sober.

The Context of Communication and Emotional Processes

Alcohol and drugs can both trigger and alter family interactional processes (Steinglass et al., 1987). Their use can bring family members together through either the relaxation of anxieties in social interactions or the creation of crises. Or they can drive people away from one another. In working with the family, the clinician will discern both the function of sober and intoxicated behaviors and the unspoken rules governing behaviors and expectations. The family therapist has to ask questions about *who does what with whom when and how and why* in relation to the drinking or drugging and codependent behaviors. What part do drugs or alcohol play in triggering one family member to pay attention to another? Who pays the most attention to the behavior? The least? How do they pay attention? What do they *not* pay attention to? What other family issues get attached to or brought out by the drinking or drugging behavior? What issues get suppressed? What would be going on in the family if drinking or drugging were not going on? What issues are they in most conflict about? The least conflict about? What part does the drug or alcohol use play in causing the conflict or trying to avoid conflict? Who goes to whom when there is a problem? How does the use of substances help create better emotional boundaries or open them inappropriately (sexual abuse)? When and how do the substances help out with intimate behaviors? When do they interfer with them? What are the underlying needs of each family member that contribute to these behaviors? In short, what needs to be changed about the "who, when, how, and why" of the way family members communicate their feelings so that they can develop interactional processes that do not rely on alcohol or drugs? The clinician's work is to formulate hypotheses about the function of the chemicals and codependent behaviors in creating and regulating these patterns of communication and then to intervene in such a way as to help the family solve the problems they present for treatment (Treadway, 1989).

TREATMENT

Organizing a Treatment Plan

Treatment is a process of interaction between a therapist and a family in which the therapist's behaviors, actions, language, directives, and interventions are focused on influencing and persuading family member's individually and the family as a whole to alter their beliefs, behaviors, ways of interacting and communicating, and ways of perceiving and experiencing one another. There is a "gift exchange" (Ritterman, 1983) that takes place between the way a family presents their pain and the way a therapist helps them reframe and transform the pain utilizing as resources their emotional experience, intelligence, and prior capacities to alter their experience (Lankton & Lankton, 1983, 1986). The organization of the treatment plan is the therapist's return of "the gift" in a form that empowers the family to do something about their problems.

Studies of addictions treatment for individuals (Hester & Miller, 1989) show that plans that are adapted to each person are more effective than generic programming. Similarly, each family needs to be seen as unique and treatment plans need to be flexible. The length of therapy, the number of sessions, and the speed of work and change have to be guided by the way each family system handles the incorporation of interventions and recommendations into its cognitive–affective system. Some families change quickly, using brief therapy effectively and comfortably, while others change slowly, requiring steady, patient work on the part of the therapist.

Paradoxical Interventions

Paradoxical interventions developed as a way of dealing with human ambivalence about whether and how to change familiar and predictable patterns of behavior and longstanding patterns of perception (beliefs and attitudes). There are complex binds between a desire to change and a desire to have things stay the same. Paradoxical interventions use the ambivalence families experience about change to respectfully and safely help the family change.

By the time substance-abusing families come to treatment, their lives are rife with paradoxes and contradictions. The therapist has to respect the fact that the family is wrestling with ambivalence, complex contradictions, and fear of change. Thoughtfully constructed paradoxical interventions place the fear, ambivalence, and negativity in a positive frame, affirming the family's strengths and the way their negative behaviors have connected them (Palazzoli, Boscolo, Cecchin, & Prata, 1978). Such interventions affirm the power of the symptomatological behaviors and guide the family in a careful consideration of the many other changes that might have to take place during the treatment process.

Paradoxical interventions are not gimmicks or tricks. They will not work if they do not match the family's ambivalence about change. The therapist creates each intervention out of a realization that family members are doing what they know how to do and that they are not going to change magically without some bridge between the known and the unknown. Each paradoxical intervention has to include a prescription to continue to do something the old way while they consider or try out new behavior. This flexibility (Lankton & Lankton, 1986) allows the therapist to avoid a rigid posture as the "agent of change" struggling with the family's "resistance." If a family does not want to change much, or wants to work in smaller or different steps from those the therapist is recommending, they are free to do so without a great "loss of face" (Treadway, 1980). A therapist might tell a family in early recovery to "continue to distrust one another while each of you carefully considers what would have to be different in the way you treat one another so trust can be redeveloped." In this intervention, the therapist encourages family members to continue to think or behave in a way that affirms their fear and anxiety by not demanding that they change too quickly, and simultaneously, encourages the family to extend their distrustful thinking in such a way as to consider trust. Or a therapist may point out how the behaviors, as dysfunctional as they often are, have come to have a stabilizing effect in the family; thus family members ought not to rush headlong into change without considering how they will be affected.

When therapists align themselves with the "no-change" side of the family's ambivalence, they help to create a safe context for the family. More securely anchored, the family can then consider the possibility of change. It is also important to know when not to use paradox. If family members are willing to participate directly in the process of change, then they may not need the bridging function of the paradoxical intervention.

Contracting

The first step is to develop a treatment contract with the family. This involves determining the goals of therapy—the differences the family wants to effect in their lives. While a family's stated goals may not be the only goals for therapy, they do have to be considered primary. Based on the assessment, the therapist may have additional thoughts about changes in attitudes and beliefs that the family needs to make to handle their current life-cycle stage; the realigning of the family structure (hierarchy and boundaries) and ways of experiencing and communicating affect; changes in social- and gender-role behaviors; changes in identity definitions; alterations in age-appropriate intimacy behaviors; development of more effective discipline to accomplish the simple and complex tasks of daily life; and cognitive changes in their thinking about themselves (Lankton & Lankton, 1986). The therapist may suggest these goals directly or indirectly, through story, and return to discuss them periodically throughout treatment, to be sure they are being addressed in a way the family wants them to be.

Each step in contract development and renegotiation of contract goals has to respect family members' right to choose (Wegscheider-Cruse, 1989) and convey to the family that the purpose of therapy is to help them expand their experience of choice, not lose it (Lankton & Lankton, 1983). If they have emphasized and clarified the principle of choice, therapists are less likely to be perceived as "speaking out of both sides of the mouth" when they say one thing to one member of the family and something else to another member—for example, directing the substance abuser to try controlled drinking because he or she has a right to choose to drink or drug, while encouraging the codependent spouse to set limits for him- or herself because he or she has a right to care for self and to be skeptical of the partner's capacity to control substance use. Throughout the assessment and treatment process, the therapist has the right to request that there be no drinking or drugging on the day of the session.

A directed, problem-solving approach (de Shazer, 1985, 1988; Haley, 1987; O'Hanlon & Weiner-Davis, 1989; Treadway, 1989) is usually most effective. Families rarely seek help for their underlying issues. More typically families are experiencing immediate emotional and interpersonal pain that has to be addressed promptly. It is useful for the therapist to think in terms of getting to specific outcomes or solutions (de Shazer 1985, 1988; O'Hanlon & Weiner-Davis, 1989) and of the steps that family members can take to actualize their goals from session to session (Treadway, 1989). Accomplishment of specifically agreed-upon behaviors that a therapist can support, positively affirm, and help the family to continue to work on can be one of the more effective ways to build self-esteem.

Treating Direct Presentations

When a family seeks help directly with a substance abuse problem, the first order of business is to create a contract focusing on the presenting problem. It is best to establish abstinence as a goal. If, however, the severity of physiological dependency is unclear or the denial of substance abuse is strong, then the therapist may introduce a carefully structured, contolled-use drinking or drugging contract. Such a contract is an agreement to cut the use of the substance(s) back to a pattern of minimal, random, social drinking or drugging. Through this approach, the clinician joins the substance abuser in denial and helps the abuser determine for him- or herself whether a substance abuse problem exists. It is best to recommend that such controlled, minimized, and randomized drinking or drugging be done for a minimum of 5 years to determine genuine remission from addiction. Most substance-dependent individuals will find this impossible. For theraputic effectiveness, the clinician may use a controlled drinking contract twice, accepting the person's rationalizations for the failure of the first effort and encouraging the person to try harder with the second effort.

After the failure of the second effort, the therapist will be in a much stronger position to say, "I don't think the issues are your willpower or any external factors but the fact that your central nervous system is addicted and the best choice you can make for yourself is one of abstinence." Or "Look, you've made a genuine effort and I think your body is trying to tell you something—it's addicted to this substance and wants more, regardless of what your mind and ego are telling you. I think there is no choice here, for your sake and the sake of your family, but to begin to work on abstinence and accept the fact that you have an addiction." Through such an intervention the challenge to the client is built into the process; the therapist does not have to be overtly challenging or confrontative. It also offers a way for the client to save face and hit bottom safely.

The family is included in this process by positively affirming and supporting their skepticism that the substance abuser will succeed in developing control. The therapist frames such skepticism as a normal consequence of the fear and pain that has already been experienced. Encouraging the family to remain skeptical is a way of affirming and respecting their pain and their reactions to the suggestion that the substance abuser attempt controlled drinking or drugging. In rare situations the substance abuser does return to controlled alcohol or drug use. In those cases the family's fears and anxiety about such use may become the main focus of treatment. This is particularly common when the anxious family member is the adult child of parents who had addictions or depressions.

The therapist needs to help family members, particularly the codependent spouse or partner, begin a process of emotional separation from their enmeshment with (desire to control) and reactiveness to (anger that they cannot control) the substance abuser and to begin work on their own development. The therapist supports the codependents by letting them know that they have a right to change whether the substance abuser wants to or not and may suggest to them various support and/or educational groups and readings to focus on while the substance abuser works on his or her decision about abstinence. This may be the first time that family members have worked on creating emotional separation and boundaries among themselves.

If the controlled drinking contract is ineffectual or the substance abuser does not want to stop drinking or drugging but the family does want him or her to, the therapist may have to utilize the Intervention process (Johnson, 1980, 1986; Treadway, 1989; Wegscheider-Cruse, 1989), whereby the family requests that the substance abuser go to a substance abuse treatment facility. This is an emotionally demanding process that should be used only when all other means of persuasion have been exhausted. The family has to be prepared to set a limit and ask the substance abuser to leave the family if he or she does not begin abstinence. The family members also have to commit themselves to specific changes as the substance abuser works on his or her recovery. This makes the Intervention process systemic, mutual, and more fair than the usual one-sided confrontation of the substance abuser. During Interventions children's comments frequently become pivotal points in persuading the subject of the Intervention to go to treatment; thus it is always useful to include children, even young ones, in that process. Children also have to be given special attention so that they understand that they did not do something wrong that caused the drinking or drugging.

Treating Indirect Presentations

The indirect presentation of substance abuse problems presents an interesting challenge to the clinician. Rarely can a problem that is presented indirectly be confronted openly during the beginning of therapy. This is the kind of treatment situation that requires what Madanes (1984) and Haley (1987), drawing on Milton Erickson's work, refer to as "analogic treatment." The presenting problem is understood to be an analogy or metaphor for issues that are not being presented or talked about.

The therapist proceeds by treating the presenting problem while developing and creating strategies to work with his or her hunches or hypotheses about what is *not* being said. After obtaining sufficient data to indicate that alcohol or drug use is interfering with the family's capacity to solve the presenting problem, or when a family member feels safe enough to mention substance abuse, the therapist may be able to bring up the issue directly in a story. The story would be about a different family that the therapist felt stumped about until a family member told "an interesting story" about how scared and ashamed everyone was that they could not talk about "some other problems." The therapist might mention that he or she likes good mysteries—books, movies, and so forth—and move the conversation to ask what kind of mystery stories the family likes. It is important not to name the "other" problem but rather to "plant seeds," thus giving permission for family members to bring up other issues and letting them know they will be supported in an exploration of the family mysteries.

Some families may not walk through any of the doors the therapist opens to discuss the issues of addiction; they may even threaten to leave therapy or begin to miss appointments even when the therapist addresses the issue as gently and indirectly as is possible. The therapist will then need to plant a few seeds for the future so that family members will feel comfortable enough to return to therapy "if anything else comes up." The therapist can also send the families carefully worded follow-up letters to let everyone know that something important was not addressed. In those communications, the therapist can indicate respect for the successful way the family worked to keep these hidden issues out of therapy and suggest that they not to do anything about those issues until the family as a whole or individual members are ready to consider them. In the treatment of indirectly presented problems, therapy ought to help increase the family's sense of competence by affirming any changes family members make (de Shazer, 1985) that may motivate them to seek treatment at another time.

Gender

Whether male or female, it is important that the therapist be sensitive to issues of gender. It is easy to be unconsciously empathic to one gender in ways that alienate the opposite gender (McGoldrick, Anderson, & Walsh, 1989). There is not a neat formula about this issue; one simply has to pay attention, ask questions, observe what is going on, and listen to how people describe their gender- and social-role functioning in talking about themselves. As Bepko and Krestan (1985) have pointed out, the substance-abusing family is usually gender-rigid in terms of social-role expectations of its members. The therapist can comment on such rigidity during an intervention or suggestion: "You know, John, given what you said and what you seemed to imply about a woman's role, you might feel uncomfortable with the fact that I'm going to suggest that your wife begin to look for some work. The kids are growing up, and she needs to have interests for herself. If you disagree with me or have other feelings about this change, I want you to say what they are now (*pause*) . . . or, maybe after you've had an opportunity to experience how it feels to have her at work and you are sharing some of the responsibilities for the house and the kids [main point of intervention]."

Gender differences may also play a role in recovery. Women are often more remorseful than men and more likely than men to be aware of the damaging impact of their behavior on relationships. Whereas men may implicitly consider the development of addictions to be a natural part of participating in male culture, women often experience a greater sense of shame. They will generally have done more secret drinking or drugging and used more combinations of tranquilizers than men, which will leave them in a more depressed state longer in the early recovery. Substance-abusing women often experience a lower sense of self-esteem than men and may need a different kind of support and understanding to relieve their shame and allow them to reestablish themselves in the family process.

Support Systems

It is always helpful to have family members attend specialized treatment groups while in family therapy. These can be in the same clinic, with other therapists in the community, in 12-step meetings such as AA or Al-Anon, or in newer organizations such as Rational Recovery. It is also helpful to have children attend groups (Hawley & Brown, 1981). Attendance at such support groups can contribute to new understandings of the self as a separate person, with one's own unique needs and issues. It can begin to diffuse some of the shame people feel by universalizing and naturalizing some of the experiences. And it can provide support to people who generally feel quite isolated and alone.

In early recovery, the focus of family therapy may be limited to getting people to self-help meetings and working on improving communications skills. During this phase family sessions, which may take place every 2 to 6 weeks in conjunction with attendance at support groups, are focused on specific behavioral steps each person needs to take to help the family remain substance-free and rebuild trust. The longer the history of addiction and codependency, the more the emphasis should be on such stabilization steps. The family needs to be informed that complex interactive issues, conflicts, and old hurts will be explored or worked on later in therapy. The therapist can say, "Many families find this stage difficult because they want to clear everything up immediately, especially old hurts and angers, but they have to wait to just get used to one another clean and sober." The therapist may suggest that people keep "anger and hurt" journals in which they record memories of hurt, disappointment, rage, anger, grief, sadness, and violation of trust so that they will not forget them and will have them ready when the time comes to deal with those feelings in therapy.

When family members will not go to self-help groups or other specialized treatment programs, the therapist must be careful not to push them too hard to do so. One can take a supportive but skeptical position, stating that the work may be much harder without the help and support of others. Usually the therapist also has to redefine the treatment goals into smaller steps to create the possibility of a positive outcome. One solution to one small problem will help the family build trust in the therapy process and contribute to family members' trust in themselves and willingness to consider other suggestions of the therapist.

Children

Finding ways to include children in treatment can be a challenge if they are not the focus of treatment. Parents will often deny that their behaviors have had an impact on their children. To overcome this resistance, therapists can tell parents that it is a routine part of the clinic's or the therapist's treatment procedures to have children in family treatment (Zilbach, 1986). If a child's problem is presented, it is useful to work with the parents to help them create a solution to it. The therapist can also look for opportunities to praise the parents for effective parenting, thus alleviating some of their fear and shame. This rebonds the family by doing something constructive and empowering.

The therapist can also include children in a way that empowers them and helps the family by enrolling them as "cotherapists" or "consultants" who can "help" the therapist understand which one of the parents will be more likely to implement a change the family has discussed. This reversal of hierarchy (Madanes, 1981) conforms with the way parents are already reversing the hierarchy by using their children in parental ways. This procedure can be effective by adding some humor and consciousness to the process, detoxifying the shame the parents feel in using their children in those ways, building trust, and beginning to realign the hierarchy in an appropriate structure. This approach can only be used when it is clear that no emotional or physical retribution will be directed at the children once the family is out of the office.

Physical and Sexual Abuse

Issues of child and adult physical and sexual abuse have to be addressed directly. Children's safety is of the utmost importance. In reporting the family to the child protection authorities, a therapist may have to take a "bad cop, good cop" position, making the state regulations the bad cop and the clinician the good cop who "hates to do this." The clinician must emphasize that the family is seeking help and that this is a positive step and must encourage the family to stay in treatment. This is especially important for codependents who feel shame if they have failed to protect their children. In cases of domestic violence, the therapist has to help the family members feel safe—for example, by involving other family members whose presence may reduce or prevent the violence; or by recommending separate residence for some family members while continuing family therapy and working on such issues as safety, boundaries, apologies, and forgiveness. The therapist has to help the family stop the violence and help them learn how to respect and express love to one another (Haley & Madanes, 1986; Madanes, 1990).

Distrust

Clinicians can include the existing distrust as a part of therapy by describing it as a normal aspect of the beginning stages of recovery. The therapist may state: "You ought not to expect to trust one another too much or too soon. It is natural for people not to trust one another after they have been through a painful time, the way you have been. What is really going to matter here is the way you begin to treat one another in this family." Utilizing the concept of congruency, the therapist teaches the family that trust is built not only with words but also with actions.

A useful intervention is to assign distrust days that are marked on a calendar. These can be every other, third, or fourth day. The therapist tells the family to work seriously at distrusting one another on "distrust days" while working at trust on the other days—and see which they like better. All family members are given permission, indeed encouraged, by the therapist to swear under their breath, to think all sorts of angry, hurt, sad, and distrustful thoughts, and to do a complete review of the past on the distrust days. Such an approach includes what will happen anyway (this is one kind of paradoxical intervention); but this approach brings it under therapeutic control and, more often than not, gives an edge of playfulness to a process that would otherwise happen covertly and be quite painful. It also validates family members' experiences of hurt and anger, increases self-esteem, and decreases shame and guilt by making negative feelings acceptable. The therapist may have to say something seemingly even more absurd, such as "Look, you and I both know you're feeling all this distrust anyway so I want you to practice it and get good at it; I don't believe anybody should do anything in a half-hearted way." Sometimes this approach undermines the family members' distrust of one another and bonds them together against the intrusive "outsider" with these strange ideas. Rather than being "fooled" by this pseudo-closeness of the family and their "rejection" of the "outsider," the therapist positively points to the closeness as progress and builds on it by having the whole family or dyads do something together—go to the movies or a sports events, go shopping, take a walk or a hike, do projects around the house, and so forth—thus building on and maintaining the closeness between sessions.

Communication

Substance-abusing families frequently need help in developing communication skills. The therapist may have to create experiential exercises that help the family understand the behaviors of effective communication, such as speaking in "I" terms, learning the difference between report and command communication, learning how to change questions that are hidden statements into statements of "I want," "I need," or "I would appreciate it if. . . ." For example, the therapist can direct the family to talk with one another for 15 minutes each or every other night. They are expected to report on their day without saying anything provocative about one another. The therapist often has to help the family feel comfortable with the difference between report communication, which is often unfamiliar to them, and the more familiar experience of either command communication or cold, stony silence.

Generally family members use "you" terms to project many of their thoughts and feelings onto other family members. Learning to speak directly in "I" terms and in nonmanipulative, direct request statements instead of ones that are veiled as questions can be awkward for some individuals who were raised among people speaking to one another indirectly. People from cultural heritages in which speaking in "I" terms is considered impolite may be told that such ways of speaking help the other person, who will then know they are speaking about themselves, and not suspect them of being self-centered. For people who are bitter and use "you" phrasing to be attacking, the therapist can explain that by thinking about "you" all the time, they are projecting all their power to determine their own experience onto the other person, which leads to even more feelings of disappointment, fear, and frustration.

Conflict Management

Most chemically dependent families lack knowledge of how to handle and express conflict, for example, the negotiation of needs, disappointments, and anger. Often the basic rules of conflict management (Bach & Wyden, 1968; Fisher & Ury, 1991) have to be explained and practiced during a session: Family members have to learn how to say what they are feeling without raising their voices in too much anger to gain power and how to think what about what they are wanting and needing. The needs a person is looking to have met have to be thought about in specific behavioral terms—what behavior are they looking for in another family member during their interactions.

Most families in early recovery fail to reassure one another that they are willing to try to work things out, which provokes feelings of abandonment, fear, failure, and shame. Anger and conflict are often associated, from the viewpoint of the family's experience, with a "wet," or intoxicated, state. The substance abuser only allowed him- or herself to express angry, conflicted feelings when stoned or drunk. During treatment, discussion of conflictual situations evokes painful memories and associations for the family members. In worst case scenarios, the angry feelings can provoke an emotional state in substance abusers known as a "dry drunk," a state in which they feel intoxicated or are as emotionally negative as when they were drunk or drugged, even though they have no substance in their systems. These issues can be anticipated in the treatment planning by utilizing relapse prevention planning (Daley, 1989) so that each family member will have specific plans for how to behave if such situations begin to occur.

Working on New Behaviors

The therapist has to discuss in the next session how family members did in practicing new behaviors they agreed to try out. An effective frame for such discussion is to tell family members that they are expected to do only "a little right" and to be sure to make a few mistakes. This can help alleviate some of the self-consciousness family members may experience in trying out new behaviors. Since promises to change have usually been made and repeatedly broken in substance-abusing families, it is helpful for the therapist to encourage the family to have low expectations and take things in small steps. In conjunction with the distrust and conflict management work of early recovery, the therapist can encourage family members to observe one another's mistakes but not to say anything to them. They are to use their desire to criticize other family members as inspiration "to do their own behavior all that much better." Or, using a journal, they can write down all their criticisms and bring them to therapy, where the therapist alone will read them, saying to the family member: "I'll keep these till the end of therapy. Then we'll go over what has and hasn't changed, and what in these concerns is still true for you. They may even be a good reference to see how far things have come." Such an approach introduces hope by suggesting that there will be a future in which these issues are no longer a problem; it also offers family members a safe place to contain and "leave" the criticism and anger. In addition, it uses feelings of competition and distrust to solve two problems simultaneously: It "captures" the capacity for disappointment, anger, and criticism, and it alleviates the shame attached to experiencing the competition and the desire to criticize by prescribing it and turning it into a more focused attention to self-process and self-development. Letter writing—of hopes, fears, expectations, needs, and wants—is another effective way to slow down process, to create reflective consciousness and better boundaries, and to give people more chances to respond in nonreactive ways to manage distrust in the development of new behaviors.

The therapist may wish to create experiential exercises within a session, using directed practice of new behaviors, role playing, and storytelling/metaphor work (Combs & Freedman, 1990; Lankton & Lankton, 1986, 1989). Since family members will frequently have no internal references or role models for the suggested behaviors, the therapist may need to be directive (Haley, 1987; Madanes, 1981, 1984), giving specific and detailed instructions for the development of behaviors, cognitive frameworks (beliefs), and affective experiences that aid family members in accomplishing particular "homework" exercises. The role-play in the office helps family members anchor each suggested behavior with a referent memory image. For example, instead of having a father and a daughter snarl at each other when dad arrives home, the therapist may ask dad and daughter to teach each other how they want to be spoken to, including voice tone, facial expression, and degree of physical closeness. The therapist usually has to comment on the self-consciousness people feel about acting out what they want and help them relax with it. Once again, the therapist prescribes the distrust, predicting its presence and diffusing its impact. Indirectly, the therapist also nurtures, or "reparents," the parents by instructing them in how to display a friendly, specific, and supportive manner that may be dramatically different from the disrespectful, authoritarian, and even abusive ("just do it!") way their parents directed them. Storytelling is also effective because it allows instructions to be given to family members in a nonthreatening way (Combs & Freedman, 1990; Lankton & Lankton, 1989). The therapist describes how other families made similar changes or even made other changes they were not expecting to make.

During each session, it is important to include everyone who attends: to review how they are doing; to determine what they think about what is going on; and to find a way to connect each person's experience to the experience of the family as a whole. The therapist role-models for the family the process of inclusion and fairness, since these are usually new behaviors in substance-abusing families. Family members have to be supported to do no more than they feel ready to do, and they usually have to be directed in how to set boundaries and limits by assertively saying "I've had enough" or "No, I won't do that." Since addictions could be called the "disease of too-high expectations," helping people understand limits helps them understand new ways to manage disappointment, which is the emotional by-product expectations that are too high or too numerous.

Affirmation, appreciation, apology, and forgiveness will be new behaviors and attitudes for a substance-abusing family and will take much practice on a regular basis, since the family will have accumulated much cynicism and bitterness by the time they have come in for therapy. It is important to go over, in a form of paradoxical prevention, all the ways in which family members can forget to demonstrate affection and appreciation after they have worked on ways to be appropriately affectionate and tender. This validates their worst fear—that the affection will just disappear—and makes that fear more acceptable. It is useful to go over how the men will forget, and how the women will be lying-in-wait for the men to forget, and how the children are convinced that both parents will fail to "get it right." Affirming, noncondescending praise of every effort to change is important. Given the exaggerated, defensive, and false pride of many substance abusers and substance-abusing families, it is useful to remind people not to take one another for granted, to learn to apologize when they make mistakes, and to learn to say thank-you for the positive steps toward change the other family members do take.

Completing the Contract

The termination of family therapy is usually done simply and gracefully. The therapist and family agree that the work they contracted to do is done. When the therapist has reviewed successes and praised their accomplishments throughout the therapy, there is little need to do more than reiterate some of the praise and affirmation as part of the goodbye. Some families like a ritual, a formal way of symbolizing the end of the work, which may include a review of everything that was and was not accomplished and a formal, solemn goodbye handshake. Some families just like to say, "Thanks and goodbye." The termination generally has to be consistent with the family's social conduct in the therapy.

It is useful to let a family know that if they want to come back they can. Or, as they do in the Milwaukee Brief Therapy Project, that if they call back, the therapist will review with them what they might be forgetting to do so they can remember to do it and stay out of therapy (de Shazer, 1990). This often adds a touch of humor and supports the family in remembering that they are empowered to help themselves now. Another way to terminate with families that have had difficulty in learning new behaviors is to playfully but seriously suggest that they go home and see how many ways of forgetting their new behaviors and attitudes they can remember.

Another useful way to terminate is to have them go home and do a "remember when" or "remember how bad it was" exercise, either writing it down or tape-recording it. The family is directed to be sure that they become as sad as they can "and to be sure they go over every painful memory to make sure they have forgiven each other in proper proportion to the pain they experienced." This exercise is particularly useful with families that experienced violence, abuse, and severe shaming behaviors. The therapist will want to conduct this session in the office as a closing session if it seems likely that the family could not do it at home. It clears out most vestiges of shame and grief, completes the grieving process, creates a boundary with the past, and directs the family toward the future.

CONCLUSION

Families in which alcohol and drug addictions develop become systems that are bound in progressively debilitating processes of poor communication, power struggles, conflict, disorganization, and financial, social, and psychological chaos. These processes profoundly affect each family member individually and the family as a whole. A multidimensional assessment and differential treatment plan is necessary to undertake this challenging and complicated work and to aid the clinician and the family members in beginning to heal the wounds experienced in the development of the addictions. A willingness to revise and update one's assessment and treatment plans to fit new information, a capacity for developing many specific experiential exercises that help people learn new attitudes and behaviors that they never thought they could learn, a good sense of humor, a willingness to let go when things are not working and try something different, a willingness to take creative risks and to listen carefully to what a family is saying about what is and is not working, a capacity to set limits and not become a codependent oneself to family members who do not want to change, a capacity to make and apologize for mistakes, reliable colleagues to consult with, and a vision of all the best that is possible in relationships are necessary components in sustaining and supporting the therapist as he or she helps the family. As Michael Elkin (1991) is fond of saying, "We are often helped in our own growth by our families as much as we help them in theirs." Good therapy, like a good life, is demanding, challenging, risky, interactive, and respectful of the fact that each step along the way is unique, requiring a responsive creativity to each moment of time.

Acknowledgment. The author wishes to thank the editor for her support and her consistently good-natured feedback. The spirit of the process only enhanced the work of shaping the complex material of the chapter.

REFERENCES

Bach, G. R., & Wyden, P. (1968). *How to fight fair in love and marriage.* New York: Avon.

Bepko, C., & Krestan, J. (1985). *The repsonsibility trap: A blueprint for treating the alcoholic family.* New York: Free Press.

Berenson, D. (1975). Alcohol and the family system. In P. Guerin (Ed.), *Family therapy: theory and practice.* New York: Gardner.

Black, C. (1981). *It'll never happen to me!* Denver: M. A. C.

Bowen, M. (1978). *Family therapy in clinical practice.* New York: Aronson.

Brown, S. (1985). *Treating the alcoholic.* New York: Wiley

Brown, S. (1988). *Treating adult children of alcoholics.* New York: Wiley.

Brown, S. (1991). Personal communication, National Consensus Symposium, Airlie Conference Center, Airlie, VA.

Carter, B., & McGoldrick, M. (Eds). (1989). *The changing family life cycle: A framework for family therapy.* New York: Gardner.

Combs, G., & Freedman, J. (1990). *Symbol, story, and metaphor: Using metaphor in individual and family therapy.* New York: Norton.

Cork, R. M. (1969). *The forgotten children.* Toronto: Addictions Research Foundation.

Daley, D. C. (Ed.). (1989). Relapse: Conceptual, research, and clinical perspectives. *Journal of Chemical Dependency Treatment,* 2(2).

de Shazer, S. (1985). *Keys to solution in brief therapy.* New York: Norton.

de Shazer, S. (1988). *Clues: Investigating solutions in brief therapy.* New York: Norton.

de Shazer, S. (1990). *Brief therapy: Constructing solutions.* Seminar presentation, American Association for Marriage and Family Therapy, Washington, DC.

Elkin, M. (1984). *Families under the influence.* New York: Norton.

Elkin, M. (1991). Personal communication.

Fisher, R., & Ury, W. (1991). *Getting to yes: Negotiating agreement without giving in.* New York: Penguin.

Haley, J. (1973). *Uncommon therapy.* New York: Norton.

Haley, J. (1987). *Problem solving therapy.* San Francisco: Jossey-Bass.

Haley, J., & Madanes, C. (1986). Love and violence training seminar sponsored by the Family Therapy Institute of Washington and Boston University, Boston.

Hawley, N., & Brown, E. (1981). Children of alcoholics: The use of group treatment. *Social Casework,* 62(1), 40–46.

Hester, R. K., & Miller, W. R. (Eds). (1989). *Handbook of alcoholism treatment approaches.* Elmsford, NY: Pergamon.

Jackson, D. (1967). The eternal triangle. In J. Haley & L. Hoffman (Eds.), *Techniques of family therapy.* New York: Basic Books.

Jackson, J. (1954). The adjustment of the family to the crisis of alcoholism. *Quarterly Journal of Studies on Alcohol,* 15(4), 562–586.

Jacobs, J., & Wolin, S. J. (1991). *Resilient children growing up in alcoholic families.* Paper presented at the National Consensus Symposium on COAs and Codependence, Airlie Conference Center, Airlie, VA.

Jess, R. C. (1989). *Children in recovery: Healing the parent–child relationship in alcohol/addictive families.* New York: Norton.

Johnson, V. (1980). *I'll quit tomorrow.* San Francisco: Harper & Row.

Johnson, V. (1986). *Intervention: How to help someone who doesn't want help.* Minneapolis, MN: Johnson Institute Books.

Kaufman, E. (1985). *Substance abuse and family therapy.* New York: Grune & Stratton.

Lankton, S. R., & Lankton, C. H. (1983). *The answer within: A clinical framework of Ericksonian hypnotherapy.* New York: Brunner/Mazel.

Lankton, S. R., & Lankton, C. H. (1986). *Enchantment and intervention in family therapy.* New York: Brunner/Mazel.

Lankton, C. H., & Lankton, S. R. (1989). *Tales of enchantment.* New York: Brunner/Mazel.

Lankton, S. R., Lankton, C. H., & Matthews, W. J. (1991). Ericksonian family therapy. In A. S. Gurman & D. P. Kniskern (Eds.). *Handbook of family therapy* (Vol. 2). New York: Brunner/Mazer.

Madanes, C. (1981). *Strategic family therapy.* San Francisco: Jossey-Bass.

Madanes, C. (1984). *Behind the one way mirror: Advances in the practice of strategic therapy.* San Francisco: Jossey-Bass.

Madanes, C. (1990). *Sex, love, and violence: Strategies for transformation.* New York: Norton.

McGoldrick, M., Anderson, C., & Walsh, F. (1989). *Women in families: A framework for family therapy.* New York: Norton.

Minuchin, S. (1974). *Families and family therapy.* Cambridge, MA: Harvard University Press.

O'Hanlon, W. H., & Weiner-Davis, M. (1989). *In search of solutions: A new direction in psychotherapy.* New York: Norton.

Palazzoli, M. S., Boscolo, L., Cecchin, G., & Prata, G. (1978). *Paradox and counter-paradox.* New York: Aronson.

Ritterman, M. (1983). *Using hypnosis in family therapy.* San Francisco: Jossey-Bass.

Seixas, J. S., & Youcha, G. (1985). *Children of alcoholism: A survivors manual.* New York: Crown Publishers.

Seventh reports to Congress. (1990). Washington, DC: National Institute on Alcohol Abuse and Alcoholism and National Institute on Drug Abuse.

Stanton, M. D., Todd, T. C., & Associates. (1982). *The family therapy of drug abuse and addiction.* New York: Guilford.

Steinglass, P., Bennett, L., Wolin, S., & Reiss, D. (1987). *The alcholic family.* New York: Basic Books.

Steinglass, P., Weiner, S., & Mendelson, J. H. (1971). A systems approach to alcoholism: A model and its clinical application. *Archives of General Psychiatry, 24,* 401–408.

Straussner, S. L. A., Weinstein, D. L., & Hernandez, R. (1979). Effects of alcoholism on the family system. *Health and Social Work, 4*(4), 111–127.

Subby, R., & Friel, J. (1982). *Co-dependence.* Deerfield Beach, FL: Health Communications.

Treadway, D. (1980). Communications in a 2-year family therapy training seminar sponsored by Intervention, Inc., Lincoln, MA.

Treadway, D. (1989). *Before it's too late: Working with substance abuse in the family.* New York: Norton.

Wegscheider-Cruse, S. (1989). *Another chance: Hope and health for the alcoholic family.* Palo Alto, CA: Science and Behavior Books.

Zilbach, J. J. (1986). *Young children in family therapy.* New York: Brunner/Mazel.

11

Treating the Partners of Substance Abusers

Elizabeth Zelvin

The spouses and lovers of alcoholics and drug abusers constitute an almost forgotten class in the treatment of chemical dependency. Traditionally, wives of alcoholics in particular were considered to have a preexisting pathology that led them to select an alcoholic partner and continue to derive secondary gains from his drinking. The formation of Al-Anon in 1951, the work of Kellermann (1974), and the emergence of the concept of codependency in Minnesota in the early 1970s briefly focused attention on the partner of the chemical dependent as someone adversely affected by alcoholism or addiction and in need of help. Before long, however, the term "codependent" was co-opted by the fast-growing movement of adult children of alcoholics. It became synonymous to many with "adult child," and the spouse or partner became a less important figure in the burgeoning chemical dependency literature. In the 1980s, not only were books on addiction and recovery written for a general readership receiving increasing professional respect, but the works of Beattie (1987), Woititz (1983), and Norwood (1985) were to be found on popular best-seller lists. In contrast, a 1989 literature search through the National Clearinghouse for Alcohol and Drug Information on spouses or partners of alcoholics and other kinds of substance abusers turned up only three articles specifically on spouses of alcoholics, a few more on treatment of the alcoholic or chemically dependent family, and none on partners of cocaine abusers or other addicts. While the necessity of arresting the enabling behavior of the spouse is a given in addiction treatment and the acknowledgment of codependency as a primary and widespread disorder is a highly visible popular trend, somehow the special plight of the wife, husband, or lover of the alcohol or drug abuser as an individual with his or her own pain, concerns, and treatment needs has not been of very great interest to either the professional community or the booming network of recovery self-help programs. This chapter discusses how the codependent partner is affected by alcoholism or substance abuse and addresses the treatment needs of this important and neglected population.

HOW THE PARTNER IS AFFECTED

Beliefs about how the spouse or partner is affected by chemical dependency have changed over the past 20 years. Today we can make a distinction between enabling, the protective and controlling behaviors that inadvertently encourage the alcoholic or addict to continue abusing substances; coalcoholism or coaddiction, the adverse consequences to the partner of living with chemical dependency; and codependency, a condition or disorder affecting the whole personality and all relationships that arises, in part, from living with chemical dependency.

Myths

The traditional myth about the wives of alcoholics was that they needed their husbands to go on drinking in order to meet their neurotic needs. Many, including the wives themselves, believed the drinking was all their fault. The alcoholic's projection of blame onto his "controlling" partner and her acceptance of that blame was and is a key element in the alcoholic–codependent denial system. Societal reinforcement of this assumption is evident in the traditional socialization of women to be loyal, accepting, and not overly assertive. Women have also traditionally been held responsible for the social and emotional deficiencies of men, especially their husbands and sons. (As for the husbands of alcoholics, these were hardly supposed to exist, thanks to the myth that there were few alcoholic women.) Less obvious, perhaps, was the concurrent myth that the wives of alcoholics were saints who martyred themselves to their husbands' addiction; did not lose identity, self-esteem, or ability to function because of it; and were able to adapt without much difficulty when their husbands got sober. This is nowhere more evident than in the "Big Book" of Alcoholics Anonymous (*Alcoholics Anonymous*, 1976), first written over 50 years ago, in which recovering alcoholics recount in story after story how they disappointed and shamed the finest wife and family a man could hope to have. It is well known that Lois W., the wife of the founder of Alcoholics Anonymous (AA), worked for years in a department store to support the fledgling fellowship, coming home to cook for a houseful of drunken "prospects" her husband had taken in, none of whom ever seemed to get sober (*Alcoholics Anonymous Comes of Age*, 1957)—a prime example of what we now call "enabling" by both Lois and Bill W.

The wives of drug addicts seem not to have been mythologized in the same way, perhaps because professional attention was so focused on the addict himself. By the late 1970s, family treatment, usually systems-oriented, had quietly found its way into a majority of drug treatment programs (Stanton, 1979), but the notion of the partner as a primary patient who could be helped professionally for her own sake was a product of the Minnesota model of chemical dependency. This model suggested that drug addiction, whether to heroin, cocaine, or prescription pills, is a disease process parallel to and including alcoholism and requiring spiritual as well as physical and behavioral recovery—a view still not shared by all substance abuse theoreticians and purveyors of treatment.

The current myth about codependent partners contradicts the original mythology in some ways and paradoxically restates it in others. The notion of the spouse's preexisting neurosis was rejected by the modern family disease model, and it was acknowledged that living with alcoholism or addiction caused significant damage to the partner's emotional, mental, physical, and social well-being. This also disposed of the sainthood myth. It was further acknowledged that a recovery process was necessary for the partner even if the drinking stopped or the addict left. However, more and more, the codependency theorists have been attributing this condition to the dysfunctional family of origin, seeing the choice of an alcoholic or addicted partner as a reenactment of the preexisting family dysfunction. Of the best-known writers on codependency, only Schaef (1986) gives due weight to the role of society in producing the addictive process and perpetuating codependency, pointing out that "the Ideal American Marriage [has] exactly the same elements as . . . an addictive relationship" (p. 35). Zelvin (1988) agrees that "novels, theater, movies, and television support a view of the mutually dependent relationship characteristic of alcoholism as not dysfunctional but rather 'romantic' and desirable" and adds that "alcoholism itself and its attendant codependency are often viewed in literature and the media as grand and tragic rather than pathological and treatable" (p. 101). Zelvin (1988) and Schutt (1985) both observe that not every codependent spouse comes from a dysfunctional family. The latter states: "Some women come from functional families that were relatively happy and stress-free. Yet, if they too fall in love with an alcoholic, they are at risk for developing the dysfunctional behavior that characterizes codependent wives" (p. 9). She adds that, given treatment, spouses with such a background may recover more rapidly than other codependents. It is noteworthy that Schutt, writing in the mid-1980s for the same publisher as Wegscheider-Cruse (1985) and Woititz (1983), has not become a media star. The myth that virtually all codependents come from dysfunctional families has been reinforced by the powerful "adult children" movement. This myth needs to be challenged in both the interests of differential diagnosis, prognosis, and treatment of codependency

and the need to hold society to some extent accountable for this phenomenon.

Enabling

The term "enabling" is used to describe the ways the nonaddicted partner
inadvertently perpetuates the drug or alcohol use. Until recently, "enabler"
was considered an adequate label for the partner of a chemical dependent. It
is important to stress that what this individual *is*, in diagnostic terms, is a
codependent (described below). "Enabler" is merely the maladaptive, ho-
meostatic role the partner plays in relation to the loved one's addiction—
and, by extension, to other dysfunctional family behaviors. It is enabling to
cover up for a chemical dependent's inability to function socially or vocation-
ally. It is enabling to take over financial and organizational management of
the family if these are normally the addict's roles. These protective behaviors
reinforce the dependent's denial by removing the consequences of his or her
chemical abuse. It is also enabling to berate or reproach the abuser, since the
remorse, guilt, and shame it arouses in the substance abuser inevitably trigger
either chemical use or projection of blame and responsibility, or both, to
defend against these feelings. It is enabling to rescue an addict from the
consequences of his or her addiction in any way, no matter how frightening
these consequences may appear to the person who loves the addict—for
example, giving money to a cocaine user who claims the dealer has threatened to break his legs. It is also enabling to attempt to control the addict's
behavior—for example, to pour liquor down the sink, measure the level in
the bottle, or extract promises about whether or how much he or she will
drink on a particular occasion. Such behaviors arouse defiance and opposition in the substance abuser, allow the abuser to project responsibility for the
consequences onto the enabler, and reinforce the erroneous belief that the
uncontrollable—the drug or alcohol dependency—can be controlled.

Coalcoholism or Coaddiction

If enabling is how the spouse or lover attempts to deal with the drinking or
drugging, and codependency is a primary disorder that may result from
social and developmental factors as well as the addictive relationship, let us
use the terms "coalcoholism" and "coaddiction" to describe how the partner
is *affected* by living with someone who is chemically dependent. It is all too
easy to slip from acknowledging "enabling" as the partner's contribution to
the systemic dysfunction to using it as a blaming label, in effect making the
partner responsible for the continuing chemical abuse. Without wanting to

encourage the spouse to play the passive role of victim, we must remember that he or she is indeed a victim of the bizarre, irrational, and socially unacceptable behavior that can result from substance abuse. It must not be forgotten that the major symptom of chemical dependency is denial. Alcoholics or addicts may deny that they are drinking or using at all, that they have problems at all, that the chemicals have anything to do with the problems, or that they are responsible for the problems. Nonaddicted partners may deny that the drinking or drugging is going on, minimize its extent, deny their problems as well as the addict's, be oblivious to the relationship between the substance abuse and the problems, or deny that their behavior has anything to do with the friction in the relationship. Both may deny the label "alcoholic" or "addict," saying that the alcoholic "just has a little drinking problem" or "likes his schnapps," that the addict uses cocaine or marijuana "recreationally," or that the daily Valium or Xanax was prescribed by a doctor and is for the abuser's "nerves."

As a result of all this denial, the coalcoholic or coaddict gradually develops an unnaturally high tolerance for bizarre, irrational, and unacceptable behavior. Worse, he or she feels confused, fearful, guilty, angry, anxious, depressed, and often even "crazy." As Woititz puts it: "You don't know what to believe or what to expect. . . . Your sense of what is real becomes distorted" (1979, p. 41). Woititz lists the end products of the disease progression for the partner as lethargy, hopelessness, self-pity, and despair. In order to hide the pain, shame, and despair, as well as minimize the impact of the bizarre behavior on others, the couple isolate themselves (Straussner, Weinstein, & Hernandez, 1979). Potential sources of support and help, such as family, friends, and professionals, are cut off. Some marriages are characterized by rage, violence, and mutual recriminations; others bolster the mutual dependence with an image of the couple as a doomed, romantic "two against the world." Rothberg, looking at the couple from a systems perspective, points out: "People in an alcoholic dyad feel powerless . . . to control each other and are involved in a useless, exacerbating, roller-coaster-like attempt to achieve power and/or control" (1986, p. 73).

Coalcoholics or coaddicts will turn to chemicals themselves or to compulsive behaviors to bring themselves closer to the substance abusers, to attempt to control them, or to sedate their own feelings. One wife pours wine from her husband's glass into her own at dinner parties to keep his intake down. Another, distressed by her husband's belligerence when drunk, encourages him to smoke marijuana because it "makes him cheerful." She smokes along with him nightly, "keeping him company" and also sedating her anxiety and terror about her out-of-control marriage and unmanageable life. Neither of these women is necessarily chemically dependent. Their substance abuse may cease when their husbands achieve sobriety. Further exploration of their drinking patterns, chemical use, and family history would be needed to diagnose or rule out chemical dependency.

Because of both denial and enabling, coalcoholics or coaddicts often appear to be very much in control of their lives. They perform their own and their partners' tasks, have many opinions and much advice for others, and may express a great deal of confidence in their own coping abilities. They are convinced that they need no help and that no one can be trusted to take care of things as well as they can. In fact they trust no one, and they are rigidly controlling in order to defend against their belief that if they let go one iota for one second, their whole world will fall apart. This constant need for universal control causes their lives to "become unmanageable," as they will learn to say in Al-Anon. The smallest tasks may feel overwhelming because they are invested with so much magical importance. Says one recovering coalcoholic: "It got so getting a parking space was as much of a major crisis as getting married."

Codependency

"Codependency" is the currently popular term—castigated by some, overused by others, but undeniably useful—for an exaggerated dependence upon a loved object or, by extension, external sources of fulfillment. It is characterized by incomplete development or loss of identity, neglect of self, and low self-esteem. As previously suggested, it can result from membership in a dysfunctional family, a relationship with an alcoholic or addict, and/or socialization to expect external sources of fulfillment and the derivation of identity and self-esteem from a love relationship. Not surprisingly, some theorists consider 96% of Americans to be codependent. To be used this broadly, the concept of codependency must be considered along a continuum from the most severe case (such as someone who clings to a physically and emotionally abusive relationship in spite of being offered viable alternatives) to the most mild (such as the highly functional adult child who apologizes when someone steps on his foot). Codependents are "people-pleasers" who have an acute need for approval, are terrified of abandonment, fear risk taking, and are unable to express anger. They may also be controlling, rigid, perfectionistic, and overresponsible. They are typically nurturing, while it might be said that addicts are typically egocentric: This may be the best way to distinguish which disorder is primary or needs more attention in treatment when dealing with someone who is both. Codependents tend to rescue others at the expense of their own needs. Obversely, they tend to control as a way of distracting attention from their own needs and deficiencies. Codependents feel as if they are always right and, simultaneously, that they are always wrong. They care deeply what others think, often have difficulty identifying what they want or like, and in relationships tend to be attracted by neediness, unavailability, or a recklessness that complements their own fear of risk. These three attributes are often found in alcoholics or addicts. One recovering codependent is amused to remember that it seemed perfectly normal to explain her attraction to her alcoholic by saying, "I'm moved by his problems." Codependents are often described as "addicted to addicts" or "addicted to relationships." They are obsessed with the beloved object and often believe that their survival or their partner's depends on maintaining the relationship. In recovery they must learn to maintain boundaries; identify and express needs; make healthy relationship choices, which they often perceive as "dull" or "boring"; deal with solitude as well as intimacy; and find resources for fulfillment and happiness within themselves.

If enabling is "about" the drinking or drugging behavior and coaddiction is "about" the relationship with the addict, codependency is most emphatically "about" the codependent him- or herself. It pervades every relationship and attitude toward life; it is easily portable from relationship to relationship and from situation to situation. Codependency does not disappear when the codependent leaves the alcoholic, addict, or dysfunctional family. Nor does it disappear when the addict recovers. A coaddict may stop the enabling behavior and remain codependent. In a recovering relationship, a couple may work hard to reduce their codependency with each other but find that each is still codependent in family, work, or social relationships. Finally, most alcoholics and addicts themselves are also codependents. Often from dysfunctional families, frequently choosing other addicts as friends and lovers, and usually surrounded by other addicts even in recovery—as well as living in our society, which so profoundly enables codependency—they do not shed codependency when they give up alcohol or drugs nor even as they work on their sobriety. Recovery from codependency depends on its being acknowledged and treated, professionally and in self-help groups, as a primary, pervasive, and insidious disorder in its own right.

TREATING THE CODEPENDENT PARTNER

The conditions of treating the codependent partner may vary according to whether the chemically dependent partner is in treatment or is actively drinking and drugging. Treatment tasks range from stopping the enabling behavior to resolving core codependency issues. Obstacles to treatment include the pretreatment personality of the codependent partner, which tends to arouse countertransference in the therapist. Addictions and other pathology may also be present in the codependent. A variety of treatment and self-help modalities may be integrated for effective treatment.

When the Chemically Dependent Partner Is in Treatment

Alcoholism and substance abuse treatment professionals have found that even when an institutionalized commitment to treating families and significant others exists, it is often very difficult to engage the partner of an addicted client in treatment. The response of one wife when told her husband was an alcoholic ("How can I help?"), while classically codependent in that it assumed an ability to rescue and focused the need for help on the alcoholic, is unfortunately rare. (In this case, an alert therapist responded, "You can go to Al-Anon," which the wife did, quickly becoming engaged in her own recovery.) More often, the spouse's response is either to deny the problem altogether or refuse to participate in treatment because it is not his or her problem, but the addict's. Denial can be extreme: One wife, after compliantly sitting through a family education series and a review of the facts of her husband's three driving-while-intoxicated (DWI) convictions with high blood alcohol levels, still believed that her husband drank only an infrequent "one or two beers" and that alcohol had caused no problems in their lives. Ironically, spouses who have remained committed to their marriages through many years of embarrassment, neglect, and abuse often choose the moment when the substance abuser finally enters treatment to declare that they have had enough. Some leave, while others cite all the times they have "helped" to no avail to justify their refusal to cooperate with family treatment planning.

Partners differ widely in their feelings toward the substance abuser at the moment he enters treatment. Some are codependently bonded with the addict and obsessed with his treatment and recovery, as they are with every other aspect of his drinking or drugging. Others are furious at the chemically dependent partner. The approach taken to engage the codependent partner must be carefully tailored to the individual. If she claims she will do anything to get her partner sober, she must be told that the most helpful thing she can do is seek recovery for herself. If she resents and blames the chemically dependent partner, she may be told that she deserves support and understanding in her difficult position and that this may be found in self-help and family treatment.

On an institutional level, the individual therapist's work to engage the partner must be supported by massive outreach, counselor training in family issues and engagement techniques, and institutionalization of outreach procedures. Advocacy with administration and funding sources must also take place, especially since treatment of the family may not be considered cost-effective.

Too often therapists, whether recovering alcoholics or addicts themselves or trained to work with an identified patient rather than systemically, resist making real efforts to engage the significant other. If the therapist feels that it would violate the patient's boundaries or the therapeutic relationship to reach out to the partner, the partner will remain untreated, subject to his or her continued suffering, and liable to sabotage the substance abuser's recovery by continued enabling and codependency. Further, the responsibility for engaging the significant other sometimes falls between the cracks among intake worker, primary therapist, and family worker, depending upon the structure of the treatment program.

Deborah had been married for 3 years when her husband, Michael, was mandated to chemical dependency treatment by his company's employee assistance program. He attended a 28-day rehab program, and she attended weekly family sessions with Michael and his therapist and groups with other partners. At the end of rehab, Deborah was invited to join an aftercare group for significant others at the agency's outpatient facility. She did this, and attended regularly for more than a year. Initially reluctant to attend Al-Anon, which was strongly recommended by the agency, she began going more frequently after she completed aftercare; 2 years later, she was a regular and enthusiastic member of the fellowship, which she saw as ongoing support for her own recovery from codependency.

For every case like the one above, there are several like the following.

Peter entered therapy with an alcoholism specialist after several years of sporadic AA attendance without ever achieving more than 90 days' sobriety. His wife, Bonnie, refused several invitations to attend a session, but finally came once. The therapist attempted to engage her by joining with her, and Bonnie reported afterward that she liked the therapist. Peter remained sober for several months, until the therapist's vacation. While she was away, he relapsed. When he came to his first scheduled session on her return, he admitted that he had been drinking; he considered the therapy a failure and refused to return to treatment. He reported that he had concealed his relapse from his wife. Several weeks later, Bonnie called the therapist and requested an appointment. She stated that her husband was drinking and that she wanted help for herself. She also inquired about planned intervention, indicating that several concerned family members and friends were willing to participate. The therapist referred Bonnie to an intervention specialist and also began seeing her weekly. Before an intervention could be made, Peter recommitted himself to AA and became sober again. For several weeks Bonnie continued to attend treatment, but had difficulty finding anything to talk about, as things were "going fine"; she eventually dropped out of treatment.

It is common for partners, even when their own family backgrounds are dysfunctional or they have long histories of codependent relationships, to be out of touch with their feelings unless a crisis is in progress and to feel that they themselves have no problems and therefore need no help.

When the Chemically Dependent Partner Is Active

When substance abusers are still drinking or drugging, their partners typically seek treatment not for themselves but for the addict. They want to know how to make them get into treatment, what they should do to make them stop, or whether they should leave the relationship. Again the first task is engagement of the partner as the primary client by joining with either her anger or her concern for the dependent. Howard and Howard (1978) stress: "*The person who seeks assistance becomes the primary client.* . . . Traditionally, the significant other has been regarded as a "bridge," a means of getting the alcoholic to consent to treatment. . . . The person who walks [in] . . . becomes . . . our first concern. . . . Nine times out of ten, it is the female spouse of the male alcoholic" (p. 142). While refocusing codependent clients on their own pain and dysfunction, it is appropriate to tell them that changes in their behavior *may* bring about improvement in the partner.

> Luanne, a registered nurse, came in seeking help for her husband, an active alcoholic. She was offered individual treatment and encouraged to attend Al-Anon. After her first meeting, she reported she disliked Al-Anon because the people there seemed "selfish" and talked only about their own concerns and not about the alcoholic. Her therapist explained that these people were all in Al-Anon because, like Luanne, they loved somebody, and "putting the focus on themselves" instead of being preoccupied with their loved one's behavior was their "medicine," as it was hers. The therapist also suggested changes in Luanne's enabling behavior, which included controlling, extracting promises, and participating in violent arguments. Luanne immediately began making these changes, and 3 weeks later her husband entered detox.

It is equally important to make it clear that an outcome of sobriety for the partner cannot be guaranteed.

> Pamela came into treatment because her husband's drinking bothered her and she was concerned about its effects on her three young children. She was an impeccable housekeeper and devoted mother who had "no time" for herself because she "had to" perform an infinite number of tasks. She also had fits of anger when she fought with her husband and verbally abused her children. Her goal on entering treatment was an immediate, impulsive "geographic" in which she would move to another state and find a job while living with her one friend there; it was clear

that she might easily agree to include her husband in the plan, even though its purpose was to get away from him. Early in treatment, she had a pseudo-hallucinatory episode in which she "saw herself" murdering her husband in a variety of ways; when she called the therapist to report it, she was unsure whether she would act on it and unable to assess the probable consequences realistically. In 18 months of treatment, Pamela learned to express her anger verbally in more appropriate ways; became a regular participant in Al-Anon; found a full-time job and began building financial independence; developed constructive ways of relating to her children and began educating them about the disease of alcoholism; relinquished many household tasks and allowed them to remain undone if other family members shirked their responsibilities; stopped remaining awake all night if her husband was out drinking and demanding where he had been on his return; ceased attending family parties at which all her husband's relatives were drunk; refused to get in the car with him if he insisted on driving after drinking; and allowed herself regular outings in which she practiced doing what she liked and enjoying her own company. At the same time, her husband's alcoholism progressed. When he impulsively quit his job, thereby losing their apartment, which came with it, Pamela was able to find an apartment for herself and the children and leave the marriage.

Treatment Tasks

When the partner of an alcoholic or addict is willing to be engaged, the first task is to change the enabling behavior. Untreated codependents can enable as destructively in early recovery as in the active situation: by trying to control the dependent's treatment and AA attendance, by continuing to monopolize decision making in the family, by giving or withholding money, by continuing to express mistrust and contempt, and in a host of other ways. Monitoring the client's engagement in self-help—Al-Anon, Nar-Anon, Co-Anon, Families Anonymous, or Codependents Anonymous—and processing resistance to these programs is also a crucial early and ongoing counseling task.

If the codependent comes from a dysfunctional family of origin, exploration of this may begin fairly early, at first gently with psychoeducational information and gradually in more depth. In cases where the dysfunctional family is an actively destructive element in the client's current life, this issue must be addressed more quickly. In other cases, the psychic damage the client has sustained as a child may far outweigh the stresses of the current relationship. Here, too, it would be dangerous to delay addressing the family issues. Many clients, however, are in denial about the impact of their early life on their current relationships and choices. Only after more than a year of treatment was Pamela, for example, beginning to understand that her early loss of an alcoholic father and the codependency of her rigid, controlling mother had affected her.

If coaddiction is the primary problem, work on the current relationship, especially enabling behavior, will take precedence for a while over core codependency issues. The goal, however, is to lead the client toward a recognition of codependency as a problem of self, irrespective of the chemically dependent relationship. Ideally, the client will recognize codependency issues in all his or her past and present relationships and his or her way of interacting with the world and will accept needing treatment and ongoing self-help whether or not he or she remains with the substance abuser and whether or not the addicted partner achieves sobriety. And of course, working on taking responsibility for one's feelings, not rescuing or controlling the addict or obsessing about the partner to the point of self-neglect is in fact making a start on recovery from codependency.

Treatment Modalities

Inpatient treatment for the partners of substance abusers is limited. The most progressive chemical dependency programs have a family week, which at best brings the significant others together to focus on their codependency and also begins to rebuild the relationship by fostering communication between chemically dependent individuals and their partners. Some inpatient programs limit family involvement to a few brief sessions of education and discharge planning. Traditionally, telling the partner to go to Al-Anon has been expected to compensate for the deficiencies in family treatment; in reality, getting to Al-Anon and using it effectively, for some clients, is a process that benefits greatly from informed professional help. There is little inpatient care for codependents whose partners are active substance abusers, although there are a few excellent programs for codependents and adult children that focus on healing the wounds of early family dysfunction.

Outpatient programs usually use psychoeducation and group therapy as their primary modalities for significant others (Honig & Spinner, 1986). Individual, couple, and family therapy may also be offered. It is important to ensure that family education is focused on codependency rather than on alcoholism and chemical dependency. While partners need to be informed about the disease and what to expect, they are all too eager to learn about the addict's problem while continuing to ignore their own. It is essential that treating staff guard against reinforcing the codependent pathology by putting the alcoholic or addict and his or her sobriety in the center of the frame when working with significant others. Similarly, group and individual therapists may find that they must constantly refocus discussion as it drifts inevitably toward the substance abuser's behavior and progress.

The Role of Self-Help

The 12-step programs—Al-Anon and its more recent sister fellowships—are essential adjuncts to effective treatment, which should be used if at all possible. The combination of cognitive–behavioral change and spiritual comfort that they provide cuts the therapist's work in half and makes progress in the codependent's recovery more rapid, more effective, and more lasting. Unfortunately, many therapists share the resistances to self-help that codependents bring to treatment. They may believe the client's claim that Al-Anon is "just a gripe group" or "not for people who are not religious." The remedy is for treating professionals to be well informed about the program and about the character of specific meetings in their area. Many addiction professionals are themselves untreated codependents and adult children of alcoholics or other dysfunctional families who may bring this hidden pathology to the workplace and the therapeutic relationship. On the other hand, an increasing number of workers in the field are addressing their own issues and using the concepts of "putting the focus on yourself" and "detachment with love" not only to help their clients but also to eliminate codependency from their helping and professional relationships.

Obstacles to Treatment

In addition to client resistance, the absence or inadequacy of services, and professional lack of understanding or commitment to the partner's needs, a major obstacle to treatment is the difficulty therapists notoriously have in empathizing with the codependent spouse. One therapist, herself a recovering codependent, says: "I went into the field specifically to advocate for this population, but sometimes I feel so frustrated working with these clients that I want to bang their heads against the wall." Codependent partners typically are angry, self-righteous, impatient, hostile to the therapist, rigid, controlling, critical of their partners, and convinced they have no need to seek help or to change anything about themselves. They are also convinced that they are sensitive, perceptive, self-aware, good at intimate relationships, and more than tolerant of their partners' shortcomings, although they may feel intolerably victimized by them. It is very hard for them to see, for example, that giving up the victim role means not only that they "won't stand for his (her) doing that to me any more" but also accepting that the way they feel is not the product of what the chemically dependent partner "did to" them but is their own responsibility. It is equally hard for them to give up the controlling, critical, "right" stance because it is their defense against self-blame and terror. The therapist must keep firmly in mind that the controlling is not a willful obnoxiousness but an unconscious defense against pain and fear, a symptom of the disease that is as far beyond the codependent's control as bingeing is beyond the alcoholic's. In exchange for the control they must relinquish, codependents must be offered support and the opportunity to improve their self-esteem.

ADDICTIONS AND OTHER PATHOLOGIES OF THE CODEPENDENT PARTNER

Frequently one partner's greater alcohol or drug consumption or more obvious acting-out behavior masks an alcohol or drug problem in the other.

> Ted and Gina, who were engaged to be married, came in together with a presenting problem of Ted's heroin addiction. He had been clean for 2 months on his own at the time of the first session. He wanted individual therapy and refused to consider inpatient care. Gina claimed that she was willing to help in any way she could, including paying for the treatment. On questioning them, the therapist discovered that Gina had a history of 2 years of heroin addiction as a teenager, which she had ended on her own; that her father was an alcoholic; and that both she and Ted were daily drinkers. Both Ted and Gina had had a couple of drinks right before the session.

There is no distinction between the identified substance abuser and the codependent partner when it comes to the precept that therapy cannot be done in the presence of chemicals. Before any work could be done, both Ted and Gina had to be educated about the disease process of chemical dependency, contract to abstain from all mood-altering chemicals, including alcohol, and start attending AA.

Since anxiety and depression are symptoms of codependency, especially in the acute and chronic stages of a chemically dependent relationship, Valium or other benzodiazepines and sugar are frequently the codependent's drugs of choice. In assessing the codependent partner, questions must routinely and searchingly be asked about the client's use of prescribed mood-altering medications and eating patterns. It must be remembered that eating disorders are not necessarily signaled by bulimia, anorexia, or obesity and that there is a great deal of denial, both societal and individual, associated with pathological relationships to food. In settings where the presenting problem is not a partner's alcoholism or substance abuse, such as mental health clinics, routine questions should be asked of clients presenting with depression or anxiety about their own and their partners' drinking and other chemical use as well as about their dieting and eating patterns.

Depression and anxiety may persist, in some cases, for a significant period even though the client is abstaining from chemicals and other mood-altering substances; refraining from other compulsive behaviors, such as shopping, gambling, or compulsive sex; attending self-help groups and treatment regularly; and detaching emotionally from the addict to the best of his or her ability. In such cases, an additional diagnosis may be made and alternatives should be explored. These may include psychiatric consultation and possible use of psychotropic medications; inpatient codependency treatment; and more focused spiritual or stress-relieving work, such as biofeedback, meditation, physical exercise, or therapeutic body work.

THE RECOVERING RELATIONSHIP

There seems to be some controversy not only about whether the relationship as well as the recovering individuals should be treated but also about whether and to what extent this is being done. Stanton (1979) states that "treating the drug abuser and his family members separately or concurrently does not appear to be as promising or efficacious as treating them *together*, i.e. in a situation where their interactions and relationships can be directly observed and altered" (p. 143). Kaufmann and Kaufman (1979), describing the treatment of addict–spouse couples in long-term inpatient drug treatment, state: "In most cases, the couples who have reached the stage of couple therapy have a relationship which is evaluated as potentially constructive. Thus the spouse is not encouraged to detach emotionally or physically, but . . . to establish a mutual, loving relationship between partners" (p. 101). Sullivan (1985), advocating for "putting the relationship on the shelf," claims that "there is a tendency to recommend relationship-oriented interventions, such as marriage counseling or couples groups, whenever there is a significant level of tension between the dependent and the codependent" (p. 22). He makes a case for focusing on individual recovery, offering as one reason that this allows more room to focus on the codependent's needs.

In fact, it appears that currently, especially in the alcoholism and chemical dependency model based on the 12-step philosophy as well as professional sources, it is more usual to direct the codependent into separate treatment. In many programs, special family workers, usually social workers, deal only with significant others, and the alcoholic's or addict's counselor has minimal contact with the partner. Many alcoholics are told in AA and treatment to "put the relationship on the shelf." At the same time, the codependent partner who tries to talk about his or her marriage in Al-Anon or a codependency group may be told to "put the focus on yourself." The pitfall in this approach is that a relationship that has been wracked by chemical dependency has problems that are not solved by sobriety or codependency treatment, just as codependency issues are not resolved by work on sobriety alone. The recovering person who is trying to deal with the day-to-day difficulties of an established relationship while being told by therapist, sponsor, and recovering friends to ignore it is bound to feel unsupported, bewildered, and angry.

Certainly in some cases the disease has caused such a rift that the best way to avoid conflict is to direct the partners to their separate recoveries. Equally, if the marriage is in such acute crisis that sobriety is threatened, marital conflict must be addressed immediately. For example, some intervention must be made to deal with violence that does not stop with abstinence. But in some cases, the counselor and other helpers may be overlooking or minimizing an underlying factor of genuine love in the relationship or even dismissing it contemptuously as a manifestation of pathology. The therapist who, on the contrary, learns to recognize and acknowledge this love, where it exists, has a powerful treatment tool. Codependency is often confused with love; however, the love that remains when the excessive dependency of the active situation is removed can be framed as a strength. It is then possible to rebuild the relationship while supporting the individual recovery and autonomy of both partners. If the relationship is not addressed, dysfunctional patterns continue even as individual recoveries progress, and the partners may become increasingly alienated from each other. Kaufmann and Kaufman (1979) point out: "In the addict–spouse pair, there is frequently competition over who is the sickest and most needy. This may be the source of many quarrels and continues when the addict is drug-free" (p. 101). There may also be acute competition over whose recovery is more important and who is working the program better. Couples in individual recovery only may see each other's program as threatening, feel hostile to it (a very counterproductive attitude if the codependent has a hidden addiction problem or the alcoholic has codependency issues that must be addressed later on), and escalate hostility by accusing each other of "taking my inventory."

An acknowledgment that the couple is an entity that needs and deserves its own recovery is more productive in cases that have at least a hint of a positive prognosis, however buried under resentment and disappointment it may be. In deciding whether a recovering couple can be treated successfully, that spark of love can be used as a diagnostic tool. Rothberg (1986) lists the following as positive outcomes in treatment of the alcoholic–codependent couple: "reduced isolation, a sense of love, focusing on common goals, reduced blame, and less defensiveness. Treatment implications suggest personality change in both spouses" (p. 73). The therapist must support the recovery of both partners and refrain from allying with one and scapegoating the other—as in any systems therapy. Working with recovering couples can be both challenging and rewarding. Treatment issues include trust, communication, accepting differences, sexuality, money, and families. These seem to be universal, whether the addict is male or female, or indeed both partners are addicted, whether the couple is married or in a committed relationship, whether they are gay or straight. The therapist has the opportunity to be very concrete and prescriptive in helping the partners learn to communicate directly, express feelings, and speak from an "I" perspective instead of accusing, criticizing, and blaming.

A remarkable and little-known resource available in some areas is the 12-step program Chapter 9. Based on AA and Al-Anon but not affiliated with either, it provides an opportunity for couples to pursue their recovery together in the company of others addressing the same issues. Like other 12-step programs, it provides a model of recovery and potentiates behavioral and attitudinal change.

SUMMARY

While family treatment has become an increasingly important element of the chemical dependency model, the specific needs of the spouses and partners of alcoholics and substance abusers have been inadequately addressed. The partner may be viewed simultaneously as enabler, coalcoholic or coaddict, and codependent. As enabler, the partner contributes to the chemical abuse by rescuing and controlling behaviors. As coaddict, he or she is adversely affected by the disease, experiencing pain, confusion, anger, fear, guilt, anxiety, and depression. Codependent pathology is independent of any single relationship. It may come from the dysfunctional family, the chemically dependent relationship, the society, or from all of these. It is characterized by low self-esteem, a dependence on outside objects for identity and fulfillment, neglect of one's own needs, rescue and control of others, approval seeking, perfectionism, fear of risk, and denial of feelings.

Codependency must be treated as a primary disorder and the codependent partner as a primary client who needs and deserves help for his or her own sake. The partner may be treated whether or not the alcoholic or substance abuser seeks help. A variety of modalities are available. Obstacles to treatment include client resistance, professional denial and ignorance as well as the therapist's unresolved codependency issues, a lack of institutional support for codependency or family treatment, and the unattractive presenting personality of the untreated codependent, whose symptoms may include rigidity, self-righteousness, and control. Self-help programs, such as Al-Anon and Chapter 9, are an invaluable adjunct to treatment.

REFERENCES

Alcoholics Anonymous (3rd ed.). (1976). New York: Alcoholics Anonymous World Services.

Alcoholics Anonymous comes of age. (1957). New York: Alcoholics Anonymous World Services.

Beattie, M. (1987). *Codependent no more.* Center City, MN: Hazelden Foundation.

Honig, F., & Spinner, A. (1986). A group therapy approach in the treatment of the spouses of alcoholics. *Alcoholism Treatment Quarterly, 3*(3), 95–105.

Howard, D. P., & Howard, N. T. (1978). Treatment of the significant other. In S. Zimberg, J. Wallace, & S. B. Blume (Eds.), *Practical approaches to alcoholism psychotherapy.* New York: Plenum.

Kaufmann, P. N., & Kaufman, E. (1979). From multiple family therapy to couples therapy. In E. Kaufman & P. N. Kaufmann (Eds.), *Family therapy of drug and alcohol abuse.* New York: Gardner.

Kellermann, J. L. (1974, Fall). Focus on the family. *Alcohol Health and Research World,* pp. 9–11.

Norwood, R. (1985). *Women who love too much.* New York: Pocket Books.

Rothberg, N. M. (1986). The alcoholic spouse and the dynamics of codependency. *Alcoholism Treatment Quarterly, 3*(1), 73–86.

Schaef, A. W. (1986). *Codependence: Misunderstood—mistreated.* New York: Harper & Row.

Schutt, M. (1985). *Wives of alcoholics: From codependency to recovery.* Deerfield Beach, FL: Health Communications.

Stanton, M. D. (1979). Family treatment of drug problems: A review. In R. I. Dupont, A. Goldstein, & J. O'Donnell (Eds.), *Handbook on drug abuse.* Rockville, MD: National Institute on Drug Abuse.

Straussner, S. L. A., Weinstein, D., & Hernandez, R. (1979). Effects of alcoholism on the family system. *Health and Social Work, 4*(4), 112–127.

Sullivan, D. J. (1985). Putting the relationship on the shelf. *Focus on Family and Chemical Dependency, 8*(4), 22–23, 30.

Wegscheider-Cruse, S. (1985). *Choice-making.* Deerfield Beach, FL: Health Communications.

Woititz, J. G. (1979). *Marriage on the rocks: Learning to live with yourself and an alcoholic.* New York: Delacorte.

Woititz, J. G. (1983). *Adult children of alcoholics.* Deerfield Beach, FL: Health Communications.

Zelvin, E. (1988). Dependence and denial in coalcoholic women. *Alcoholism Treatment Quarterly, 5*(3/4), 97–115.

12

Dynamics and Treatment Issues with Children of Drug and Alcohol Abusers

Roberta Markowitz

It has been estimated that there are more than 7 million children under the age of 20 growing up in homes with at least one alcoholic parent and nearly 21 million adult children of alcoholics (Department of Health and Human Services, 1988). It is conceptually useful to explore children of alcoholics (COAs) or substance abusers (COSAs) as a special population, even though such children do not constitute a monolithic group. Among these children (as among substance abusers) one can find every diagnostic category. Nevertheless, certain commonalities in the behavior of alcoholic and other drug-abusing parents tend to lead to some common pathological outcomes that can seriously diminish the quality of life for their children, even long after they have left the parental home. This chapter examines the pathogenic circumstances, the dynamics of the resulting impairments, and various treatment issues with this population. As the research and clinical literature on COAs is much more comprehensive than that on children of other drug abusers, this chapter by and large directly refers to COAs. Much research remains to be done on children of other substance abusers, as even statistics on prevalence vary widely. Etiology and psychodynamics appear to be essentially similar to those of COAs, the chief differences flowing largely from the illegality surrounding the use of other drugs.

ETIOLOGY AND DYNAMICS

In the literature on COAs one frequently sees lists of attributes (such as inability to trust, fear of intimacy, external locus of control, and need for control) that are said to characterize this population. These characteristics, however, are certainly not unique to COAs, a fact that has led some to question what substance-abusing families have in common with other types of dysfunctional families that might lead to similar outcomes.

The core commonality in all types of dysfunctional families centers on the existence of some significant degree of impairment in empathy on the part of at least one parent (or primary caretaker), and the dynamics of COAs can best be understood as a special case of narcissistic injury suffered at the hands of empathically impaired parents.[1] What makes this a special case is the intermittent presence of behaviors induced by mood-altering drugs in parents whose non-drug-involved personalities may be dramatically different from what they appear to be "under the influence." Children have neither the knowledge nor the experience with which to understand the physiology and behavioral effects of a chemical dependency. In addition to the parent's behavior being directly distorted by the effect of drugs, the parents may value their drugs more than their child. As such, the normally powerful parent–child attachment, in which the child is extremely highly valued by the parent, may be supplanted by the parent's attachment to the drug as the chiefly valued object. Since the availability of the substance becomes an all-consuming preoccupation for the abuser, the needs and well-being of the child becomes a secondary concern; indeed, the degree to which the abuser values the child may be dependent on whether the child facilitates or interferes with the parent's use of the substance and related needs. Some spouses may attempt to protect their children from some of the direct consequences of the substance abuse and thereby soften the impact. Many others, however, are as preoccupied with the substance abuser's behavior as the abuser is with the substance; still others simply withdraw or turn to substance abuse themselves, thus becoming similarly unavailable to the child.

Such narcissistic use of the child may or may not be part of a parent's premorbid personality. When sober and drug-free during recovery, many parents will express great sorrow and shame in recalling their earlier treatment of their children. However, where substance abuse is present, some degree of empathic impairment is inevitable. This occurs in a number of ways. First, mood-altering drugs affect ego functioning and alter the balance among all the psychic structures. Even in those cases where abusers behave in a mellow and affectionate way, they are preoccupied with their own inner sensations and narcissistic needs and thus are not really available to the children. Second, during periods of physical withdrawal or when the drug is not having the desired effect, abusers experience the kind of narcissistic withdrawal that always accompanies illness, making them simply emotionally unavailable. The increase in anxiety, depression, tension, and irritability

---

[1]Compare this with Cermak and Rosenfeld's (1987) conception of adult children of alcoholics as suffering from post-traumatic stress disorder.

during these periods increases the likelihood of such parents' displacing the source of these feelings onto the children, who may then be unfairly blamed and punished. This arouses anxiety, confusion, guilt, and anger in the children, who also experience a sense of being "unseen." Third, the occurrence of blackouts—during which the parents will not recall anything that may have been discussed with the children—can also create enormous confusion, fear, and anger, again resulting in the children's feeling "not seen." Fourth, the substance use often loosens inhibitions and severely impairs parents' social judgment. At such times, the children may become the direct victim of inappropriate and possibly abusive behavior. Even if not directly victimized, if the children see or hear about such behavior, they are likely to experience a sense of helplessness, shame, and humiliation. Finally, nonabusing parents cannot be relied upon for relief, since they are usually overwhelmed and preoccupied with trying to manage the chaos engendered in the family and trying to maintain the illusion of normal functioning. Keeping the "family secret" (i.e., hiding the family shame) makes a mockery of the children's reality testing insofar as it demands selective inattention to portions of reality, both events and feelings. There is little permission for—indeed, there is often overt discouragement of—the expression of feelings generally.

According to Kohut (Kohut & Wolf, 1978), the development of a coherent, well-integrated self requires the presence of responsive-empathic selfobjects[2] who can meet the normal mirroring and idealizing needs of the child. As a consequence of minor, nontraumatic failures in the responses of mirroring and idealized selfobjects, the child begins to develop a mature self by gradually taking over the functions of the selfobjects. Archaic mirroring and idealizing needs are transformed into normal self-assertiveness and normal devotion to ideals. Faulty interactions between the child and the self-objects result in a damaged self.

For reasons described above, in a family with alcohol or other drug dependency one or both parents will be rendered unavailable to meet the normal needs of the child for mirroring and idealizing. This perspective is particularly illuminating with regard to the deep sense of shame experienced by most COAs as well as the powerfully felt need to maintain the alcoholic family secret. The substance abuser may not be able to exercise a normal degree of control—may stumble, vomit, soil him- or herself, or act foolish.

---

[2]"Self-objects are objects which we experience as part of our self; the expected control over them is, therefore, closer to the concept of control which a grown-up expects to have over his own body and mind than to the concept of control which he expects to have over others. There are two kinds of self-objects: those who respond to and confirm the child's innate sense of vigour, greatness and perfection; and those to whom the child can look up and with whom he can merge as an image of calmness, infallibility and omnipotence. The first type is referred to as the mirroring self-object, the second as the idealized parent imago" (Kohut & Wolf, 1978, p. 414).

Such failures are particularly linked to shame, and to some degree COAs are identified with this (Hibbard, 1987). The parent appears degraded in the child's eyes, so that in addition to the likelihood of having been directly shamed, the child's need to identify with an idealized parent is thwarted, leading to a deeper sense of shame.

In order to understand some of the effects on the child of parental empathic failure, it is helpful to examine what happens in healthy or "good enough" families.

> Jamie has just had one of the most glorious experiences a 9-year-old boy could have: He hit the winning home run in a baseball game. When he arrives home, his mother notices he is glowing and asks him in an interested and animated way what happened at school to make him look so happy. He shares the episode with his mother, relishing the retelling. As he speaks, his mother's eyes are open wide, she is smiling and attentive. When he finishes speaking, she congratulates him enthusiastically, praises him for doing so well, and reflects back to him that she can now see why he looked so delighted when he arrived home.

This exchange has a number of effects on Jamie, and he learns a number of things from it. In having his feelings of exhilaration, power, and grandiosity mirrored by his mother, they are validated and Jamie is able to sustain the good feelings and internalize them. He receives confirmation that what he was feeling was the correct thing to be feeling under the circumstances, which adds to the integrity of his sense of self and further enhances his self-esteem. He has learned that he can trust an important person to reflect his feelings accurately and that sharing such feelings can multiply the pleasure— there is pleasure in the original experience, in the safety of the retelling, in his mother's reflections of his own pleasure, and in his having pleased her directly.

What happens when such empathic responsiveness is lacking?

> Sarah, a 10-year-old girl, has been told by a visiting author at school that her story is one of the most charming she has ever read. Sarah is "walking on air," filled with her achievement. On the way home from school, however, some of her excitement begins to be edged out by anxiety because she is not sure in what condition she will find her alcoholic mother when she gets home. On arriving home, she finds her mother up and in the kitchen. Although her mother has not yet begun drinking that day, she is depressed, tense, and irritable because of her craving for alcohol. Sarah's arrival reminds her mother that Sarah had left yesterday's discarded clothing on the floor of her room rather than putting it in the hamper. Sarah attempts to tell her mother about the compliment she had received at school. Her mother replies sarcastically

that that's great, but if she can put words in such good order on paper, why can't she put her clothing in proper order at home, and proceeds to berate her for being such a "difficult, sloppy child." In her growing anger, her mother starts slamming cabinet doors, pours herself a drink as though to underscore how difficult it is to cope with her daughter, and stomps out of the kitchen. Sarah wonders whether her mother will be able to prepare dinner later.

All the self-enhancing experiences of Jamie's interaction with his mother are absent in this episode. On the contrary, the central experience is one of anxious anticipation followed by anger and a precipitous drop in self-esteem. Furthermore, Sarah gets the message that she is responsible for her mother's drinking because she is "such a bad girl." Sarah learns that it is not safe to share positive feelings with her mother, since chances are they will be shattered; with repeated experiences such as this one, she learns that it is not even safe to allow herself to *feel* such feelings, since it leads to such serious disappointment. She denies her feelings of rejection and abandonment by focusing on a concrete problem.

   The experience of the precipitous drop in self-esteem is so very painful that many such children learn to numb their responses to positive experiences: It is felt to be safer to exist in a chronic state of low self-esteem and moderate depression than to take the risk of feeling good about oneself, only to set oneself up for a fall. Since they ward off the positive and self-esteem-enhancing feelings that normally accompany compliments or satisfying achievements, there is little to counteract their feeling of being basically bad or flawed. The conviction of being flawed in some very deep, abiding, and fundamental way (which has both conscious and unconscious components) may become an organizing fantasy that can shape much of their lives, expressing itself in excessive feelings of shame. It may be acted out directly or via a grandiose reaction formation and exhibitionism.

> Mr. B., the adult child of an alcoholic father, is a very successful business-man who makes unreasonable demands that everything around him be elegant and perfect. Despite the fact that his wife also works and has primary responsibility for the children, he insists she arrange for their linens and towels to be changed daily. He fights with his colleagues because of periodic demands for special indulgences—such as having a fine bone china tea service for his office. If his wife should bring home a bag of potatoes from the market with one rotting potato in it, he flies into a rage, becoming verbally abusive and throwing things around. At times he becomes depressed and has difficulty getting up for work in the morning.

The conviction of being flawed or damaged is typically projected, so that in addition to feeling "I'm lousy," the adolescent or adult COA feels, "You will look at me and see how lousy I am." The sense of exposure is intolerable; it is not unusual for the resulting feelings of mortification to be dealt with by social withdrawal and isolation, by rages, or by self-medicating with alcohol or other drugs.

If there is any kind of real bodily defect, even one that is quite minor, the sense of being flawed may be projected onto it. Ms. A., for example, was born with a bump on her head that is visible only to herself and her hairdresser. Yet, in telling her therapist about it at the age of 40, she broke into tears, recalling her belief that no one liked her as she was growing up because of that bump. In the absence of any real external defect, the fantasy of being flawed and/or damaged may remain unconscious and can assume many different forms—many women, for example, experience themselves as hopelessly stupid or inept, or focus on their imperfect body shape, which leads them to an eating disorder. Perfectionism and a desperate need to seek approval develop as a means of warding off any hint of inadequacy or rejection, either of which could trigger the painfully precipitous drop in self-esteem.

COPING MECHANISMS

Just as a dependent child needs to have certain basic physical needs met in order to survive, so too must certain psychological needs be met for adequate nurturing, holding, balance of stimulation and soothing, empathic responsiveness, and reasonable consistency. When these are not sufficiently forthcoming, overwhelming anxiety, rage, depression (and, in extreme cases, failure to thrive), as well as deficits in the sense of self, may result. The child generally concludes that he or she is at fault and bad and will seek to have his or her needs met in whatever ways possible. Many authors have pointed out that COAs develop a variety of coping skills to survive in situations where life may be chaotic, unpredictable, frightening, and dangerous (e.g., Black, 1981; Seixas & Youcha, 1985; Wegscheider, 1981).

One coping technique that COAs frequently develop is to become overly attuned to the parental needs and wishes. In this reversal of roles, children discover that by pleasing or taking care of parents they can glean at least a facsimile of the nurturing they crave. In addition to becoming confidant(e), comforter, adviser, and supporter of the parents, these children develop a special sensitivity to unconscious signals manifesting the needs of others (Miller, 1981). As with other survival mechanisms that are learned, this one can be very adaptive and provide many secondary gains. Such children are appreciated by friends, in school, or later on the job for their sensitivity, hard work, strongly developed sense of responsibility, desire to please, and need to rescue others (they are represented in large numbers in the helping professions). But these gains come at a high price: the repression of their own wishes, feelings, and needs. These COAs may look very successful on the outside, but they suffer powerful feelings of emptiness and aloneness. Not having access to their own feelings, they have difficulty finding sources of satisfaction or tapping creative resources. Such things as making career choices or finding a hobby, for example, can be confusing and frustrating. Since inadequate parental empathy causes COAs to feel it is unsafe to act on the basis of their own feelings and needs, they learn to regulate their feelings and actions based on their perception of the feelings and needs of others, leading to boundary confusion and enmeshment. Internal resources for self-comforting are inadequate, leaving COAs largely dependent on an external source to feel complete. This may help explain the frequency with which ones sees a variety of compulsive behaviors among COAs, including eating disorders, substance abuse, gambling, compulsive shopping, and/or addictive relationships. As with many of the coping mechanisms that enable COAs to survive their difficult and frightening early years, being overly attuned to others—while continuing to bring some rewards—brings with it serious maladaptive consequences later in life: The role reversals, continuing dependence upon external sources for self-regulation, excessive fears about the parents' health and well-being, perfectionism, desperate need for approval, and reaction formation against anger often make it difficult for COAs to separate from parents in reality as well as intrapsychically.

> After years of therapy, Ms. C. was finally able to bring herself to leave her parents at the age of 29 and to get married. Both parents were alcoholic, although she was not aware of her mother's alcoholism until, soon after the wedding, her mother developed a life-threatening illness that the doctor declared to have been caused by her drinking. The illness further undercut Ms. C's attempts at separation. She became depressed, and even months after the crisis had subsided, Ms. C. continued to feel obligated to spend considerable time with her parents, making biweekly trips to visit them—no easy feat, since they had moved 1,200 miles away! Shortly afterwards, Ms. C. became pregnant. Her father, who continued to drink daily, complained bitterly that he could not cope with the limitations his wife's illness had placed on their lifestyle and thought about ending his grief by suicide. Ms. C. believed he would never hurt himself while she was pregnant. She was aware that she had conceived her child as a gift for her father, in order to counter the threatened loss and separation.

Related to the separation issue is the fact that the moods of adult children of alcoholics (ACOAs) are frequently regulated by the feelings of others.

When Ms. C. decided to skip one of her biweekly trips, her father called her four times a day because of his own difficulties with separation and infantile dependence. She noticed that she was feeling better than she had in months and realized it was because her father sounded "pretty good" on the phone. She was struck by the degree to which her moods were dependent on her father's state of mind.

Cermak and Rosenfeld (1987) point to the extreme need to maintain control as a central and critical issue for COAs. This too begins as a coping mechanism that can facilitate survival in a chaotic and unpredictable environment but that, because of its rigidity, has maladaptive consequences. Exerting control often enables COAs to play a role in holding the family together, and this may become a source of realistic pride. But they often cling to the illusion of being in a position to control their substance-abusing parent's behavior. They ascribe the cause of their intermittent abandonment to their own "badness" so that they can continue to view the parent as good (and thereby continue to hope for the caring and connectedness they seek). This perpetuates the illusion and sustains the hope that they can influence the parent's moods and behavior by adjusting their own behavior.

Ms. C. reported receiving nightly spankings up until the age of 10. Although she reported that these spankings were not severe, she recalled that, when intoxicated, her father was quite volatile and explosive and that he would throw and break things including tearing the heads off her dolls. She reported these episodes with inappropriate affect—smiling, almost laughing—and attempted to minimize their horror by pointing out how guilty her father would later feel. She added that she distinctly remembered deliberately doing naughty things in order to provoke these spankings, as though to say, "You see, it really was my fault, after all, not his."

In a frightening and out-of-control world, Ms. C. had found the one area in which she could experience herself as exerting control. In her reports of these spankings (which were clearly sexualized, thus adding to her guilt), Ms. C. attempted to deny her own anxiety, minimize her father's culpability, and ascribe the cause to her own "badness": If only she were better behaved, her father would have had no cause to hit her. In writing about his work with a severely abused population, Shengold (1989) finds a similar dynamic.

When one parent can tyrannize, the need for a loving and rescuing authority is so intense that the child must break with the registration of what he or she has suffered, and establish within the mind (delusionally) the existence of a loving parent who will care and who really must be right.

. . . (In the adult, there may be a good deal of intellectual awareness of what the parent is like, but the delusion of goodness continues underneath and surfaces when needed.) The child takes on the guilt for the abuse, turning inward the murderous feeling that is evoked by the traumata. . . . The child denies what has happened, sometimes but not always with orders from the tormentor. The parent is right and good; the child must be wrong and bad. (pp. 73–74)

Shengold (1989) explains that the child's need to "break with the registration of what he or she has suffered" results in a kind of compartmentalizing of contradictory images, which are never permitted to coalesce. This kind of "vertical splitting" transcends diagnostic categories.[3] It has powerful implications for the understanding and treatment of this population. Healing can begin to take place only when the client can responsibly own his or her full ambivalence and can truly accept that that which is fervently wished for—to have had a good and loving parent—never existed and can never be re-created. Golden and Hill (1991) point out the paradox in the task of those who need to mourn that which was never enjoyed, as many ACOAs do:

Childhood may have been endured, may be remembered, or may be denied, but it has not been mourned, because mourning requires letting go. These patients cannot yet let go of the desire for good and loving parents. The recognition that what has been lost in childhood has been lost forever revives the threat of childhood despair which appears to be every bit as devastating now as it was then. (p. 24)

Faced with the chronic overstimulation and emotional deprivation that are typical in chemically dependent families, some COAs cope through a constellation of acting-out behaviors. They may turn to running away from home, abusing substances, promiscuity, suicidal ideation and behavior, bullying or belligerency with peers, uncooperativeness at school, and antisocial or criminal activities. These behaviors may represent, among other things, direct discharge of overwhelming affect, seeking of attention and limit-setting, identification with the aggressor, reaction formation against feared helplessness, and the turning of passivity into activity. Difficulty dealing with anger is typical. Inability to discharge anger in appropriate ways at appropriate times leads to the building of a well of anger that can be touched off by even small triggers. The resulting overreaction is frightening and leads to more determined efforts to further suppress anger. One client aptly described her experience of her own anger: "It feels like a hard core inside me—like kryptonite—it's toxic and it weakens me."

---

[3]For an excellent discussion of the contributions of the object relations school and Kohut and the self psychologists to this topic, see Wood (1987).

Dissatisfaction and failure in interpersonal relationships are extremely common complaints among ACOAs. Fear of intimacy and lack of trust are frequently cited as contributing to this. Equally a problem is *blind trust*. If a child has experienced rejection, abandonment, or abuse, the powerful need for love and attachment will prevent the normal unraveling of the archaic idealization of the parent. This idealization is transferred onto potential love objects during adolescence and adulthood, so that inadequacies and failures in these partners, which may be evident to outside observers, go unperceived by the ACOA.

It is common for ACOAs to find partners who are themselves alcoholics or drug abusers, or who are emotionally unavailable for other reasons. Sometimes these attachments seem to blaze into existence precipitously—the ACOA may report "love at first sight"—but they are often based on dependency and neediness rather than a relationship of adult mutuality. Sensing the partner's neediness, the ACOA feels temporarily safe from rejection—a rejection he or she has come to fear but to expect as normal and inevitable. The partner does inevitably withdraw, based on his or her own fears or conflicts, but the ACOA, who was blind to the danger signs to begin with, assumes the guilt for this rejection and responds with feelings of badness, a painful drop in self-esteem, depression, and such symptoms as difficulty eating and sleeping or gastrointestinal problems (Norwood, 1985). These painful interactions represent repetitions of the early parent–child relationship.

As in the childhood experience, the ACOA sees no relief from the painful affects other than by reuniting with the partner. This scenario may be played out again and again despite repeated abandonments or even abuse. In addition to the denial and inability to give up this idealization, part of the "blindness" to the character of the partner may be due to the ACOA's perception of his or her childhood experiences as normal, since there may have been little else with which to compare it. A further motivation for the repetition may be a wish to achieve mastery—the hope that this time it will work out all right, that the trauma can be avoided. Most compelling of all, the need to escape from a pervasive and desperate sense of emptiness almost ensures that the ACOA will seek to reunite with the very partner who has precipitated the immediate distress. Without outside help, the ACOA may remain endlessly trapped in a vicious circle with the disappointing yet yearned-for partner—or series of such partners.

TREATMENT

Since parental substance abuse in and of itself leads (at the very least) to impaired parental empathy and therefore narcissistic injury to the children, the first question that arises is whether all COAs require some form of intervention or treatment.

There has not been sufficient research to allow us to identify clearly which COAs would be most at risk, and we need to understand more about those factors that seem to mitigate the negative influences of parental pathology. There are certain "resilient" individuals who appear to function successfully despite an apparently traumatizing upbringing (Heller, Sher, & Benson, 1982). Nevertheless, there are two types of intervention that all COAs should have access to: the first is simply the information that growing up in a chemically dependent home creates an at-risk situation; the second is some basic education about alcoholism and other chemical dependencies. Making such information available alerts COAs to specific potential difficulties (this is especially important given our understanding that there is a genetic component to certain types of alcoholism); and it opens the door to individuals to seek help by reducing the shame that is so commonly part of the baggage carried by COAs. Self-help movements like Al-Anon, ACOA, and codependency groups that have burgeoned in recent years are playing an enormously important role in meeting this latter need, as are the national conferences for and about COAs that appear to be drawing ever-increasing number of participants. In addition, the wide availability of such information may contribute to more responsible decision making on the part of those anticipating parenthood: Damage to the fetus as a result of alcohol or other drug use during pregnancy can be considerable and is completely preventable (Nadel, 1985, Straussner, 1989).

WORKING WITH YOUNG CHILDREN
OF SUBSTANCE ABUSERS

Children or adolescents living in a substance-abusing family often benefit from participation in a group, which can reduce their isolation, provide peer support, and prepare them for involvement in self-help groups for adolescent children such as Alateen or Narateen. Therapists can use all the usual techniques for creating an atmosphere of trust—a critical aspect of beginning treatment—but can enhance this process by demonstrating an understanding of common characteristics of parents who abuse alcohol and other drugs, children's feelings about them, and consequent behaviors. Substance abuse education is an important component of treatment. Concrete suggestions for coping can be provided, for example, steps the child might be able to take to avoid getting into a car with an intoxicated parent. In addition, it is important to provide the message that the child is not alone, is not responsible for the parent's drinking or drugging, and cannot control the parent's substance abuse (Richards, Morehouse, Seixas, & Kern, 1983).

Treatment for children and adolescents can help them overcome denial of the parents' difficulties and allow for ventilation of anger. The child needs to know that it is normal to feel angry under certain circumstances and may need help understanding the distinction between wishes and fantasies on the one hand and action on the other: To wish one's parents dead need not give rise to the kind of guilt one would feel if one were to act on that wish. Therapists need to be sensitive to the child's ambivalence, however. A child might be feeling unjustly treated and murderously angry, but at the same time be feeling very worried about and fearful of losing the abusing parent. Conscious fears can include arrest, accident, illness, or death of a parent. Unconsciously, realistic dependence and need for parental protection make loss of the parent's love a terrifying prospect. This frequently gives rise to powerful rescue fantasies. It is important for the therapist to assist the child in accepting his or her ambivalence and to point out the unrealistic nature of the wish to rescue the parents.

Children of substance-abusing parents are frequently treated inconsistently and given confusing and conflicting messages, making it difficult for them to trust their own judgment. Therapists can help by providing validation for the child's feelings and perceptions and feedback on what is normal.

TREATING ADULT CHILDREN OF ALCOHOLICS

When ACOAs do present themselves for treatment, certain types of issues commonly arise despite the fact that, as mentioned earlier, ACOAs are represented in the full range of diagnostic categories. These issues include proneness to experiencing guilt and shame, fear of anger, an inadequate or damaged sense of self, use of denial, and possibly substance abuse or other forms of compulsive behavior.

Since ACOAs are at increased risk for all types of substance abuse as well as eating disorders and other types of compulsive behaviors, it is important that careful assessments be made of all of these areas and appropriate interventions planned. Not infrequently, ACOAs exhibit the early stages of alcohol or drug abuse, since they have learned to turn to chemicals as a form of self-medication for painful affects. In these cases relatively minimal intervention—in the form of some alcohol and drug education and advice—is often all that is required to help them give up their use of chemicals, since it has not yet become a long-term, chronic problem with its typically entrenched defenses of rationalization and denial.

Low self-esteem and proneness to excessive shame sometimes present obstacles in the beginning of treatment. ACOAs may perceive their very need for treatment as corroboration of their deeply held conviction of being flawed or damaged in some way. This may interfere in their ability to form a therapeutic alliance, since they fear and fully expect that if they open themselves up they will be rejected by a therapist who will be seeing and judging all their flaws. This problem needs to be addressed early on by interventions, offered in an empathic and accepting way, that clarify and illuminate the nature of this anxiety. The clinician also needs to help clients transform excessive shame or guilt from ego-syntonic to ego-alien experiences: the client needs help in redefining the problem from "I *am* so bad and stupid" to "I am *too quick to feel* bad and stupid." Furthermore, defenses against shame need to be interpreted so that more adaptive behaviors can take their place. By allowing clients to share shameful feelings about the self in a therapeutic environment that is accepting and understanding, the clinician can bring clients to experience themselves as worthwhile, valuable human beings (Potter-Efron, 1987).

Damage to self-esteem is a specific problem endured by ACOAs; damage to one's very sense of self is a more global difficulty for many ACOAs. Questions such as "what kinds of things do you enjoy?" or "Do you have any hobbies?" are sometimes initially met with surprise and resistance since (1) ACOAs have cultivated the art of repressing their own feelings, wishes, and needs; (2) they may be convinced they could not possibly be good at anything; and (3) sharing positive feelings may be felt to be too dangerous since, in their experience, it has often been followed by a precipitous drop of self-esteem. When such clients are able to overcome their own resistance to examining their feelings, one may hear surprising examples of interests, hobbies, or desires long suppressed. Simply being asked the questions provides permission for them to own their own feelings.

Boundary confusion resulting from damage to the sense of self is frequently an ongoing treatment issue. It may manifest itself in a variety of ways, such as preoccupation with and a tendency to overreact to the behavior, thoughts, and feelings of others, including those of the therapist, to the exclusion of the ACOA's own needs. This may become a resistance in the treatment when, for example, the client uses it to avoid focusing on him- or herself. The therapist should be careful not to disclose personal information in an effort to keep the boundaries clear and to facilitate the client's gaining an understanding of this difficulty. The client needs to be enabled to progressively relinquish efforts at regulating his or her feelings through enmeshment with others and to work toward establishing a sufficiently coherent, differentiated, and well-integrated sense of self that can tolerate differences and separation.

Early in her treatment, Ms. C. complained that her husband made critical remarks about her brother and parents and expressed the wish that "he should be nicer to them." In response to the therapist's request for clarification, she admitted that his comments were warranted, then exclaimed in considerable dismay, "But my parents have been the biggest influence in my life! I am my parents; my parents are me! Am I supposed to change at this point in my life and become like my husband?"

Ms. C. experienced her husband's criticism of her relatives as though he were criticizing her. It was hard for her to imagine that she did not need to be like her parents *or* her husband—that she could be herself!

Helping ACOAs deal with anger and repressed rage is usually a pivotal issue in treatment. They dread the anger of others, since that brings with it the threat of rejection, abandonment, or attack; and they dread their own anger, since that threatens the destruction of the loved object. When the love or attachment of parent or partner seems somewhat secure, ACOAs may engage in provocative behavior as a way of testing their full expectation of rejection. At other times anger may either be suppressed or expressed in very ineffectual or self-defeating ways. All of these fears about and modes of dealing with anger may be acted out within the context of the therapy as well as in the client's life in general. For example, the client may not show up for an appointment if he or she is feeling angry at the therapist. If the therapist is able to demonstrate to the client how he or she is handling such feelings, the client may experience considerable relief and, with support, become freed up to find more adaptive ways of dealing with anger.

Certain difficulties of ACOAs, when acted out in relation to the therapist, may contribute to countertransferential reactions on the part of the therapist. For example, it is painful for many ACOAs to acknowledge their dependency wishes. Their expectation is that their needs will never be met, and it is therefore difficult to trust the therapist's implicit offers of help, however much that help may be desired. They may powerfully defend against any display of vulnerability, holding the therapist at arm's length. Therapists who do not understand the dynamics of this may feel thwarted and frustrated. Another example involves the many ways in which anger may be acted out. For instance, anger at childhood deprivations may contribute to a sense of entitlement. This may be expressed in therapy as dissatisfaction with or denigration of helpers in general or the therapist in particular. Again, not understanding these dynamics could cause the therapist to feel personally attacked or inadequate. As in any treatment, if the client is arousing uncomfortable feelings within the therapist, it is vital that the therapist not allow him- or herself to act out those feelings (e.g., by expressing impatience or acting rejecting toward the client). Rather, the therapist must take the time to examine his or her feelings, try to understand the source as it is rooted in the client's conflicts, and demonstrate to the client how he or she is acting out conflicts in a maladaptive manner.

Sensitive treatment by a therapist who demonstrates empathy, patience, and a wish to understand, in a setting that provides consistency and clear boundaries, can make it safe for clients to rediscover a hope of finding relationships of genuine mutuality with truly available partners. They can accomplish this by acknowledging their deprivation, working through their sense of shame, and transforming their despair into the kind of mourning that allows them to let go of the *illusions* of empathic, caring parents (and thereby working through the compulsive need to reenact the childhood trauma). The self that has been injured, frightened, and hidden away can thus emerge as an authentic self capable of autonomy and a full range of feelings.

CONCLUSION

Given the large numbers of young and adult children of alcoholics and other substance abusers, given the degree of pain they suffer in childhood and the continuing painful consequences for many of them in adulthood, it is critical for therapists to be aware of the dynamics common to this population. Appropriate treatment can help clients to overcome excessive shame, guilt, boundary confusion, disabling need for control and approval, and the tendency to repeat their traumatic early experiences. The narcissistic injury and damage to the sense of self sustained as a result of impaired parental empathy can begin to be worked through with the help of informed, empathic therapists.

REFERENCES

Black, C. (1981). *It will never happen to me.* New York: Ballantine.

Cermak, T., & Rosenfeld, A. (1987). Therapeutic considerations with adult children of alcoholics. *Advances in Alcohol and Substance Abuse, 6*(4), 17–32.

Department of Health and Human Services, Office for Substance Abuse Prevention. (1988). *Children of alcoholics.* Maryland: National Clearinghouse for Alcohol and Drug Information.

Golden, G., & Hill, M. (1991). A token of loving: From melancholia to mourning. *Clinical Social Work Journal, 19*(1), 23–33.

Heller, K., Sher, K. J., & Benson, C. S. (1982). Problems associated with risk overprediction in studies of offspring of alcoholics: Implications for prevention. *Clinical Psychology Review, 2*(2), 183–200.

Hibbard, S. (1987). The diagnosis and treatment of adult children of alcoholics as a specialized therapeutic population. *Psychotherapy, 24*(4), 779–785.

Kohut, H., & Wolf, E. S. (1978). The disorders of the self and their treatment: An outline. *International Journal of Psycho-Analysis, 59,* 413–425.

Miller, A. (1981). *The drama of the gifted child.* New York: Basic Books.

Nadel, M. (1985). Offspring with fetal alcohol effects: Identification and intervention. *Alcoholism Treatment Quarterly, 2*(1), 105–116.

Norwood, R. (1985). *Women who love too much.* New York: Simon & Schuster.

Potter-Efron, R. (1987). Shame and guilt: Definitions, processes and treatment issues with AODA clients. *Alcoholism Treatment Quarterly, 4*(2), 7–24.

Richards, T., Morehouse, E., Seixas, J., & Kern, J. (1983). Psychosocial assessment and intervention with children of alcoholic parents. In D. Cook, C. Fewell, & J. Riolo (Eds.), *Social work treatment of alcohol problems.* New Brunswick, NJ: Journal of Studies on Alcohol.

Seixas, J., & Youcha, G. (1985). *Children of alcoholism: A survivor's manual.* New York: Crown.

Shengold, L. (1989). *Soul murder.* New Haven, CT: Yale University Press.

Straussner, L. (1989). Intervention with maltreating parents who are drug and alcohol abusers. In S. Ehrenkranz, E. Goldstein, L. Goodman, & J. Seinfeld (Eds.), *Clinical social work with maltreated children and their families: An introduction to practice.* New York: New York University Press.

Wegscheider, S. (1981). *Another chance: Hope and health for the alcoholic family.* Palo Alto, CA: Science and Behavior Books.

Wood, B. (1987). *Children of alcoholism: The struggle for self and intimacy in adult life.* New York: New York University Press.

Special Issues and Special Populations

V

13

Treating the Adolescent Substance Abuser

BEVERLY FEIGELMAN AND WILLIAM FEIGELMAN

Adolescent drug abuse has had a great impact on our society with its connections to crime, suicide, automobile fatalities, and a host of other social ills. Past research tells us family problems often provide the backdrop that brings forth drug abuse. Perplexing as youth drug problems may be, they are not without hope of remediation.

This chapter reviews recent research data on adolescent alcohol and drug use and abuse patterns in the United States. It looks at ways to assess, motivate, and treat adolescent substance abusers, discusses the available treatment alternatives, and reviews specific techniques that work best with adolescents.

HISTORICAL PERSPECTIVES

Although adolescent substance abuse is regarded as a modern problem, throughout American history there has been evidence of young people with alcohol abuse problems. During early colonial history, youth often left their parental homes to learn trades from craftsmen in distant towns. Estranged from their families, these adolescents often felt lonely and oppressed by their powerful masters. After working long hours these youngsters often congregated together: "The lads and wenches met when they wished, they drank rum at the taverns and they danced till late in the night. Reproved, they threatened to burn the town down" (attributed to a contemporary observer, Haskins, 1976, p. 37).

In the 1890s, Jacob Riis, studying the living conditions of the urban poor, attempted to document the incidence of drinking among children. He counted the number of children who entered a saloon and emerged with beer jugs during one 3½-hour period:

> Ten boys and a girl under ten years of age, and three girls between ten and fourteen years. . . . There was not the least concealment about the transactions in any of the fourteen cases. The children were evidently old customers. (cited in Haskins, 1976, p. 39)

In the early 1900s most teenage alcohol abusers were of low social status and little concern was expressed about this problem. Later, during Prohibition years, drinking became fashionable for many middle- and upper-class youth. After Prohibition, although drinking was somewhat less stylish and still illegal, youth alcohol consumption remained as an accepted practice.

The 1960s represented a turning point for American youth. Although alcohol had always been the chief drug of abuse among teenagers, during the 1960s there was a spectacular rise in illicit drug use when many college and high school students first began experimenting with marijuana and a variety of other psychedelic drugs (Abelson & Fishburne, 1973).

The 1970s witnessed soaring youth-crime rates and unprecedented rises in the incidence of drug-related criminal activity. It also saw a new type of drug-abusing adolescent: the polydrug abuser. Thereafter, drug abuse extended beyond the lower-class minority community and became pervasive in white middle-class suburbs as well (Mandel & Feldman, 1986).

CURRENT SUBSTANCE USE AMONG ADOLESCENTS

While the perception that youth drug use and abuse has never been as pervasive as it is now, most recent research evidence suggests that illicit drug use among teenagers may have stabilized or declined since the mid-1970s.

The annual series of systematic, large-sample surveys of drug taking among American high school seniors conducted by the University of Michigan Survey Research Center have shown a continuing decline in the use of most illicit drugs, down to just under a third of the students in 1990, compared with a high of 66% in 1979. Marijuana use showed a decline from its 1979 peak of 60% of students, as did the use of cocaine and crack, which peaked in 1986 (Treaster, 1991).

Alcohol remains the predominant drug among teenagers. Two-thirds of high school seniors considered themselves current drinkers, with 35% reporting having five or more drinks at a sitting during the previous 2 weeks.

And one-third also reported that all or most of their friends got drunk at least once a week (Johnston, O'Malley, & Bachman, 1988). Despite overall evidence showing falling youth drug use, the population of youth drug abusers still remains a significant one.

Unfortunately, many youngsters engaging in high alcohol and drug consumption tend to drop out of school prematurely or establish patterns of persistent truancy; consequently, many of these problem-prone youth may not be included in the school-based surveys. Nor may others be included in household surveys if they are living on the streets, are in jail, or are institutionalized in a variety of mental health or drug rehabilitation centers.

Every year more than 50,000 teenagers enter one or another form of care for their problems of drug dependency (Beschner & Friedman, 1985). What drives young people into the dangerous course of drug dependency?

WHAT ATTRACTS ADOLESCENTS TO SUBSTANCE USE?

The developmental tasks of adolescence place tremendous burdens on young people. For many, the use of mood-altering chemicals seems to be a way to facilitate, deny, or deal successfully with some of these expectations. Young people are required to understand and accept their biological changes, to come to terms with their emerging sexuality, to select an occupational identity, and to begin the process of separation and individuation from their parental homes.

In addition, adolescents are expected to integrate the values of the adult community with their own thoughts and feelings and are obliged to accept the limited opportunities society makes available to them. As a group and like other minorities, they lack money, power, and freedom of movement. In many instances, illegal drugs, alcohol, and tobacco may be among the few "adult" pleasures available to them.

For the adolescent substance abuser, impulsivity becomes the dominating factor. Very often behavioral choices are made purely on the basis of "what feels good." For other teenagers less habituated to drug consumption, drugs may relieve much of the status anxiety they collectively experience during this turbulent period.

Much has been written about the high correlation between low adolescent self-esteem and substance abuse (George, 1990). The development of self-esteem begins at an early age, engendered by the significant people in the young child's life, especially the parents. For preadolescents, a dramatic shift takes place: Their peers become increasingly significant role models. In most teenage peer groups youngsters are expected to engage in at least some alcohol and drug consumption.

Some teenagers may feel impelled to become drug or alcohol abusers in response to peer rejection. Lacking intimate acceptance, they may feel driven to join up with other rejects who find solace together taking drugs and engaging in other forms of antisocial conduct. Some, especially those with low self-esteem, may be provoked to engage in dangerously high levels of drug consumption.

Drug use is also influenced by media glorification of alcohol, tobacco, and the quick relief promised by many over-the-counter drugs (Gold, 1986). Many other factors have also been mentioned as important in accounting for the phenomenon of youth drug abuse: parental drug abuse, parent–child conflict, family instability, parental inconsistency, and genetic factors (see Goode [1989] or Kandel [1980] for a thorough review of much of this literature). The social acceptability of alcohol to the adult culture is yet another factor contributing to youth drug abuse (Unger, 1978).

STAGES OF ADOLESCENT ALCOHOL AND DRUG USE

While the use of drugs is pervasive among teenagers, abuse is more atypical. Sketched out below are the stages one may pass through on the way from awareness and curiosity about drugs to drug dependency. This model was adapted from MacDonald (1984) and Henricks (1989).

Awareness and Curiosity

Children of elementary school age may not be using any drugs; however, they are acutely aware that alcohol and drug use is pervasive in our society. They also possess much curiosity about what drugs are like and what kinds of effects they have on people. At this time, prevention programs in the schools and drug-free role modeling by parents may be especially important in guiding children toward a drug-free lifestyle.

Experimentation

Students of junior high school age, especially boys, are particularly prone to experimentation with mood-altering substances (glue fumes, alcohol, marijuana, etc.). Although some will discontinue use at this stage, many others will continue to explore and become regular users. If the experiences are positive, the youngster is likely to continue. If, however, experimentation results in negative consequences, such as physical illness or parental or school discipline, the adolescent will be less likely to continue.

Social Use

At the beginning of this stage adolescents incorporate drugs into their social activities, becoming "weekend drinkers" or "social users" of marijuana. Rules are usually developed for when drug use is appropriate. When drugs are around, the adolescent enjoys getting high. Later on, the adolescent may actively seek the high and arrange to have his or her own supply of drugs.

Preoccupation

During this stage, adolescents use drugs as a major part of their lives. Their focus usually is on how or when they can next get high; at this stage, one may use whatever drugs are available. Selling (dealing) drugs, shoplifting, stealing, sexual promiscuity (often in order to obtain drugs), school dysfunctionality (fights, failing grades, suspensions for misconduct) are now common correlates of high drug consumption.

Youngsters at this time often have problems with the police: vandalism, shoplifting, and drunk driving are offenses commonly encountered. They may also be inclined to fight almost constantly with their parents. Frequently, they may feel depressed and ashamed. They may also be prone to suicidal thoughts and possible suicide attempts.

Teenagers may stop drug use for a brief period during this phase, usually as a result of parental, police, or school intervention, and delude themselves into thinking they can stop using drugs any time they wish; yet most will resume drug use.

Dependency

At this stage the young person "needs drugs just to feel normal" (Henricks, 1989, p. 12). At this time, they usually use drugs alone, rather than with friends, and stay drugged most of the time. These young persons have low self-images and often project their self-hate as rage toward their parents. There is accompanying physical deterioration: weight loss, increase of somatic illnesses, memory problems, and depression. Such persons pose high risks for successful suicide.

Previously, it was believed that it would take several decades of drinking to reach a serious level of mental and physical deterioration. However, more recent literature (Bennett, Chafetz, Fitzsimmons, Fox, & Ottenberg, 1975; Royce, 1981) suggests that adolescent drinking may be more dangerous than formerly believed. According to Unger (1978):

> because of the more critical nutritional needs during body growth, disorders which would usually take ten years to form in an adult might take only two or three years to develop in an adolescent. (p. 29)

In addition, with a much wider array of potentially dangerous drugs now available and the high incidence of polydrug abuse, individuals can experience severe physical and emotional deterioration after only a few years of substance abuse.

WARNING SIGNALS

Substance abuse therapists recognize a variety of indications suggesting the presence of youth substance abuse, such as frequent moodiness and outbursts of hostility. While one or two of these symptoms may not be conclusive, several together should arouse suspicions.

During adolescence it is normal for teenagers to draw away from their families and to become more attached to their peer groups. For many, home becomes a pit stop—a place to eat, take a shower, and sleep before venturing forth again with their peers. It therefore may be difficult for parents to distinguish some of the early signs of drug use from ordinary adolescent rebelliousness and separation. Parents sometimes become the last ones to recognize their child's drug dependency. This is especially true with drug-dependent females (Vandor & Demirjian, 1990).

Gold (1986) identifies the following set of clues to substance abuse: (1) chronic lying, (2) sudden disappearance of money or valuables from the home, (3) marked mood changes, (4) abusive behavior toward the self and others, (5) frequent outbursts of hostility, (6) auto accidents, (7) frequent truancy, (8) deterioration of academic performance, (9) evidence of drug paraphernalia and preoccupation with drugs, (10) association with drug-involved peers, (11) chronic fatigue, (12) chronic sore throat or cough, and (13) chronic conjunctivitis.

MOTIVATION

Inspiring adolescents and their parents to become engaged in drug rehabilitation therapy represents one of the most demanding challenges for the clinician. Not only must one induce the adolescent patient to accept care; but caregiving efforts will never fully succeed without some level of participation from the child's parents.

Motivating the Adolescent

Motivating adolescents to get help for drug and alcohol problems is difficult. Most come into treatment under duress because parents, schools, or the criminal justice system have applied pressure. The drinking or drugging has usually come to light in connection with some undesirable behavior, such as theft, fighting, poor school performance, or some other acting-out behavior. Given this difficult beginning, one attempts to engage an adolescent in treatment by "beginning where the client is." Most adolescents will admit that some things are not all that positive in their lives, and some may even express some relief that someone is willing to listen to their side of the story. It is important to engage the adolescent and develop a relationship in which the adolescent feels comfortable talking.

For some youngsters the confines of an office may be too threatening and a less traditional therapeutic setting may be more suitable, for example, talking together while taking shots on a basketball court or on a walk doing an errand.

The adolescent's difficulty in accepting the slow and arduous task of therapy may necessitate shorter sessions, especially in the beginning. When Nina, age 15, first started treatment she said she did not want any individual sessions. Later, she asked how long these private sessions would last. Her social worker told her she could decide on any time up to 45 minutes. She selected 10 minutes. After the first 2 weeks, Nina "renegotiated" to extend her session time.

This example also illustrates how power and control issues often intermingle with the scheduling of therapy. Such accommodations on the part of the therapist can, conceivably, reduce a teenager's acting-out behavior.

In the assessment phase it is most helpful to begin with questions that arouse the least amount of anxiety; the social worker might begin with such areas as eating and sleeping habits and medical history, only later shifting to more anxiety-laden topics, such as family relations, school, or social functioning. Finally, one obtains the history of drug and alcohol use, remaining as objective and nonjudgmental as possible. It is very important to ascertain problems that may have come about as a result of drug and alcohol use, such as fights with parents or declining grades. During the earliest stages of treatment, adolescent clients often remain wary and uncommitted to the therapeutic enterprise. It therefore becomes necessary to minimize their anxiety and to help foster the development of their commitment to accepting professional help.

Adolescents' denial of drug or alcohol problems can be cut through more effectively by obtaining and using their own factual information. For example, Lisa, age 17, described how she used to think about going to college to become a nurse but now did not know if she would graduate from high school on time. Lisa had previously described her many drinking and drugging parties in the park; yet she had denied having a drug problem. When Lisa was questioned about her graduation date, a look of knowing recognition came over her face when she realized that her drug taking was interfering with the progress of her studies.

Therapists can also successfully motivate adolescents through the use of peers. Many programs use peer orienters, big brothers or sisters, and adolescent groups, claiming that the peer group can sometimes be more successful in motivating adolescents to enter treatment than one-to-one interactions with a professional.

Motivating the Family

Practitioners and researchers usually agree that adolescent drug therapy without familial involvement rarely succeeds (Feigelman, 1990; Hendin, Pollinger, Ulman, & Carr, 1981; Huberty, 1975; Reilly, 1975).

Some parents enter treatment not entirely convinced of the seriousness of their child's substance abuse problems. Others feel enmity toward their child for disrupting the family's equilibrium. When parents eventually acknowledge their child's drug problem, they often feel shame and guilt about having failed as parents. During the early stages of treatment it is important for parents to get social support for their feelings of humiliation and inadequacy.

> Mr. and Mrs. Orman brought their son Todd into treatment because of his problem with cocaine use. The treatment program recommended a drug- and alcohol-free home for at least the early stages of treatment in order to give Todd a message of complete support and to assess the importance of alcohol to the family. Mr. Orman resented the absence of alcohol in the home, blamed his current misery on his son, and took every opportunity to point out his displeasure to his wife. Mrs. Orman, while pleased with Todd's recovery, complained about the excessive amounts of food he consumed now that he was off drugs and at home during the evening hours. The parents met with their social worker, who encouraged them to share their feelings in their parent group and get support from other families who could relate to their experiences. Marital counseling sessions were also offered to the couple as a way to help them work on their relationship, which had been sorely neglected for a long time.

TREATMENT APPROACHES FOR ADOLESCENTS

There are a variety of therapeutic possibilities for dealing with teenage substance abuse. Drugs used, patterns of abuse, and the degree of psychosocial dysfunctionality are the primary criteria for recommending one or another available treatment modality.

Prevention: Psychoeducational Approaches

One of the first-line defenses against youth substance abuse is to stop misuse before it starts. Good psychoeducational programs with preadolescent populations can play an important role in insulating youngsters from the persuasive influences of their drug-taking peer groups. Psychoeducation is not easily done in a society that forbids drug use for youngsters but accepts certain kinds of dangerous drug taking among adults. It is very hard to induce young people not to use drugs when their parents and significant others tell them, "Do as I say, not as I do."

Previous research has found little success in reducing drug consumption by offering informationally oriented fear-arousing approaches. However, factual information about the hazards of drug use, which may be ignored when presented by teachers and parents, is taken more seriously when presented by peer leaders (Botvin & Wills, 1985).

Programs that enhance the development of self-esteem and interpersonal competence, that teach adolescents how to resist social pressures to use drugs, that enhance their awareness of feelings and the appropriate expression of feelings, and that teach stress management and employ positive identification figures have been found to be helpful in instilling prosocial adaptations among youth (Carroll, 1986).

Assessment

Before treating the adolescent, the clinician needs to make a thorough assessment of the patient and family. Morehouse (1989) mentions three important components to the assessment process. First, before seeing the patient, the practitioner should obtain as much information as possible from the referral source about the patient's use of alcohol and drugs as well as other pertinent details. Second, a comprehensive history of the adolescent should be acquired. This should cover the patient's physical, social, psychic, family, and school functioning, as well as experiences with law enforcement institutions. Of course, a detailed history of the patient's drug and alcohol use should also be obtained, consisting of information on the quantity, frequency, duration, patterns, and perceived health and mental consequences of the drug use. Lastly, a monitored urine test should be a component to the initial screening process, since adolescents may admit to alcohol consumption but, not wishing to upset their parents, deny any other drug use.

Treatment Modalities

There is a considerable and growing body of literature on the effects of various youth drug and alcohol treatments. A great deal is now known about most all therapeutic modalities, including the shorter- and longer-term outcomes of treatments (Collier & Hijazi, 1974; DeLeon, 1984; Hubbard, Rachal, Craddock, & Cavanaugh, 1984; Maddux & McDonald, 1973; Pin, Martin & Walsh, 1976; Simpson & Sells, 1982; Stimmel, Goldberg, Cohen, & Ratkopf, 1978; Vaillant, 1978).

Study results clearly show that, whatever the particular mode—whether methadone maintenance, therapeutic community, or outpatient drug-free programs—treatment usually succeeds (Tims, 1981). Most of these studies measure treatment successes in terms of three elements: reduction in the use of drugs, reduced criminality, and increased productive activity, such as holding a job or attending school. However, it has been more difficult to gauge the effectiveness of 12-step programs for adolescents.

Although there are a wide range of services available today, it is best to consider the least intrusive or disruptive types of approaches first, and then, if necessary, move onto more intrusive types of treatments.

Outpatient Care

Outpatient care permits the client to function in his or her home environment and to attend the treatment facility regularly for psychotherapy, counseling, or advising. In most outpatient programs for teenage drug abuse, parents are also expected to participate in the treatment process. Family therapy is often provided in addition to the diverse individual treatments. Outpatient therapies are usually available to clients whose level of abuse is judged as less acutely problematic to society and to themselves.

While the existing body of research suggests that most who undergo outpatient drug-free treatment are likely to be helped by it, the research also shows that many former patients resume some form of drug taking after treatment (Hubbard et al., 1984; Sells & Simpson, 1979). Usually the drug taking subsequent to treatment involves use of "soft" drugs, such as marijuana and alcohol. However, even these drugs may be used in smaller quantities than before treatment.

Detoxification

Detoxification may be a component of other forms of treatment, or it may be considered as a form of treatment in its own right. Hospital detoxification may be necessary for adolescent alcohol abusers who have developed such a physiological dependence that abstinence would result in serious withdrawal symptoms, such as convulsions. Detoxification is mandatory in some cases of drug dependency, such as for heroin and amphetamine addictions.

Residential or Therapeutic Community Approach

Inpatient programs, such as therapeutic communities (TCs) and hospital-based or free-standing treatment facilities, are usually reserved for those whose drug dependencies or social environment are more acutely problematic. The length of treatment varies with the facility and can range anywhere from several days to 2 or more years.

Morehouse (1989) lists several conditions that may indicate a need for an adolescent inpatient rehab or residential program:

1. The presence of a serious emotional problem in addition to alcohol and drug abuse (for example, suicidal behavior, anorexia nervosa, bulimia, or psychosis)
2. The presence of a serious medical condition
3. Physical addiction to alcohol or another drug
4. An unsuccessful experience in outpatient treatment
5. The absence of family members who support abstinence and treatment
6. The absence of appropriate and affordable outpatient programs
7. The risk that a slip or relapse would result in serious consequences, such as incarceration or physical harm

Therapeutic community programs tend to provide longer-term treatments, usually in drug-free settings. For many young drug abusers who lack internal controls, this complete extrication from their drug-using peer groups may be absolutely necessary. Also, residential treatment readily regulates the amount of association between adolescent patients and their families, which, in cases of extreme conflict, provides a respite for all family members.

Residential treatment facilities use any number of therapeutic approaches: conventional psychotherapies, peer confrontation, behavior conditioning, academic and vocational counseling, drug education programs, and milieu therapies. If the residential program is within traveling distance of the patient's family, they, too, can be direct participants in the therapeutic process and can begin to work on improving family functioning.

When referring an adolescent to an inpatient setting, several important treatment issues require consideration, such as whether the facility is appropriate for and sensitive to an adolescent's needs and whether the young person will feel alienated in a ward full of adult patients. Another concern involves the potential for secondary gains. As a psychiatric or drug rehab inpatient, one may be entitled to a variety of "perks," such as solicitous responses from friends and family, gifts, and being relieved of various household chores. For some youngsters, hospitalization may appear to be a way out of a difficult situation, as illustrated in the example below:

> Kevin, a 16-year-old, with an extensive history of polydrug abuse, was seen in an intensive after-school treatment program. A behavioral contract was drawn up with certain conditions, including no drugs and no truancy. If Kevin did not comply, he would be recommended for daycare treatment for a minimum of 8 months. Kevin violated all of the conditions of his contract. When his parents attempted to have him begin daycare, Kevin threatened suicide. His parents, in fear and desperation, had Kevin admitted to an inpatient psychiatric hospital. Kevin appeared to enjoy his stay at the hospital. He no longer had to follow the house rules, was visited regularly, and received phone calls and some gifts from relatives. After 28 days, Kevin was discharged back into the community; shortly thereafter he resumed drug use.

Although in this particular case, Kevin's threats of suicide were merely a device to control his treatment, suicidal ideation and gestures should always be taken seriously and evaluated professionally. This is especially true among adolescents, whose judgment and impulse control are often wanting.

One of the problems in applying an inpatient approach is in reconciling the heavily regulated atmosphere of the treatment center and the less restrictive civilian society. Many patients encounter difficulty in readjusting to the society outside the treatment facility. This issue is frequently addressed by creating any number of transitional stages of "reentry" status, preparing the individual for conventional social participation. Yet despite such interim stages, many adolescents still encounter difficulties in changing from successfully adapted clients into drug-free civilians.

Daycare: A Middle-Ground Approach

Daycare represents a middle ground of treatment for adolescents: Daycare patients are supervised at the treatment facility during weekdays, then return to their homes on evenings and weekends. The treatment regimen usually consists of many of the same elements offered in residential programs: conventional psychotherapies, peer confrontation, behavioral conditioning, psychotropic medication, and so forth. This treatment mode, although a more intrusive intervention than outpatient care, is a far less all-encompassing approach than residential treatment.

To accomplish its objectives, adolescent daycare may rely heavily upon parents to monitor the progress of therapy and to help in the realization of treatment goals when clients are not at the treatment facility. Daycare treatment, obviously, is not appropriate for many adolescent drug abusers; those lacking available and committed parents are not likely to be successful with it.

Because of its particular requirements, daycare is not a common form of drug treatment for teenagers. Beschner and Friedman (1986) indicate that there are only about 50 such programs nationally, compared to the countless number of residential and outpatient treatment facilities.

12-Step Programs

Although not considered treatment per se, 12-step programs must be included in any comprehensive discussion of recovery from addictions. All 12-step programs are based on the original self-help concept of Alcoholics Anonymous (AA). Morehouse (1989) lists several benefits to adolescents who participate in 12-step programs: seeing role models who have "made it"; reducing shame by sharing experiences with others who have "been there"; becoming involved with caring and empathic adults—a second-chance family; educational involvement with a sponsor; continuous and ongoing support; and as an activity to fill the void left by not using drugs.

Much has been written about adolescent resistance to self-help groups. Not having faced many serious life crises, they cannot relate to stories shared at meetings by older AA members and say: "I'll do something about it when it gets that bad." A generation gap may impede many adolescents from engaging themselves in these groups.

Some youth resistance may also stem from the reluctance of many professionals to endorse 12-step groups for adolescents. Afraid of diluting the therapeutic relationship, many counselors express misgivings about the value of sponsorship and other aspects of 12-step fellowships. Yet more young people apparently are participating in these self-help groups. This was demonstrated in a 1983 random sample survey of 7,611 AA members; 20% of the group were under 30 years of age, a 5% increase over the 1980 survey result (Graeber, 1985).

Fortunately, many adolescent drug treatment programs now incorporate the 12-step model and either facilitate on-site meetings or recommend that their teenage clients seek them out in their home communities. Group therapy can help youngsters become more comfortable in self-help groups such as AA (Morehouse, 1989). Another positive benefit of 12-step referrals is that a counselor who refers an adolescent to self-help is also sending a message: "I am not all-powerful; I accept my limitations and reach out for extra support." This role modeling may enable an adolescent to accept their own dependency needs more realistically (Unger, 1978).

SUBSTANCE ABUSE AND PSYCHIATRIC DISORDERS

In recent years the lines demarcating substance abuse from psychiatric disorders have begun to blur. Increasing numbers of patients with obvious mental health problems are beginning to enter drug treatment centers. Similarly, increasing numbers of mental health patients are showing signs of substance abuse and dependency.

One 800-COCAINE survey showed that 68% of the teenage callers reported being depressed, with 28% having active thoughts of suicide and 12% reporting suicide attempts (Semlitz & Gold, 1987). Another 800-COCAINE survey showed that 22% of the teenage callers met DSM-III-R criteria for bulimia (Jonas, Gold, Sweeney, & Pottash, 1987). In mental health facilities similar trends are being observed; a study of 300 chronically mentally ill young adults showed that 37% had a known history of marijuana abuse, 37% had a known history of alcohol abuse, and 28% had a known history of other drug abuse (Pepper, 1985).

Many teenagers treated in drug or alcohol programs also experience psychiatric symptoms, such as depression and suicidal ideation. Others have been observed to possess a variety of psychiatric problems, including affective disorders, anxiety disorders, eating disorders, conduct disorders, and attention-deficit disorders, among other psychiatric difficulties. Chemical dependency and mental illness mutually affect each other. Many chronically mentally ill teenagers use drugs and alcohol in an effort to medicate themselves and to deny their psychiatric illnesses. Others may be inclined to pursue suicidal or hostile impulses under the influence of drugs or alcohol. Among mentally ill young adults, chemical abuse can precipitate the onset of psychiatric difficulties and can interfere with efforts to treat psychiatric disorders.

If not properly diagnosed, psychiatric illness may interfere with the effectiveness of any drug treatment program. Therefore a thorough biopsychosocial assessment must include not only patients' substance use but also their own history of psychiatric illness and a family history of substance use and psychiatric illness(es).

Most drug treatment professionals will want the patient completely detoxified of all drugs before making anything more than a tentative psychiatric diagnosis or before offering a prescription for any psychotropic medication. It may be impossible to judge the need for and the effect of medication in a young person whose body and nervous system are still under the influence of mood-altering street drugs.

THE ROLE OF THE SOCIAL WORKER IN ADOLESCENT SUBSTANCE ABUSE TREATMENT

When working with adolescents, the counselor needs to be a real person—with thoughts, ideas, feelings, hobbies, and interests. Fischer (1987) describes this as "getting down" to the level of the patient, talking about music, sports, fashion, and the other subjects of interest to youth. Fischer also suggests the use of humor, frivolity, and silliness. Humor can go a long way to diffuse a potentially sensitive or explosive topic, as the following example demonstrates:

> During an outpatient group session for adolescents, Peter, age 15, spoke of his anger toward his father: "He puts me down all the time." When the group asked for an example, Peter said his father often called him "an asshole." Members of the group supported Peter's anger. He became more visibly incensed, preparing himself for a fight when he went home that evening.
>
> The social worker decided to take another stance to reduce the tension. She suggested that Peter's father was actually paying him a compliment: "After all, an asshole is an extremely useful thing to have. Imagine what we'd all look and feel like, if after a week or two of eating, we didn't have assholes." The group and Peter first looked at the social worker in stark amazement and then broke out into hysterical laughter.

Social workers also need to be actively involved with their adolescent clients; a laid-back, passive approach is usually doomed to fail. As counselors participate in activities with their clients, accompanying them to court appearances, visiting them in hospital emergency rooms, and so forth, clients begin to place more trust in them and to gain more benefits from therapy.

Many activities with adolescents take place outside the agency premises—recreational events, fieldtrips, cultural activities, and so forth. One social worker recalled spending a day riding in the back of a crowded agency van, surrounded by wet bodies and damp pillows, and listening to loud heavy metal music after an aborted rock-climbing trip ended with a rainy cookout. Despite the frustrated plans, the kids loved the day. After the worker recovered from her fatigue, she acknowledged her own enjoyment too and sensed that a deeper bond had been established with the youngsters during the day's misguided adventures; she later found group therapy sessions with these youngsters far more meaningful and effective.

Workers need to be in close touch with their own feelings and adolescent experiences, yet distant enough not to get caught up in power struggles with the youngsters or to overidentify to the detriment of advancing therapeutic goals.

Workers need to be open to adolescent recovery issues. Sexuality is one such concern. Early sexual acting out among substance-abusing adolescents is a familiar pattern. At the same time, paradoxically, many of these adolescents may know little about their bodies and of genuine intimacy.

Also, in many families with a history of alcohol abuse there is often a high incidence of incest or other manifestations of sexual victimization. The worker needs to reduce the feelings of guilt and self-blame that often accompany sexually abused adolescent drug patients. Frequently, such sexual guilt and abuse can precipitate drug abuse and other acting-out behavior. If the patient remains at risk of continued sexual victimization, he or she must be protected through legal and environmental interventions.

The worker needs to be able to teach social skills and relapse-prevention techniques. For most teenagers, social maturation stops when drug use starts. Adolescents need to be taught alternative ways of dealing with stress, of resisting social pressures, and of reducing impulsivity. For example, impulse control might be taught to an agitated adolescent by encouraging him or her to find a quiet place to "cool off" before letting anger turn into uncontrollable rage. Once calm, the adolescent is then taught to use verbal communication rather than action to express feelings and resolve conflict. The adolescent is also encouraged to practice these techniques in dealing with family difficulties. This skill training helps adolescents acquire appropriate socialization skills, stress management techniques, and communication proficiency.

CONCLUSION

Treating the adolescent substance abuser is a challenge of immense proportions to the social work practitioner. The restless energy and emotional intensity of troubled adolescents frighten many clinicians away from this population. Yet for those who are undaunted, the work can be extremely exciting and fulfilling. With the great potential for change and growth during the dynamic years of adolescence, even modest interventions can make a durable impact on a young person's life. For the teenager, a little help, purposefully focused, can go a long, long way. Thus serving this population with appropriate interventions can provide clinicians with a rich bounty of treatment successes.

REFERENCES

Abelson, H., & Fishburne, P. (1973). Drug experience, attitudes and related behavior among adolescents and adults. In National Commission on Marijuana and Drug Abuse, *Drug use in America: Problem in perspective* (Vol. 1, pp. 488–861). Washington, DC: U.S Government Printing Office.

Bennett, J. A., Chafetz, M. E., Fitzsimmons, M., Fox, V., & Ottenberg, D. (1975). Who will help the teenage alcohol abuser? *Patient Care*, 9(16), 88–117.

Beschner, G., & Friedman, A. S. (1985). Treatment of adolescent drug abusers. *International Journal of the Addictions*, 20(6 & 7), 971–993.

Beschner, G., & Friedman, A. S. (Eds.). (1986). *Teen drug abuse.* Lexington, MA: Lexington Books.

Botvin, G., & Wills, T. (1985). Personal and social skills training: Cognitive-behavioral approaches to substance abuse prevention. In C. Bell & R. Battjes (Eds.), *Prevention research: Deterring drug abuse among children and adults* (NIDA Research Monograph No. 63, pp. 8–49). Rockville, MD: National Institute on Drug Abuse.

Carroll, J. (1986). Secondary prevention: A pragmatic approach to the problem of substance abuse among adolescents. In G. Beschner & A. S. Friedman (Eds.), *Teen drug abuse* (pp. 164–184). Lexington, MA: Lexington Books.

Collier, W. V., & Hijazi, Y. A. (1974). A followup study of former residents of a therapeutic community. *International Journal of the Addictions*, 9, 805–826.

DeLeon, G. (1984). *The therapeutic community: Study of effectiveness* (Treatment Research Monograph Series, DHHS Pub. No. (ADM)84-1286). Rockville, MD: National Institute on Drug Abuse.

Feigelman, W. (1990). *Treating teen age drug abuse in a day care setting.* New York: Praeger.

Fischer, J. (1987). Psychotherapy of adolescent alcohol abusers. In S. Zimberg, J. Wallace, & S. Blume (Eds.), *Practical approaches to alcoholism psychotherapy* (2nd ed., pp. 295–313). New York: Plenum.

George, R. L. (1990). *Counseling the chemically dependent: Theory and practice.* Englewood Cliffs, NJ: Prentice-Hall.

Gold, M. D. (1986). *The facts about drugs and alcohol.* New York: Bantam.

Goode, E. (1989). *Drugs in American society* (3rd ed.). New York: Knopf.

Graeber, L. (1985). *Are you dying for a drink?* New York: Messner.

Haskins, J. (1976). *Teen age alcoholism.* New York: Hawthorn.

Hendin, H., Pollinger, A., Ulman, R., & Carr, A. (1981). *Adolescent marijuana abusers and their families* (NIDA Research Monograph No. 40). Washington, DC: U.S. Government Printing Office.

Henricks, L. (1989). *Kids who do/kids who don't: A parent's guide to teens and drugs.* Summit, NJ: PIA Press.

Hubbard, R., Rachal, J., Craddock, S., & Cavanaugh, E. (1984). Treatment outcome prospective study (TOPS): Client characteristics and behaviors before, during and after treatment. In F. Tims & J. Ludford (Eds.), *Drug abuse treatment evaluation: Strategies, progress and prospects* (NIDA Research Monograph No. 51, pp. 42–68). Washington, DC: U.S. Government Printing Office.

Huberty, D. J. (1975). Treating the adolescent drug abuser: A family affair. *Contemporary Drug Problems*, 4, 179–194.

Johnston, L., O'Malley, P., & Bachman, J. (1988). *Illicit drug use, smoking and drinking by America's high school students, college students, and young adults, 1975–1987.* Washington, DC: U.S. Government Printing Office.

Jonas, J. M., Gold, M. S., Sweeney, D. S., & Pottash, A. L. C. (1987). Eating disorders and cocaine abuse: A survey of 259 cocaine abusers. *Journal of Clinical Psychiatry*, 48(2), 47–50.

Kandel, D. (1980). Drug and drinking behavior among youth. *Annual Review of Sociology, 6,* 235-285.

MacDonald, D. I. (1984). *Drugs, drinking, and adolescents.* Chicago: Yearbook Medical Publishers.

Maddux, J. F., & McDonald, L. K. (1973). Status of 100 San Antonio addicts after admission to methadone maintenance. *Drug Forum, 2,* 239.

Mandel, J., & Feldman, H. W. (1986). The social history of teenage drug use. In G. Beschner & A. S. Friedman (Eds.), *Teen drug abuse* (pp. 19-42). Lexington, MA: Lexington Books.

Morehouse, E. (1989). Treating adolescent alcohol abusers. *Social Casework, 70*(6), 355-363.

Pepper, B. (1985). The young adult chronic patient: Population overview. *Journal of Clinical Psychopharmacology, 5*(3) (Suppl.), 75-82.

Pin, E. J., Martin, J. M., & Walsh, J. F. (1976). A followup study of 300 ex-clients of a drug free narcotic treatment program in New York City. *American Journal of Drug and Alcohol Abuse, 3,* 397-407.

Reilly, D. M. (1975). Family factors in the etiology and treatment of youthful drug abuse. *Family Therapy, 2,* 149-171.

Royce, J. (1981). *Alcohol problems and alcoholism.* New York: Free Press.

Sells, S. B., & Simpson, D. D. (1979). Evaluation of treatment outcomes for youths in the drug abuse reporting program (DARP): A followup study. In G. M. Beschner & A. S. Friedman (Eds.), *Youth drug abuse: Problems, issues and treatments* (pp. 571-613). Lexington, MA: Heath.

Semlitz, L., & Gold, M. S. (1987). Diagnosis and treatment of adolescent substance abuse. *Psychiatric Medicine, 3*(4), 321-335.

Simpson, D. D., & Sells, S. B. (1982). Effectiveness of treatment for drug abuse: An overview of the DARP research program. *Advances in Alcohol and Substance Abuse, 2*(1), 7-29.

Stimmel, B., Goldberg, J., Cohen, M., & Ratkopf, E. (1978). Detoxification for methadone maintenance: Risk factors associated with relapse to narcotic use. *Annals of the New York Academy of Sciences, 311,* 173-180.

Tims, F. (1981). *Effectiveness of drug abuse treatment programs* (Treatment Research Monograph Series, DHHS Pub. No. (ADM)81-1143). Rockville, MD: National Institute on Drug Abuse.

Treaster, J. B. (1991, January 25). Drop in youths' cocaine use may reflect a societal shift. *New York Times,* p. A-18.

Unger, R. (1978). The treatment of adolescent alcoholism. *Social Casework, 59*(1), 27-35.

Vaillant, G. (1978). A 20-year followup of New York narcotic addicts. *Archives of General Psychiatry, 29,* 237-241.

Vandor, M., & Damirjian, A. (1990, April). Yes I can't—Confusion and drug use during adolescence. *New York Department of Substance Abuse Services Newsletter,* p. 20.

14

Issues in Assessment and Intervention with Alcohol- and Drug-Abusing Women

PATRICIA A. PAPE

Since ancient times, women who are alcoholics or have other drug dependencies have been the victims of extreme stigma and stereotyping. An old Romulus law decreed women who engaged in adultery and drinking could be sentenced to death. Even today, female alcoholics and drug addicts are often treated with rejection, disgust, prejudice, or apathy and indifference.

The purpose of this chapter is to review the research on substance-abusing women, including differences between men and women and also among women themselves. Issues related to assessment and treatment are discussed.

PREVALENCE OF ALCOHOL AND DRUG ABUSE IN WOMEN

Although estimating the magnitude of alcohol and other drug abuse among females is difficult, national and special surveys consistently point to the fact that substance abuse is a serious problem among American women today. It is estimated that of the 15.1 million alcohol-abusing or alcohol-dependent individuals in the United States, approximately 4.6 million are women. (National Institute on Alcohol Abuse and Alcoholism [NIAAA], 1990). Studies of drug and alcohol prevalence in the workplace indicate that at least 8½% of the total female work force is alcoholic or drug addicted.

Johnston, O'Malley, and Bachman's (1987) national study of college students indicates the annual prevalence rate for females for substances other than alcohol is as follows: marijuana, 37%; tobacco, 26%; cocaine, 15%; stimulants, 11%; LSD, 2%; heroin, 1%; barbiturates, 1%; and opiates other

than heroin, 1%. The National Institute on Drug Abuse (NIDA, 1989) estimates that of women of childbearing age (15–44 years of age), 15% are
current substance abusers, and as many as 375,000 babies each year may be
born to mothers who used drugs while they were pregnant.

DIFFERENCES BETWEEN ALCOHOLIC MEN AND WOMEN

Recent research has indicated significant differences between men and
women in how their bodies handle alcohol and how alcohol dependency
progresses in each (Straussner, 1985). Studies have shown that since wom-
en's bodies have more fatty and less muscle tissue (and therefore less water),
they tend to absorb alcohol faster and become intoxicated sooner on the
same amount of alcohol compared to men of equivalent body weight. Studies
also show that the level of sex hormones in the body determines the effect
alcohol has on women. Thus women are more easily intoxicated just prior to
their menstrual period. Women using birth control pills have an additional
complication. Since both alcohol and birth control pills metabolize in the
liver, causing alcohol to remain in the body longer, women who take birth
control pills will have higher blood alcohol levels.

Alcohol dependency also has been found to progress more quickly in
women—the "telescoping" effect—and the progression itself may be different from that of men. With lower intake and fewer years of drinking than
men, women will incur more fatty liver, hepatic cirrhosis, hypertension,
anemia, malnutrition, and gastrointestinal hemorrhage. They experience
more negative moods, more drinking to relieve tension and depression, and
more solitary drinking during menstruation. Heavy drinking among women
correlates with infertility, lack of sexual functioning, inability to reach or-
gasm, and other obstetric and gynecologic dysfunctions (Blume, 1988).

Chronic abuse of alcoholic beverages during reproductive years has
been reported to be associated not only with irregular menstrual cycles but
also with early menopause. Alcohol abuse during the postmenopausal years
increases estrogen levels and thus raises the risk of osteoporosis and cardiovascular disease (Gavaler, 1990).

Women more often state that their heavy drinking began as a result of a
specific psychological stress or circumstance, often involving a loss or perceived threat of loss. In comparison to men, who often drink to be sociable,
women's drinking and drug use is more of a self-medication to escape
tension, anxiety, and problems (Straussner, 1985). Often cited as antecedents
to problem drinking are issues related to sex-role conflicts, sex-role confusion, and sexual identity problems. Also, a significant number of women
report sexual dysfunction, menstrual difficulties, and a history of other

gynecologic problems. Whether these precede or result from heavy alcohol and drug use needs to be further addressed.

Numerous studies of women in treatment indicate that women who abuse alcohol or drugs are more likely than their male counterparts to come from families with a history of alcoholism. Gomberg (1976, 1980) states there is more loss, more depression, and a greater number of other psychiatric problems in their families than in those of male abusers. She also found that a high percentage were children of alcoholics. These women had poor relationships with their mothers and had exhibited more emotional and behavioral problems as children than had substance-abusing men.

Studies estimate that 20% to 75% of adult women and 71% to 90% of teenage girls in treatment have been sexually abused (Gomberg & Lisansky, 1984; Rohsenow, Corbitt, & Devine, 1988). Sexual victimization has a direct effect on adolescent drug use whereas physical abuse has an indirect effect, the latter resulting in self-medication for low self-esteem (Dembo et al., 1987).

Studies also show that women are more apt than men to attempt suicide—usually by overdosing with legally prescribed pills, and have more primary affective disorders. Both the use and abuse of pills, especially minor tranquilizers and sedative–hypnotics, tend to be higher among alcoholic women than alcoholic men or women in the general population (Straussner, 1985). The following data reported by Davis (1990) illustrate the growing problem: 60% of all prescribed tranquilizers, 71% of all antidepressant prescriptions, and 80% of all amphetamines are prescribed for women. While drug-related emergency room visits for men are likely to be a result of using street drugs, for women they are due to using prescription drugs. The tendency for women to be more open about seeking help for emotional problems combined with a possible greater tendency for physicians to prescribe medication for women is potentially a deadly combination.

DIFFERENCES AMONG SUBGROUPS
OF ALCOHOLIC WOMEN

In addition to differences between male and female alcoholics, there are differences among subgroups within the female population according to a variety of variables: socioeconomic status, employment status, sexual preference, age, minority status, racial or cultural variables, and differential diagnosis. A summary of some of these findings related to alcohol is reported by Wilsnack (1990) and Straussner (1985).

In terms of socioeconomic status, rates of drinking (nonabstention) tend to be higher among women at higher levels of education and income, but rates of drinking problems and alcohol dependence symptoms are not consistently related to socioeconomic levels.

Black women have higher rates of abstention than do white women. However, the tendency of black female drinkers to drink more heavily than white female drinkers may have disappeared during the last decade. Hispanic women are more likely to be abstainers and less likely to be heavy drinkers than either non-Hispanic women or Hispanic men. Available data suggest that American Indian women experienced higher rates of fetal alcohol syndrome and higher rates of alcohol-related deaths, including death from liver cirrhosis, than either black or white women.

Most surveys have found higher rates of heavy drinking and drinking problems among women who are divorced or separated or who have never married than among women who are married or widowed. Also, cohabiting women are more likely to drink heavily or have drinking problems. Also at risk are women experiencing depression, sexual dysfunction, or reproductive disorders; those with nontraditional gender-role orientations or nontraditional sexual behavior; and those who have heavy-drinking significant others.

Wilsnack (1990) found little recent evidence to support the once-popular belief that women with multiple roles (married women with paid employment outside the home) are at especially high risk for alcohol abuse. In fact, women combining marital and employment roles may have lower rates of alcohol problems than women who lack these roles (unmarried, unemployed, employed part-time). "Role deprivation"—a lack of meaningful social roles—may increase women's risk for unrestrained or self-medicative use of alcohol and/or other drugs.

EFFECTS OF MARIJUANA, COCAINE, AND HEROIN ON WOMEN

The effects of alcohol abuse on women have been fairly well documented and researched. Less researched are the effects of other often-abused drugs: marijuana, cocaine, and heroin. Much of the research is focused on the harm done by alcohol or drugs to the unborn fetus in pregnant women, and less on the women themselves.

Marijuana is generally found to be the top-ranking illegal drug of abuse among adolescent and adult women. There are more than 421 chemicals in marijuana, including some 70 cannabinoids or psychoactive elements. The most significant cannabinoid, delta-9-tetra-hydrocannabinol (THC), causes the familiar marijuana "high," or state of intoxication. The potency of marijuana is determined by the amount of THC it contains. Marijuana today has up to ten times more THC than that used in the 1970s and therefore is more potent and more harmful (Moulton & Moulton, 1984).

All cannabinoids, which are fat-soluble, react on living cells by interfering with the cell's ability to manufacture pivotal molecules. The body is rich in fat and fat-like materials (called lipids), and women have more fat content than men. So the body—especially a woman's body—can store a lot of THC. THC slows down the production of DNA, RNA, and protein replacement. This causes cellular activity to decrease and eventually to stop, leading to cell death. This would seem to present more of a problem to women, with their higher content of body fat, than to men.

Studies also show that the effects of marijuana on female reproduction may be long-lasting (Moulton & Moulton, 1984). An infant girl is born with a lifetime supply of eggs, and if these are damaged, there is no replacement. THC can irreversibly damage the entire supply of the ovaries' eggs.

Cocaine acts on the central and peripheral nervous systems. It prevents the reuptake of norepinephrine, prolongs catecholamine stimulation of the receptors, and acts to increase dopamine concentration. The increase in concentration of norepinephrine may cause a marked rise in blood pressure, vasoconstriction, and tachycardia (Creglar, 1989). Cocaine also lowers the seizure threshold (Johnston et al., 1983). In pregnancy, cocaine use has been associated with placental abruption (Chasnoff, Burns, Schnoll, & Burns, 1985).

Many cocaine-abusing females exhibit symptoms common to all substance-abusing women: impairment of their capacity to recognize and regulate emotions, lowered self-esteem, and difficulties in their relationships. Krystal (1982) talks about an inability to differentiate various feeling states that occurs particularly with cocaine-abusing women. Khantzian (1987) also sees cocaine-abusing women as suffering from "related painful affect states" that are unique to cocaine addicts and that interact with the psychotropic effects of cocaine to make these affect states powerfully compelling. It is the intensity of this compulsion that makes the cocaine-addicted woman particularly prone to relapse.

Heroin, produced by the acetylation of morphine, has two to four times the analgesic power of its parent drug and has become one of the major drugs of abuse. The toxic effects of heroin are related to the method used for preparation. Quinine is one of the more popular diluents, and quinine toxicity damages internal organs (Sternbach, Moran, & Eliastram, 1980). Subcutaneous injection of heroin, "skin popping," common in female addicts, results in abscesses and cellulitis (Jaffe & Martin, 1985).

Heroin and other opiates act centrally at the hypothalamic level to alter hormone secretion and to disrupt the menstrual cycle (Gawin & Kleber, 1985). Secondary amenorrhea is common in female heroin abusers, as is severe dysmenorrhea and venereal disease. Sexual dysfunction in the intravenous drug abuser has been well documented, as has lack of sexual desire and decreased performance (Smith et al., 1982).

The increasing problem of the risk for HIV infection to women who are intravenous drug users (IDUs) warrants special attention. The National AIDS Demonstration Research (NADR) Project (NIDA, 1989) produced data on 5,280 female sexual partners of IDUs. These data confirm that women who are sexual partners of IDUs are at multiple risk for HIV infection. Few women (less than 10%) reported using condoms during vaginal, oral, or anal sex. A large proportion had not used new or bleach-cleaned needles, yet a high proportion had shared needles with two or more persons, with many injecting daily. Over half of the women had further compromised their immune systems, as well as their judgment, by use of alcohol. A majority of these women are in their prime childbearing years, and many have substantial child care responsibilities.

Why do these women continue to put themselves at risk by practicing unsafe sex with multiple partners? The answers lie in the issues of sexual abuse, violence, and victimization. These women tend to have low self-esteem, dissociate frequently, experience phobic reactions, and have difficulty with intimate relationships. A history of painful or victimizing experiences, combined with fear of a currently abusive partner, will interfere with a woman's ability to assert herself and to reduce HIV risks. Until she feels empowered to make choices, she is at high risk to continue in ongoing victimizing relationships and therefore to be subject to ongoing risk for HIV infection.

IMPACT OF ALCOHOL AND OTHER DRUGS ON FETAL DEVELOPMENT

Ethanol and its metabolites can cause a wide range of physiologic and neurologic disturbances in fetal development. The most extreme manifestation of alcohol's effects, fetal alcohol syndrome (FAS), includes growth retardation, facial dysmorphology, central nervous system anomalies, and morphologic abnormalities. Less severely affected people are considered to have fetal alcohol effects (FAE). Incidence figures for FAS are estimated to be 1.9 per thousand live births (Abel & Sokol, 1987), and it is the third leading cause of mental retardation. It is likely that FAE occurs three times more frequently than FAS.

The following are some of the effects of other drugs on the babies born to mothers who used these drugs during their pregnancies:

1. Marijuana users gave birth to babies who were, on average, 3 ounces lighter and one-fifth of an inch shorter than babies of nonusers. These babies also had a smaller head circumference, pointing toward possible problems with brain development. These findings indicate that the pot smoker may not only be damaging her own mind and body, but may be playing genetic roulette with her unborn children (Moulton & Moulton, 1984).

2. Cocaine-using mothers have five times as many babies with birth defects as nonusing mothers, and the rate of sudden infant death syndrome (SIDS) is more than ten times higher in this population than in the general population (17% compared to 1.6%). Their babies were even lighter and shorter than those of marijuana users. Cocaine precipitates miscarriage or premature delivery by raising blood pressure and increasing uterine contractions. It also causes premature separation of the placenta, which can produce life-threatening hemorrhaging. The drug constricts arteries leading to the womb, thus diminishing the amount of blood, hence oxygen, reaching the fetus. In the extreme, it can cause fetal stroke. Cocaine-exposed infants are at high risk for motor developmental dysfunction.

3. The rate of SIDS is five to ten times than that of the general population among the infants of women who use opiates.

4. Infants exposed to narcotics undergo a characteristic withdrawal sequence called the neonatal abstinence syndrome (NAS). These newborns show increased sensitivity to noise, irritability, poor coordination, excessive sneezing and yawning, and uncoordinated sucking and swallowing reflexes. If the symptoms persist, they may require medication. These babies tend to have smaller head circumferences, raising questions about brain growth, which could affect such mental functions as memory.

ISSUES RELATING TO FAMILIES OF ALCOHOL- AND DRUG-ADDICTED WOMEN

Three major issues relating to the families of the alcoholic- or drug-addicted woman are: (1) family-of-origin issues, (2) the effects of her substance abuse on her present family, and (3) the high correlation between alcohol or drug abuse and domestic violence.

Alcohol- and drug-addicted women have a higher percentage of alcoholic relatives than women who develop other problems. Women most at risk are those with a family history of alcoholism on both sides of the family, especially those with an alcoholic biological mother (Bohman, Sigvardsson, & Cloninger, 1981). Studies indicate that women with alcoholic fathers have higher rates of depression, inability to make friends as children, somatoform illness, and eating disorders, as well as a high propensity to marry an alcoholic male.

Ackerman (1987), in his research on adult children of alcoholics found that women with an alcoholic father have greater problems with intimacy, whereas women with an alcoholic mother have higher rates of chemical dependency. Early childhood risk factors for substance abuse in women appear to be one or both parents with a drinking problem, poor relationships with their mothers, lack of approval from parents, feelings of childhood deprivation, lack of social support, sexual and physical abuse, and family role reversals wherein daughters feel responsible for their parents' well-being and marriage.

Several dynamics are commonly perceived in a substance-abusing women's current family: Men are more likely to leave their addicted wives (whereas women stay with their addicted husbands); an addicted woman is emotionally, and sometimes physically, unavailable to her children; and family denial and protectionism generally are higher, and the rules and roles in these dysfunctional families perpetuate the dysfunction, the denial, and the keeping of secrets.

Substance-abusing women and those involved with substance abusers are frequently the victims of family violence. Problem drinking was reported by 85% of battered women using a crisis hotline (Seligman, 1975). Other statistics show that 65% of batterers abused alcohol and two-thirds of assaults were alcohol-related (Fojtik, 1977–1978). In violent lesbian relationships, 35% of batterers were under the influence of alcohol or other drugs at the time of the abuse (Renzetti, 1988). Batterers with histories of substance abuse were more frequently violent and produced more serious injuries than those without histories of substance abuse (Browne, 1987).

Battered women who abuse alcohol tend to be older (Eberle, 1982). Those who reported the heaviest drinking patterns were those in relationships with men who also abused alcohol (Walker, 1979). Substance-abusing battered women face special dangers, since the chemicals make them less able to respond or to escape injuries. Moreover, they may be rejected at domestic violence shelters because of their substance abuse. These women face the double stigma of being an addicted as well as a battered woman.

As many as 85% of children from such homes tend to abuse alcohol (as early as age 11), and 50% abuse other drugs. They use drugs to gain self-respect with peers and to take the edge off facing the violence at home (Weisinfluh & Aniolkowski, 1988).

BARRIERS TO TREATMENT

For the most part, women do not get identified through our legal and criminal justice systems. One of the major reasons for this is the "male protectionism" and enabling by male police officers. While alcohol-related traffic accidents and fatalities are more common among men than among women, the number of female drivers in such fatal traffic accidents increased 37% between 1977 and 1985 (Zobeck, Grant, Williams, & Bertolucci, 1987), with younger women most likely to drive after drinking. Despite these statistics, approximately 90% of those entering drunken driver programs are men (Laign, 1987).

Furthermore, women are neither being identified nor entering treatment at the same rate as men. This "disgraceful discrepancy" (Pape, 1986) has been documented in much research literature. Estimates based on a National Drug and Alcoholism Treatment Unit Survey and national prevalence data indicate that 1 of 3 (perhaps 1 of 2) alcoholics in the United States is a woman, yet only 1 of 20 of these women is in treatment in a given year. Of the other drug users, 2 of 5 are women but only 1 of 50 of these women is in treatment in a given year. In spite of the consistent call for specialized treatment programs for women, only 27% of treatment units offer such specialized programs, and the proportion is not increasing (Chatham, 1990).

Employee assistance programs (EAPs) are also recognizing alcohol and drug abuse problems in the workplace earlier and more often in men than in women. Sullivan's (1979) study of company alcoholism programs found that only 3% of clients referred for treatment were women, although women represented 22% of the employee sample. She concluded that "when 50 percent of alcoholics are women, and 47 percent of the American workforce are women, it appears that alcoholism/employee assistance programs have not impacted the working woman as significantly as they have the working man" (p. 20).

One reason for the "gender gap" appears to be the fact that women tend to be stuck in low-level jobs, working below their potential and capacity. Another reason may be due to behavioral differences in female alcoholics and addicts, as well as gender-related deficiencies in the systems used to identify and treat them. Correcting this will require modification of EAP assessment procedures, improved supervisory training, and better or different models of referral (NIAAA, 1980). An increase in female EAP counselors and administrators will help to bring about needed changes.

While detection of early-stage alcohol and drug abuse problems is difficult in general, it is even more difficult among women because of their high levels of guilt and shame. Women try harder to hide their alcohol and drug problems, and they often succeed. Because many women are stuck in low-level jobs, it is often easier to replace them than to treat and retain them. Women are often less valued as employees; companies have less invested in their training. Female employees cooperate in this process by quitting rather than seeking help for their alcohol and drug problems. Family, friends, coworkers, and supervisors help protect and cover up these problems because they, too, are embarrassed or do not know what to do—and the denial goes on and on.

Women tend to present with problems other than substance abuse—most often family or relationship problems. Clues to female substance abuse often lie in the area of inconsistent, rather then substandard, job performance. Other indicators are deterioration in personal grooming, bruises, puffiness of the face, frequent illnesses combined with vacation days impulsively taken, and moody or irritable behavior. For women who work under close supervision, absenteeism is a good identifier.

Some research indicates that the traditional "confrontation" model is not as appropriate for women as for men. Confrontation can reinforce a woman's sense of powerlessness and further lower her self-esteem. Women appear to need a great deal of support in order to be willing to enter treatment. One study indicated the need for varied approaches. Among women under 30 with higher self-esteem and more positive self-images, direct confrontation was used successfully; with women aged 30 to 45, who had lower self-esteem, avoiding confrontation and stressing strong support groups was preferable (Pape, 1990).

One of the major barriers to women's getting the treatment they need is the lack of education of the community gatekeepers: law enforcement officials, social service personnel, clergy, and health care providers. Since we know that women are apt to seek help from these professionals for their "emotional problems," we must begin to target these professionals and educate them. Other barriers to treatment include the woman's own denial of the problem, her family's strong denial and opposition to treatment because they need her at home, and the lack of spousal or parental support due to their own substance-abuse problem.

One of the consistent reasons given by women for not seeking treatment is lack of available child-care resources. In addition to their guilt for not being available to their children, sometimes women fear they will lose custody of them. Barriers in the workplace include lack of trust in the confidentiality of EAPs, fear of job termination, not having enough sick time or vacation time to take off for treatment, and the lack of insurance coverage.

We need to reach out to these women with educational materials where they are: in their homes, laundromats, supermarkets, health clinics, psychiatrists' offices, emergency rooms, and obstetricians' or gynecologists' offices. Literature about the consequences of substance use and abuse, as well as lists of community resources that treat these problems, need to be given to all women as they frequent these locations.

More studies need to be done on women who never get to treatment so that we can better understand the circumstances preventing women from accessing community resources.

TREATMENT NEEDS OF WOMEN

For women, alcohol and drug addiction is a triple stigma; this associated stigma is often a barrier to their being identified and getting the needed treatment. First, there is the general stigma of alcohol or other drug dependency. Despite the acceptance in 1956 of alcoholism as a disease by the

American Medical Association, many people still assume that alcoholics drink and addicts use drugs out of choice, lack of willpower, and moral weakness. The second stigma is a result of the fact that moral standards for women are often higher than those for men. To "drink like a man" and occasionally get drunk is often viewed as humorous; a woman who is drunk is viewed with disgust. The third stigma relates to the continued association of drinking and drug use with sexual promiscuity. In reality, research indicates that female alcoholics and drug addicts have decreased sexual desire; what actually increases is their chance of being sexually victimized, because they are considered acceptable targets for male aggression.

Because women are raised and socialized in the same society, and with the same values as everyone else, they are acutely aware of the triple stigma. And, in fact, they turn it against themselves, internalize it, and create two major issues with which they must deal in their recovery: guilt and shame.

Treatment studies support the value of all-female treatment groups that address the special issues and needs of women during early recovery. Such groups prevent women from taking on the usual roles and behaviors they assume with men: passivity, nonassertiveness, and caretaking. They allow women to talk about issues they might not feel free to talk about in the presence of men: physical and sexual abuse, incest, rape, and other sexual problems in their relationships with men. The issue of sexual preference needs to be addressed, and addicted lesbian women need a place to talk about their special problems.

ISSUES IN ASSESSMENT OF WOMEN

As substance-abusing women tend to exhibit more physiological problems than substance-abusing men, a thorough physical examination (including a gynecological exam and a pregnancy test for sexually active women) is extremely important. As with any alcohol- or drug-abusing client, an extensive alcohol and drug history needs to be taken, paying particular attention to the use of prescribed medications such as tranquilizers, barbiturates, sedatives, and amphetamines. Treatment professionals need to be alert to any delayed withdrawal symptoms from other sedatives—particularly the benzodiazepines, which are longer-acting due to their half-lives.

In assessing and diagnosing women, it is important to focus not only on the quantity of alcohol or drugs consumed (women tend to drink and use less than men) but also on the chemical use patterns and the effects on both personality and personal functioning.

It is also important to perform a thorough differential diagnosis in order to determine if there is *primary* substance use disorder or if it is *secondary* to a preexisting diagnosable psychopathological state. In females, depression, anxiety disorders (panic disorders or agoraphobia are the most common), and eating disorders often coexist with alcohol abuse. In the case of dual diagnosis, the treatment should begin by addressing the chemical dependency, with the goal of total abstinence from *all* mood-altering substances.

A complete family history going back two or three generations is important, noting particularly any mental illness or chemical dependency. Involving family and/or significant others from the beginning of treatment is crucial. Part of the reason for this is the priority women have placed on relationships and the importance of their roles as wife and mother to their own identities. The entire family—everyone who lives in the home, including any young children—needs to be involved in treatment.

Research indicates that women gain a great deal of value from both structure and education. Treatment programs need to build in structure and provide a variety of forms of education—audiovisual presentations with discussion, reading materials (particularly about other chemically dependent women), and continued education in support and therapy groups.

> Susan, a 35-year-old single parent, came in as a self-referral to her company EAP. She had three children, ages 5, 7, and 12, and her 12-year-old daughter was getting into trouble at school. Susan talked about the stress related to her career advancement in the company, attending school to finish her MBA, and trying to parent her three children by herself. She had no extended family, no support system, and no leisure time in her life. Her "reward" for getting through her days was to "relax after the kids are in bed with a couple of brandies and a good book before I fall asleep." Often she could not fall asleep, and so a few months ago her doctor had prescribed sleeping pills, to take only occasionally when she "needed them."
>
> Upon further questioning, the following information was gathered: Susan's father and grandfather were alcoholics; the "couple of brandies" were 4 ounces each—more than she used to need to relax, since she had developed a tolerance for alcohol; she occasionally had blackouts the next day; she was now taking at least one, sometimes two, sleeping pills each night in order to sleep (further evidence of tolerance); and, finally, she had promised herself the month before that she would stop taking the pills but suffered such anxiety and inability to sleep that she had returned to using them.
>
> The diagnosis for Susan was polysubstance dependence (DSM-III-R 304.90). Treatment recommendations included an outpatient chemical dependency program where she would receive education about the disease; family therapy to work on the problems involved with single parenting; and a women's sobriety group and attendance at Alcoholics Anonymous (AA) meetings. Today, Susan has been abstinent for 2 years,

is successfully parenting her three children, still attends AA, and is involved in an Adult Children of Alcoholics (ACOA) therapy group to address the effects of growing up with an alcoholic father.

TREATMENT ISSUES

Some of the major issues that women bring into treatment include low self-esteem, dependency, identity confusion, guilt and shame, socialization related to their role as nurturers of others, inability to identify and express their own feelings (especially anger), inability to identify their needs and get them met, and learned helplessness and passivity. They also have such practical problems as child care, housing, finances, and employment. Often they have the unrealistic expectation that others should know and meet their needs without their having to ask, because that is what they have done for others for years. Some women have become very isolated and resist group therapy. They often do not like or trust other women and have a particular resistance to any women's group, either professional or self-help. Many state that they find it easier to relate to men than to women—they know the "rules of the game" and find it more difficult to "con another woman."

Women in treatment need to become involved in a 12-step program such as AA or Narcotics Anonymous (NA) for their ongoing support and recovery. The 12-step programs appear to be the best modality for dealing with the issue of shame (so prevalent among female alcoholics and addicts), and it is generally accepted that the combination of professional treatment and a self-help group is the ideal treatment for addiction.

If necessary, a structured intervention may be needed for other family members who may also be chemically dependent. Many women coming into treatment are married to alcoholics or addicts, have significant relationships with addicted men, or have teenage children who are abusing or addicted to alcohol and other drugs. Often the spouses will not become involved in treatment; this represents a high risk for relapse if the women stay in relationships with them.

A brief family systems therapy approach combined with the addictions model of treatment is successful in conducting family therapy. A major goal is to get family members to focus on themselves, their feelings, and their treatment needs—and to stop focusing on the chemically dependent woman. Family members also need both professional treatment and recovery in a self-help group such as Al-Anon, Nar-Anon, Alateen, or ACOA.

It is important for the family to talk about their losses during the active drinking or using (for example, the unavailability of the chemically dependent female) and also their losses during recovery (for example, she is more assertive now, takes care of her own needs too, is enforcing the rules) as well as the feelings related to these losses.

Two other major areas that need to be addressed in family therapy are familial roles and rules. Parents need to be in charge, appropriate boundaries need to be established, and children need to be relieved of the responsibilities of taking care of their parents. These changes can precipitate a sense of loss in a child who may have gotten self-esteem from being responsible for younger children and/or the home.

Rules in the chemically dependent family have generally been inconsistent, unspoken, and shame-producing. There may have been "drinking rules" (chaotic and unreliable) and "hangover rules" (permissive and guilt-produced). Children have learned to survive and to manipulate the system, but at a cost to their healthy development. There need to be clear, specific behavioral rules and consequences that the parents consistently enforce.

Finally, an area often overlooked in treatment is fun and recreation. Members of a chemically dependent family do not know how to play! Planning such activities together can be a way to improve communication, problem solving, decision making, and conflict resolution. Planned weekly activities can promote healing within the family.

Isolation is characteristic of chemical dependency. The use of group therapy begins to overcome this isolation, as well as providing a forum for education, support, the learning of new interpersonal skills, and the receiving of feedback.

The overall focus of group therapy needs to be on addiction, with a primary goal of total abstinence from all mood-altering chemicals. A female therapist will often become a role model; her attitudes about chemical dependency and about being a woman are important. The first 12 months are especially crucial in building a solid foundation for an ongoing recovery program. Understanding the disease concept of addiction, grieving for her losses, and arriving at very specific concepts of her acceptance of her disease are vital.

Developing a very structured and specific recovery plan is often helpful. Such things as commitments to the women's therapy group, family therapy, a specific number of AA or NA meetings weekly, readings, improved nutrition (eliminate caffeine; reduce sugar), and reflection or meditation at the beginning and end of each day begin to structure her time in a positive manner.

Much of early treatment needs to be cognitive and behavioral, dealing with the real world. Women need to learn to manage people, places, things, and feelings in order to reduce the risk of relapse. They need to learn relapse cues, both internal and external, that are specific to them. Women need permission to be assertive and to put their own needs first.

A common problem is the single woman in a relationship with a male addict and her frequenting places where alcohol and other drugs are available. Often she needs to end this relationship, but this takes time and does not usually happen until she has found other, more satisfying relationships.

Many women talk about a "spiritual void" or "emptiness." The solution for this will eventually be the development of a new set of recovery-based beliefs and values and some sort of spirituality or sense of purpose, meaning, and connectedness with others. Often this happens through attending a self-help group and working the 12 steps of a recovery program.

Women need to begin to set career, vocational, or school goals. Much of the literature points to the importance of setting goals in the areas where they are competent and can experience self-mastery and pride in their accomplishments. This will lead to feelings of independence, personal power, and security, as well as a willingness to take responsibility for their own lives. (This is contrary to women's socialization, which teaches them to sacrifice their own needs and to take care of others' need first!)

Treatment issues specific to women addicted to opiates begin with legal issues. The Harrison Act of 1914 marked the beginning of the criminalization of the use of narcotics. The history of a heroin addict is one of the reduction of life options. The heroin-addicted woman often turns to illegal work to support her habit, thus entering the world of crime. Such work is usually sex-related, often selling sexual favors for money to buy drugs; she thus becomes locked into a deviant lifestyle.

Methadone maintenance is a phenomenon in and of itself (Rosenbaum & Murphy, 1990). The initial phases involve the surrender of control as the woman is put on a structured routine: mandatory clinic attendance, payment of fees, urinalysis, and counseling, Often there is a sense of relief. In the next stage—"stabilization"—the correct dosage is arrived at and she begins her lifelong relationship with the drug. If she is a "success," she breaks from her deviant lifestyle and reenters conventional life. A "failure" continues in the heroin world and uses methadone as a fall-back drug and lifestyle. The final phase—"disillusionment"—involves her resentment of the controls, such as mandatory reporting and travel restrictions. She also experiences health concerns and parenting and identity problems (being a "half-junkie"). Paradoxically, being a successful methadone patient can impede detachment from methadone. The most pervasive obstacle to getting off methadone is fear—of long-term withdrawal symptoms, of emotional vulnerability, and of losing the social life that her clinic attendance and going out for coffee with other clients has provided.

Outcomes of treatment for heroin addiction appear to be linked to social class. For the working and lower classes, life options are reduced in both the deviant and the conventional world. Therefore, their ability to remain drug-free is decreased. In general, women have more difficulty plugging into the conventional world—they carry a deeper stigma and as a consequence find it more difficult to secure and keep jobs. Treatment outcomes are better for middle-class addicts who have more options, although there are generally fewer for women than for men. And finally, women IDUs and their risk of AIDS make them the outreach worker's and treatment personnel's greatest challenge. Issues concerning sex roles and stigma make IDU women the most difficult to reach at-risk population!

Although cocaine-abusing women exhibit symptoms common to all substance-abusing women, the intensity of their compulsion to use makes them prone to particularly high relapse rates. Three major treatment issues— grief, sexuality, and assertion—have a major impact on positive treatment outcomes (Eisenstadt, 1990).

Although dealing with grief, guilt, and loss is important in all treatment, cocaine addicts exhibit a more intense bonding with their drug of choice; they are "in love with their drug." The memory of the pain of their addiction is overshadowed by the memory of the pleasure. They are giving up the most intense love affair they have ever known. They need to be educated to the stages of the grieving process so they understand that the intensity of many of their emotions is directly related to their grieving over the loss of cocaine.

The unspoken sexual concerns these women bring into treatment can impede their progress more than anything else. They must be educated to realize that their numerous and unusual sexual encounters are the norm for cocaine-abusing women; and their guilt, anger, and humiliation must be worked through. Some of their guilt and shame comes from their embarrassment at having enjoyed some of those experiences and their belief that, were they to share this with others, they would be seen as "sick" and "perverted." Part of this has to do with their love of the drug and part of it has to do with the fact that sex was never as pleasurable or intense as when they were using cocaine. Women-only groups provide the safe and respectful atmosphere needed to work on these issues.

Basic assertion training, necessary for all women's treatment, can be a powerful treatment modality in working with real-life problems. It opens up a new world of options, enhances their self-esteem and self-respect, and helps them cope when they find themselves in risky situations. Cocaine-abusing women are often the sexual partners of IDUs; and while IDUs comprise the largest group of women at risk for AIDS, the sexual partners of IDUs are the second largest group of women at risk (Mondanaro, 1987). "Just saying no" does not work, but learning and rehearsing *how* to say "no" without jeopardizing their self-esteem can be very effective and can literally save their lives!

IMPLICATIONS FOR SOCIAL WORKERS

What are some of the implications for social workers? First and foremost, we must look at ourselves and our own denial, which supports and helps maintain societal denial, and our own tendencies to buy into the myths and stereotypes related to chemically dependent persons in general and women in particular. Many helping professionals are oldest children—family heroes—caretakers from chemically dependent family systems. If these issues have not been acknowledged and worked through, both in therapy and in a 12-step recovery program, they will surely get in the way of our attempts to help others. Our countertransference issues will prevent us from being effective in our treatment of our clients.

In general, research has failed to demonstrate which particular treatment strategies are more or less effective for which kinds of patients. With the general push toward health care cost containment in our society today, the concept of individualized treatment plans takes on a new importance.

Also, there needs to be more and different research relating to treatment outcomes for women. The whole idea that women have special treatment needs that are not being served has not received support in the research literature. One reason for the failure of existing research to support such a view may be that very few treatment outcome studies have focused on women. Harrison and Belille (1987) estimate that only 8% of the studies published between 1970 and 1984 are about women. Even when studies include women, findings for women are rarely presented separately from findings for men.

During the past decade, the abuse of alcohol and other drugs by women has been recognized by many as the number-one health problem in the United States today. We owe it to ourselves—and to our clients—to take all the necessary steps to enhance our potential to be able to help this population.

REFERENCES

Abel, E. L., & Sokol, R. J. (1987). Incidence of fetal alcohol syndrome and economic impact of FAS-related anomalies. *Drug and Alcohol Dependence, 19,* 51–70.

Ackerman, R. J., (1987, January/February). A new perspective on adult children of alcoholics. *EAP Digest, 7,* 25–29.

Blume, S. B. (1988). *Alcohol/drug dependent women.* Minneapolis, MN: Johnson Institute Books.

Bohman, M., Sigvardsson, S., & Cloninger, R. (1981). Maternal inheritance of alcohol abuse: Cross-fostering analysis of adopted women. *Archives of General Psychiatry, 38,* 965–969.

Browne, A. (1987). *When battered women kill.* New York: Macmillan.

Chasnoff, I. J., Burns, W. J., Schnoll, S. H., & Burns, K. A. (1985). Cocaine use in pregnancy. *New England Journal of Medicine, 313,* 666–669.

Chatham, L. R. (1990). Understanding the issues: An overview. In R. C. Engs (Ed.), *Women: Alcohol and other drugs* (p. 7). Dubuque, IA: Kendall/Hunt.

Cregler, L. L. (1989). Adverse health consequences of cocaine abuse. *Journal of the National Medical Association, 81,* 27-38.

Davis, D. J. (1990). Prevention issues in developing programs. In R. C. Engs (Ed.), *Women: Alcohol and other drugs* (pp. 71-77). Dubuque, IA: Kendall/Hunt.

Dembo, R., Dertke, M., La-Voice, L., Borders, S., Washburn, M., & Schmeidler, J. (1987). Physical abuse, sexual victimization and illicit drug use: A structural analysis among high risk adolescents. *Journal of Adolescence, 10*(1), 13-34.

Eberle, P. (1982). Alcohol abusers and non-users: A discriminate functional analysis. *Journal of Health and Social Behavior, 23,* 260.

Eisenstadt, B. L. (1990). Cocaine. In R. C. Engs (Ed.), *Women: Alcohol and other drugs* (pp. 119-123). Dubuque, IA: Kendall/Hunt.

Fojtik, K. M. (1977-1978). The NOW domestic violence project. *Victimology, 2,* 653-657.

Gavaler, J. S. (1990). Alcohol and hormones: Reproductive and postmenopausal years. In R. C. Engs (Ed.), *Women: Alcohol and other drugs* (pp. 43-48). Dubuque, IA: Kendall/Hunt.

Gawin, F. H., & Kleber, H. D. (1985). Neuroendocrine findings in chronic cocaine abusers: A preliminary report. *British Journal of Psychiatry, 147,* 569-573.

Gomberg, E. S. (1976). Alcoholism in women. In B. Kissin & H. Begleiter (Eds.), *Social aspects of alcoholism* (Vol. 4, pp. 117-165). New York: Plenum.

Gomberg, E. S. (1980). Risk factors related to alcohol problems among women: Proneness and vulnerability. In *Alcoholism and alcohol abuse among women: Research issues* (NIAA Research Monograph No. 1, USDHEW Pub. No. (ADM 80-835). Washington, DC: U.S. Government Printing Office.

Gomberg, E. S. L., & Lisansky, J. M. (1984). Antecedents of alcohol problems in women. In S. C. Wilsnack & L. J. Beckman (Eds.), *Alcohol problems in women: Antecedents, consequences, and intervention* (pp. 233-259). New York: Guilford.

Harrison, P. A., & Belille, C. A. (1987). Women in treatment: Beyond the stereotype. *Journal of Studies on Alcohol, 48*(6), 574-578.

Jaffe, J., & Martin, W. (1985). Opioid analgesics and antagonists. In A. G. Gilman, L. S. Goodman, T. W. Rall, & T. Murad (Eds.), *The pharmacological basis of therapeutics* (7th ed., pp. 491-531). New York: Macmillian.

Johnston, L. D., O'Malley, P. M., & Bachman, J. G. (1987). *National trends in drug use and related factors among American high school students and young adults, 1975-1986.* Rockville, MD: National Institute on Drug Abuse.

Khantzian, E. J. (1987). Psychiatric and psychodynamic factors in cocaine dependence. In A. Washton & M. Gold (Eds.), *Cocaine: A clinician's handbook* (pp. 229-237). New York: Guilford.

Krystal, H. (1982). Alexithymia and the effectiveness of psychoanalytic treatment. *International Journal of Psychoanalytic Psychotherapy,* 353-378

Laign, J. (1987, September/October). How far have we really come baby? Women's addiction treatment in 1987. *Focus on Chemically Dependent Families,* pp. 14-30.

Mondanaro, J. (1987). Strategies for AIDS prevention: Motivating health behavior in drug dependent women. *Journal of Psychoactive Drugs, 19*(2), 143-149.

Moulton, C., & Moulton, O. (1984, March). Biological effects of marijuana. *Drug Abuse Newsletter.* Issue No. 6.

National Institute on Alcohol Abuse and Alcoholism. (1990). *Alcohol alert*. Rockville, MD: Author.

National Institute on Alcohol Abuse and Alcoholism. (1980). *Women's occupational alcoholism demonstration project: Phase I*. Rockville, MD: Author.

National Institute on Drug Abuse. (1989, June). *Capsules*. Rockville, MD: Author.

Pape, P. A. (1985). Removing the shroud from female alcoholism. *The Almacan, 15*(4), 14-16.

Pape, P. A. (1986). Women and alcohol: The disgraceful discrepancy. *EAP Digest, 6*(6), 49-53.

Pape, P. A. (1990, May). *Does age make a difference?* Paper presented at the Alcohol and Drug Problems Association Women's Conference, Syracuse, NY.

Renzetti, C. M. (1988). Violence in lesbian relationships: A preliminary analysis of causal factors. *Journal of Interpersonal Violence, 4*, 381-399.

Rohsenow, D. J., Corbitt, R., & Devine, D. (1988). Molested as children: A hidden contribution to substance abuse? *Journal of Substance Abuse Treatment, 5*(1), 13-18.

Rosenbaum, M., & Murphy, S. (1990). Opiates. In R. C. Engs (Ed.), *Women: Alcohol and other drugs* (pp. 111-117). Dubuque, IA: Kendall/Hunt.

Seligman, M. (1975). *Helplessness: On depression, development and death*. San Francisco: Freeman.

Smith, D. E., Moser, C., Wesson, D. R., Apter, M., Buxton, M. E., Davison, J. V., Orgel, M., & Buffum, J. (1982). A clinical guide to the diagnosis and treatment of heroin related sexual dysfunction. *Journal of Psychoactive Drugs, 14*, 91-99.

Sternbach, G., Moran, J., & Eliastram, M. (1980). Heroin addiction: Acute presentation of medical complications. *Annual Emergency Medical, 9*, 161-169.

Straussner, S. L. A. (1985). Alcoholism in women: Current knowledge and implications for treatment. In D. Cook, S. L. A. Straussner, & C. Fewell (Eds.), *Psychosocial issues in the treatment of alcoholism* (pp. 61-74). New York: Haworth.

Sullivan, J. (1979, June). *The working alcoholic woman: Separate and unequal*. Paper presented at the 25th International Institute on the Prevention and Treatment of Alcoholism, Tours, France.

Walker, L. (1979). *The battered woman*. New York: Harper & Row.

Weisinfluh, S., & Aniolkoski, C. (1988, May). *Substance abuse among battered women: Developing a model for identification and intervention of domestic violence victims*. Paper presented at the Alcohol and Drug Problems Association Second National Conference on Women's Issues, Columbus, OH.

Wilsnack, S. C. (1990). Alcohol abuse and alcoholism: Extent of the problem. In R. C. Engs (Ed.), *Women: Alcohol and other drugs* (pp. 17-30). Dubuque, IA: Kendall/Hunt.

Zobeck, D., Grant, B. F., Williams, G. D., & Bertolucci, D. (1987). *Trends in alcohol-related fatal traffic accidents, United States, 1977-1985* (Surveillance Report No. 6). Rockville, MD: National Institute on Alcohol Abuse and Alcoholism.

15

The Borderline Substance Abuser

EDA G. GOLDSTEIN

With increasing interest in the differential assessment and treatment of individuals who present with a dual diagnosis (Attia, 1988; Blume, 1989; Brown, Ridgely, Pepper, Levine, & Ryglewicz, 1989; Evans & Sullivan, 1990; Mulinski, 1989; Osher & Kofoed, 1989), there has been scant attention in the substance abuse literature to a particularly vexing group of patients who show borderline disorders. While exact numbers are lacking, there is ample clinical evidence to suggest that a large percentage of those who are chemically dependent also show borderline pathology (Kiesler, Simpkins, & Morton, 1991). Leading lives of not so quiet desperation, borderline individuals generally are angry, volatile, impulsive, and self-destructive. Highly contradictory in their feelings and behavior, they show severe identity disturbances and may develop brief psychotic episodes. They are plagued by fears of abandonment and become panicked when separated from those upon whom they are dependent.

With characteristic problems in managing their feelings and impulses, borderline individuals are highly prone to substance abuse. Yet their use of alcohol and drugs does not always follow a typical pattern. It usually is intermittent and may seemingly appear to be under better control at times when they engage in other types of compulsive behavior that center, for example, on food, gambling, or love relationships (Evans & Sullivan, 1990). The etiology of this addictive behavior may have multiple sources, and the substance abuse often takes on a life of its own.

What is the nature and cause of borderline disorders? How can practitioners recognize borderline pathology and its presence among those who abuse alcohol and other substances? What types of treatment do borderline substance abusers need? What are the obstacles to successful treatment? After briefly reviewing contrasting perspectives on the nature and causes of borderline disorders and their main clinical features, this chapter discusses an integrated treatment approach that combines elements of mental health and substance-abuse models.

CONTRASTING PERSPECTIVES

Since the emergence of the term "borderline" (Stern, 1938), there has been controversy about its exact definition. Originally it referred to a diverse group of ill-defined disturbances that did not seem to fit traditional diagnostic criteria and were more severe than the neuroses and less severe than the schizophrenias (Goldstein, 1990). While now there is general agreement that borderline pathology constitutes a type of personality disorder that reflects entrenched maladaptive coping patterns, considerable disagreement remains about its exact nature, origins, and successful treatment.

There are currently four major models in the study of borderline disorders: the DSM-III-R model, the psychodynamic or developmental model, the family model, and the biological model. The social environment, however, provides a crucial context in which these frameworks must be viewed. No single model does justice to the complexity of this disorder, and an integration is required.

The DSM-III-R Model

The revised third edition of the *Diagnostic and Statistical Manual of Mental Disorders* (American Psychiatric Association, 1987) classifies borderline conditions on Axis II as a type of personality disorder if at least five of the following eight characteristics are present:

1. a pattern of unstable and intense interpersonal relationships characterized by alternating between extremes of overidealization and devaluation
2. impulsiveness in at least two areas that are potentially self-damaging, e.g., spending, sex, substance use, shoplifting, reckless driving, binge eating . . .
3. affective instability; marked shifts from baseline mood to depression, irritability, or anxiety, usually lasting a few hours and only rarely more than a few days
4. inappropriate, intense anger or lack of control of anger, e.g., frequent displays of temper, constant anger, recurrent physical fights
5. recurrent suicidal threats, gestures, or behavior, or self-mutilating behavior
6. marked and persistent identity disturbance manifested by uncertainty about at least two of the following: self-image, sexual orientation, long-term goals or career choice, type of friends desired, preferred values

7. chronic feelings of emptiness or boredom
8. frantic efforts to avoid real or imagined abandonment . . . (p. 347)

While the DSM-III-R attempts to use clear-cut, nonoverlapping criteria for the borderline designation, not everyone agrees with its atheoretical conception of this disorder (Kernberg, 1984; Kroll, 1988; Stone, 1987).

The Psychodynamic or Developmental Model

From a psychoanalytic developmental perspective, the main controversy regarding borderline pathology is whether it reflects a type of intrapsychic defensive structure that arises to ward off conflict and that must be modified, usually through a highly confrontative, interpretive, and limit-setting approach (Kernberg, 1975, 1984; Masterson, 1972, 1976; Masterson & Rinsley, 1975), or whether it reflects developmental failures that result in deficits or underdeveloped elements in the personality and that require treatment that builds, strengthens, and consolidates internal structure (Adler, 1985; Blanck & Blanck, 1974, 1979; Buie & Adler, 1982; Kohut, 1971, 1977, 1984). Neither the conflict or deficit model sufficiently takes into account, however, the mounting evidence documenting the traumas of sexual abuse and violence in the histories of female borderline individuals (Herman, Perry, & van der Kolk, 1989; Kroll, 1988; Wheeler & Walton, 1987).

The Family Model

Family-oriented theorists view the family of origin and current interpersonal interactions as generating and sometimes perpetuating borderline pathology. Borderline family characteristics include primitive defenses such as splitting, denial, idealization, and projective identification; conflicts around autonomy and dependence; enmeshment and overinvolvement; and neglect and rejection (Goldstein, 1981a; Grinker, Werble, & Drye, 1968; Gunderson, Kerr, & Englund, 1980; Shapiro, Shapiro, Zinner, & Berkowitz, 1977; Walsh, 1977). Couple dynamics show collusion, distortion, and vicious circles of mutual frustration (Schwartzman, 1984; Slipp, 1988; Solomon, 1985; Stewart, Peters, Marsh, & Peters, 1975).

The Biological Model

The older view that borderline disorders were linked genetically to schizophrenia has been replaced by the belief that they reflect an underlying affective or mood disorder (Akiskal, 1981; Klein, 1977). The evidence for viewing borderline pathology as a form of affective disorder treatable with antidepressants is not conclusive, although it seems clear that some borderline patients also may present with a depressive disorder and may benefit from medication (Kroll, 1988).

THE SOCIAL CONTEXT

While there is no clear evidence that minorities or socioeconomically disadvantaged individuals show more borderline disturbances, there is general agreement that racism and other forms of discrimination and absence of positive role models engender low self-esteem, self-hatred, and negative self-concepts that may complicate personality development. Blacks and Hispanics, other ethnic and racial minorities, women, and gays and lesbians are examples of groups within the society who experience oppression. In many instances, an individual's self-destructive behavior, self-directed anger, feelings of worthlessness, and sense of hopelessness may be misdiagnosed as borderline pathology rather than seen as a result of psychologically assaultive societal attitudes and policies and a lack of social justice that engender feelings of impotence and retaliatory aggression (Beverly, 1989; Chestang, 1980; Comas-Diaz & Minrath, 1985; Lewis, 1984).

ASSESSING BORDERLINE PERSONALITY DISORDER

While substance abuse does not cause borderline disorders, it can cause and intensify borderline traits or it can mask actual borderline pathology. Consequently, the diagnosis of whether a "true" borderline disorder exists requires a careful assessment. If one suspects the presence of borderline pathology alongside substance abuse, it is more useful to think of borderline disorders and substance abuse as coexisting rather than to try to establish whether one disorder is primary and one is secondary or whether one is causing the other.

Evans and Sullivan (1990) suggest several guidelines for determining whether substance abuse is accompanied by a psychiatric disorder generally: (1) when the maladaptive traits or symptoms existed prior to the substance use; (2) when the traits and symptoms are qualitatively different from those usually encountered among most substance abusers; (3) when the individual continues to show difficulties after a period of abstinence (4 weeks); (4) when there is a positive family history for mental disorder; (5) when there is a history of multiple treatment failures; and (6) when improvement results from use of nonaddictive neuroleptic medications. Unfortunately, in assessing borderline substance abusers, these decision rules are less certain than with other types of psychiatric disorders. Because of borderline defenses that distort their inner experience and external perceptions of others and the world, it is difficult to get an accurate history from these individuals. Likewise, because of their identity problems and shifting states, it is hard to get a sense of who the borderline individual really is. Substance use begins very early, during and sometimes even before adolescence in borderline individuals. While in some instances it intensifies anxiety, depression, as well as self-destructive and violent behavior, in other cases it may be used to quell strong feelings and thus may dampen these tendencies. Diagnosing such individuals during abstinence or inpatient treatment can be misleading, since borderlines appear better when they are in structured settings or are not stressed by life demands, separations, interpersonal closeness, and so forth. Their chronic storms generally are episodic in nature, and they may show good control in between. Consequently, it may take some time before one can observe their characteristic difficulties. Further, when they become stressed, their inability to soothe themselves makes them vulnerable to slips and ongoing problems in maintaining abstinence. By this time, they may be discharged and lost to follow-up.

The data on family history of mental disorder in borderlines are not conclusive. While many come from overtly dysfunctional families in which there is physical, sexual, and substance abuse, others come from families in which there are more subtle though nevertheless malignant difficulties. It is not clear that borderline substance abusers are distinctive with respect to family histories from other substance abusers. Further, except in alleviating depression where there is an affective disorder or mild disorganization, neuroleptics usually are contraindicated in the treatment of borderline individuals and do not alter their characteristic difficulties in any case.

The best assessment tools are an accurate history and systematic observation over time. It is usually necessary to obtain information from multiple sources and to focus particularly on how the patient copes during periods in which he or she is not using drugs and on the triggers for and patterns of drug use. The following 13 major characteristics are common in borderline individuals (Goldstein, 1990).

Identity Disturbances

Borderline individuals are confusing and unpredictable. They tend to portray themselves either as "all good" or "all bad," making it difficult to get a three-dimensional sense of who they are. They may repeatedly use others for a sense of identity. Abrupt and radical shifts in feelings, attitudes, and behavior may occur within hours, days, or weeks, seemingly without reason.

Splitting and Other Related Defenses

Splitting, the main defense of borderline individuals, keeps apart two conscious, contradictory feeling states, such as love and anger or admiration and disappointment, so that a friend, family member, or therapist who is viewed as all "good" suddenly may be seen as all "bad." Selected personality traits become associated with "goodness" or "badness"; thus, for example, an individual may view assertiveness negatively and compliance favorably or may acknowledge his or her submissiveness and cooperativeness while denying the existence of independent or rebellious thoughts, feelings, or behavior.

Other related borderline defenses are (1) denial, in which there is an inability to acknowledge selected aspects of the self or others that conflict with one's image of the self or of others; (2) idealization, in which there is a tendency to see oneself or others as totally "good" in order to ward off frightening impulses; (3) devaluation, in which there is a penchant to see oneself or others as all "bad"; (4) omnipotent control, in which a person with a highly inflated sense of self attempts to control others totally; and (5) projective identification, in which a person continues to have an impulse, generally an angry one, which, at the same time, is projected onto another person, who then is feared as an enemy who must be controlled.

Problems in Impulse Control

Borderline individuals generally are impulsive in one or more areas of their lives. Their impulsiveness may be chronic and seemingly without environmental triggers, or it may be episodic in response to internal or external events, such as blows to self-esteem, loss, or the threat of abandonment. In addition to substance abuse, such impulsiveness often shows itself in eating disorders, self-mutilation, at-risk sexual behavior, manipulative suicidal threats and acts, financial mismanagement or gambling, physical abuse, and violence.

Problems in Anxiety Tolerance

Many borderline individuals are anxious most of the time or they have recurrent, disabling bouts of diffuse anxiety. They may experience dread when they awake or awake in the middle of the night. Increases in stress are disorganizing or overwhelming. They may experience panic reactions intermittently in response to life events, especially separations.

Problems in Affect Regulation

Borderline individuals often escalate rapidly in their feelings; thus, for example, irritation becomes rage, sadness becomes despair, loneliness becomes aloneness, and disappointment becomes hopelessness. They become overwhelmed by positive or negative feelings that are too intense. Seemingly happy at one moment, they plunge into a painful depression the next. They often show intense and inappropriate anger, temper tantrums, or affect storms. When these displays are coupled with impulsiveness, borderlines can become frightening, physically violent, or self-destructive.

Negative Affects

Often complaining of chronic depression, many borderlines show persistent feelings of anger, resentment, dissatisfaction, and envy. Sometimes they experience inner emptiness and feel bereft of positive or meaningful connections to others or even to themselves.

Problems in Self-Soothing

Borderline individuals lack the capacity for self-soothing. They are at the mercy of any upsurge of uncomfortable feelings and have "no money in the bank" to draw upon in moments of stress. They become overwhelmed by feelings of panic, rage, and aloneness. Even minor separations such as leaving a therapy session can generate panic that prompts the patient to engage in desperate efforts to make contact. Some individuals immerse themselves in activities of all sorts or engage in addictive or other types of self-destructive behavior in order to escape from their feelings.

Abandonment Fears

Borderline individuals commonly show fears of abandonment. Some attempt to merge with others in efforts to deny or ward off their aloneness and to reassure themselves that they will never be abandoned. They seek constant proximity to or contact with those upon whom they are dependent and want to know their exact whereabouts or minute details of their activities. At the same time, most borderline individuals have a need–fear dilemma that makes them ward off or withdraw from the positive experiences with others for which they long and show an oscillating cycle of clinging and distancing behavior. When they are not feeling intense loneliness, many borderline individuals manage their abandonment fears by regulating interpersonal closeness and engage in many superficial relationships, avoiding intimacy.

Problems in Self-Esteem Regulation

Borderline individuals are extremely dependent upon others and upon external approval. Consequently, their self-regard is highly vulnerable and may undergo radical swings as a function of the feedback they receive or the degree to which they live up to their own perfectionist standards. Some borderline individuals show either highly grandiose or devalued conceptions of their abilities and talents and tend to feel either very entitled to special treatment or unworthy of help; sometimes they fluctuate between these extremes. Even seemingly minor disappointments or comments can lead to rage reactions; feelings of worthlessness, shame, or humiliation; and fits of self-loathing.

Superego Difficulties

While some borderline individuals show an absence of guilt and empathy in their dealings with others and are capable of ruthless and exploitative acts, many experiencing remorse, self-contempt, and self-recrimination after they mistreat others. Nevertheless, they find themselves unable to stop the very behavior that they hate.

Intense and Unstable Interpersonal Relationships

Intimacy is a problem, since the borderline tends to merge with others or to regulate closeness so that it is not threatening. Moodiness, possessiveness, insecurity, and highly charged interactions are common. Fights, accusations, and sudden breaks frequently occur and are usually related to feelings of being rejected or abandoned. Feelings of victimization are frequent. Separations are difficult, however, and cause anxiety and severe depression. They may lead to desperate and often seemingly manipulative and attention-getting behavior, such as suicidal threats and attempts or other types of acting out.

Reality Testing and Psychotic-Like Features

While borderline individuals show distorted perceptions, these usually are not bizarre and the capacity for reality testing is maintained. For example, they may be highly suspicious of friends and associates. Some may have psychotic-like beliefs or a loosening of ego boundaries. For example, they may seem convinced that they are psychic and can predict the future, are dying of an incurable illness, or are being punished for their success. When more reality-based explanations for their perceptions are presented, such individuals often become more realistic. Showing problems in their sense of reality, as evidenced by feelings of depersonalization and derealization, borderlines may experience themselves as outside of their bodies or may feel as if they are walking on a strange planet. Distortions of body image, such as feeling too fat, are common.

Problems in Self-Cohesion

Some borderline individuals are vulnerable to psychotic decompensation under stress. They have a profound lack of self-cohesion that leaves them susceptible to transient periods of fragmentation that can be quite disturbing. When in equilibrium, borderline individuals can maintain their self-cohesiveness by regulating the degree of intimacy in their relationships and thus avoid the loss of ego boundaries involved in closeness.

THE NEED FOR AN INTEGRATED TREATMENT APPROACH

Because of their underlying developmental deficits, particularly in the area of self-soothing, it is more difficult to treat borderline substance abusers than substance abusers who are not borderline. Often biased toward seeing substance abuse as a form of self-medication for underlying personality difficulties, mental health practitioners have tended to neglect treating the substance abuse directly when they see borderline individuals in psychotherapy. Conversely, substance abuse programs often ignore borderline individuals' personality problems, since staff are focused on the chemical dependence itself, lack knowledge about the nature of borderline pathology, and do not provide appropriately structured services; this adversely affects their potential for recovery. Borderline substance abusers find it difficult to maintain a stable sobriety, or they resort to other types of dysfunctional behavior. They constitute a large number of those who are treatment failures or who drop out of or are asked to leave such services because of their seeming "noncompliance." Despite the success of 12-step programs with many borderlines, some have trouble adhering to such programs.

Even those borderline individuals who are engaged in treatment that is specifically geared to their needs, however, have difficulties in developing and maintaining a therapeutic alliance, which often shows a stormy course.

They arouse strong emotions in therapeutic personnel and challenge our usual notions about what is supposed to occur in treatment. They present frequent crises, miss appointments, threaten to leave, mutilate themselves, threaten and attempt suicide, do not comply with agency or therapeutic requirements, and request personal information, additional time, or extra-therapeutic contact. Consequently, therapists frequently experience insecurity and the feeling that they are "walking a tightrope" in the treatment.

Staff collaborative difficulties are common in work with borderline substance abusers, and this is particularly evident in inpatient or residential settings. Disputes typically center on how to work with a particular patient, who is likely to be viewed by some staff members as dependent, fragile, and in need of empathy or special treatment and by others as hostile, belligerent, and requiring firm limits and structure. In settings that contain substance abusers who reflect a range of other psychiatric disorders, including dual diagnosis units, borderlines often are at the center of conflict among other patients as well as staff because of their need and ability to evoke special treatment or to provoke conflict. Family relationships of borderline individuals also present problems. Couple interactions are turbulent and conflicted; parent–child relationships generally are characterized by either rejection or enmeshment.

In working with borderline substance abusers, an integrated approach is necessary (Minkoff, 1989). It is generally advisable to treat both the underlying personality disorder and the substance abuse, since it is potentially just as futile to assume that substance abuse will cease with psychotherapy alone as to believe that abstinence will suffice or even be possible in the presence of such profound ego and self deficits. There are differences of opinion, however, as to how to accomplish this complex task. Further, in order to implement such an approach the usual dichotomy between the mental health and substance abuse treatment models needs to be bridged (Mulinski, 1989; Ridgeley, Goldman, & Willenbring, 1990; Wallen & Weiner, 1989). A flexible and experimental, rather than doctrinaire, treatment approach is necessary.

Individual Psychotherapy

Long-term individual psychodynamically oriented psychotherapy is the most frequently used modality in the treatment of borderline individuals. Specific therapeutic models differ, however, in whether they emphasize confrontation, interpretation, limit-setting and structure, or empathic understanding and responsiveness, ego-building, and corrective experiences (Goldstein, 1990). Recently some clinicians have utilized a cognitive–behavioral psychotherapy that focuses on altering the patient's dysfunctional ways of thinking and behavior (Rush, 1984).

In working with borderlines who are also substance abusers, individual psychotherapy should be used even in the earliest stages. A crucial focus of the first phase of treatment is to help borderline substance abusers develop better ways of dealing with their pressing needs and impulses so that sobriety can be attained and maintained. In later stages of the treatment, more reparative work can be done.

Establishing a Therapeutic Holding Environment

Because borderline individuals generally are chaotic, impulsive, and prone to radical shifts in their feelings, the establishment of a therapeutic environment that helps them to feel safe and to contain their impulses is essential in the beginning stage of treatment. While stability, consistency, clarity about expectations, and limits are important in achieving these goals, the treatment framework should be individualized, flexible, and empathic rather than mechanistic. Borderline clients who are angry, provocative, demanding, impulsive, or disorganized can benefit from strict rules to help them maintain control of their behavior, while those who are anxious, fearful, depressed, dependent, or volatile may need more access to the therapist or other staff and a more flexible approach. Since lack of object constancy and absence of self-soothing capacity propel borderlines into impulsiveness and panic, therapists will need to find ways of helping patients maintain their positive connections with them and managing their intense feeling states between sessions. Some authors (Wells & Glickauf-Hughes, 1986) have suggested using transitional objects, journals, and visualization to achieve these purposes.

Whether to expect total abstinence as an immediate goal with borderlines is a controversial question. The answer is clearer when substance abuse is out of control and is having obvious and immediate destructive consequences for the individual or others. In these instances, steps must be taken to enable the patient to become free of alcohol or drugs. While this may be possible on an outpatient basis in some instances, in most situations an inpatient phase of treatment will be necessary. When the substance abuse is erratic, even though severe, and the patient shows more denial, the therapist's timing in placing expectations for sobriety on the client and the use of a stepwise therapeutic process are important in the treatment. The therapist may need to wait until the therapeutic alliance is stronger and he or she has more leverage with the patient before making abstinence a clear condition of the treatment. Waiting does not imply inactivity or the ignoring of the patient's substance abuse. It is advisable (1) to let the patient know that abstinence is a goal; (2) to keep the negative consequences of substance abuse in the forefront of the treatment; (3) to identify the defenses that protect the abuse; (4) to identify the underlying problems in self-soothing, abandonment fears, and so forth that give rise to the abuse; (4) to acknowledge and explore the gratification obtained from the abuse; (5) to explore fears of and resistance to abstinence; and (6) to problem-solve with the patient about the ways of controlling the abuse. The therapist must be vigilant about his or her own fears of raising these issues with the client or the erroneous belief that eventually the patient will gain control of his or her substance abuse as a matter of course. Unfortunately, therapists can unwittingly become "enablers" too (Levinson & Straussner, 1978). Usually it is necessary to pressure the patient to take decisive action at some point, but it may take a long time before this tactic can be effective (Chernus, 1985).

The Use of Limits and Structure

Unfortunately, borderline individuals' fears of abandonment, problems with closeness, absence of self-soothing mechanisms, and panic and rage reactions—all of which make them feel more alone and alienated—do not easily permit them to experience being "held" by a therapist's consistency, accessibility, empathy, or limits. The patient's actual life circumstances may also present stresses that stimulate impulsiveness and that overshadow the therapeutic holding environment, especially at the beginning of treatment. Some individuals may require active and protective interventions, such as the use of hospitalization, day treatment, 12-step programs, or other types of external structure. To the degree that limits and structure are needed, it is important for the therapist to engage patients collaboratively in a problem-solving effort about what will enable them to contain their impulses and self-destructive behavior. While the use of contracts with consequences spelled out is helpful, the therapist working with borderline individuals needs to recognize their vulnerability to slips and crises. There should be sufficient flexibility in the treatment structure to help patients through these crises without their being discharged or terminated from treatment.

Confrontation and Empathy

Some authors have stressed the confrontation of defenses in treating borderline personalities (Kernberg, 1975, 1984) and in work with substance abusers generally (Chernus, 1985; Fewell & Bissell, 1978; Wallace, 1978), while others have emphasized a more empathic approach (Brandchaft & Stolorow, 1984; Levin, 1987). Clinicians in the latter group argue that too great an emphasis on pointing out and controlling maladaptive defenses and behaviors may escalate rather than diffuse aggressive outbursts or other forms of self-destructive behavior, since patients are likely to feel attacked. It is important that those who work with borderline individuals see beyond their often angry, provocative, grandiose, and seemingly manipulative behavior to their underlying anxiety, desperation, diminished self-esteem, fears of abandonment, feelings of being unlovable, and hopelessness. A nonjudgmental attitude is needed. It is important that those who work with borderline patients address their self-defeating behavior, but it is generally preferable to do so in ways that show an understanding of their inner states and difficulties in soothing themselves. This can be accomplished through empathically relating to the urgent needs that clients experience, through exploring the origins of these needs in the client's early life, and through pointing out negative consequences of behaviors that the individuals may have learned in order to survive early neglect, abuse, or other kinds of trauma. The therapist should employ "experience-near empathy" (Kohut, 1984; Kohut & Wolf, 1978; White & Weiner, 1986; Wolf, 1988) in which one tries to feel what it is like to be in the client's shoes. For example, the therapist might say that the client's need to get immediate relief from his or her emotional pain through the use of a chemical is understandable, particularly since no one in the client's early life ever responded to his or her feelings or offered needed protection. This effort to understand a person's subjective experience will be calming and soothing to a disturbed client.

Ego-Building

Most of us take for granted certain capacities that borderline individuals often lack, such as the ability to recognize and verbalize feelings, soothe themselves, maintain positive connections when alone or frustrated, and empathize with others' motivations and feelings. These deficits impair their ability to cope effectively. Treatment must attempt to help the individuals restore, develop, or strengthen their adaptive coping mechanisms or restructure the environment to be more responsive to their particular personalities (Blanck & Blanck, 1974, 1979; Goldstein, 1984; Weick, Rapp, Sullivan, & Kisthardt, 1989). While such an approach may initially focus on here-and-now issues and must consider the patient's ability to tolerate exploration of his or her feelings and past traumas, it is inadvisable to attempt to help patients manage their emotional states only through cognitive or behavioral means or consistently to divert the focus of treatment away from their feelings. Helping borderline substance abusers to get in touch with what is disturbing to them, to track the relationship between their feelings and their use of substances, and to get validation for their needs can have soothing and ego-strengthening effects.

The Therapist's Use of Self

The traditional view that therapists should remain neutral and frustrating needs to be reexamined when working with borderline substance abusers.

Since these clients are so profoundly developmentally arrested, this stance may reexpose them to the neglect they experienced early in life. At times therapists may need to be more genuine rather than neutral and to meet the client's needs rather than to interpret the client's efforts to get those needs met as manipulations. This does not mean that one always gratifies the client's requests, since this may put the therapist in the position of being an enabler, stimulate regressive behavior, or eventually lead to burnout or anger and withdrawal. What is important is providing a type of "optimal responsiveness" (Bacal, 1985) based on what will help the client function more adaptively. For example, the therapist may indicate his or her availability to clients for brief telephone calls between sessions but clearly specify when these calls may occur.

Managing Countertransference

There is general consensus that therapists are especially vulnerable to problematic reactions that can obstruct their work with borderline individuals because of the impact of the client's urgent needs, aggressive behavior, and primitive defenses. There has been a tendency to say that borderline patients "induce" particular responses in those around them in order to rid themselves of uncomfortable feelings. There is a risk in assuming that this is always the case, since this perspective tends to hold the patient responsible for what the therapist is feeling. While a client's provocative and even obnoxious behavior may result in a therapist's becoming angry, helpless, or rejecting, the therapist may have contributed to the client's behavior with an insensitive or harsh comment or may be feeling particularly defensive because of having had a hard day. Even if the client is inducing a reaction in the therapist, it is important to explore the reasons for this rather than to act on one's feelings.

An important requirement of clinical staff is that they refrain from retaliating in anger to patients' provocative and attacking behavior, giving too much to the point of exhaustion or frustration, or withholding or withdrawing in the face of overwhelming demands. In order to provide a therapeutic holding environment, staff must understand the treatment philosophy that guides their work and have ample opportunity for open communication, sharing and examination of their work, support in managing their intense reactions to patients, and help in recognizing and dealing with borderline clients' needs and primitive defenses, such as splitting and projective identification. When patient–staff interactions seem too "real," countertransference acting out occurs. For example, staff may become polarized and fight about their perceptions and management of a patient, resulting in a therapeutic stalemate. Staff–patient meetings, rounds, and team meetings that embody an atmosphere of openness and acceptance can provide opportunities for all those involved in the care of patients to share their impressions and to plan individualized treatment strategies.

The Role of Psychotropic Drugs

While the common view is that psychotropic drugs do not help borderline substance abusers and are generally contraindicated because they tend to be abused, there are some positive indications for the use of medication with clients who show depression, panic states, or disorganized thinking (Zweben & Smith, 1989). A rule of thumb is to give antidepressants for a concurrent affective disorder or panic states and small doses of major tranquilizers for pathology that is close to the psychotic range of symptoms (Berger, 1987; Pack, 1987). Psychotropic drugs should always be used cautiously with borderlines. Minor tranquilizers should be avoided; while they relieve anxiety, they are addictive. Major tranquilizers, while not abused and sometimes helpful in small doses, often have serious side affects. Antidepressants, while potentially effective with those who have affective disorders, are highly lethal when used with other substances or as part of a suicide attempt, and sedating antidepressants are often abused. Lithium is quite toxic when combined with alcohol. Noncompliance with drug regimens as well as abuse are common, since borderline patients tend to use drugs in their acting out of their intense feelings. Prescribed medications also have meaning beyond their specific utility: They can be seen as an unwanted intrusion, a transitional object, a sign of caring, a magical substance that instills hope, or an indication that there is no hope (Meissner, 1988).

The Role of Psychiatric Hospitalization

Many borderlines are admitted to psychiatric hospitals following suicide attempts, psychotic episodes, or self-destructive behavior. Hospital treatment is usually short-term and focuses on resolving the immediate crisis leading to hospitalization (Friedman, 1969; Nurnberg & Suh, 1978), although some settings do provide long-term treatment. For many borderline substance abusers, a phase of inpatient treatment may be essential to beginning their recovery (Chernus, 1985; Evans & Sullivan, 1990). When treatment is short-term, a multifaceted, active treatment approach with partialized goals is necessary. Family must be involved in the treatment from the beginning, not only as part of the problem but also as part of the solution. Medication for target symptoms may be used as part of a holistic approach. Since borderline patients typically are admitted to hospitals at times of crisis, when they are extremely agitated, impulsive, or disorganized, the short-term model emphasizes the control function of the setting (Nurnberg & Suh, 1978). It tries to limit disruptive behavior by maintaining a firm, highly structured, unified, and predictable atmosphere in which patients must obey all rules and meet all expectations. In order to provide "optimal holding," it is equally important for staff to relate empathically to, rather than distance themselves from, patients' panic and aloneness (Adler, 1985). Education about substance abuse should be provided, and treatment needs to embody the principles that have been discussed so far. Discharge planning is paramount, often requiring creativity, advocacy, systems negotiation skills, and persistence. Patients and families need to be involved in this process, and much of the groundwork can be done by family members. Linkages to community resources, such as Alcoholics Anonymous, vocational training, or outpatient settings, generally should be made prior to the time the patient leaves the hospital. There should be ample time to discuss reactions to the plan and specific services.

Couple and Family Treatment

There are many instances in which therapeutic success with borderline individuals necessitates work with the family system (Goldstein, 1983). In addition to showing interlocking pathology, family members experience shame, guilt, low self-esteem, frustration, fatigue, helplessness, and hopelessness that escalate their sometimes angry and demanding behavior. An approach that is sensitive to the family's needs and defenses and that respects their needs for information and rights as consumers will lessen their more extreme reactions and lead to a therapeutic alliance (Anderson, Hogarty, & Reiss, 1980; Goldstein, 1981b). The family of the borderline patient requires a therapeutic holding environment that helps them contain their anxiety and become true collaborators in the treatment process. Preventing power struggles, being accessible, providing information, and involving family members in decision making facilitates their engagement. While many family members may require treatment of their own, they may be threatened by such efforts and, without the necessary support, will resist and act out, often undermining the primary patient's recovery.

Group Intervention

Arguing that unstructured groups mobilize regression and stimulate volatility and defensiveness in borderline individuals, most clinicians have cautioned against the use of intensive group therapy with this population. Supportive, structured, and task-oriented groups, however, can be used effectively with many borderlines to promote ego functioning and interpersonal relationships. Task-oriented groups can provide opportunities for the exercise of autonomy and the expansion of ego and social functioning.

12-Step Programs

While many therapists have tended to see the philosophies of 12-step programs and psychotherapy as polarized, the borderline substance abuser's participation in such programs generally is a necessary but not sufficient part of recovery. When treatment is on an inpatient basis, it is easy to mandate attendance at such meetings. When treatment is on an outpatient basis, it may take longer to motivate borderlines to make the commitment to attending such a program. Furthermore, there are some aspects of 12-step programs that are difficult for many borderlines. For example, because they live in the moment, lack trust and a sense of continuity with others, are out of control, and have trouble dealing with their feeling states, a focus on powerlessness, trust in a Higher Power, and doing a moral inventory may stimulate regressive and overwhelming feelings (Evans & Sullivan, 1990). They may need help in translating some of the steps to where they are and in "taking what they can and leaving the rest." The clinician who works with patients attending 12-step programs must be knowledgeable about and comfortable with them and able to help the patient integrate the generally compatible but sometimes conflicting foci of the two approaches (Winegar, Stephens, & Varney, 1987). For example, in early stages of sobriety, patients may get the message from 12-step programs that they are not to dwell on their feelings and will question the therapist's effort to explore emotion-laden issues. The therapist needs to know when it is supportive of patients to minimize or suppress such exploration in order to promote their sense of control and ability to take action, and when it is necessary to help them get in touch with, verbalize, and get validation for their feelings so as not to become overwhelmed by them.

CONCLUSION

Borderline pathology is common among those who are chemically dependent, and both the borderline disorder and the substance abuse need to be addressed in the treatment process. This chapter has described the main characteristics of borderline pathology that can be identified through a systematic assessment and the elements of an integrated treatment approach with borderline substance abusers. The need to individualize the treatment of borderline substance abusers challenges mental health and substance abuse professionals and staff to overcome some of the barriers to integrated service delivery that currently exist and to experiment with creative solutions in work with this vexing population.

REFERENCES

Adler, G. (1985). Borderline psychopathology and its treatment. New York: Aronson.

Akiskal, H. S. (1981). Subaffective disorders: Dysthymic, cyclothymic and bipolar II disorders in the borderline realm. Psychiatric Clinics of North America, 4, 25–46.

American Psychiatric Association. (1987). Diagnostic and statistical manual of mental disorders (3rd ed., rev.). Washington, DC: Author.

Anderson, C., Hogarty, G. E., & Reiss, D. J. (1980). Family treatment of adult schizophrenic patients: A psychoeducational approach. Schizophrenia Bulletin, 6, 490–505.

Attia, P. R. (1988). Dual diagnosis: Definition and treatment. Alcoholism Treatment Quarterly, 5, 53–63.

Bacal, H. A. (1985). Optimal responsiveness and the therapeutic process. In A. Goldberg (Ed.), Progress in self psychology (Vol. 1, pp. 202–227). New York: Guilford.

Berger, P. A. (1987). Pharmacological treatment for borderline personality disorder. Bulletin of the Menninger Clinic, 51, 277–284.

Beverly, C. (1989). Treatment issues for black, alcoholic clients. Social Casework, 70, 370–374.

Blanck, G., & Blanck, R. (1974). Ego psychology in theory and practice. New York: Columbia University Press.

Blanck, G., & Blanck, R. (1979). Ego psychology II: Psychoanalytic developmental psychology. New York: Columbia University Press.

Blume, S. (1989). Dual diagnosis: Psychoactive substance dependence and the personality disorders. Journal of Psychoactive Drugs, 21, 139–144.

Brandchaft, B., & Stolorow, R. D. (1984). The borderline concept: Pathological character or iatrogenic myth. In J. Lichtenberg, M. Bornstein, & D. Silver (Eds.), Empathy II (pp. 333–358). Hillsdale, NJ: Analytic Press.

Brown, V., Ridgely, M., Pepper, B., Levine, I., & Ryglewicz, H. (1989). The dual crisis: Mental illness and substance abuse. American Psychologist, 44, 565–569.

Buie, D. H., & Adler, G. (1982). The definitive treatment of the borderline personality. International Journal of Psychoanalytic Psychotherapy, 9, 51–87.

Chernus, L. A. (1985). Clinical issues in alcoholism treatment. Social Casework, 66, 67–75.

Chestang, L. (1980). Character development in a hostile environment. In M. Bloom (Ed.), Life span development: Bases for preventive and interventive helping (pp. 40–50). New York: Macmillan.

Comas-Diaz, L., & Minrath, M. (1985). Psychotherapy with ethnic minority borderline clients. Psychotherapy, 22, 418–426.

Evans, K., & Sullivan, J. M. (1990). Dual diagnosis: Counseling the mentally ill substance abuser. New York: Guilford.

Fewell, C. H., & Bissell, L. (1978). The alcohol-denial syndrome: An alcohol focused approach. *Social Casework, 59,* 6-13.

Friedman, H. (1969). Some problems of inpatient management with borderline patients. *American Journal of Psychiatry, 126,* 47-52.

Goldstein, E. G. (1981a, March). *The family characteristics of borderline patients.* Paper presented at the annual meeting of the Americn Orthopsychiatric Association, New York.

Goldstein, E. G. (1981b). Promoting competence in families of psychiatric patients. In A. Maluccio (Ed.), *Building competence in clients: A new/old approach to social work intervention* (pp. 317-342). New York: Free Press.

Goldstein, E. G. (1983). Clinical and ecological approaches to the borderline client. *Social Casework, 64,* 353-362.

Goldstein, E. G. (1984). *Ego psychology and social work practice.* New York: Free Press.

Goldstein, E. G. (1990). *Borderline disorders: Clinical models and techniques.* New York: Guilford.

Grinker, R. R., Werble, B., & Drye, R. (1968). *The borderline syndrome.* New York: Basic Books.

Gunderson, J. G., Kerr, J., & Englund, D. W. (1980). The families of borderlines: A comparative study. *Archives of General Psychiatry, 37,* 27-33.

Herman, J. L., Perry, J. C., & van der Kolk, B. (1989). Childhood trauma in borderline personality disorder. *American Journal of Psychiatry, 146,* 490-495.

Kernberg, O. F. (1975). *Borderline conditions and pathological narcissism.* New York: Aronson.

Kernberg, O. F. (1984). *Severe personality disorders.* New Haven, CT: Yale University Press.

Kiesler, C., Simpkins, C., & Morton, T. (1991). Prevalence of dual diagnosis of mental and subtance abuse disorders in general hospitals. *Hospital and Community Psychiatry, 42,* 400-405.

Klein, D. F. (1977). Psychopharmacological treatment and delineation of borderline disorders. In P. Hartocollis (Ed.), *Borderline personality disorders* (pp. 365-384). New York: International Universities Press.

Kohut, H. (1971). *The analysis of the self.* New York: International Universities Press.

Kohut, H. (1977). *The restoration of the self.* New York: International Universities Press.

Kohut, H. (1984). *How does analysis cure?* Chicago: University of Chicago Press.

Kohut, H., & Wolf, E. S. (1978). The disorders of the self and their treatment. *International Journal of Psycho-Analysis, 59,* 413-425.

Kroll, J. (1988). *The challenge of the borderline patient.* New York: Norton.

Levin, J. D. (1987). *Treatment of alcoholism and other addictions: A self-psychology approach.* New York: Aronson.

Levinson, V., & Straussner, S. L. A. (1978). Social workers as "enablers" in the treatment of alcoholics. *Social Casework, 59,* 14-20.

Lewis, L. A. (1984). The coming out process for lesbians: Integrating a stable identity. *Social Work, 29,* 464-469.

Masterson, J. F. (1972). *Treatment of the borderline adolescent.* New York: Wiley.

Masterson, J. F. (1976). *Treatment of the borderline adult.* New York: Brunner/Mazel.

Masterson, J. F., & Rinsley, D. (1975). The borderline syndrome: The role of the mother in the genesis and psychic structure of the borderline personality. *International Journal of Psycho-Analysis, 56,* 163–177.

Meissner, W. W. (1988). *Treatment of patients in the borderline spectrum.* New York: Aronson.

Minkoff, K. (1989). An integrated treatment model for dual diagnosis and addiction. *Hospital and Community Psychiatry, 40,* 1031–1036.

Mulinski, P. (1989). Dual diagnosis in alcoholic clients: Clinical implications. *Social Casework, 70,* 333–339.

Nurnberg, H. G., & Suh, R. (1978). Time-limited treatment of hospitalized borderline patients: Considerations. *Comprehensive Psychiatry, 19,* 419–431.

Osher, F., & Kofoed, L. (1989). Treatment of patients with psychiatric and psychoactive substance abuse disorders. *Hospital and Community Psychiatry, 40,* 1025–1030.

Pack, A. (1987). The role of psychopharmacology in the treatment of borderline patients. In J. S. Grotstein, M. F. Solomon, & J. A. Lang (Eds.), *The borderline patient* (Vol. 2, pp. 177–186). Hillsdale, NJ: Analytic Press.

Ridgeley, M., Goldman, H., & Willenbring, M. (1990). Barriers to the care of persons with dual diagnoses: Organizational and financing issues. *Schizophrenia Bulletin, 16,* 123–132.

Rush, A. J. (1984). Cognitive therapy. In T. B. Karasu (Ed.), *The psychiatric therapies.* Washington, DC: American Psychiatric Press.

Schwartzman, G. (1984). Narcissistic transferences: Implications for the treatment of couples. *Dynamic Psychotherapy, 2,* 5–14.

Shapiro, E. R., Shapiro, R. L., Zinner, J., & Berkowitz, D. (1977). The borderline ego and the working alliance: Implications for family and individual treatment. *International Journal of Psycho-Analysis, 58,* 77–87.

Slipp, S. (Ed.). (1988). *The technique and practice of object relations family therapy.* Northvale, NJ: Aronson.

Solomon, M. F. (1985). Treatment of narcissistic and borderline disorders in marital therapy: Suggestions toward an enhanced therapeutic approach. *Clinical Social Work Journal, 13,* 141–156.

Stern, A. (1938). Psychoanalytic investigation of and therapy in a borderline group of neuroses. *Psychoanalytic Quarterly, 7,* 467–89.

Stewart, R. H., Peters, T. C., Marsh, S., & Peters, M. J. (1975). An object relations approach with couples, families, and children. *Family Process, 14,* 161–172.

Stone, M. H. (1987). Systems for defining a borderline case. In J. S. Grotstein, M. F. Solomon, & J. A. Lang (Eds.), *The borderline patient* (Vol. 1, pp. 13–36). Hillsdale, NJ: Analytic Press.

Wallace, J. (1978). Working with the preferred defense structure of the recovering alcoholic. In S. Zimberg, J. Wallace, & S. B. Blume (Eds.), *Practical approaches to alcoholism therapy* (pp. 19–29). New York: Plenum.

Wallen, M., & Weiner, H. (1989). Impediments to effective treatment of the dually diagnosed patient. *Journal of Psychoactive Drugs, 21,* 161–168.

Walsh, F. (1977). Family study 1976: 14 new borderline cases. In R. R. Grinker & B. Werble (Eds.), *The borderline patient* (pp. 158–177). New York: Aronson.

Weick, A., Rapp, C., Sullivan, W. P., & Kisthardt, W. (1989). A strengths perspective for social work practice. *Social Work, 34,* 350–354.

Wells, M., & Glickauf-Hughes, C. (1986). Techniques to develop object constancy with borderline clients. *Psychotherapy, 23,* 460–468.

Wheeler, B. K., & Walton, E. (1987). Personality disturbances of adult incest victims. *Social Casework, 68,* 597–602.

White, M. T., & Weiner, M. B. (1986). *The theory and practice of self psychology.* New York: Brunner/Mazel.

Winegar, N., Stephens, T. A., & Varney, E. D. (1987). Alcoholics Anonymous and the alcoholic defense structure. *Social Casework, 68,* 223–228.

Wolf, E. S. (1988). *Treating the self: Elements of clinical self psychology.* New York: Guilford.

Zweben, J., & Smith, D. (1989). Considerations in using psychotropic medication with dual diagnosis patients in recovery. *Journal of Psychoactive Drugs, 21,* 221–228.

16

Substance Abuse among the Homeless

SHELLEY SCHEFFLER

It is rare nowadays to walk down a city street, or ride on a train or bus, without seeing the most obvious social problem of this era, homelessness. The actual number of homeless at any given time is difficult to assess, and the estimates range from a quarter-million to 3 million (Lam, 1987). The general belief is that the rate of homelessness has been and is increasing and that this population includes people not previously associated with homelessness, particularly women and children. Part of the difficulty in accounting for the number of homeless is the varying definitions of homelessness. For some, homelessness is simply defined as being without a permanent residence, while for others the lack of social ties and relationships is a key issue. For the purposes of this chapter, the definition of homeless individuals is that put forward by Baxter and Hopper (1981), which states that the homeless are "those whose primary nighttime residence is either in publicly or privately operated shelters or in the streets, doorways, etc., or other hidden sites known only to their users" (pp. 6–7).

A 1987 survey by the Urban Institute estimated that the number of homeless in the United States was between 500,000 and 600,000. This survey found that 81% of the homeless were male and 19%, female. Forty-six percent were white; 41%, African-Americans; 10%, Hispanic; and 3%, other. The breakdown according to age showed that 51% were 31 to 50; 30%, 18 to 30; 16%, 51 to 65; and 3%, 66 and over (Burt & Cohen, 1989).

A study done by a leading epidemiologist found that alcoholism rates among the homeless are as much as nine times higher than among the general population and that alcoholism is about 10% to 20% higher in shelters than on the streets (U.S. Department of Health and Human Services [USDHHS], 1989).

This chapter addresses the issue of homelessness; the role of alcohol and drug abuse within the homeless population, particularly among the homeless utilizing the shelter system; and the role of social workers in working with these clients.

THE HISTORICAL RELATIONSHIP BETWEEN HOMELESSNESS AND ALCOHOL ABUSE

Historically, alcohol was considered an inherent factor in homelessness. Homelessness in America can be traced back to the settlement of the western frontier, where unattached men, often cowboys, loggers, and so forth, went to work. However, once the frontier was developed, the number of employment opportunities was reduced and some of the men took to the road in search of work. They were called "hoboes," a name applied to those who wandered and worked, as opposed to "tramps," who wandered but did not work. Life on the road was often romanticized, and hoboes were depicted as individuals who were not willing to comply with prevailing social norms (Cumming, 1974).

The economic depression of 1873 caused widespread unemployment and resulted in homelessness and the growth of run-down areas that provided cheap shelter, such as flophouses. These areas came to be known as "skid row," a term taken from Seattle's Skid Row, which was a street where horses skidded logs to a sawmill and whose inhabitants were primarily lumberjacks. The area was filled with saloons, brothels, and flophouses, all the institutions usually associated with homeless men. "Skid row" soon became the generic term for run-down areas in cities across the nation. Studies of the skid row areas during that time indicate that alcohol played a major role in the lives of their inhabitants and often served as the context for social interaction (Garrett, 1989).

The economic prosperity of the 1920s saw a decline in homelessness, only to be followed by the devastating Great Depression of the 1930s, which created widespread poverty and an increased transient population. The United States pulled out of the Depression in the late 1930s, and "those who remained homeless in the economic boom years and after World War II tended to be middle aged male alcoholics and persons with deep emotional and psychological problems" (Leepson, 1982, p. 802).

Up until the 1960s, the public inebriate was considered a criminal and a moral degenerate, frequently going from street to jail, then back to the street or a flophouse. This mostly male population often used the jails for housing, getting themselves arrested for vagrancy or public intoxification when they wanted temporary relief from the stress of living on the streets. With the decriminalization of public drunkenness in the 1970s, homeless alcoholics were no longer jailed. The result was an increasing number of individuals on the street and the growing need for public shelters.

Prior to the 1980s, disaffiliation was the key concept in describing homelessness. The homeless individual was characterized by the absence of family and friends; he was usually a white, middle-aged male, a loner whose primary social activity was participating in a bottle gang. Drinking was described as a way to adapt to and be accepted by the subculture of skid row (Bahr, 1973).

Some researchers have explored the extent to which alcohol problems are an antecedent to homelessness. Bahr and Garrett (cited in Garrett & Schutt, 1987) each studied this question by comparing homeless individuals identified as heavy drinkers with other homeless respondents. Neither study clearly established that alcohol problems were a factor causing homelessness. Furthermore, patterns of disaffiliation did not differ significantly between homeless individuals who drank heavily and those who did not.

A study by Calsyn and Morse (1991), which examined the relationship between problem drinking and homelessness within a male population, found that the length of time spent homeless and the degree of transience were not predictive of alcoholism. The most significant finding of this study was the relationship between stress and alcoholism. The study did not clarify whether the high levels of stress existing prior to homelessness overwhelm an individual's adaptive coping ability—subsequently leading to drinking—or whether a preexisting drinking problem precipitates life crises ultimately resulting in homelessness.

Throughout the history of homelessness, there is a marked absence of literature on homeless women. The limited studies done in the 1960s and 1970s found that while fewer in number, homeless women were similar to their male counterparts on skid row. They were characterized as isolated, emotionally disturbed, alcoholic, and plagued with numerous health problems (Lam, 1987).

In the late 1970s the characteristics of homeless women began to change. In comparison to their male counterparts; homeless women of the 1980s presented a picture of more relatedness and interconnection. No longer characterized solely as "bag ladies" or "isolated alcoholics," the women reported having had intimate relationships in their lives, and many had children with whom they were still in contact. These homeless women were more likely than homeless men to have grown up in an institutional or foster care setting (Crystal, 1982).

THE NEW HOMELESS

The changing economy and social systems of the 1980s and 1990s have brought forth "the new homeless." Included in this group are higher rates of women, children, and adolescents, as well as those with severe psychiatric disorders. The new homeless population tends to be younger and more frequently African-American or Hispanic.

The number of alcohol abusers among the homeless has remained fairly constant at approximately 30% over the years. However, use of drugs such as marijuana and cocaine, which first emerged around the 1970s, and crack, the drug of the 1980s, has increased in prevalence, especially among younger homeless people (Crystal, 1982).

The use of alcohol and drugs among the new homeless is viewed "as a badge, or a ritualized affirmation of (even a disgraced) identity; as a functional adaptation—an anodyne—to the emptiness and listlessness of street and shelter life; as a modality of self medication for both physical and psychiatric ills" (Fischer, 1987, p. 28).

The most frequently used substances among today's homeless are alcohol, marijuana, cocaine, and crack (USDHHS, 1989). Although few accurate statistics are available, the drug currently seen as the most harmful is crack. Reports on a men's shelter in New York City housing an average of 850 men claim that crack abuse affects approximately 85% of the population (Barbanel, 1988). This figure, however, does not indicate the extent of individual use.

The chronically mentally ill are reportedly one-third of the homeless population. Many of these individuals also abuse drugs and alcohol. A study of patients in the Alternatives to Hospitalization Program in Los Angeles found that 68% of the 53 homeless mentally ill patients had a history of serious substance abuse (Koegel & Burnam, 1987).

EFFORTS TO HELP THE HOMELESS

Clearly the most immediate need of the homeless population is for food and shelter. In response to the increasing numbers of people who are homeless, cities across the country have been forced to provide emergency shelter. According to the U.S. Department of Housing and Urban Development, by 1984 there were more than 1,800 shelters throughout the United States (Schutt, 1987).

These facilities vary widely; some are publicly funded and operated, while others are run by voluntary agencies. Some provide only minimum service, such as a bed, food, and showering facilities for the night, often requiring early-morning departure. Others are more comprehensive, including social services and medical treatment.

In addition to publicly run shelters, local community and religious groups have responded to the needs of the homeless by setting up voluntary shelters. These can range from cots laid down in a church basement on a cold winter night to large buildings operated by such organizations as Volunteers of America.

Many homeless individuals view the public shelters as unsafe and imposing too many restrictions, preferring the more humane feeling of the smaller community-run shelter. Others reject the shelter system entirely and choose to remain on the streets, frequently inhabiting such places as train and bus stations. In a study done in Boston's Long Island Shelter, it was found that those with psychiatric and alcohol problems were more frequent users of shelters and social services and were more likely to have been arrested than other homeless people (Schutt, 1987).

THE STRESS OF SHELTER LIFE

The daily struggle of homelessness affects every area of functioning, whether an individual is residing on the streets or in an emergency shelter. Often drugs and alcohol serve as a major coping device to get through the day by anesthetizing feelings and giving a false sense of security. It is not uncommon for a group of homeless individuals to buy and share a bottle. This can be viewed as a frequent form of socializing among homeless individuals.

The nature and design of municipal emergency shelters often support the lowest level of functioning. More often than not, there is no privacy and users are lodged in huge, open rooms with little space to store belongings. Bathroom and shower facilities tend to be without doors, creating a frightening feeling of vulnerability. As in other institutions, "survival of the fittest" prevails, which often causes the more vulnerable homeless to choose to live on the streets. Shelter residents tend to develop patterns of survival, in a process that has been called "shelterization." It is characterized by a decrease in interpersonal responsiveness, a neglect of personal hygiene, increasing passivity, and an increasing dependency on others (Grunberg & Eagle, 1990).

Drugs and alcohol often play a major part in the economy of shelter life. Drugs are frequently sold or exchanged for favors, and it is not uncommon for an able-bodied resident to go to the liquor store for an elderly alcoholic in exchange for a "taste."

THE SHELTER AS AN ENABLER

Substance abuse is characterized by dependence, tolerance, progression, loss of control, and denial (Evans & Sullivan, 1990). Because of the denial, it is difficult to motivate a substance abuser to acknowledge the problem and seek treatment. Often individuals are motivated toward sobriety through their ties with the world, for example, pressure from employers or family members. On the other hand, it is not uncommon for the system around the individual to change to accommodate the drinking or drugging, hence joining the denial. For example, as the individual's drinking interferes with usual responsibilities, other family members cover for him or her, thus enabling the substance abuse to continue (Levinson & Straussner, 1978).

In the absence of family, friends, and work, the network of the homeless living in a shelter includes other shelter residents and staff, who may become the enablers. Shelter employees are often the major feedback system of the residents. They are the first to see residents in the morning and the last at night, sometimes being the only person to have verbal contact with them. Those residents who pose no problem and tend to be engaging often gain favors and special privileges, which may include overlooking the issue of drugs or alcohol.

Most shelter systems have rules against using drugs or alcohol on-site. However, this does not prevent shelter residents from entering the facility drunk or high. As long as they are not posing any behavioral problems, they may be permitted entry. Regulation of substance abuse tends to be more stringent in private shelters since these facilities are usually smaller, makeshift dorms staffed by volunteers and therefore more affected by an intoxicated guest.

Shelters are not designed to be treatment centers. Food and shelter are provided unless a resident becomes unruly. Therefore the shelter often functions as the enabler, accommodating to the residents' drinking and covering the consequence of it. This is exemplified in the following case.

Ruth is a 53-year-old white female who came to the shelter system 10 years ago. She has a 19-year-old son in a psychiatric institution. Although she speaks about him often, she does not know which hospital he is in and has made no request for help in finding him. Ruth drinks daily, frequently appearing to be drunk in the late afternoon. She denies any drinking problem vehemently, although she talks about the sadness of her life.

Ruth describes her early childhood as very happy. She states that she attended an exclusive residential school with children whose parents were connected to the United Nations. She does not speak about her parents, emphasizing instead the privilege she had of attending such a school. It is believed that the school she is referring to was, in reality, a home for abandoned children.

Ruth's daily life consists of doing laundry, ironing clothes, and participating in the shelter work program. She assists the supervisor of the work program with processing timesheets and answering phones. She has gained recognition because of her extreme efficiency, on which she prides herself. Her drinking begins primarily late in the day, and she can function until early afternoon. Since this is not a regular paying job, the supervisor tolerates her lateness and absenteeism. In the midst of shelter residents who often have either severe psychiatric problems or negative, hostile attitudes, she is seen as a high-functioning, valued resident. During her stay in the shelter, Ruth has refused offers to help her get a job or alternate housing, although she holds tight to her wish to get a decent apartment in a decent neighborhood. At one point, she briefly became involved with an on-site case management program at the shelter, but she quickly left when the social worker addressed her drinking problem.

The case of Ruth highlights many factors associated with alcohol and drug problems among the homeless. She experienced early loss of her family, although the reasons are unknown, and grew up in an institution. Unable to sustain herself in the community and burdened with all the stress and failure related to having a son with psychiatric problems, she came to the shelter. In the shelter she is able to feel superior to other residents, and this sense of superiority is supported pharmacologically with the use of alcohol.

The shelter is a setting where many people function in a minimal and bizarre fashion. Within this context Ruth appears as a high-functioning person, and she uses this to support the denial of her alcohol problem. Outside of the shelter setting, it would be unlikely that Ruth's daily drinking habits would be acceptable to any employer. As long as she remains in the shelter, she will continue to receive praise for her work while her drinking problem remains largely unaddressed. Consequently, Ruth needs to remain in the shelter in order to maintain any feelings of value about herself and in order to be able to continue to drink with relatively little external pressure to stop.

MOTIVATION FOR TREATMENT

Homeless alcohol abusers often continue to be in a state of denial, attributing their continued homelessness to everything but drinking. It is also not uncommon to meet younger clients who are experiencing similar losses and deterioration due to crack. The toll of crack is a heavy one. Individuals will deny their use, even though using, and will spend all their money to purchase the drug, even when they may have been thrown out of their homes because of their crack abuse. On the nights that the shelter work program pays residents a $12.50 stipend for working 20 hours a week, crack dealers may walk up and down the street waiting for their customers, offering a quick, ostensibly cheap, remedy to a dismal life of deprivation.

The need for self-esteem, the need for access to physical and material well-being, and the need for relief from psychic pain are issues that are vital in motivating this population. Treatment must be geared to addressing these issues in order to be successful.

In working with homeless substance abusers, addressing a hierarchy of needs must be central to efforts to engage them in treatment. In a study done of 817 New York City shelter residents, the following hierarchy of needs was identified: (1) finding a place to live; (2) securing a steady income; (3) improving physical and mental health status and family relationships; (4) resolving problems with alcohol and drugs; and (5) dealing with issues such as transportation, self-protection, and the police (Struening, 1987). In another study by Ball and Havassy in San Francisco (cited in Breakey, 1987), the homeless population studied listed the following needs in ranked order: (1) affordable housing; (2) financial entitlements; (3) employment; (4) free-time activities and social contacts; (5) food; (6) alcohol cessation; (7) supportive counseling; (8) money management; (9) interpersonal skills; and (10) storage for possessions.

In line with these expressed needs, a nationwide survey of services to the homeless alcoholic showed that exemplary programs have shifted their emphasis from detoxification and staff-intensive residential recovery program activities to housing and other support services aimed at homeless alcoholics (Wittman, 1989).

Realistic strategies for engaging the homeless substance abuser need to include assistance in obtaining basic services for a stable environment, including housing, financial assistance, food, and clothing. Frequently the ability to aid the individual in concrete ways will help to begin to repair the hopelessness that often accompanies the damaging effects of homelessness.

Programs that have been successful in reaching treatment-resistant individuals start with the most apparent needs as a means of developing trust and a bridge to other services. Treatment agencies that go out to the streets, using food as their motivating tool, are one example of this. Another example is provided by those treatment agencies that offer a continuum of services from detoxification to sober living environments, such as the Comprehensive Homeless Alcohol Recovery Services (CHARS) in Alameda County, California. This is a National Institute on Alcohol Abuse and Alcoholism demonstration project that includes an alcohol crisis center, two multipurpose drop-in centers, seven residential recovery centers, a transitional housing program, and permanent sober housing (Bennett, Weiss, & West, 1990).

It is important to keep in mind that a homeless substance abuser will not be successful in treatment without access to a safe place to live; at the same time, housing the homeless substance abuser without treatment leaves them vulnerable to the same problems that may have caused their homelessness.

While many individuals may as a rule resist treatment, they may become more amenable to social work intervention when feeling the discomfort of their substance abuse. Often they will be motivated by medical problems to enter detoxification units. Usually they return to the streets or shelter feeling better, only to return to the hospital at a later date. Moreover, it is not uncommon for homeless substance abusers to use detoxification services as a respite from the streets, just as the people in the past used jails for the same purpose. Nonetheless, hospitalization for a medical problem or for detoxification might be the point of entry into long-term treatment if designed to meet the needs of the homeless individual. For instance, the prospect of an alcohol-free living center may seem more appealing than returning to the shelter.

Initial approaches to the homeless substance abuser frequently require extensive outreach efforts. Mobile vans, drop-in centers, and strategically positioned outreach workers are often the essential ingredient in motivating an individual toward treatment. This is exemplified in the following case.

John, a 27-year-old black male, had watched social workers from the municipal outreach office interview men at the local deli, where many homeless men hang out during the day. One day he approached a worker to find out why he was there and stated that he had been using crack for the past 2 years, resulting in being thrown out of his home. He had been hanging out with a buddy of his, who was also addicted to crack. Together they had committed petty crimes, and whenever possible they would use the money for drugs and a room, although recently they both had been living in the subways. Lately it seemed that his friend was getting more and more dysfunctional, starting fights on the street, using drugs openly, and basically jeopardizing their tenuous existence. John was concerned that he was heading in the same direction. He stated that he wanted help but was not sure where to begin. The worker assessed his most obvious need, which was food, clothing, and shelter. Since John made it clear that he was terrified of the public shelters, the worker referred John to one of the smaller men's missions. He made an appointment to see him the following week at the home office of the outreach team, located in a local hospital.

John did well at the mission; he was drug-free that week and kept his appointment with the social worker. After several weeks, during which he kept all his appointments and stayed drug-free, the worker introduced the idea of getting involved in a drug program. Initially John refused, stating that he saw his primary problem as the need for money. However, as John began to trust the worker, he became more open to the worker's recommendation of an outpatient day treatment drug program that offered both educational and vocational services as well as housing assistance (Billington, 1991).

In this case, the social worker was able to interest the client in treatment through concrete services. By addressing his most obvious need for food and shelter, the worker was able to engage and motivate the client to obtain further treatment.

INTERVENTION WITH SUBSTANCE-ABUSING HOMELESS

The alcohol- and drug-abusing homeless population face many problems. Within this group, some may have become homeless because of their substance abuse, while others may have become homeless first, increasing their substance use in response to their homelessness. Yet the difficulties that they face are the same; they are a group without resources, finding quick relief in the use of alcohol and drugs.

Traditional substance abuse treatment services are not prepared to deal with the issues that homelessness presents. Addressing the problems of this group can no longer be limited to a singular focus on intrapsychic issues and the belief that once the individual changes, the environment will change. Although the chances of lifestyles improvement certainly increase with sobriety, the solution to homelessness does not lie solely with the individual. Increasingly over the past 20 years, low-cost housing options have been significantly reduced due to economic and political reasons. Therefore even when a person is motivated toward recovery, once he or she has become homeless the return to normal functioning is full of obstacles.

Moving from a state of homelessness is not a simple act. In so affluent a culture, it is often difficult to understand the extensive assistance necessary to enable an individual to move from homelessness. For instance, housing requires proof of identity as well as sufficient funds for security and the first month's rent. Landlords will not rent to those who present themselves shabbily dressed, unclean, or smelling of alcohol. To obtain work, a person needs adequate clothing, a way to clean him- or herself, and carfare for transportation. Sufficient funds to live during the initial week of work are needed until the first paycheck arrives. Telephones and addresses are often necessary to receive information from a potential employer or a potential landlord. These resources are not readily available to the homeless, nor are they easily obtained.

Moreover, the adaptive strategies necessary to maintain oneself on the street or in the shelter are often skills that are not valuable in facilitating reentry to the mainstream. All these issues are compounded when an individual has a substance abuse problem. Some of the factors that have been associated with homelessness, such as disaffiliation and mistrust of service organizations, often prevent people from getting treatment. Availability and accessibility of treatment services often are the key issue in whether a homeless individual enters treatment. For example, most outpatient substance abuse clinics work by appointment. A homeless person may have difficulty keeping an appointment without owning a watch or having another way to determine the day or time. Furthermore, if a person is living in a shelter, his or her schedule is determined by the regulations of the shelter. Carfare, which is distributed in the public shelters, may or may not be given out on time, therefore determining whether the person arrives for his or her appointment on time or at all.

Substance abuse agencies working with the homeless population have tailored their services to meet the needs of this population, as exemplified above in the case of John. Outreach and case management services are essential features in helping an individual into the treatment system. Outreach places workers in areas where the homeless congregate, making themselves available and known to those who may want assistance. The function of the case manager is to assess the client's needs, make referrals, coordinate services, and facilitate communication between client and various agencies. Often the relationship with the worker serves as the constant, sustaining force in the reentry efforts of the client, providing support, encouragement, and hope. The case manager is responsible not only for initiating and sustaining connection to services but also for follow-up in the progression of recovery.

In addition to performing case management functions, programs treating the homeless must develop sensitivity to the issues of homelessness. For instance, in a demonstration project in Boston, it was found that 5 days in a detoxification unit are not sufficient time for the homeless chronic abuser; longer periods are necessary for the restoration of physical and cognitive functions (McCarty, Argeriou, Krakow, & Mulvey, 1990).

A relatively new approach to helping the homeless alcohol abuser is the alcohol-free living center. These centers are designed to provide a low-rent, alcohol-free environment for recovering alcoholics who have small, steady incomes and wish to enter into independent living arrangements with peers. The emphasis in this environment is reliance on support and pressure from peers who have been in recovery, rather than on classes and counseling (Koroloff & Anderson, 1989).

WORKERS' ROLES AND EXPECTATIONS

Denial, low rates of recovery, and the inherent dynamic of relapse among the substance-abusing population pose difficult challenges for most social workers. These problems, coupled with the extensive problems of homelessness, have tended to increase social workers' pessimism about actually being able to help.

Workers find that it is often difficult to engage the homeless substance abuser because of distrust of authority and wariness of service providers. In addition, the lifestyle of the homeless is not compatible with treatment services. When they do come for help, it is rarely a simple case; extensive intervention and creativity in connecting them up to different services are usually required (Breakey, 1987).

Working with this population demands much flexibility in the social work role. As stated previously, the ability to engage individuals in treatment requires extending help in a wide variety of areas. Therefore the worker may need to make referrals for entitlements or locate a nearby soup kitchen in order to meet the needs of the client. At the same time, the worker needs to address the problems of substance abuse and often has to work with a client who may be physically repulsive due to lack of clean clothing and bathing facilities.

Workers need to be prepared to be patient in approaching clients and to realize that it may take an extraordinary amount of time to build any trust. Prognosis is often poor, and it is important to keep expectations based in reality.

The plight of the homeless often taps into some of the deeper, darker fears that we, as humans, carry with us. The fear of being alone in the world, without friends or family or the ability to alter our situation, is often the underlying fear that makes workers reluctant to become involved with this population. Even for those who do become involved, such counter-transferential reactions make it difficult for them to continue this kind of work for any length of time.

Supervison and staff support can often mediate some of the stress from working with this population. It is important for workers to be able to identify countertransferential issues as they arise and to ventilate them with the support and understanding of others. The foreknowledge that these issues may arise is often helpful in building in safeguards. In addition, efforts to balance caseloads with both hopeful and difficult client helps to prevent some of the hopelessness occasionally felt by workers.

The truly positive aspect of working with this population is that some do recover and return to a reasonably normal life. Being part of the process of helping someone who is often coming from the depths of desperation can be an inspiring experience. In working with a population whose needs are so great, any intervention, even one as small as getting a client a meal, imme-diately alleviates a piece of the misery of that person's life.

CONCLUSION

The issue of loss has always been a part of the progression of substance abuse, whether it be loss of family, friends, work, or material goods. Today, included among these many losses is the possible loss of a permanent place to live. Given current economic, political, and social factors, once a person has become homeless the options for returning to a reasonable place to live have become increasingly limited.

It is crucial that social workers be aware of the devastation that becoming and being homeless creates and begin to intervene in appropriate ways. This is a sensitive issue, since subtance abusers frequently need to experience the consequences of their drinking and drugging before becoming motivated for treatment. Workers need to explore the interventions appropriate for helping the homeless without also becoming an enabler in the process.

It is also important that substance abuse treatment agencies make themselves more aware of the problems of homelessness and develop the necessary services to aid clients who are both substance abusers and homeless. The task of helping homeless substance abusers cannot be relegated only to those already working with the homeless; services need to be integrated in order to be comprehensive.

REFERENCES

Bahr, H. M. (1973). *Old men drunk and sober*. New York: New York University Press.

Barbanel, J. (1988, February 18). Crack use pervades life in a shelter. *New York Times*, p. A-1.

Baxter, E., & Hopper, K. (1981). *Private lives/public spaces*. New York: Community Service Society.

Bennett, R. W., Weiss, H. L., & West, B. R. (1990). Alameda County Department of Alcohol and Drug Programs Comprehensive Homeless Alcohol Recovery Services (CHARS). *Alcoholism Treatment Quarterly, 7*, 111–128.

Billington, C. (1991, May 12). Interview.

Breakey, W. R. (1987). Treating the homeless. *Alcohol Health and Research World, 2*, 42–47.

Burt, M. R., & Cohen, B. E. (1989). *America's homeless numbers, characteristics, and programs that serve them* (Urban Institute Report 89-3). Washington, DC: Urban Institute Press.

Calsyn, R. J., & Morse, G. A. (1991). Correlates of problem drinking among homeless men. *Hospital and Community Psychiatry, 42*, 721–725.

Crystal, S. (1982). *Chronic and situational dependency: Long-term residents in a shelter for men*. New York: Human Resources Administration.

Cumming, E. (1974). Prisons, shelters and homeless men. *Psychiatric Quarterly, 48*, 496–504.

Evans, K., & Sullivan, J. M. (1990). *Dual diagnosis: Counseling the mentally ill substance abuser*. New York: Guilford.

Fischer, P. (1987). *Alcohol problems among the contemporary homeless population: An analytic review of the literature* (Report to the Committee on Health Care for Homeless People). Washington, DC: National Academy of Sciences, Institute of Medicine.

Garrett, G. R. (1989). Alcohol problems and homelessness: History and research. *Contemporary Drug Problems, 16*, 301–330.

Garrett, G. R., & Shutt, R. K. (1987). The homeless alcoholic, past and present. In *Homelessness: Critical issues for policy and practice* (pp. 29–32). Boston: Boston Foundation.

Grunberg, J., & Eagle, P. F. (1990). Shelterization: How the homeless adapt to shelter living. *Hospital and Community Psychiatry, 41* 521–525.

Koegel, P., & Burnam, M. (1987). Traditional and nontraditional homeless alcoholics. *Alcohol Health and Research World, 2,* 28–35.

Koroloff, N. M., & Anderson, S. C. (1989). Alcohol-free living center: Hope for homeless alcoholics. *Social Work, 34,* 497–504.

Lam, J. (1987). *Homeless women in America: Their social and health characteristics.* Unpublished doctoral dissertation, University of Massachusetts.

Leepson, M. (1982). *The homeless: Growing national problem.* Washington, DC: Editorial Reasearch Reports.

Levinson, V. R., & Straussner, S. L. (1978). Social workers as "enablers" in the treatment of alcoholics. *Social Casework, 59,* 14–20.

McCarty, D., Argeriou, M., Krakow, M., & Mulvey, K. (1990). Stabilization services for homeless alcoholics and drug addicts. *Alcohol Treatment Quarterly, 7,* 31–45.

Schutt, R. K. (1987). Shelters as organizations: Full fledged programs or just a place to stay? In *Homelessness: Critical issues for policy and practice* (pp. 43–52). Boston: Boston Foundation.

Struening, E. L. (1987). *A study of residents of the New York City shelter system: Report to the New York City Department of Mental Health, Mental Retardation and Alcoholism Services.* New York: Epidemiology of Mental Disorders Research Department, New York State Psychiatric Institute.

U.S. Department of Health and Human Services. (1989). *Homelessness, alcohol and other drugs.* Rockville, MD: National Institute on Alcohol Abuse and Alcoholism.

Wittman, F. D. (1989). Housing models for alcohol programs serving homeless people. *Contemporary Drug Problems, 16,* 483–504.

17

Assessment and Treatment of Clients Dependent on Cocaine and Other Stimulants

DAVID M. OCKERT AND ARMIN R. BAIER, JR.

The abuse of stimulants presents a problem of such enormous scope and proportion from social, psychological, and medical perspectives that we have only begun to assess its impact. Psychomotor stimulants include cocaine (in the form of powder, freebase, or crack) and the amphetamines (including amphetamine, methamphetamine/"ice", crystal Methedrine/"crank"). The devastating effects of these substances, most apparent in major metropolitan areas (National Institute on Drug Abuse [NIDA], 1991), affect every age group, including the unborn. In many cases the consequences of stimulant abuse are psychosis, brain damage, and death.

Why, then, do stimulant abusers run such risks? One answer is that stimulants produce an intense pleasure during early phases of dependence that strongly reinforces any behaviors necessary to allow continued use. This immediate, reinforcing euphoria is more powerful in controlling behavior than is the realization that, in the long run, chemical dependency can impair and may even destroy life.

Complex political, economic, and psychosocial factors determine what substances are used and abused in society today. An analysis of the influence of the political and economic climate on the drug problem is beyond the scope of this chapter. Nevertheless, this climate exists and must be understood by treatment professionals, as well as policy makers, in order to design effective strategies for prevention as well as for early intervention and treatment.

The purpose of this chapter is to present the history and current status of cocaine and other stimulant dependence in the United States; to emphasize the need for an understanding of an integrated multimodal approach addressing stimulant-related biological, psychological, and social (biopsychosocial) factors that have an impact on the individual in both assessment and treatment; and to present a case study of an integrated multimodal approach in assessment and treatment.

HISTORY AND EPIDEMIOLOGY

For centuries South American Indians have chewed the leaves of the coca plant to obtain a mild stimulant effect, apparently without any resulting dependence. Cocaine, the chief active ingredient in the leaves of the coca plant, was first isolated in alkaloid form in 1844 (Brecher & the Editors of Consumer Reports, 1972; *Remington's Pharmaceutical Sciences*, 1970). During the latter half of the 19th century, those European and American physicians and pharmacists aware of its stimulant effect began to use cocaine medicinally in various elixirs and tonics (such as the original form of Coca-Cola) and for the treatment of catarrhs (in snuff-like powdered form). Sigmund Freud and other physicians used cocaine, injected under the skin, to treat depression and chronic fatigue. However, they soon discovered that daily use could cause full-fledged symptoms of mental disturbance similar to those seen in delirium tremens (Brecher et al., 1972; E. Jones, 1953).

Recreational use of cocaine in the United States, which began around 1890, was legally restricted in 1914 with the passage of the Harrison Act (Courtwright, 1991). As cocaine use declined, amphetamines, a large group of synthetic stimulants including methamphetamine and crystal Methedrine, were marketed in the United States. Although restricted, amphetamines were easily found on the black market, and their use steadily increased following World War II. Despite further attempts to restrict illegal sale, the use of a nonsanctioned amphetamine called "speed" increased explosively during the 1960s. By the 1970s successful police action against illegal manufacture and sale of amphetamines had led to a resurgence of cocaine importation and use (Brecher et al., 1972).

During the 1970s cocaine, used intranasally, began replacing amphetamines. At this time, cocaine was claimed to be a relatively safe, nonaddicting euphoriant agent (Greenspoon & Bakalar, 1980). This perception was reinforced by reports from two national commissions on drug abuse, which concluded that amphetamines cause substantial morbidity but that cocaine does not (Gawin & Ellinwood, 1988; National Commission on Marijuana and Drug Abuse, 1973; Strategy Council on Drug Abuse, 1973). This erroneous conclusion, and the popular notion that cocaine is safe, derived in large part from the fact that cocaine dependence results in mostly psychological, rather than physical, withdrawal symptoms (Gawin & Ellinwood, 1988).

By the late 1970s cocaine was also being used in a smokable form called "freebase" or "base," which proved to have the greatest dependence liability of all drugs. The introduction of crack (a smokable form of cocaine similar to freebase but diluted with an inert filler and sold in small, inexpensive quantities) resulted in a rapidly escalating number of cocaine users during the 1980s. (Crack was originally called "rock" in the western United States.) Shortly thereafter, a crystalline, smokable form of methamphetamine, called "ice," began to appear in certain areas of the country.

The 1990 National Household Survey on Drug Abuse (NIDA, 1991) reports that while cocaine experimentation and use of "other stimulants" has decreased generally, crack use has remained stable. However, this survey also reports that there are continued high rates of frequent or intense cocaine use and that higher rates of use are found among certain segments of the population—young adults aged 18 to 25, blacks, individuals in large metropolitan areas, those living in the western United States, and the unemployed. Household surveys of illegal drug use contain inherent methodological problems that call into question their reliability and validity. Consequently the survey data must be viewed guardedly in order to avoid underestimating the extent of cocaine and other stimulant abuse.

EFFECTS OF COCAINE AND OTHER STIMULANTS

A neurobehavioral theory of cocaine and stimulant dependence rests on an understanding of the neurochemical impact these drugs have on the brain and the resulting effect on behaviors. This section discusses stimulant dependence in terms of neurobehavioral theory as a link to understanding the neurobehavioral model of assessment and treatment of stimulant dependence (Rawson, Obert, McCann, Smith, & Scheffey, 1989).

Neurochemical Impact of Stimulants

While cocaine and the amphetamines are structurally dissimilar, their neurochemical and clinical effects are similar, with the exception of duration of action (Gawin & Ellinwood, 1988). Cocaine has a half-life (the time required for half the amount of a substance introduced into the body to be broken down or eliminated by natural process), and thus a duration of euphoria, of less than 45 minutes (R. T. Jones, 1985), while amphetamines have a half-life up to eight times longer (Gunne & Anggard, 1973). Consequently intranasal cocaine use is characterized by readministration of the drug at intervals of 10 to 20 minutes, causing rapid and frequent mood changes. When amount and duration of cocaine use are comparable to high-dose amphetamine use, the psychological and behavioral effects of each are indistinguishable (Gawin & Ellinwood, 1988).

At the heart of the neurobehavioral model is the recognition that the highly complex set of behaviors required by humans to function effectively are assembled and maintained by reinforcement contingencies. Certain brain mechanisms mediating pleasure and its reinforcing quality are required to support this process. These are the mechanisms that are affected by substances of abuse in ways that create the problems of drug dependency.

What are these ways? One of the reinforcement mechanisms in the brain manufactures and utilizes the biochemical dopamine. These dopamine mechanisms can be induced by stimulants to magnify the pleasure experienced in most activities, thereby reinforcing maladaptive behaviors (such as social withdrawal) and interfering with adaptive behaviors (such as social responsibility). The dopamine system may also be involved in mediating dependencies involving many other substances of abuse. For example, recent research has identified an avenue by which nicotine predisposes susceptibility to cocaine recidivism (Wise, 1988). Similar interactions between cocaine and alcohol have been suggested (for a general review, see Carlson, 1991). This explains the fact that a client with a history of dependence on one substance can also have a history of dependence on many other substances. This raises the question of whether the proclivity for becoming chemically dependent is a basic psychological or neurophysiological characteristic or whether early exposure to one substance biases the system toward susceptibility to other substances. But whatever the answer, it seems that many of the reinforcement mechanisms in the brain involved in substance dependence share a common response to a broad class of substances.

These mechanisms, when overstimulated (as they are when bombarded by substances of abuse), compensate by decreasing their responsiveness. Higher doses of these substances are then required to induce pleasure. This development of tolerance often leads to elevated dosages and/or more frequent use (Gawin & Ellinwood, 1988; Gawin & Kleber, 1985, 1986b; Siegel, 1985).

When an individual has developed tolerance to a drug, these pleasure mechanisms are unable to maintain normal levels of positive affect. The experience of daily life as lacking pleasure (anhedonia) sets in during periods of abstinence, and the memory of the extreme euphoria induces an intense craving for it. Cocaine is a most effective reinforcer: Studies of primates that were provided with unlimited access to cocaine, food, and water show that they were most likely to select cocaine repeatedly over food and water, even to the point of death (Pollin, 1984). The reinforcing effects of cocaine appear to be directly proportional to the rapidity of onset of euphoria. Administering cocaine intravenously and inhaling freebase or crack are more reinforcing routes of administration than intranasal use and incur a greater vulnerability for dependence. Two to five years of snorting cocaine may be required for dependence to develop (Schnoll, Karrigan, Kitchen,

Daghestani, & Hansen, 1985; Siegel, 1985); however, smoking freebase or crack, which allows for diffusion and absorption in the large pulmonary area, shortens the time required to develop dependence to weeks (Gawin & Ellinwood, 1988). High-dose use produces disinhibition, impaired judgment, feelings of grandiosity, impulsiveness, and hypersexuality (Gawin & Ellinwood, 1988).

A most alarming effect of regular use of cocaine or amphetamines is increased incidence of psychotic behaviors: hallucinations, delusions of persecution, mood disturbances, and repetitive behaviors. These symptoms so closely resemble those of paranoid schizophrenia that a trained mental health professional cannot distinguish them unless aware that the client has a history of chemical dependency.

A psychotic reaction caused by the use of cocaine or amphetamines will usually subside with abstinence. However, the exposure to stimulants appears to produce long-term changes in the brain that make the person more likely to display psychotic symptoms if he or she takes the drug later, even months or years later (Sato, 1986; Sato, Chen, Akiyama, & Otsuki, 1983).

Stimulant Use and Dependence

Cocaine use progresses through a series of phases. In the introductory phase, the positive aspects of use outweigh the negative. During episodes of intitial use, increases in energy, sexual function, status, confidence, work output, popularity, thinking ability, and euphoria are reported. At this point, the negative aspects are the financial cost and illegality. As dependence on cocaine develops, the negative aspects increase: vocational disruption, relationship problems, and financial crises. There may be temporary relief from depression and lethargy; euphoria at this phase occurs only on initial administration. As dependence further intensifies, nosebleeds, infections, financial jeopardy, relationship disruption, family distress, and impending job loss may result. Finally, only momentary relief from depression and fatigue is experienced. In the final stages, weight loss, seizures, impotence, severe depression, paranoia, psychosis, loss of family and loved ones, unemployment, bankruptcy, isolation, and even death are likely consequences (Rawson et al., 1989).

Stimulant Abstinence

When a stimulant abuser discontinues use, weeks or months of stimulant abstinence are required for pleasure mechanisms, made tolerant by drug use, to begin to readjust their lowered responsiveness to levels adequate for maintaining stable and optimistic moods. Stimulant abstinence syndrome refers to the physical and psychological symptoms that the dependent person experiences following the initiation of abstinence from cocaine or other stimulants. Stimulant abstinence proceeds through three stages: crash, withdrawal, and extinction.

Crash

The crash is an extreme exhaustion that immediately follows a binge and can continue in lessened form for up to 15 days (Gawin & Kleber, 1986a; Kramer, Fischman, & Littlefield, 1967; Siegel, 1985). Initially there is intense depression, agitation, and anxiety (Ockert, Coons, Extein, & Gold, 1985). Severe depression is often accompanied by suicidal ideation, which can manifest itself at any time from 1 to 8 hours after abstinence is initiated. Over the first few hours, the craving for stimulants is supplanted by a craving for sleep (Gawin & Kleber, 1985, 1986a). This often leads to the use of benzodiazepines, sedatives, opiates, marijuana, or alcohol to reduce agitation and induce sleep. Prolonged hypersomnolence (excessive sleep) and, during brief awakenings, hyperphagia (excessive eating) may follow. The mood returns to normal after the hypersomnolence, although some residual dysphoria may linger (Gawin & Kleber, 1986a; Post, Kotin, & Goodwin, 1974; Smith, 1969).

Withdrawal

Withdrawal symptoms are the opposite of stimulant effects, as decreased energy limits ability to experience pleasure (Castellani, Petrie, & Ellinwood, 1985; Gawin & Ellinwood, 1988; Gawin & Kleber, 1986a). Clinical observations have shown that the withdrawal period can be subdivided into distinct phases, including an early "honeymoon phase" (10 to 45 days following initiation of abstinence) characterized by overconfidence, inability to initiate change, episodic cravings, and alcohol use; a second phase, the "wall" (45 to 120 days into abstinence), characterized by an intense and often sudden onset of increased anhedonia, mood swings alternating between intense agitation and depression, thoughts of relapse justification, and cognitive rehearsal; and finally the "adjustment phase" (120 to 180 days into abstinence), characterized by vocational dissatisfaction, relationship problems, and lack of goals (Rawson et al., 1989).

Extinction

As the cues (or "triggers") associated with the craving for stimulants cease to be satisfied by the production of a euphoric state, the intensity and frequency of the craving is gradually diminished and anhedonic fatigue and dysphoria recede. Despite the fact that cravings may be diminished, renewed cravings can occur months or years after the withdrawal period (Ellinwood & Petrie, 1977; Gawin & Kleber, 1986a).

ASSESSMENT

Cocaine and other stimulant dependence requires a comprehensive initial assessment. The history of a client's drug use is necessary to establish the severity of the drug dependence and the consequent disruption in biopsychosocial areas of his or her life. Other important variables are age of onset, duration of drug use history, and level of dosage.

In addition to medical and psychosocial assessment, the clinician might find it helpful to use an instrument such as the Addiction Severity Index (ASI), a structured 40-minute interview designed to assess the severity of adjustment problems in medical, legal, psychiatric, drug abuse, alcohol abuse, employment, and family areas (McLellan, Luborsky, Woody, & O'Brien, 1980).

Historical and Current Drug Use

A complete history of all drug and alcohol use (licit and illicit use, age of onset, and the span of time that drugs have been used) is necessary to begin an assessment. It can generally be assumed that the higher the dose and the longer the period of either chronic or binge use, the more biopsychosocial problems will have been incurred. Periods of extensive multiple drug use are of particular importance.

An important aspect of assessment is to determine which drug is the primary substance of dependence and which drugs are secondary. Stimulants can be either primary or secondary. When stimulants are primary, the route of stimulant administration will affect the pattern of use of other drugs. For example, cocaine snorters and users of amphetamines (either in crystalline or pill form) typically use alcohol, benzodiazepines, marijuana, or sedative-hypnotics. Stimulant injectors may use a mixture of stimulants and opiates injected simultaneously ("speedball"). Crack, freebase, and "ice" smokers are more likely to discontinue stimultaneous or independent abuse of other drugs but are likely to use sedating drugs (such as large amounts of alcohol) to self-medicate the acute effects of the stimulant crash. In time, however, this ameliorating use of sedating intoxicants can develop into a new dependence (Gawin & Ellinwood, 1988). Secondary use of stimulants typically occurs among severe alcoholics or opiate addicts in order to increase alertness and to offset the sedating effects of the primary intoxicant.

Severity of Use

An essential first question in an assessment is whether the client believes that the current use of cocaine or other stimulants constitutes a problem. It is extremely common for stimulant users to believe that, because their use is not daily but rather follows a weekly or biweekly binge cycle, they are not "addicted" and consequently do not need therapeutic intervention. It is useful at this point to elicit from the client a description of biopsychosocial dysfunctions and to evaluate the extent to which the client can attribute the problems in living directly to drug use. The reason for seeking treatment is often the best material to initiate this discussion.

There are four basic questions to use in determining the severity of stimulant use. How it is taken? How much? Where? and When?

How Is the Stimulant Administered?

Briefly restated, clients may be using stimulants in a variety of forms and methods: loose cocaine or "crank" (used intranasally); stimulants in pill form (taken orally); cocaine or other crystaline amphetamine cooked with water (intravenously injected); and freebase, crack, or "ice" (smoked). As indicated previously, intravenously injected cocaine, freebase, crack, and "ice" have a more immediate and powerful impact on the entire brain and are more likely than cocaine used intranasally to result in daily administration (Adams, 1982).

How Much Stimulant Is Used?

Cocaine in loose form is sold in grams or fractions of a gram. An eighth of an ounce ("eightball") is considered a very high dose if all of it is consumed within 24 hours, regardless of the mode of administration. However, if smoked in freebase form, it creates a more potent, acute event. Cocaine amounts in crack vary, depending on the amount of additives. Crack is usually sold in relatively inexpensive amounts packaged in vials or bags, which provide approximately two brief euphoric events ("rushes") per vial or bag. The use of 10 to 40 vials of crack in a period of 1 to 3 days would be considered a high dose. Amphetamines in pill or smokable form provide effects of varying degrees and duration, depending on the dosage.

When Are Stimulants Used?

Use typically begins as a weekend or party event. As dependence increases, use is likely to be determined more by availability and financial resources than by any other factors. "Payday habits" are extremely common, and compulsive, uncontrolled use increases as cocaine binges become more intense and frequent.

Where Are Stimulants Used?

During the introductory phase, cocaine is usually used at parties, on special occasions, and at gatherings of friends or coworkers. With continued use, there is a tendency for people to use drugs in isolation or in more impersonal locations, such as "crack houses."

By gathering such information as that discussed above, the clinician can more accurately assess the severity of the problem and determine the appropriate treatment plan.

History of Attempts at Abstinence

As with any assessment of substance abuse, it is important to ascertain the client's previous attempts to terminate use and to determine the extent of success of failure. This will involve an assessment of what made periods of abstinence possible, including previous treatments, changes in life circumstances (e.g., a new job), and external threats (e.g., pending bankruptcy, arrest, homelessness, job loss, or divorce), as well as an assessment of the client's subjective experience of attempts at abstinence (e.g., are attempts doomed to failure?).

Psychological Assessment

As discussed above, stimulant abuse can cause certain psychological symptoms: depression, agitation, paranoid delusions and hallucinations, suicidal ideation and attempts, violent impulses, and such cognitive dysfunctions as loss of concentration and memory. It is essential that all of these possible symptoms be explored; generally the more severe the symptoms, the more progressed is the stimulant dependence. Stimulant users are likely to progress from paranoid delusion, to auditory, then visual, hallucinations during intoxication, and finally to hallucination and delusion when not intoxicated.

Since these symptoms of stimulant abuse are similar to symptoms of psychopathology not related to use of intoxicants, assessment of underlying psychopathology is crucial. Treatment approaches that focus exclusively on drug use and neglect the relevance of social-psychological pathology are bound to fail and may simply reinforce dysfunctional drug-using behavior (Brook, Kaplan, & Whitehead, 1974). Findings suggest that persons with affective disorders and residual attention-deficit disorders (formerly termed "hyperactivity") are overrepresented among the drug-abusing population (Gawin & Ellinwood, 1988; Gawin & Kleber, 1985, 1986a; Weiss, Mirin, Michael, & Sollogub, 1986).

The use of stimulants as self-medication for depression has been posited since Freud cited the drug's antidepressant activity in 1884 (Weiss et al., 1986). The evidence for this hypothesis comes from several areas: the profound euphoria induced by cocaine (F. Jones, 1953; NIDA, 1979; Resnick & Resnick, 1985; Weiss et al., 1986); the ability of cocaine, like antidepressant drugs, to increase noradrenergic activity in the central nervous system (Blanken & Resnikov, 1985; Weiss et al., 1986); and the pharmacological similarity of cocaine to amphetamines, which have been used effectively in the treatment of some depression (Brecher et al., 1972). There are several reports of termination of stimulant use by patients with affective disorders after psychotropic medication appropriate to their psychopathology was administered (Gawin & Ellinwood, 1988; Khantzian, Gawin, Kleber, & Riordan, 1984; Utena, 1966; Weiss & Mirin, 1986).

Distinguishing stimulant-induced symptoms from symptoms of underlying pathology is not simple or straightforward under any circumstances, and in some cases it may not be possible until the client has remained drug-free for a significant period following termination of acute cocaine withdrawal. However, time and circumstantial factors can make distinctions of symptom causes somewhat more reliable. The age of onset is the most obvious factor: Are the symptoms premorbid, that is, did they exist prior to the use of cocaine? It is necessary to note that prior use of other intoxicants, such as alcohol, marijuana, or tranquilizer's, can also be a cause of depression. Similarly, symptom occurrence that is seasonal or periodic might indicate seasonal affective disorder or cyclical or recurrent affective disorder. Specific onset or increase in symptoms following a significant life crisis or the onset of a major stressor might signal the existence of a reactive depression or post-traumatic stress disorder. Finally, symptoms that occur during extended periods of abstinence from stimulants are more likely to be non-stimulant-related.

Any assessment must of course take into account the client's personality development and any personality dysfunction. Such issues with respect to stimulant use are not significantly different from those presented by other substance abuse and need not be discussed at length here. Substance abusers' emotional development is often arrested in certain respects at the age of onset of use (Kleber & Gawin, 1987), and any other developmental inhibitions such as serious problems resulting from unresolved separation–individuation (Resnick & Resnick, 1985) are likely to be exacerbated by stimulant use. These factors may be important considerations in determining a clients ability to tolerate life stressors in the absence of stimulants and/or ability to handle treatment in group settings.

It is worthwhile to note here that Resnick and Resnick (1985) found that compulsive cocaine users commonly had Axis II diagnoses of borderline or narcissistic personality disorder. Clients exhibiting characteristics of borderline personality disorder may require a more restrictive treatment environment in order to limit the negative impact of impulsivity. Narcissistic clients may require a less confrontive treatment environment in order to avoid excessive narcissistic injury.

Sexual behavior in relation to stimulant use is of particular importance in the psychological evaluation (Washton, 1989). Many clients state that sexual arousal appears to increase during the euphoria of initial stimulant use. Accordingly, sexual activity may trigger the thought of stimulant use. Indiscriminate sexual activity and extended periods of sexual involvement often result from stimulant use and must be addressed as a treatment issue. Moreover, the exchange of sexual favors for stimulants has become an increasingly common feature within the stimulant-using population. Because sexual activity is indiscriminate, clients may be at greater risk of sexually transmitted infections, including HIV, and this at-risk behavior will necessitate further assessment and counseling. In addition, sexual activity often leads to an experience of shame, which should be explored in the course of treatment.

Medical Evaluation

Medical evaluation is necessary for a number of reasons. First, chronic stimulant use causes many physical injuries; some of the most common are scar tissue on the heart muscle, arrhythmia, and high blood pressure. Liver damage is possible with use of multiple drugs. Alcohol has long been known to be hepatotoxic, as are substances used to "cut" cocaine and heroin in order to increase volume. These injuries may need to be addressed in treatment. Second, other medical causes need to be eliminated as competing explanations for stimulant-related symptoms. Elevated liver enzymes, for example, may cause fatigue and nausea, which might otherwise be viewed as symptoms of depression. High body temperatures can cause mental states that can also be symptoms of psychopathology, for example, hallucinations and disorientation. Elevated blood sugar serum levels can cause mood swings not unlike those caused by the stimulant abstinence syndrome. in fact, many illnesses have been shown to be accompanied by depression. This alone might make the allure of stimulants all the more compelling. In order to proceed with the assessment and make appropriate treatment choices (psychotherapeutic and/ or pharmacological), the clinician must have adequate information. Finally, indiscriminate sexual behavior associated with stimulant use requires the medical evaluator to consider all the sexually transmitted diseases.

An evaluation of current physical status should include a blood chemistry profile (liver enzyme levels, white blood cell count, etc.), tests for sexually transmitted diseases, an electrocardiogram (EKG) to determine heart rhythm, and an electroencephalogram (EEG) to assess brain wave activity.

Assessment of Social, Legal, and Employment Areas

The assessment requirements regarding the social, legal, and employment issues that accompany stimulant abuse are basically identical to those accompanying any other substance abuse. Several aspects of stimulant abuse, however, do have a specific effect on these areas and need to be addressed here.

As discussed earlier, stimulant and especially crack dependence can develop rapidly. Consequently it is not unusual for crack or freebase abusers to present at intake the irreparable loss of all savings, assets, housing, employment, and extended family support networks—indeed, the basic necessities of life—within the period of a year or, in extreme cases, within a period of months. This will not only place the client in individual crisis but can have disastrous effects on many of the client's significant others.

Thus prompt and complete assessment of the status of the client's family and social networks is crucial. At the time of assessment, the client's family may be so dysfunctional, overburdened with crises, and/or on the brink of dissolution that immediate intervention may be necessary to secure the continuation of family life. This is especially important because the significant others may be the only available source of external limitations on the client's stimulant use (e.g., by controlling the client's income, cashing the client's paycheck, etc.). Immediate intervention may also be necessary to prevent or encourage the removal of children from the client's care.

Legally, clients often find themselves facing prosecution for illegal acts (especially buying, selling, and/or holding illegal substances; theft; and prostitution) committed under the influence of the stimulant that they could not conceive of doing when not using drugs. Clients may be extremely reluctant to divulge information they experience as shameful. Care must be taken to elicit such information in a nonjudgmental manner, so that appropriate use can be made of it in treatment.

Illustration of Assessment

The following case history exemplifies the assessment process with a typical stimulant-abusing client.

Louis, a 30-year-old, married school maintenance worker, set up an appointment at an outpatient stimulant treatment facility after reading an advertisement in the local Yellow Pages. At the intake session, he stated that he was seeking help because he was spending too much money on cocaine and that although he felt his cocaine use was not all that severe, the urge to use it was increasing. He did not identify alcohol or any other drug as a problem.

However, a thorough history of drug use revealed that from age 14 through 19 he smoked marijuana daily. Upon his entry to the Marines at age 19, he began drinking 1 to 2 pints of rum every other day, a habit he continued after discharge from the service at age 24. At age 25, he began to snort cocaine occasionally with drinking buddies in the neighborhood. At age 28, his alcoholic father passed away, causing Louis to become depressed and to stay indoors for 2 weeks, drinking steadily. His next paycheck was spent entirely on cocaine and crack, which he tried then for the first time and liked immensely. His biweekly payday became the occasion for increasingly lengthy crack binges with neighborhood drug-abusing acquaintances. Alcohol use began to take on a new pattern, increasing at the start of the crash following each crack binge and continuing heavily (2 pints of rum per day) through the week following the binge. To this pattern Louis added heroin, which he had snorted five times in the year prior to the intake, each time to alleviate the effects of the cocaine crash.

At the time of intake, he was using approximately 10 to 15 vials of crack per weekend, postpayday binge and occasionally used 1 or 2 vials on other days if he had sufficient cash. Louis managed to give rent and food money to his wife before he set off to meet his drug-abusing acquaintances at the local grocery, which sells crack under the counter. This group had become his sole social outlet. They usually smoked their crack in someone's automobile or apartment. Louis's cousin, who also had a severe crack problem, had recently been arrested while purchasing drugs on the street. Louis felt it could just as well have been him, and he was afraid that he would be the next to be arrested.

Louis had first sought treatment from the local Veterans Administration hospital 6 months earlier. He was treated in the inpatient alcohol rehabilitation program for 15 days and discharged with the instruction to participate in community Alcoholics Anonymous meetings. He began using cocaine and alcohol again 1 week after discharge. This was the only period of voluntary abstinence he had experienced since the onset of alcohol use.

At the time of intake, Louis had not used cocaine for 5 days but had been drinking from 2 beers to 2 pints of rum daily. He was very talkative, joking occasionally, but more often restless in his seat and apparently somewhat agitated. He denied feeling depressed and stated that he was always tense or anxious. He admitted being quick to anger, but never violent or suicidal. He had no prior history of psychiatric treatment. He stated that he had always been restless as a child and that his 9-year-old son had recently been diagnosed as hyperactive. He described his mother as having been "depressed a lot." Louis had become aware in the previous year that he had an increasingly difficult time concentrating and that he was sometimes confused when attempting to make a decision. Although he was able to fall asleep after drinking in the evening, his sleep was short and he woke often during the night. In his recollection, he had had sleep problems all of his life. He denied having hallucinations but admitted to mild paranoid delusions (e.g., falsely assuming that the police were at the door) during cocaine use.

Louis was evaluated by a physician at the outpatient facility and was found to have no current medical illness or physical dysfunction. Accordingly, physical illness was ruled out as a source of his symptoms.

In Louis's case, although alcohol had for some time been his primary drug of abuse, it had taken a secondary position to cocaine over the course of several years. Louis's crack use had reached a severe level, a fact that he attempted to minimize. His symptoms of agitation, low tolerance for frustration, sleep disturbance, and mild confusion are typical symptoms of the crash from heavy crack use. Because of his history of continuous drug and alcohol use, there was no period of adult life with which to accurately compare his present symptoms. There may have been indications in his personal and family history of underlying psychiatric problems, but the intake history alone was insufficient to distinguish any possible underlying factors from drug-use symptoms.

TREATMENT

Based both on current research and on clinical treatment for cocaine- and other stimulant-dependent clients, it is becoming apparent that an integrated multimodal approach (the neurobehavioral model) addressing each patient's drug-related social, psychological, and biological problems is needed if treatment is to succeed. This treatment approach relies on a joint consideration of neurochemical and psychosocial mechanisms. The most effective treatment plan for such clients is based on the client's therapeutic needs and ability to function at each stage of the stimulant abstinence syndrome: initiation of abstinence/crash, the honeymoon phase, the wall phase, and finally the adjustment phase. The case of Louis, discussed above in terms of assessment, will be used later to illustrate the application of a multimodal approach in the context of these phases.

Before the phases of treatment are discussed, it is important to note that the modalities of treatment—medical, psychological, and social—need to be addressed in different ways depending on the needs of a particular client at a particular phase in treatment. The treatment approach with each client will depend on an ongoing assessment of his or her ability to master each phase of treatment. One treatment professional needs to be responsible for coordinating the treatment priorities of a client as problems and assets change throughout the treatment process. Medication, physical exercise, individual behavioral as well as cognitive and insight-oriented psychotherapies, group therapy, family and couples sessions, and community resources are tools that can be combined in a dynamic, strategic array that is uniquely suitable to the individual client. This individualized approach to a drug dependency problem will result in variations in sequence, frequency, and variety of services delivered.

Initiation of Abstinence/Crash

Treatment can only begin with the initiation of abstinence. Since stimulants produce no medically dangerous withdrawal symptoms, hospitalization is usually unnecessary and can be avoided in most instances (Gawin & Ellinwood, 1988). However, hospitalization is recommended for clients with a history of repeated failed attempts to abstain during the 5- to 10-day crash period; those with severe and unresponsive depression, paranoid delusional thinking, or suicidal ideation or attempts; and those who completely lack a structured living environment.

In many cases, however, clients can weather the crash phase without relapse if they have appropriate treatment supports. Treatment should be intensive during this phase, preferably on a daily basis and with additional opportunities for telephone contact whenever necessary and/or possible. Individual treatment enables the therapist to make an ongoing assessment of the client's relapse potential and to help the client address the myriad individual crises that invariably occur in early abstinence. Initially, treatment interventions should be primarily behavioral in approach: How can the client change his or her behavior to avoid access to, and the opportunity to use, stimulants? It is also important to establish external controls on the client's access to money and free time.

Group treatment can play an important corollary role by focusing on educational concerns, that is, by remedying the client's lack of knowledge with information on the nature of stimulant dependence, the phases of the stimulant abstinence syndrome, and the behavioral requirements of early abstinence. Another goal of group involvement should be introducing the client to 12-step self-help support groups, such as Narcotics Anonymous and Cocaine Anonymous. Such meetings may be held within the context of group treatment at the treating facility, and/or clients may be instructed or encouraged to attend such meetings in the community individually or with fellow group members. Certainly, any day during this initial phase that does not contain a scheduled treatment visit ought to include a 12-step meeting.

Family involvement focuses on instructing significant others about the nature of the client's stimulant dependence, especially the compulsive, uncontrolled response to stimulating triggers (such as cash or the sight of cocaine and the paraphernalia of use) that users experience. When significant others understand this compulsivity, their defensive condemnation and blame can sometimes be diminished; in addition, they can often be encouraged to provide external control, as appropriate. Crisis intervention and appropriate referral to community assistance may also be indicated.

A recent and significant innovation in treatment during early abstinence is the prescription of low doses of antidepressant medications to counteract the disruption of neurotransmitter release and reabsorption (Ockert, 1984; Ockert, Extein, & Gold, 1987; Rosecan, 1983; Tennant & Rawson, 1982). This emotionally stabilizes the client and decreases the severity of such crash symptoms as insomnia, anxiety, depression, and inability to concentrate, all of which can trigger the conditioned need for more stimulants. Furthermore, by treating despondency and attentional deficits, these medications make clients more accessible to talk therapy. This is important because such therapy is the principal avenue by which we can best address certain sociosituational, as well as historical and current emotional, factors that often lie at the root of addiction. Medications used include the tricyclic antidepressants, such as imipramine hydrochloride (Rosecan, 1983) and desipramine hydrochloride (Tennant & Rawson, 1982), which also have a serendipitously useful sedative side effect, as well as a relatively new class of antidepressants that are serotonin-specific, such as fluoxetine hydrochloride (Prozac) and sertraline hydrochloride (Zoloft).

The Honeymoon Phase

Six to 15 days into abstinence, clients usually present a gradual lessening of dysphoric symptoms, begin to feel a sense of returning to "normal," and often express an overconfidence in their ability to remain drug-free. This phase is popularly known as the "pink cloud" in 12-step programs.

At this point, treatment focus usually shifts markedly. In both individual and group sessions, greater attention must be paid to the various phases of stimulant withdrawal and recovery, especially to the fact that the honeymoon phase is followed by the wall phase and that, without proper preparation, clients are prone to relapse when the change occurs. The cognitively and behaviorally oriented relapse prevention theories of Marlatt and Gordon (1985), among others, are especially appropriate at this stage. Clients need to assess their unique patterns of drug use and to begin to fashion a relapse prevention strategy for themselves that allows for the experience of self-efficacy through use of schedules, cognitive preparation, behavioral techniques, and measures of success. Fundamental to this approach is the client's understanding of relapse as a series of events that can, but need not, result in using the drug (Marlatt & Gordon, 1985). In this conception, the process of recovery is an educational process of learning, often by examining one's mistakes, how and when to intervene to prevent movement toward drug use and away from abstinence. Clients may be asked to contract for behavioral change (especially in the areas of participation in 12-step programs, scheduling of leisure and work hours to focus on abstinence, and avoidance of situations with cocaine associations) and to terminate all alcohol and marijuana use. It is best to collect and test urine several times a week to insure treatment compliance and to intercept relapse behavior at the earliest possible opportunity.

It is essential that clients be encouraged to continue psychotropic medications when indicated despite (and precisely because of) their mood improvement. This is especially true in light of the often sudden onset of mood swings in the subsequent wall phase and the time lag of several weeks before most psychotropics reach an adequate blood level for depression relief. In addition, whether or not clients are taking medications, regular aerobic activity (such as running, jogging, swimming, or bike riding) should be strongly emphasized at this point. Aerobic activity is very useful in establishing control (or in supplementing the antidepressant medication in establishing control) over the emotional symptoms of the stimulant abstinence syndrome (Siegel, 1985). Sufficient aerobic activity causes the subjective experience of a "second wind" or "runners' high," in which the physical stress of the activity forces the neurochemical system to produce and release more enkephalins (such as endorphins), which in turn counteract for a short period the neurochemical deficiencies induced by stimulant dependence.

Family treatment at this phase typically involves continuing education about the phases of recovery (especially the soon-to-be-experienced difficulties of the wall phase). In addition, the stimulant-dependent person is assisted in reorienting to his or her appropriate role in the family system. Other areas of social function are also addressed, especially addressing issues of work performance, dealing with demands for recompense for past behavior (paying drug debts, handling legal proceedings, etc.), and helping children cope with sudden and perhaps unsettling changes in the drug-abusing parent.

The Wall Phase

About 1½ months after the initiation of abstinence, the wall phase (sometimes popularly termed the "gray wall") commences, usually with the sudden and inexplicable onset of increased anhedonia and mood swings between agitation and low-energy depression. Relapse potential is greatly increased during this phase. Clients begin to express significant frustration and discouragement with treatment. It is important to address the discouragement openly in group and individual sessions (or to elicit its verbal expression if it is being expressed in acting-out behavior) by reemphasizing the biochemical causes of this change in mood. Any misattribution of this phase to personal deficiencies, treatment inadequacies, or fatalistic worldviews must be firmly and repeatedly shown to be incorrect. Instead, the group and individual treatment agenda should readdress the previously discussed relapse prevention concepts and techniques, using specific examples of relapse-oriented behavior that the clients currently present. For example, as clients begin to disclose their seemingly justified failures to attend 12-step meetings, to continue their exercise routines, to limit the availability of cash, or to make scheduled treatment appointments, these events can be cognitively reframed in terms of relapse behavior patterns and prompt behavioral interventions can be proposed. Efforts should be made to enhance the positive reinforcement of the experience of efficacy that will result from the client's behavioral intervention by encouraging group recognition of the achievement.

The likelihood of actual stimulant use at this stage needs to be addressed in two ways: first, by initiating cognitive rehearsal of circumstances in which clients are likely to find themselves confronted by opportunities for drug use; and second, by discussing what needs to be done if such use actually occurs. It is crucial to instruct clients that a slip to drug use means not that further relapse is necessary or justified but rather that immediate return to the treatment environment is the most effective intervention, will prevent further relapse, and will allow them to learn how not to make the same mistake in the future. Relapse must be dealt with in a nonjudgmental, nonpunitive manner on the part of both treatment staff and fellow clients.

Psychotropic medication dosages may need to be reevaluated by medical staff if the current dosage does not seem adequate to address the increased depression and other anhedonic symptoms that arise. In addition, conjugal and family counseling may need to be intensified to address increased tensions that result from mood changes and low tolerance of frustration. Significant others need to be informed at this point of the reasons for the changes and the behavioral steps the client needs to take to reassert control over his or her progress in recovery.

The Adjustment Phase

Most clients gradually emerge from the extreme depression of the wall phase somewhere from 120 to 180 days into abstinence. However, the anhedonia often continues as clients become less focused on their uncomfortable moods and increasingly confront the problems they face in living, some of which are self-inflicted by a history of drug use. Clients are often bewildered by the prospect of rebuilding failing marriages, handling vocational dissatisfaction, and learning to establish a drug-free social network and lifestyle.

Group and individual treatment can begin to address underlying emotional issues such as anger, guilt, isolation, boredom, and low self-esteem. It is hoped that by then clients may have attained sufficient emotional capacity to undertake an insight-oriented psychotherapy, or in some cases a goal-oriented one. Rational-emotive approaches have been found to be useful with some clients in this and later phases as they start constructing a new emotional vocabulary.

Couples and family therapy may also begin to take a more constructive approach, as significant others are required to do less damage control and can establish goals for the future of the family system. Vocational counseling may also be appropriate in some cases.

It is best to continue psychotropic medication protocols through the sixth month of abstinence. At that time, treatment staff and client can mutually agree to initiate a planned trial off medication to evaluate whether any further depressive condition exists.

Illustration of Treatment

The case of Louis (whose assessment was described previously) illustrates the various stages of treatment and recovery.

Initiation of Abstinence

Louis did not appear at the intake to have any of the factors that would have made an inpatient detoxification necessary. Therefore the assessment team, consisting of the medical director, the clinical director, and the primary individual counselor, established a treatment plan that addressed medical, social, and psychological aspects of the initial phase of recovery. Louis was given a schedule of required appointments that assured his participation in either individual or group treatment during each workday of the first week of treatment.

After a medical evaluation conducted the same day as the intake, he was given a prescription for imipramine hydrochloride antidepressant (initial dose 50 mg per day, increasing to 150 mg per day over a period of 7 days). Louis took his initial dose that same evening. His sleep improved somewhat the first night, and by the third day of treatment he was expressing a greater sense of calm and a more positive outlook.

Following intake, Louis met with the social worker who would serve as his individual counselor, and plans were devised to keep him as far as possible from those people, places, and things (especially money) that would make it possible for him to use alcohol or cocaine during the first week of abstinence. At the educational group meeting that he attended the next day, the importance of 12-step programs was presented and each group member was asked to study a meeting schedule and choose the meetings they would attend prior to the next group session. Louis was asked to give a urine sample at each session for laboratory analysis, and he was told that this would continue during his entire time in the program.

The Honeymoon Phase

In his twice-weekly individual treatment sessions. Louis's counselor focused on discovering the specific details of Louis's drug use, with the goal of identifying behavioral patterns that needed to be changed in order to prevent opportunities to use alcohol and drugs. These included the usual persons, places, and things, as well as certain emotional states or interpersonal interactions that preceded the actual use. For Louis, this meant learning to identify the sequence of events from the beer at lunch with coworkers, to the trip past his hangout spot on the way to park the car, to the angry interaction with his wife, and finally the escape from the house and the walk to the hangout spot. Ways to intervene behaviorally were discussed, and a plan for implementation was devised and agreed on. Louis agreed to keep a written schedule of his daily activities in order to plan in advance for the steps he needed to take to avoid drug use. Since his wife had refused to come in for a family session, Louis and his counselor discussed ways to communicate with her and to provide materials for her to read in order to educate her about his drug dependence.

After several weeks Louis was beginning to feel that he was no longer susceptible to the dangers of further use, since he was not troubled by strong urges to use cocaine. He admitted to having had wine at a family gathering and with much prodding stated that others felt he had drunk too much. He was resistant to the idea that alcohol might lead him to using cocaine again. Furthermore, he had been inconsistent in attending his Narcotics Anonymous (NA) meetings. During staff meetings, the counselors decided to have a thorough discussion of the dangers of alcohol use during group meetings. Using formal written worksheets and informal discussion, the group began to put alcohol use into the context of a series of events that could lead to relapse. The group helped Louis identify how he could intervene to prevent further movement toward the use of cocaine.

Group members were also asked to account to one another for their plans to attend 12-step meetings and failures to follow through with those plans. Louis's reluctance to attend meetings was partially alleviated by the offer of a group member to take Louis to a favorite NA meeting. Both individual and group sessions also focused on the need to recognize the symptoms of the wall phase, which he would be soon approaching. Louis responded by taking his exercise regimen more seriously, a change for which he received much praise from fellow group members.

Because family treatment was still not agreeable to Louis's wife, family issues were emphasized in individual treatment. In fact, his improved mood and behavior had already begun to create a new sense of harmony at home.

The Wall Phase

In the eighth week of treatment Louis began to cancel every other appointment at the last minute, claiming that, with the approach of the Christmas holidays, his job required additional overtime work. The urine left the following Monday tested positive for marijuana use. When confronted with this information, Louis at first denied the possibility, then admitted he had smoked marijuana with his brother-in-law after work on the prior Friday. He attributed this use to the need to be high to escape the frequent quarrels he was having with his wife. On further inquiry, it became clearer that for a week he had been out of sorts, feeling increasingly irritable at work and at home and unable to follow his established schedule for meetings or exercise. He sometimes forgot to take the antidepressant medication. His individual counselor immediately reemphasized the need for Louis to intervene to stop this movement toward relapse and reacquainted him with the nature of the wall phase and its likely effects. Louis agreed to take further steps to improve his situation, all the while insisting that he had no intention of using cocaine. He subsequently failed to appear for the next group session. Messages were left for him, which he did not return. The counselor finally reached Louis shortly before the next individual session. He stated that he had used cocaine, to which the counselor responded with sympathy and strong invitations to come to the scheduled session. Louis arrived at the session accompanied by his wife. He explained that the previous Friday he had used 2 vials of crack after drinking with friends at his hangout spot. Far from being the ecstatic return to cocaine he had anticipated, his drug experience had been rather painful because of his guilt and disappointment with himself. His wife had refused to talk to him until the previous night, when he told her that he was too ashamed to return to treatment. She had accompanied him to make sure that he did not detour on his way to the session. Both Louis and his wife were praised for having come in immediately to process this cocaine use despite any despair or disappointment they might be feeling. The counselor quickly educated them both about the nature of Louis's mood swings, urges, and possibilities for continued abstinence. The relapse was framed as an educational opportunity, a way to discover what mistakes had been made in order to act differently in the future and to avoid further mistakes. Both Louis and his wife expressed some relief on hearing this, and they left with a renewed sense of direction and understanding. An agreement for further couple sessions was made.

In the following group session, Louis was encouraged to describe his experiences to the group in terms that emphasized the learning opportunities it had presented. The group responded favorably.

The individual counselor consulted with the medical staff, and it was decided that an increase in the antidepressant medication dose was appropriate at this time. Louis reported mood improvement within a few days at the increased dose.

Adjustment Phase

By the middle of the fifth month of treatment, Louis had become less prone to mood swings and much more adept at spotting relapse-related symptoms in order to take steps to prevent drug use. He began to open up in his group about the conflicting emotions he felt toward his ailing father, which stimulated extensive discussions about relationships with older parents and the effect this had on behavior toward their own children. In individual sessions, Louis became increasingly aware of his underlying feelings of low self-esteem. He and his counselor were able to contract to focus more specifically on this issue over a number of sessions.

A trial period off the antidepressant medication was planned to determine whether further use was needed. Louis showed no significant deterioration in mood for a month after the medication was removed, and a mutual decision was made to discontinue it.

After two more couple sessions, Louis's wife had decided not to come in for further meetings. Louis was disappointed with this, and it was necessary to deal with this extensively in his individual sessions. He completed the planned treatment program 7 months after he began it. He continued his involvement with his 12-step program and also continued to see his individual counselor on an as-needed basis.

CONCLUSION

Louis, in the foregoing example, represents just one client among a wide variety of stimulant abusers, all of whom face considerable odds in the struggle to achieve and maintain abstinence. Cocaine or other stimulant abuse simultaneously causes severe biological, psychological, and social dysfunction. It is necessary, then, to embrace the complexity of this problem by viewing stimulant dependency from a multifaceted and interactive perspective. This in turn demands the creation of an integrated multidisciplinary treatment approach. Such treatment, when designed to address the various phases of the stimulant abstinence syndrome and tailored to the needs of the individual, is capable of fulfilling client needs and effecting better outcomes. Undoubtedly, our understanding of stimulant dependence will increase as our knowledge of biochemistry and its impact on psychological processes continues to develop. New treatment methods will consequently incorporate this information to increase the probability of relapse prevention and to improve the prognosis for recovery from dependence.

REFERENCES

Adams, E. H. (1982). Abuse/availability trends of cocaine in the United States. *Drug Surveillance Reports, Division of Epidemiology and Statistical Analysis, National Institute on Drug Abuse, 1*(2), 49–71.

Blanken, A. J., & Resnikov, D. C. (1985). *National drug and alcoholism treatment utilization survey summary report on drug abuse treatment units.* Rockville, MD: National Institute on Drug Abuse.

Brecher, E. M., & the Editors of Consumer Reports. (1972). *Licit and illicit drugs.* Boston: Little, Brown.

Brook, R., Kaplan, J., & Whitehead, P. C. (1974). Personality characteristics of adolescent amphetamine users as measured by the MMPI. *British Journal of Addiction, 69,* 61–66.

Carlson, N. R. (1991). *Physiology of behavior* (4th ed.). Boston: Allyn & Bacon.

Castellani, S., Petrie, W. M., & Ellinwood, E. H. (1985). Drug induced psychosis: Neurobiology mechanisms. In A. I. Alterman (Ed.), *Substance abuse and psychopathology.* New York: Plenum.

Courtwright, D. (1991). The first American cocaine epidemic. *Newsletter of the Cocaine/Crack Research Working Group, 1*(1), 3–5.

Ellinwood, E. H., Jr., & Petrie, W. M. (1977). Dependence on amphetamine, cocaine and other stimulants. In S. N. Pradhan (Ed.), *Drug abuse: Clinical and basic aspects.* St. Louis: Mosby.

Gawin, F. H., & Ellinwood, E. H. (1988). Medical progress: Cocaine and other stimulants. *New England Journal of Medicine, 318*(18), 1173–1182.

Gawin, F. H., & Kleber, H. D. (1985). Cocaine use in a treatment population: Patterns and diagnostic distinction. *National Institute on Drug Abuse Research Monograph Series, 61,* 182–192.

Gawin, F. H., & Kleber, H. D. (1986a). Abstinence symptomoatlogy and psychiatric diagnosis in cocaine abusers. *Archives of General Psychiatry, 43,* 107–113.

Gawin, F. H., & Kleber, H. D. (1986b). Pharmacological treatments of cocaine abuse. *Psychiatric Clinics of North America, 9,* 573–583.

Greenspoon, L., & Bakalar, J. B. (1980). Drug dependence: Non-narcotic agents. In H. I. Kaplan, A. M. Freedman, & B. J. Sadock (Eds.), *Comprehensive textbook of psychiatry.* Baltimore: Williams & Wilkins.

Gunne, L. M., & Anggard, E. (1973). Pharmacokinetic studies with amphetamines—

Relationship to neuropsychiatric disorders. *Journal of Pharmacokinetics and Biopharmaceutics, 1,* 481–495.

Jones, E. (1953). *The life and work of Sigmund Freud* (Vol. 1). New York: Basic Books.

Jones, R. T. (1985). The pharmocology of cocaine. *National Institute on Drug Abuse Research Monograph Series, 50,* 34–53.

Khantzian, E. J., Gawin, F., Kleber, H. D., & Riordan, C. E. (1984). Methylphenidate treatment of cocaine dependence: A preliminary report. *Journal of Substance Abuse Treatment, 1,* 107–112.

Kleber, H. G., & Gawin, F. H. (1987). Cocaine withdrawal. *Archives of General Psychiatry, 44,* 298.

Kramer, J. C., Fischman, V. S., & Littlefield, D. C. (1967). Amphetamine abuse: Patterns and effects of high doses taken intravenously. *Journal of the American Medical Association, 201,* 305–309.

Marlatt, A. J., & Gordon, J. R. (Eds.). (1985). *Relapse prevention: Maintenance strategies in the treatment of addictive behaviors.* New York: Guilford.

McLellan, A. T., Luborsky, L., Woody, G. E., & O'Brien, C. P. (1980). An improved diagnostic evaluation instrument for substance abuse patients: The addiction severity index. *Journal of Nervous and Mental Disease, 168,* 26–33.

National Commission on Marijuana and Drug Abuse. (1973). *Drug use in America: Problem in perspective: Second report of the National Commission on Marijuana and Drug Abuse.* Washington, DC: National Institute on Drug Abuse.

National Institute on Drug Abuse. (1979). *Quarterly report: Data from the Client Oriented Data Acquisition Process (CoDap)* (Statistical Series D, No. 12). Washington, DC: U.S. Government Printing Office.

National Institute on Drug Abuse. (1991). *National household survey on drug abuse: Population estimates 1990.* Washington, DC: U.S. Government Printing Office.

Ockert, D. M. (1984). *A multi-modality drug abuse treatment program for high economic status patients.* Unpublished doctoral dissertation, Columbia University, New York.

Ockert, D. M., Coons, E. E., Extein, I., & Gold, M. S. (1985). Lowered drug abuse recidivism following psychotropic medication. *National Institute on Drug Abuse Research Monograph Series, 67,* 494.

Ockert, D. M., Extein, I., & Gold, M. S. (1987). Posthospital outcome in suburban drug addicts. *Psychiatric Medicine, 3*(4), 419–426.

Pollin, W. (1984). Cocaine pharmacology, effects and treatment of abuse. *National Institute on Drug Abuse Research Monograph Series, 50,* vii.

Post, R. M., Kotin, J., & Goodwin, F. K. (1974). The effects of cocaine on depressed patients. *American Journal of Psychiatry, 131,* 511–517.

Rawson, R. A., Obert, J. L., McCann, M. J., Smith, D. P., & Scheffey, E. H. (1989). *The neurobehavioral treatment manual: A therapist manual for outpatient cocaine addiction treatment.* Beverly Hills, CA: Matrix Center.

Remington's Pharmaceutical Sciences (14th ed.). (1970). Easton, PA: Mack Publishing.

Resnick, R., & Resnick, E. (1985). Psychological issues in the treatment of cocaine abuse. Proceedings of the Committee on Problems of Drug Dependence. *National Institute on Drug Abuse Research Monograph Series, 67,* 290–294.

Rosecan, J. (1983, July) *The treatment of cocaine abuse with imipramine, L-tyrosine and L-tryptophan*. Paper presented at the Seventh World Congress of Psychiatry, Vienna, Austria.

Sato, M. (1986). Acute exacerbation of methamphetamine psychosis and lasting dopaminergic supersensitivity—A clinical survey. *Psychopharmacology Bulletin*, 22, 751–756.

Sato, M., Chen, C.-C., Akiyama, K. & Otsuki, S. (1983). Acute exacerbation of paranoid psychotic state after long-term abstinence in patients with previous methamphetamine psychosis. *Biological Psychiatry*, 18, 429–440.

Schnoll, S. H., Karringan, J., Kitchen, S. B., Daghestani, A., & Hansen, T. (1985). Characteristics of cocaine abusers presenting for treatment. *National Institute on Drug Abuse Research Monograph Series*, 61, 171–181.

Siegel, R. K. (1985). New patterns of cocaine use: Changing doses and routes. *National Institute on Drug Abuse Research Monograph Series*, 61, 171–181.

Smith, D. E. (1969). The characteristics of dependence in high-dose methamphetamine abuse. *International Journal of the Addictions*, 4, 453–459.

Strategy Council on Drug Abuse. (1973). *Federal strategy for drug abuse and drug traffic prevention*. Washington, DC: U.S. Government Printing Office.

Tennant, F. S., & Rawson, R. A. (1982). Cocaine and amphetamine dependence treated with desipramine: Proceedings of the Committee on Problems of Drug Dependence. *National Institute on Drug Abuse Research Monograph Series*, 43, 351–356.

Utena, H. (1966). Behavioral aberrations in methamphetamine intoxicated animals and chemical correlates in the brain. *Progress in Brain Research*, 21, 192–207.

Washton, A. (1989, December). Cocaine abuse and compulsive sexuality. *Medical Aspects of Human Sexuality*. pp. 32–39.

Weiss, R. D., & Mirin, S. M. (1986). Subtypes of cocaine abusers. *Psychiatric Clinics of North America*, 9, 491–501.

Weiss, R. D., Mirin, S. M., Michael, J. L., & Sollogub, A. C. (1986). Psychopathology in chronic cocaine abusers. *American Journal of Drug and Alcohol Abuse*, 12 17–29.

Wise, R. A. (1988). Psychomotor stimulant properties of addictive drugs. *Annals of the New York Academy of Sciences*, 537, 228–234.

18

AIDS and Intravenous Drug Users: Issues and Treatment Implications

DIANE PINCUS STROM

M. N., a 38-year-old black woman, learned she had the AIDS virus when her 3-year-old daughter became sick. M. had stopped using drugs intravenously some 4 years earlier; she had been frightened of becoming ill. It was a shock to learn she had stopped too late. The child, in fact, subsequently died. A 4-year-old daughter also carries an AIDS diagnosis. A 7-year-old son is showing early symptoms of HIV infection. An 11-year-old, however, is completely healthy. M., who is divorced, waits for her own symptoms to develop. She prays to remain healthy long enough to see her children die; otherwise who will care for them?

C. R., a 57-year-old Puerto Rican woman, has reluctantly agreed to have her 23-year-old son live with her; in the past he has stolen from her neighbors and she is not sure he can be trusted. Now, however, he is dying of AIDS. She knows how to care for him because his two older brothers also died of AIDS, and she cared for them.

Acquired immune deficiency syndrome (AIDS), while a medical diagnosis, has broader implications than medical ones alone. It has a significant impact not only on the person with AIDS (PWA) but also on his or her family and significant others specifically and on all of society generally. Children may also be infected, as M. N.'s three younger children are, or left orphaned, as her oldest will ultimately be; parents such as C. R. are caring for their adult sons and daughters as they lay dying; hospital resources are being stretched beyond tolerance. Problems of drug use and treatment, poverty, homelessness, discrimination, and inequitable resource allocation, all longstanding social ills, have been intensified by AIDS and have called for social work intervention from the earliest days of the epidemic.

It is to the credit of the social work profession that the National Association of Social Workers issued some of the first statements by health professionals in which several areas of concern were addressed (National Association of Social Workers [NASW], 1984, 1987a, 1987b). Of major significance were recommendations regarding the development of social work services for PWAs and their significant others, the protection of individual rights (including confidentiality), and the provision of education and support to workers caring for PWAs.

Clearly most PWAs can benefit from these recommendations. Intravenous drug users (IVDUs) with AIDS or infection with the Human Immunodeficiency virus (HIV), however, because of circumstances directly or indirectly related to their drug use, may require additional social work intervention to cope with their medical status and psychosocial situation. This chapter examines the specific needs of IVDUs with AIDS or HIV infection and delineates the multiple tasks facing social workers concerned with providing services to these individuals.

BACKGROUND AND DEFINITION OF AIDS

In early 1981, unofficial sources reported that homosexual men in Los Angeles and New York were developing a rare form of pneumonia called pneumocystis carinii pneumonia (PCP). By mid-1981 a total of 26 homosexual men were officially recorded as having either PCP or Kaposi's sarcoma (KS), an equally rare form of cancer. One name for the syndrome was gay-related immune deficiency (GRID); despite this designation, by late 1981 the condition had also been identified in intravenous drug users (Shilts, 1987).

As of September 1990, 29% of the 142,426 AIDS cases reported in the United States had intravenous drug use as a factor in transmission (Centers for Disease Control [CDC], 1990). The current increase in heterosexual transmission is largely attributable to intravenous drug use, since many infected women report that their only risk factor was sexual relations with men who are IVDUs. The increasing incidence of pediatric AIDS is also related to drug use. Fifty-eight percent of the 2,379 children with AIDS born as of September 1990 were born to women who are themselves IVDUs or the sexual partners of men who are IVDUs (CDC, 1990).

The CDC (1989) defines AIDS as "a disabling or life-threatening illness caused by human immunodeficiency virus (HIV) characterized by HIV encephalopathy, HIV wasting syndrome, or certain diseases due to immunodeficiency in a person with laboratory evidence for HIV infection or without certain other causes of immunodeficiency." The definition is further divided into four classification groups: Group 1, acute infection, refers to the earliest phase, the actual time of infection, at which point the individual may or may not develop short-term viral symptoms (e.g., fever or nausea); Group 2 consists of those individuals who are in fact infected but who are completely asymptomatic; Group 3, persistent generalized lymphadenopathy (often called AIDS-related complex, or ARC), includes those with some symptoms but none sufficiently severe to be considered AIDS; Group 4 describes individuals with an array of opportunistic infections, neurological disturbances, malignancies, and other serious conditions. Only individuals exhibiting the symptoms described in Group 4 are considered to have a diagnosis of AIDS. The differentiation can be crucial in that one's category may determine the level of benefits for which one is eligible. It is also important to be aware that some people have died of conditions related to HIV infection before actually meeting the criteria in the fourth category.

HIV may be transmitted via three routes:

1. Sexual transmission may be homosexual between men or heterosexual from men to women and vice versa.
2. Exposure to blood may occur through the sharing of needles by drug users or through transfusion of blood, plasma, packed cells, platelets, and factor concentrates.
3. Perinatal transmission may occur during pregnancy, during the birth process, or during breastfeeding (CDC, 1989).

IVDUs are potentially at risk in all categories, insofar as they may share needles, be sexually active, and give birth to infected infants.

CHARACTERISTICS OF INTRAVENOUS DRUG USERS

Theories describing the genesis of addictive behavior and related personality disorders draw from a broad range of models and consider numerous biopsychosocial determinants (Chein, Donald, Lee, & Rosenfeld, 1964; Vaillant, 1975; Wurmser, 1974; Zinberg, 1975). While it is not within the scope of this chapter to examine these theories, it should be noted that some of the characteristics frequently associated with addiction may have an impact on IVDUs' capacity to cope with an AIDS diagnosis (Caputo, 1985), to avail themselves of treatments available for HIV infection, and to relate to family, friends, health care professionals, and others involved with their treatment and/or care (Flanagan, 1989). The characteristics discussed below may be particularly salient.

Intolerance of Overwhelming Affect

IVDUs frequently have difficulty tolerating anxiety, sadness, or other intense emotions (Wurmser, 1974). A positive result to an HIV test, naturally anxiety-provoking for anyone, may be totally unbearable for IVDUs. One way they may deal with this is to refrain from taking the test altogether; another is to increase drug use, despite awareness of how hazardous this may be, as a means of numbing the emotional pain.

> W. P. is a 25-year-old Puerto Rican male IVDU with AIDS. He shared needles with his older brother, who died of AIDS about 1 year prior to W.'s diagnosis. After an initial drug-free period accompanied by good medical compliance, W. resumed IV drug use. He stated that he saw no point in remaining drug-free; he was going to die whatever he might do, so why not live the time he had left free of anxiety?

Use of Maladaptive Defenses

Because of their inability to tolerate painful affects, IVDUs frequently employ defense mechanisms that allow them to distort reality and therefore avoid constructively confronting their circumstances. Two such mechanisms are denial and externalization.

Denial may keep IVDUs from examining their potential risk for HIV infection or lead them to claim that a positive result on an HIV test is a mistake. While denial is used adaptively by many people, particularly when faced with a serious medical condition, IVDUs may be able to deny reality almost to the point of delusion.

> R. J. is a 27-year-old black woman who claims to have been free of intravenous drugs for the last 6 months. She is hospitalized with fever and complains of recent weight loss. Her husband, whom she has not seen in 5 weeks, is believed to be hospitalized elsewhere with AIDS-related symptoms. R. states she has not shared needles with him, or anyone else, for the last 2 years. She is certain that she cannot possibly be infected and, in fact, must be suffering with "a virus." She does recall nodding out on many occasions and awakening to find that her husband had used her syringes and admits that he may have used them at other times without her knowledge. Nevertheless, she feels she is not really at risk for infection.

Externalization permits IVDUs to absolve themselves of responsibility related to the circumstances of their lives (e.g., HIV status, drug use, living situation) and instead to place the blame on others.

> C. S. is a 23-year-old white woman who supports her drug habit (heroin and crack) by prostitution. Although she has been an intravenous drug user for some 6 years, she believes that the cause of her HIV infection is

the sexual contacts she has had. Her partners are to blame for her situation; she is their victim. She therefore refuses to discontinue prostitution, stating, "Some guy gave this to me—what do I care if I give it to some other guy?"

Avoidance of Emotional Dependence

It is not uncommon for IVDUs to have experienced severe disappointments in their relationships with parents, other family, friends, and lovers. Drugs, on the other hand, are generally more reliable; they are neither rejecting nor critical, and as long as there is money to pay for them, they are available. Thus drug users may be apprehensive about emotionally involving themselves with people. This resistance to forming relationships may make it difficult for the social worker (or other health care professional) to establish a working alliance that can then be used to encourage compliance with medical and psychosocial recommendations.

Borderline and Narcissistic Personality Disorders

IVDUs frequently exhibit characteristics associated with borderline and narcissistic personality structures. Of particular significance is a tendency to impulsive, self-damaging behaviors; inappropriate anger; marked shifts of attitude; affect instability; and chronic feelings of emptiness (American Psychiatric Association, 1987). These characteristics frequently lead to countertransference reactions on the part of health care providers (these will be discussed in more detail later), and, perhaps more importantly, may make it difficult for IVDUs to accept the treatment that is available to them (Carpi, 1987).

Paucity of Resources

IVDUs often have neither the concrete resources nor the psychosocial stability necessary to cope with day-to-day living, much less with the stress associated with a diagnosis of AIDS. This means that the task of planning for ongoing care is arduous, since family and environmental supports may not exist. The community at large is making some good efforts in this regard, but for the most part lack of resources is a major reason for discharge delays or insufficient care in the community.

Clearly, IVDUs, hampered by many of these troubling characteristics, are ill equipped to cope with HIV infection and AIDS. It is against this backdrop that the physical, social, and emotional implications of HIV infection and its treatment for IVDUs may now be explored.

PHYSICAL MANIFESTATIONS AND IMPLICATIONS

IVDUs are at higher risk than the general population for such diseases as tuberculosis, endocarditis, and pneumonia due to their generally poor physical condition. Thus an HIV-infected IVDU who is asymptomatic for HIV disease itself may have significant medical problems and physical discomfort before developing any HIV-related symptoms. The symptoms of HIV disease and AIDS range in severity and will have different impacts on how patients look, how they feel, and how capable they are of functioning.

Appearance

Most early signs of HIV infection are not visible and, in that respect, allow the patient to feel "anonymous." Later symptoms are not as kind. Kaposi's sarcoma, for example, although more frequently found in homosexual men, is also occasionally seen in IVDUs and is manifested by skin lesions that are easily noticed. Other skin conditions (e.g., dermatitis, herpes) are also often evident. Oral thrush, characterized by multiple white nodules in the mouth, is a common symptom. Wasting syndrome, involving significant weight loss, leaves patients severly emaciated and weakened. Patients with these symptoms frequently feel "marked" and are embarrassed to leave their homes for fear of being identified as having AIDS.

Feeling Sick

The symptoms of HIV infection not only leave patients concerned about their appearance but also cause them to feel seriously ill. They may have to cope with pneumonias that lead to shortness of breath and, in the worst scenarios, are life-threatening. Other infections may result in severe headaches, blindness, unending fevers, ongoing weakness, body pain, and enlargement of the lymph nodes. Patients may become completely dependent on others for all aspects of care, including feeding, toileting, bathing, and, in some instances, movement. Dementia is another possible manifestation.

In addition to feeling ill because of AIDS, IVDUs may continue to be addicted and thus have severe physical discomfort related to drug cravings. Their ability to tolerate this distress and remain drug-free (often with the assistance of methadone or other pharmaceuticals) will ultimately influence the effectiveness of those medical treatments that are available to them.

Coping with Treatments

Treatments are available for some infections, but they may be as uncomfortable as the symptoms themselves. Some medications have side effects that leave patients weak and nauseated. Others call for the permanent insertion of catheters. In all cases patients are expected to be compliant with treatment regimes: They must keep regular appointments with their physicians and health care teams, take medications on schedule, and follow up on recommendations. These expectations may be more than many IVDUs are capable of meeting (Carpi, 1987).

IVDUs may be similarly unable to meet the expectation that they will change their behavior. Patients may understand safer sex practices, for example, but be unwilling to change their behaviors in relationships for fear of being identified as having AIDS.

> A. F., a 33-year-old single, Dominican, male IVDU who has been hospitalized on two occasions for AIDS-related infections, continues to date several women but does not practice safer sex. He has expressed fear that were he to suggest that he use condoms, he would immediately be suspected of having AIDS and no one would go out with him. He further states that, were his partner to ask him to use a condom he would do so, but since none of them has asked, he is not responsible should any of them become infected.

It may also be difficult for IVDUs to change patterns of drug use (Friedman, Des Jarlais, & Sotheran, 1986). Some patients become frightened by the prospect of infection or illness and may seek drug treatment, or they may be vigilant in their attempts either to use only their own drug paraphernalia or to employ good needle-cleaning technique. Other patients have the opposite reaction and, as discussed earlier, increase their use of drugs to cope with anxiety.

SOCIOECONOMIC RAMIFICATIONS

The effects of AIDS and HIV infection impinge on aspects of the client's life beyond physical functioning and medical symptomatology. The standard of living may be profoundly affected as well. This is further complicated when drug use is a factor (Christ & Wiener, 1985).

Financial Implications

PWAs, like most people who are chronically or terminally ill, experience financial changes that are directly attributable to their illness. These changes, which may include loss of income and insurance coverage from traditional sources of employment, also extend to IVDUs, who, although possibly working in these settings as well, are more likely be employed in "off-the-books" jobs. This increasing inability to work is significant to society as well, since, as their conditions deteriorate, PWAs will likely be eligible for benefits that are, at least in part, supplemented by governmental programs (e.g., Social Security Disability, Medicaid). The cost of treatments (e.g., hospitalizations, medications, special procedures) and services (e.g., counseling, home care, transportation) may also be prohibitive, in terms of both real dollars and labor.

Shifts in Housing Availability

The absence of adequate housing is a common problem for IVDUs, quite apart from HIV infection per se. The cost of maintaining an apartment may be more than they can afford; thus they may live with relatives, share an apartment with other drug users, or move frequently from place to place. These arrangements disintegrate should their physical condition deteriorate, either because they require too much care or because roommates reject them for fear of exposure to the virus. Individuals who do have their own housing face the loss of their homes either because they are unable to pay the rent or because they are forced out by neighbors or landlords once their diagnosis is known. While this is discriminatory and illegal, it nevertheless occurs with some frequency.

These downward shifts in income and housing, combined with the increased cost of treatments and services, can lead to an overall decrease in standard of living. However, many IVDUs report a marked increase in their standard of living as a direct result of HIV infection. This is essentially due to new eligibility for income and insurance benefits. Symptomatic individuals may also be referred for housing, allowing them to receive safe shelter for the first time in many years.

C. D., a 46-year-old Puerto Rican man, had been without housing for 8 months. While he was allowed to eat meals at the home of his aunt, he was not permitted to spend the night there. Each evening he took his pillow to the park and slept on the bench. As it became colder, he also took a blanket and stayed in the alley between two buildings where he was sheltered from the wind. Upon receiving a diagnosis of AIDS, he was given a room in a local residence hotel.

EMOTIONAL REACTIONS

PWAs face physical, economic, and interpersonal stressors armed with their idiosyncratic defense systems, coping skills, personality characteristics, and personal histories. There are, however, several reactions that PWAs may share (Christ & Wiener, 1985; Rubinow & Joffe, 1987), as discussed below.

Fears Related to Physical Deterioration, Pain, and Death

Much of the anxiety experienced by PWAs and HIV-infected individuals relates directly to the fear of death. It is also frequently focused on pain. This latter experience is particularly meaningful to IVDUs who may have begun their drug use specifically because of their inability to tolerate either physical or emotional discomfort. This intolerance may lead to frequent, seemingly unreasonable, requests for painkillers and other numbing medications.

Fear of Physical Dependence

The inability to care for oneself is frightening to most people. IVDUs, who may have been avoiding emotional dependence on others for much of their lives, are especially afraid of this prospect. This is compounded by the reality of abandonment and rejection, leaving PWAs fearful that, should they become physically dependent, there will be no one to whom they can turn for help.

Feelings of Toxicity to Others

Despite education, discussions with medical professionals, and much evidence to the contrary, HIV-infected individuals may believe they are "toxic" and deserve to be isolated from others.

> H. L., a 35-year-old black man, had been hospitalized while on a job assignment related to a work program in a low-security prison. He worried that, should he return to prison, he would be easily identified as an AIDS patient and that the authorities would not permit him to eat in the dining room, play cards, or even talk to other inmates. On the other hand, he felt that they would be correct to treat him in this way; he was, after all, an AIDS patient. During visits from his social worker he would scrub the chair before offering it to her, remind her to be careful not to touch anything in his room, and sit far apart from her so as not to "contaminate" her with his germs.

Obsessive Thinking

HIV-infected individuals may be vigilant in regard to symptoms, blood results, and so forth. This vigilance can include such things as searching the body for evidence of skin lesions, taking an HIV test monthly to confirm the result, and checking T-cell counts on a weekly basis. Some of this behavior may, indeed, be adaptive and alert the patients and medical staff to the early signs of infection. The obsessive thinking, however, may lead to a decrease in the patients' ability to function.

Self-Blame and Guilt

It is common for patients confronted with a chronic or terminal illness to ask, "Why me?" In the case of IVDUs with AIDS, the answer is too accessible: They are surrounded by many who are eager to remind them that they are somehow responsible for their condition. This knowledge is often accompanied by self-blame ("I did this to myself; no one put the needle in my arm but me") and guilt ("I deserve this for how I've lived my life; what did I think was going to happen?"). These feelings may be intensified significantly when they have infected someone else, such as a sexual partner or, in the case of women IVDUs, their children.

Helplessness and Loss of Control

HIV-infected individuals may feel helpless, without the capacity to make any difference whatsoever in the course of their illness. (This attitude meshes especially well with the tendency of IVDUs to externalize.) The feeling of losing control can be experienced in regard to relationships, emotions, finances, and other significant parts of their lives. It is also frequently accompanied by a sense of hopelessness.

Depression

Depression is a common and expectable response to these multiple assaults. Depression accompanies loss, and PWAs face losses on all fronts: loss of life, loss of physical capacity, loss of friends (either through abandonment or because they, too, have died of the disease), loss of self-esteem. Other losses are less obvious. Long-term plans (e.g., education, seeing one's children grow) are less secure. Dreams of "someday" may never come to fruition. Uncertainty becomes commonplace.

Rage

IVDUs, because of their poor tolerance of frustration, frequently react with rage when they feel frightened, ignored, or out of control. AIDS, with its accompanying feelings of helplessness and anxiety, may lead to that exact reaction. IVDUs may externalize the rage they feel at themselves, becoming unable to tolerate the health and good fortune of others as well as the insensitivities they perceive others as displaying toward them.

> D. S., a homeless 24-year-old black woman, remained in the hospital for 7 months, awaiting housing and other services. As her condition deteriorated she became increasingly agitated at the medical staff. Finally, after being told to return to her room one afternoon, she threatened the nurses with pinning them down and spitting into their mouths so that they would know what it is like to have AIDS.

Fear of Exposure

Concern about the reactions of others frequently leads HIV-infected individuals to keep their HIV-positive status a secret. Perhaps equally powerful is the fear that the high-risk behavior that led to the infection will also be exposed. This may lead individuals to deny any risk factors at all or to lie about the factors that may have led to their infection.

> M. L. is a 19-year-old Hispanic man who feared his father's reaction to his IV drug use. He told his physicians and family that he had been frequenting prostitutes and that that was the only possible source of his HIV infection. His arrest for drug dealing some weeks after discharge was an unfortunately dramatic way for his drug use to be exposed.

FAMILIES AND SIGNIFICANT OTHERS

IVDUs interact with a large network of friends, lovers, family, drug companions, employers, and so forth. The nature of these relationships inevitably changes as these significant others learn of a patient's medical condition. These changes may have both positive and negative effects on patients.

Rejection and Stigmatization

It is not unusual for family members and significant others to be afraid of contagion, feel unable to cope with patients' deterioration and death, or be worried that they will somehow be identified as being similar to the patients. Thus they may avoid patients and, in some instances, disappear from their lives altogether (Christ & Wiener, 1985). In the case of IVDUs, it is possible that this rejection has less to do with AIDS than with the patients' behavior prior to becoming ill. If patients have been manipulative, demanding, or involved in illegal activity, for example, it is possible that their friends and family separated from them long before HIV infection became a factor.

Families who choose to care for PWAs as their conditions deteriorate may hide the true nature of the illness for fear that the stigma of AIDS will be focused upon them, leading to loss of jobs, friends, and so forth. This fear of being stigmatized is closely related to feelings of shame and embarrassment concerning both the actual diagnosis and the high-risk behavior that may have been associated with transmission.

> G. D., a 32-year-old white man, had undergone drug treatment and had been drug-free for 4 years. When he became ill, his parents welcomed him into their home and cared for him devotedly until his death. Throughout this 14-month period, they refused to allow anyone in their home to visit for fear that the symptoms G. was exhibiting would be easily recognizable as AIDS. Subsequent to his death, they told other relatives that he had had cancer.

Tension and Isolation

Relationships may become characterized by an underlying tension, a sensation of "walking on eggs." PWAs may feel afraid to express themselves honestly, not wanting to alienate those around them, particularly if they are dependent upon them for care. Family and friends, in their efforts to be "upbeat," may not mention AIDS or want to talk about patients' feelings about being sick. There may also be an underlying anger at patients for becoming ill in the first place. These emotions can be so powerful that those involved may be incapable of confronting them.

The combination of the tension and the negative reactions of friends, family, and significant others (indeed, of society in general) may leave PWAs and their families feeling isolated from the outside world (as well as one another) and thus forced to face this terrifying situation on their own.

Support and Caring

Many families, friends, and lovers remain available to PWAs, providing emotional support and physical care as well as meeting concrete needs, sometimes with a devotion far beyond that which might be expected. It is also common for family members to reappear after many years of separation when they learn that the patients are ill. This may be difficult for patients to accept in some instances, especially if it reawakens old hurts and disagreements. Occasionally patients may feel they do not deserve any familial support.

> D. E., a 36-year-old black man, had grown up in a middle-class, suburban home; he said he had been loved by his parents, had had a close relationship with his brothers, and had planned to pursue a college education. He blamed himself for his drug use, calling himself a "rebel" as a teenager. He had left home after a blow-up with his father 15 years earlier and had never had contact with them again. He knew that if they were aware of his situation (homeless, ill), they would come for him. He felt he did not deserve that from them after the way he had behaved and would not allow the hospital staff to contact the family.

Alteration of Relationship Patterns

Upon learning they are HIV-infected, IVDUs may feel ready to change their lifestyles. In the best of circumstances, this may mean entering a drug treatment program where success might mean the loss of longstanding friendships with drug-using companions as well as a change in daily activities and patterns of relationships (Friedman et al., 1986). Sexual practices may also change, leading to shifts in relationships with lovers. All these changes may be puzzling to those around IVDUs and, in fact, may feel discordant to PWAs themselves.

The many factors involved in maintaining different relationships—communication, sexuality, history, emotional connectedness—are all affected by the onset of HIV infection. Whether they lead to a general deterioration or general improvement in these relationships must be evaluated on a case-by-case basis. It is clear, though, that some change is always present.

SOCIAL WORK INTERVENTIONS

Social workers must intervene on several levels in order to provide services for PWAs and HIV-infected individuals (Caputo, 1985; Mantell, Shulman, Belmont, & Spivak, 1989; Novak, 1989). These interventions consist of five general areas.

Concrete Services

As their medical conditions deteriorate, PWAs are likely to have increasing needs for such services as home care, nursing services related to the administration of special treatments, medical equipment (e.g., hospital beds, wheel-chairs), and housekeeping assistance. IVDUs, with their decreased resources, may require additional services, including housing, extended nursing care, and enrollment in income/benefit programs. In many instances IVDUs may also require some form of drug treatment, including detoxification, metha-done maintenance, or drug-free residential placement. Social workers must be knowledgeable about the services and programs available in the commu-nity and facile in negotiating these systems effectively.

Counseling

A major component of social work with PWAs and HIV-infected individuals is counseling concerning the impact of the illness on themselves, their families, and significant others as well as the mechanisms they use to cope with the situation. Counseling may take place in several modalities, including individual, couples, family, and group counseling. Some specific techniques, discussed below, are useful when counseling on an individual basis.

Active Listening

In active listening the counselor is interactive and very much a presence in the treatment. IVDUs, because of their own emptiness, cannot work with a counselor who is nondirective and silent; the counselor must be available as an understanding, motivating, confronting, and active figure.

Encouraging the Expression of Feelings

Family and significant others may be afraid to discuss the implications of an AIDS diagnosis. In their attempts to help the patients feel hopeful (and because of their own inability to deal with such intense material), they may avoid such painful topics as death and planning for those who remain. PWAs, however, may need a forum in which to safely share their thoughts and feelings about what is happening to them.

Encouraging Participation in Treatment Planning

In service of avoidance or denial, IVDUs may defer to the medical team regarding decision making, thus divorcing themselves from their own treat-ment plans. But it is crucial that they consciously make such decisions as what treatment to try, what services to request, and where to go for treatment, so as to maintain what control they have in the situation and to establish commitment to (and, potentially, compliance with) the plan. While it is appropriate for social workers to make recommendations (as when patients are unfamiliar with available resources or when they are not capable of participating fully due to severity of medical or emotional condition), PWAs can feel empowered by having input in determining the treatments and services they will receive.

Allowing Denial

The tendency of IVDUs to use maladaptive denial has been described previously. Nevertheless, there are times when denial is useful. For example, patients may believe that if they alter their lifestyles, they will be cured of the virus. Such denial may be a factor in motivating such behavior changes as decreasing drug use or shifting patterns in relationships, thus promoting a better quality of life both medically and socially.

Providing Reliable Support

IVDUs, with their histories of disappointing relationships, may find the opportunity (often for the first time in their lives) to feel emotionally supported via their relationships with social workers. This support, in turn, may help them take a chance on behavior changes that they might otherwise deem too risky. Such supportive relationships also permit them to feel safe in a situation in which they are realistically vulnerable and frightened.

Avoiding Overhelping

It is tempting to provide all-encompassing care for IVDUs with AIDS or HIV infection. They may present as helpless and desperately in need of assistance, tapping into social workers' desire to be helpful (Levinson & Straussner, 1978). Nevertheless, it is important to encourage patients to do things for themselves, despite the annoyance they may express. IVDUs with AIDS feel powerless. They may ask social workers, therefore, to attend to their problems for them. While it may actually be easier to do as they ask, in the long run it is more useful to help them feel empowered and thus capable of taking care of themselves. (The simplest example of this is to give a patient a quarter to make a telephone call rather than making it for him or her.)

Life Review

As with many terminally ill patients, PWAs may need to examine the course of their lives—their accomplishments, regrets, joys, sorrows. Social worker can provide patients with opportunities to discuss all aspects of their lives, listening for how resolved they are about each issue. IVDUs often feel saddened by how they have lived and what has happened to their relationships; they need opportunities to share what has been good and grieve for what has not been good.

Working through Unfinished Business

It is sometimes possible to resolve situations that patients feel uneasy about but are unable to cope with on their own. Social workers can be allies in this process by locating and counseling significant others, assisting with the purchase of a long-desired item, and so forth.

> J. R., aged 46, had not seen his mother for 22 years; he was not sure she was still alive, but he suspected she continued to reside in Santo Domingo. He wanted to see her, apologize for how he had hurt her years earlier—initially by his behavior, later by leaving. The social worker was able to locate her and arrange for her to come to New York, where she and her son were reunited. She remained with him for about 2 weeks. Soon after her departure, J. R. described himself as feeling peaceful and stated that he could now die without remorse. He did, in fact, die about a week after making that statement.

Maximizing Quality of Life

While some IVDUs are overwhelmed by their diagnosis and increase their substance abuse as a means of coping, others can be helped to change their behaviors, relationships, and coping mechanisms. This, in combination with the receipt of concrete benefits, enables them to change their living situation and thus their entire quality of life.

> P. M., a 40-year-old white woman, had used intravenous drugs only occasionally but had shared needles at those times. Although aware that she was at risk, she felt she would never get infected. She cared for her three children, ages 10 through 16, but was not close with them. When she learned she was HIV-infected, she abruptly stopped her drug use. She began to spend more time with her children and found that their relationship improved markedly. She tearfully wondered why it had taken so severe a circumstance to bring about this change but was grateful that she had been able to do so.

Case Management

Case management is the process of planning, organizing, coordinating, and monitoring the services and resources needed to respond to an individual's health and psychosocial care needs. Social workers with case management responsibilities have ongoing contact with patients—in hospitals, in outpatient settings, and in the community. They follow up on referrals for services within the community, have frequent multidisciplinary conferences, and act as the "clearinghouse" for planning for an individual's care.

Education

Social workers provide a broad range of educational programs to patients, families and significant others, staff members, and other professionals. They also offer preventive programs to the general public, expending particular effort to reach those individuals (e.g., IVDUs) who are at especially high risk for exposure to the HIV virus. These programs may include information on transmission, prevention, and treatment as well as on safer sex and needle-cleaning practices.

Advocacy

Social workers may be vocal regarding the needs of an individual patient (e.g., receipt of services) or of an entire group or subgroup of PWAs (e.g., homeless IVDUs). This advocacy may be limited to the setting in which a particular social worker is situated, or it may extend to activity for legislation and system changes.

REACTIONS OF SOCIAL WORKERS

IVDUs who are HIV-infected are an exceedingly difficult population with which to work. Patients who present with a combination of drug use (and the personality characteristics associated with that) and a life-threatening medical condition may evoke several reactions on the part of health care staff, including social workers (Cavrell, 1988; Dunkel & Hatfield, 1986). These reactions may, in turn, be influential in determining the course of the therapeutic relationship specifically and the treatment planning generally. The reactions discussed below are particularly common.

Fear

Fear may derive from several sources, but generally it involves irrational ideas concerning contagion. There may also be concern about the personality characteristics of IVDUs, especially when they have been threatening in some way or if they have criminal histories.

Blaming

Because the high-risk behaviors associated with HIV infection are frowned upon by society at large, it is not unusual for workers to blame PWAs for their own illness, feeling that they somehow "deserve" to be ill because of their deviant behavior.

Rejection

Fear and blaming may combine and lead to rejection. This may be subtle, manifesting itself as a decrease in the frequency of counseling sessions, slowness in processing applications for benefits, and so forth; or it may be quite obvious, as in transfering a patient to another worker or agency (Mantell et al., 1989).

Homophobia and Addictophobia

The fear, blaming, and rejection can ultimately lead to phobia regarding all homosexuals and all drug users. Should such feelings become widespread, they could lead to a decrease in services and staffing for HIV-related treatment programs.

Helplessness and Hopelessness

Social workers often berate themselves for being ultimately powerless in the face of the virus: They cannot cure their patients of AIDS. This feeling of impotence can lead the workers to feel generally hopeless about the ultimate value of their interventions in the face of the increasing prevalence of HIV infection and the growing numbers of patients needing long-term care.

S. F. is an especially talented social worker who had been working with AIDS patients for about 1 year. Although occasionally tearful when a patient died or when she felt frustrated in her efforts to plan effectively, for the most part she felt competent in and gratified by her work. While in the intensive care unit visiting with a patient she was especially fond of, she became overwhelmed with the feeling that no matter how hard she worked, she would be incapable of curing this man's condition. She felt beaten by the virus and was left with a sense of total powerlessness.

Grief

The relationship between a social worker and patient, particularly when it involves issues of death and dying, can be an intense and intimate one. Loss of patients, then, can leave workers grief-stricken and depleted.

Rage

Confronted by seriously needy patients, workers must then negotiate a system that does not sufficiently address these patients' concerns. A series of difficult cases can leave workers enraged at no one in particular for this state of events and may, at times, cause them to overreact to minor slights and insensitivities.

Guilt

Guilt can derive from several sources. First, workers are healthy and, however empathic they may be, cannot really know how it feels to be sick, especially with AIDS. Second, by virtue of being employed as social workers, it is likely that they have financial and other resources that are greater than those of their patients. Third, there are times when the provocative behavior evidenced by some IVDUs may be difficult to tolerate, and social workers may find themselves reluctant to be helpful. They may feel especially guilty about this if they have, in fact, acted out those feelings. Fourth, and more subtly, workers may find that they enjoy working with this population and are somehow energized by the excitement of working "on the edge" of life and death situations. This pleasure in their work may feel dissonant against the backdrop of death, illness, and poor quality of life (Cavrell, 1988).

Anxiety

Many social workers complain of anxiety, particularly when confronted with seriously ill clients who have minimum resources and multiple needs. Workers may worry about patients' functioning in the community (e.g., whether they are remaining durg-free, whether they are engaging in illegal activities) and about their medical condition (e.g., whether they are losing weight). Workers may be concerned about their own job performance in negotiating the numerous obstacles they confront. They may also be anxious about their own serostatus and that of people they are close to.

Depression

The constant exposure to death, illness, the broad range of emotions patients express, their own feelings of powerlessness, and the ominous sense of relentless onslaught make depression a common response. Depression is inevitably experienced in some degree, but it naturally varies depending upon each worker's coping capacity and defense mechanisms.

All these responses are normal, but they must be addressed lest they become overwhelming and lead to burnout, ultimately forcing the worker to leave the profession. It is therefore crucial that social workers have a forum in which they can express their feelings honestly. Support groups are especially successful in this regard and should be built into all programming. Supervision is another mechanism for receiving support, provided that supervisors are able to create an atmosphere in which workers feel secure enough to discuss these very difficult reactions.

SUMMARY

The provision of social work services to intravenous drug users with AIDS or HIV infection is a formidable task. Confronted with individuals whose difficulties may include a vast array of physical, social, economic, and psychological problems, social workers must intervene with services on all levels while simultaneously dealing with obstacles on all fronts, possibly including their own reactions. And yet social workers nave indeed risen to this challenge and are caring for this population with a commitment and fervor that is admirable.

REFERENCES

American Psychiatric Association. (1987). *Diagnostic and statistical manual of mental disorders* (3rd ed., rev.). Washington, DC: Author.

Caputo, L. (1985). Dual diagnosis: AIDS and addiction. *Social Work, 30,* 361–364.

Carpi, J. (1987). Treating IV drug users: A difficult task for staff. *AIDS Patient Care, 1,* 21–23.

Cavrell, D. (1988, June). *Managing countertransference: A guide for AIDS health care professionals.* Poster presented at the Fourth International Conference of AIDS, Stockholm, Sweden.

Centers for Disease Control. (1989, June). *AIDS surveillance/epidemiology.* Slide presentation.

Centers for Disease Control. (1990, September). *HIV/AIDS surveillance report,* pp. 1–18.

Chein, I. G., Donald, L., Lee, R. S., & Rosenfeld, E. (1964). Personality and addiction: A dynamic perspective. In I. G. Chein, L. Donald, R. S. Lee, & E. Rosenfeld (Eds.), *The road to H: Narcotics, delinquency, and social policy* (pp. 227–250). New York: Basic Books.

Christ, G. H., & Wiener, L. S. (1985). Psychosocial issues in AIDS. In T. V. DeVita, Jr., S. Hellman, & S. Rosenberg (Eds.), *AIDS etiology, diagnosis, treatment and prevention* (pp. 275–297). New York: Lippincott.

Dunkel, J., & Hatfield, S. (1986). Countertransference issues in working with persons with AIDS. *Social Work, 31,* 114–117.

Flanagan, N. (1989). Understanding your IVDU patients: It still helps to know the streets. *AIDS Patient Care, 3,* 23–25.

Friedman, S. R., Des Jarlais, D. C., & Sotheran, J. L. (1986). AIDS health education for intravenous drug users. *Health Education Quarterly, 13,* 383–393.

Levinson, V., & Strausssner, S. L. A. (1978). Social workers as "enablers" in the treatment of alcoholics. *Social Casework, 50,* 14–20.

Mantell, J. E., Shulman, L. C., Belmont, M. F., & Spivak, H. B. (1989). Social workers respond to the AIDS epidemic in an acute care hospital. *Health and Social Work, 14,* 41–51.

National Association of Social Workers. (1984, September). *Acquired immune deficiency syndrome* (NASW public social policy statement), Silver Spring, MD.

National Association of Social Workers. (1987a, April). *AIDS: A social work response* (proposed revised social policy statement for 1987 delegate assembly of NASW).

National Association of Social Workers, New York City Chapter Task Force on AIDS. (1987b). *New York City chapter position paper on social work practice for people with AIDS, ARC and HIV infection.*

Novak, C. (1989). Social work services. In P. Blomberg (Ed.), *Comprehensive management of HIV infection: A protocol treatment plan for HIV/ARC/AIDS patients in northern California* (pp. 228–250). Sacramento, CA: Sacramento AIDS Foundation.

Rubinow, D. R., & Joffe, R. T. (1987). Psychiatric and psychosocial aspects of AIDS. In S. Broder (Ed.), *AIDS: Modern concepts and therapeutic challenges* (pp. 123–133). New York: Marcel Dekker.

Shilts, R. (1987). *And the band played on.* New York: Penguin.

Vaillant, G. (1975). Sociopathy as a human process: A viewpoint. *Archives of General Psychiatry, 32,* 178–183.

Wurmser, L. (1974). Psychoanalytic considerations of the etiology of compulsive drug use. *Journal of the American Psychoanalytic Association, 22,* 820–843.

Zinberg, N. E. (1975). Addiction and ego function. *Psychoanalytic Study of the Child, 30,* 567–588.

19

Relapse Prevention

MURIEL GRAY

During the past 10 years there has been a proliferation of treatment providers offering a variety of levels and modalities of treatment for substance use disorders. These clinical interventions have been very effective in helping substance abusers initiate change toward a life of abstinence and a state of recovery, but they have been far less effective in helping substance abusers maintain this change for long-term recovery (Annis & Davis, 1989). For instance, while more patients are seeking, receiving, and benefiting from treatment for substance use disorders, long-term (longer than 1 year) recovery rates are estimated to be about 35% (Dolan & Olander, 1990). Therefore, relapse, or return to substance use after an apparent period of abstinence and recovery, is a major problem in the overall effectiveness of substance abuse treatment (Daley, 1987).

The focus of this chapter is on the use of clinical models and interventions in the prevention of relapse. It presents a conceptual framework, defines the major components and clinical interventions in relapse prevention counseling, presents a service delivery model, provides an annotated list of instruments, and discusses the role of social workers in the treatment of substance use disorders in general and relapse prevention in particular.

DEFINITION OF RELAPSE PREVENTION

The relationship among treatment, recovery, and relapse is currently being debated among substance abuse treatment professionals (Annis & Davis, 1989; Daley, 1987; Gorski, 1986; Marlatt & George, 1984). This debate specifically focuses on the role of relapse, or the interruption of an apparent state of abstinence or recovery, during the recovery process. Because of the prevalence of relapse, some treatment professionals accept it as a part of substance use disorders and see it as an anticipated interruption in the recovery process. Other treatment professionals, however, noting that some patients proceed to a state of uninterrupted recovery or experience very few relapse episodes, tend to view relapse as an indication of treatment failure (Annis & Davis, 1989; Washton, 1989).

Most practitioners agree that a patient cannot be in recovery and relapse at the same time. Recovery assumes a behavioral and emotional change toward health and growth; relapse assumes a reversion to a previous state of dysfunction (Annis & Davis, 1989; Gorski, 1986). Thus, relapse prevention is by definition a strategic set of clinical interventions and responses designed to help patients maintain a state of recovery and continued movement toward health and growth; it is an essential component in any form of treatment of substance use disorders (Annis & Davis, 1989; Gorski, 1986; Gray, 1989; Hester & Miller, 1989; Marlatt & Gordon, 1985).

CONCEPTUAL FRAMEWORK: CONTINUUM OF CARE

The prevention of relapse is inextricably linked to the treatment process, and since there is no known cure for substance use disorders, both treatment and relapse prevention are ongoing processes. Thus defining treatment as a singular event (e.g., detoxification only) or relapse as a singular event (e.g., resuming alcohol or drug use only) increases the likelihood that the patient will not enter a state of recovery. Social work practitioners and their patients need to view treatment, recovery, and relapse as processes and to be knowledgeable about the phases of each.

Treatment

The treatment of substance use disorders occurs in phases along a treatment continuum, with the focus of treatment changing at each phase, typically conceptualized as: pretreatment, stabilization, rehabilitation, and continuing care (Washton, 1989).

The *pretreatment* phase is the first phase of treatment, actually beginning before the patient enters a treatment program. It is the phase during which the social worker helps the client (1) identify substance abuse as a problem, (2) become motivated to change, and (3) become involved in a structured treatment regime. The focus during this phase is on getting the client involved in intensive substance abuse treatment.

The *stabilization* phase focuses on detoxifying the body of drugs (including alcohol) and monitoring the physiological and/or psychological effects of drug withdrawal, stabilizing daily functioning, resolving any immediate crises, and formulating a treatment plan (Washton, 1989) in order to help the patient be better able to respond to the next phase of treatment.

The *rehabilitation* phase is an intensive, structured period during which the physical, emotional, social, and spiritual effects of the disorder are addressed. It focuses on education about substance use disorders, the recovery process, the use of self-help groups, and ongoing personal care in order to help the patient abstain from substance use and feel comfortable living without substances. While this phase of treatment addresses the concept of relapse by developing an ongoing treatment plan aimed at relapse prevention and by teaching techniques to handle the stresses and strains of early recovery, relapse prevention is not the primary focus.

Relapse prevention is the focus of the *continuing care* phase of treatment, during which the patient makes the transition from the structured environment (either inpatient or outpatient) to a routinely unstructured outpatient environment. The focus is on helping the patient maintain the positive biopsychosocial changes made in the previous phase by applying the knowledge and techniques learned during rehabilitation. The emphasis is on educating the patient about the relapse process, helping the patient identify relapse warning signs and assess risk factors, and teaching the patient how to continue to treat the disorder in order to prevent and/or minimize relapse. A part of this education also includes the identification of and the appropriate use of supportive resources.

Recovery

Recovery also occurs along a continuum, with different foci at each phase (Gorski, 1986). The phases of the recovery continuum are typically conceptualized as early, middle, advanced, and maintained recovery (Gorski, 1986; Washton, 1989). Even though the phases are presented here as occurring at specified times, the patient's actual recovery is reflected in quality of life, lifestyle, and the successful addressing of the themes of life and recovery. Therefore the timeframe discussed is merely a rough guide to a typical patient's progress along the recovery continuum; each patient will have a unique recovery style.

Very early recovery usually refers to the first 3 months of compliance with the recovery plan. Since this is the most vulnerable time for relapse, this phase focuses on (1) monitoring the patient's reaction to postacute withdrawal (PAW) and other physiological and medical conditions; (2) developing strategies for handling PAW discomfort (which may be accompanied by depression); (3) identifying and appropriately addressing predisposing factors, such as legal, family, school, or dual diagnosis problems; and (4) identifying and appropriately addressing precipitating factors, such as high-risk situations, psychological and physiological triggers, or overconfidence. Although the introduction to self-help groups begins during the stabilization phase, involvement continues throughout the recovery process. It is important to realize that anecdotal retrospective analysis of patients' relapse patterns shows that some patients may have a high potential for relapse during this phase because they feel "too good"; as a result, they tend to see no need to comply with the recovery plan (Gorski, 1980; Ludwig, 1988).

Early recovery begins about 3 to 12 months into the recovery process. The focus in this phase is on continuing to help the patient (1) make positive, lasting lifestyle changes; (2) learn how to identify and handle emotions; (3) learn how to have fun without alcohol or other drugs; (4) learn how to deal effectively with problems, adjustments, and setbacks; (5) identify and appropriately use internal strengths; (6) identify and appropriately use external support systems; (7) increase involvement in self-help groups; and (8) heighten spiritual awareness.

Middle recovery begins 1 to 2 years into sobriety. During this phase the focus is on helping the patient (1) address issues of arrested maturity; (2) solidify adaptive coping and problem-solving skills; (3) address emotional and personality issues that affect self-esteem and so forth; and (4) identify and address areas of needed growth for both the patient and the patient's immediate family.

Advanced recovery begins during the second year into sobriety. It is somewhat open-ended, in that the issues addressed during this phase are unique to individual patients and their situations. The focus in this phase is on identifying and addressing other situations that may be obstacles to continued sobriety.

Maintained recovery is also an open-ended phase, focusing on normal life developmental issues. The main task of the patient is to maintain and share his or her recovery with others. This means continued involvement in self-help groups and continued attention to the recovery plan, but it also means that the patient should assume a more external, giving, helping role in the self-help groups in particular and in life in general.

Relapse

While it may appear that relapse is a singular event characterized by resumption of alcohol or other drug use, practitioners have noted a constellation of signs and symptoms that appear to precede a resumption of substance use (Gorski, 1980). Moreover, it has also been observed that the patterns of resumed use are often incremental and have differing consequences. Patients may "build up" to a resumption of use; if they do resume use, the pattern may be either a temporary "slip" (lapse), characterized by a brief episode of controlled use, or a full-blown relapse, characterized by an extended episode of uncontrolled use or binging.

The consequences of a relapse vary with each patient; some patterns are more deleterious than others. For instance, a relapse that is interrupted before resumption of substance use is usually not recognized as a relapse by patients and therefore may not be viewed as being deleterious.

Upon discharge from the intensive phase of primary treatment, Bob, a recovering alcoholic and drug addict, had a very positive attitude and commitment to continued recovery. He agreed to a recovery plan that included weekly attendance at a minimum of four Narcotics Anonymous (NA) and Alcoholics Anonymous (AA) meetings, weekly attendance at an aftercare group, daily exercise (either a 2-mile walk or 4-mile bike ride), daily inspirational reading, no more than 10 hours of overtime work a week, regular and nutritious meals, and weekly telephone or face-to-face contact with his NA sponsor. During follow-up interviews in the month after discharge, it was found that Bob was increasingly not engaging in the activities specified by his recovery plan. It was also noted that Bob's attitude had changed: He no longer believed he had a "serious drug problem" and had begun to question his need for the recovery plan. He became angry at the suggestion of NA meetings and questioned his need for the support of the follow-up counselor. A urinalysis and self-report indicated that Bob was abstinent.

The example of Bob shows the constellation of signs and symptoms that indicated he was moving toward relapse. While Bob did not resume drug use, in cases where a brief episode of controlled alcohol or other drug use does occur, the consequences are more psychological than physical, often manifested as anger, guilt, and shame. In other cases, an extended period of uncontrolled drug or alcohol use often results in serious physiological and social consequences as well as an array of psychological reactions.

The *process* of relapse can be interrupted at any point. Social workers can therefore intervene after any incident, whether it is one that did not include the resumption of substance use, one that involved a brief, controlled episode of substance use, or one that extended into a binge of uncontrolled use.

Relapse Warning Signs and Symptoms

Relapse can be prevented if the social worker is attuned to the symptoms that forewarn an impending episode. Among the constellation of symptoms are the following:

- anger
- poor health care
- defensiveness
- impulsivity
- dishonesty
- impatience
- self-pity
- cockiness
- loneliness
- unreasonable resentments
- depression
- irregular attendance at a self-help program
- resumption of controlled use
- resumption of uncontrolled use

It is important to remember that patients who have not resumed substance use may find it difficult to acknowledge that they exhibit signs of relapse and are not in a state of recovery. It may be even more difficult for them to understand that unless something changes, it may only be a matter of time before they resume alcohol or other drug use. In such cases, practitioners will want to assess the patient's compliance with the recovery plan or modify the recovery plan in an attempt to interrupt the relapse process.

COMPONENTS OF RELAPSE PREVENTION

Relapse prevention begins with a treatment plan, which may also be referred to as a recovery plan. It is a prescription that includes a daily regime for healthful living and is designed specifically to treat the dynamics of the disorder in the context of the patient's individual circumstances. It reinforces the treatment components of the rehabilitation phase, while recognizing and attending to the issues appropriate for each recovery phase.

Throughout each recovery phase, the plan stresses the fact that treatment of a substance use disorder is an ongoing process and it approaches recovery from a holistic perspective. Therefore, the components of relapse prevention include clinical interventions to address physical, emotional, social, and spiritual well-being (Alcoholics Anonymous [AA], 1975; Gorski & Miller, 1986; Gray, 1989; Marlatt & Gordon, 1985; Washton, 1989) as well as the monitoring of substance use through urinalysis and breath analysis.

Physical Well-Being

Substance use disorders often have deleterious physical effects, and recovery plans must reinforce the importance of maintaining physical health through regular, nutritionally balanced meals, adequate rest, and physical exercise. Since relapse specialists have found that patients are prone to relapse when they deprive themselves of food and rest, they should be specifically advised to avoid becoming too hungry or too tired. They should also be informed that certain foods (e.g., extracts) and medicines (e.g., cough syrups, painkillers) contain alcohol or narcotics and could jeopardize recovery by triggering a physiological reaction; they should therefore be encouraged to tell their health care providers (physicians, dentists, pharmacists, etc.) of their disorder.

Emotional Well-Being

Cognitive-behavioral psychotherapists have recognized that feelings and thoughts influence behavior. In the early stage of recovery, where the focus is primarily on behavioral lifestyle changes, the effect of emotions on behavior is critical. For instance, anger, frustration, loneliness, and depression are emotions often associated with relapse. Thus, "HALT" is a treatment dictum that advises patients to not get too *hungry, angry, lonely,* or *tired.* Patients are often taught how to control these emotions in recovery counseling, primary treatment, and self-help groups. Euphoric emotions, such as joy and happiness, are also associated with relapse in that they often indicate a false sense of accomplishment and excitement, referred to as the "pink cloud." Thus recovery plans need to address emotional health through the use of self-help groups, aftercare groups, family treatment, situational counseling, and other follow-up interventions.

Self-Help Groups

There are a variety of self-help groups, the most prevalent of which are 12-step programs. It is difficult to accurately and scientifically assess the effectiveness of 12-step programs because of methodological and sampling problems associated with research on Anonymous programs (McCrady & Irvin, 1989; Tournier, 1979); most of data on them are anecdotal. However, because many practitioners and patients observe a positive correlation between the quality of 12-step program involvement and the quality of recovery, involvement in a 12-step program is a basic component in relapse prevention. (For a more detailed description and discussion of 12-step programs see Chapter 9.)

Monitoring 12-step program attendance is necessary but not sufficient for social workers assisting clients in recovery. In addition to monitoring attendance by asking about the number of meetings attended, the topics of the meetings, and what they liked about the meetings, it is equally as important to assess the quality and level of patient involvement in the program. To do so and to help patients effectively use these groups, workers need to be familiar with the philosophy and structure of 12-step programs. Of particular importance are the following guidelines for patients and their families:

- Attend meetings on a regular basis (several times per week)
- Attend meetings at different locations before deciding which to attend regularly
- Attend a variety of different types of meetings
- Develop a close, confidential relationship with someone who is in recovery and has been in the program for at least 2 years (a sponsor)
- Work the program steps and respect the traditions

Even though 12-step programs are more prevalent, there are variety of other self-help and other types of support groups for substance abusers. Some of these distinguish themselves by addressing either issues that 12-step programs do not address or issues that are appropriate only for some clients. For instance, Women for Sobriety (WFS) is a self-help support group designed specifically for women. Rational Recovery is a support group based on the principles of rational-emotive therapy. There are also self-help groups for Jewish substance abusers specifically designed to offer them a way to link their Judaism to their ongoing recovery. Some of these groups are meant to complement 12-step groups rather than replace them.

Aftercare Groups

Another important component in relapse prevention is participation in aftercare groups, which usually exist under the auspices of the primary intensive treatment facility that provided the rehabilitation. These groups aid in the transition from structured treatment to unstructured community living, providing continuity between the rehabilitation and the continuing care phases of treatment.

To be most effective, aftercare groups should meet for 2 years. During very early and early recovery (3 to 12 months after the rehabilitation phase), meetings should be weekly; as recovery progresses, the frequency of meetings usually gradually decreases.

Aftercare groups focus on problem situations and emotional and behavioral reactions to life without using substances. These groups typically develop strategies and responses to troubling situations that may present obstacles to continued recovery. For example, many patients who have been in a structured treatment program (either as inpatients or outpatients) have difficulty structuring a life in the community that does not include alcohol or other drugs. This may be particularly true if family celebrations, such as weddings, holiday gatherings, or graduations, include alcohol or other drugs. The aftercare group provides the opportunity to discuss the situation, anticipate reactions, and develop a strategic plan for handling the situation.

Alumni Groups

Alumni groups are typically gatherings planned by the primary intensive treatment provider for patients who have completed the rehabilitation phase of treatment at that treatment facility. They are most often picnics, holiday parties, retreats, and other weekend activities. They provide opportunities to socialize and reminisce with those who were in treatment groups together. These groups provide not only alcohol- and drug-free social activities but also opportunities for people to support one another. Alumni groups are equally important to patients who were treated in intensive outpatient programs. Of course, patients whose primary intensive treatment did not include a group modality would not have an alumni group.

Family Treatment

Even though there is a paucity of research on this topic, treatment professionals observe that recovery seems to be best sustained when patients' significant others are both supportive of the recovery process and themselves actively involved in the treatment process (Edwards, 1982). Since 12-step programs share this belief, there are 12-step programs designed specifically for family members and others concerned with or affected by the disorder.

It is important for social workers assisting patients in recovery to encourage the involvement of family members. Even though family members may not be identified as the primary patient, as a part of the patient's social system they certainly may have an affect on recovery—as either supports or obstacles. For example, Bob, whose story was related earlier, recently completed primary intensive treatment as an outpatient. His wife was not involved in the family treatment program. During treatment Bob self-diagnosed himself as an alcoholic and an addict and accepted that appropriate continued treatment would include total abstinence. His wife was happy that Bob had benefited from treatment, but she did not understand the importance of abstinence and therefore suggested that he could drink as long as he controlled it. Not realizing that Bob may not be able to control his drinking she unwittingly undermined his recovery plan.

Individual Counseling

In addition to aftercare groups, some patients may need individual aftercare counseling. As with aftercare groups, during early recovery the focus of individual counseling is on relapse prevention. This type of recovery counseling should specifically address (Annis & Davis, 1989; Washton, 1986):

- High-risk drinking and drug-using situations
- Behavioral and psychological triggers to use
- Patient strengths and resources for dealing with such situations
- New responses to old situations
- Other familial, legal, vocational, and educational obstacles to recovery

For example, Mary, a recovering alcoholic flight attendant, had an irregular work schedule that caused her to miss several aftercare group meetings. In addition, she had a job that included serving alcoholic drinks. This aspect of her work was a threat to her recovery unless she learned specific techniques for recognizing and controlling her psychological triggers. Individual counseling in conjunction with the aftercare group was particularly helpful during her early recovery phase.

Social Well-Being

As previously indicated, the maintenance of positive treatment effects often requires new and different responses to old and comfortable situations. Such changes in life, both in style and in approach, are essential to recovery. Therefore, the patient's recovery plan needs to address housing, healthy hobbies, new friends, and employment and work relationships.

Housing

Homelessness is a major obstacle to recovery. Inappropriate housing (an environment that does not support and reinforce abstinence and recovery) is a major factor in relapse. Therefore it is critical that social workers help patients realistically assess their living situation and secure appropriate housing. For homeless patients, this may mean a recovery residence, also referred to as a halfway house or quarter-way house; these are transitional group homes specifically designed for recovering patients who need a supportive drug- and alcohol-free living environment. In some cities, certain sections are designated in public housing communities for tenants in recovery. For patients with unsupportive home environments, temporarily moving in with supportive friends or relatives may be necessary.

Hobbies

Most patients in early recovery report that they have idle time; this is the block of time that had previously been filled by substance use. Therefore a recovery plan should include alternative activities to fill that time (AA, 1975; Annis & Davis, 1989). Social workers may need to help patients select a hobby and develop a strategy for regular involvement.

Friends

Most substance abusers report that they have few friends, or very few friends, who do not use substances. But situations in which the newly recovering patient becomes lonely or is around other substance users present a high risk for relapse (Daley, 1987). Social workers need to educate patients about the importance of not becoming too lonely and help them develop strategies for dealing with old friends and skills for making new ones. Among other benefits, involvement in a self-help program can be a way to develop a new social network. However, it is important to keep in mind that not all people attending self-help program groups are abstinent. Therefore social workers need to help patients identify and associate with others who are in recovery.

Employment and Work Relationships

Employment, job performance, and quality of work relationships affect recovery. Employment is also important to a well-balanced life. To the extent that unemployment promotes an unstructured lifestyle or one conducive to substance use, to the same extent it is an obstacle to recovery. On the other hand, if a patient is employed, the threat of job loss due to a decline in job performance may be an impetus for recovery and therefore an aid in the prevention of relapse. Thus it is important for social workers to assess the role that employment may play in the recovery process.

In addition, job performance and the quality of relationships with coworkers often serve as a barometer for the quality of recovery. Therefore, to minimize the risk of relapse, social workers need to inquire about the nature and quality of the patient's work and work relationships. Job performance and relationships with coworkers will likely improve as recovery advances.

Spiritual Well-Being

Patients' beliefs and sources of inspiration are important to personal growth. Although religiosity may be a part of a spirituality, a patient's spirituality need not include organized religion. Spirituality refers to a person's beliefs about a source of inspiration outside the self.

Alcoholics Anonymous perceives substance abuse as a disorder that affects the patient's spiritual well-being; it therefore includes a focus on spirituality. However, in addition to becoming involved in 12-step programs, patients should be encouraged to become involved in activities that they find inspiring and uplifting. The specific activities will be determined by each patient's own values, but they may include daily readings, meditation, and daily affirmations.

Urinalysis and Breath Analysis

In some circumstances, the treatment plan (especially in outpatient treatment and during the continuing care phase of treatment) may include periodic chemical analysis to verify abstinence. To be most effective, such testing should occur randomly. Urinalysis is usually preferable to blood testing because it is less intrusive and less expensive. Urinalysis is used to detect use of drugs other than alcohol, while breath analysis is usually used to detect alcohol use. Both types of analysis determine the presence of the substance in the body but do not specify the degree of impairment. Should either of these test yield a positive result, a more sensitive test should be given to confirm this finding.

A RELAPSE PREVENTION MODEL: CASE MANAGEMENT

Repetitive relapse need not be a part of substance use disorders. Research has shown that the rate of relapse can be reduced with systematic treatment planning and the clinical management and coordination of such care (Foote & Erfurt, 1990). Case management models are therefore receiving much attention from those involved in the treatment of substance use disorders. Case management in its most broad form is a system of managed service delivery (Ashley, 1988). It may or may not include fiscal management, but it always includes clinical management of client services.

The functions of case management vary with different populations and service systems. However, in the treatment of substance use disorders, a balanced service system model is most frequently used. This model includes client outreach, accurate problem assessment, case planning, matching clients with the appropriate level of care, advocacy, and structured follow-up (Adelman & Weiss, 1989; Austin, 1983; Chapman & Huygens, 1988; Guiliani & Schnoll, 1985; O'Dwyer, 1984; Roberts-DeGennaro, 1987). Case management is very similar to the traditional social casework model of study, diagnosis, and treatment. However, social workers functioning as case managers, unlike traditional caseworkers, are usually not treatment providers themselves; instead they coordinate, advocate, and broker needed services on behalf of clients. Each stage of treatment and recovery is a juncture at which social workers make decisions regarding client needs. In some instances they may also be responsible for negotiating and reviewing specific costs of client services. Since relapse prevention depends on a coordinated process of treatment delivery at each stage of treatment and recovery, the case management model is particularly effective.

THE ROLE OF SOCIAL WORKERS

Social work skills have been underutilized in the treatment of substance abuse in general and in the prevention of relapse in particular. Yet social workers work in settings and situations in which substance abusers often find themselves.

Unless they are serving as case managers, most social workers assisting patients in relapse prevention will be involved during the continuing care phase of treatment, probably working with both the patient and the patient's family. It is important that the social worker have knowledge of the patient's ongoing treatment plan and enter into an agreement with the patient either to accept this plan or to modify it. Such a plan should include, at a minimum, the previously mentioned components of healthy recovery. This plan also serves as a guide for living that can help both patient and social worker assess relapse potential during structured follow-up sessions.

Technically, case management for relapse prevention may be conceptualized as a process that begins with accurate problem assessment and includes treatment matching and follow-up. However, the focus of the rest of this chapter is on the role of structured follow-up in the prevention of relapse, since research (Foote & Erfurt, 1990) has shown that structured follow-up is one of the most important clinical interventions in recovery from substance abuse and prevention of relapse.

Structured Follow-Up

The follow-up component of the case management process is probably one of the most important; yet it is the component least often provided (McAuliffe & Ch'ien, 1986). Too often treatment professionals spend considerable time getting the patient into treatment and developing treatment and/or recovery plans, only to provide minimal follow-up to ensure compliance and ongoing assessment.

Follow-up is a form of insurance. It provides the patient with the support that is critical throughout the recovery process. It provides social workers with a way to assess the patient's ongoing needs and obstacles to recovery.

The specific nature of follow-up should be determined near the end of the rehabilitation phase and incorporated into the recovery plan. Therefore it should be included as a part of discharge planning. Ideally, the social worker should be actively involved in this discharge planning process in addition to performing the extended follow-up.

The focus of follow-up is on providing support and guidance toward the maintenance of positive treatment effects (Miller, 1989).

The frequency of follow-up should be mutually agreed upon by worker and patient, and determined by the patient's compliance with the recovery plan. Most treatment professionals recommend that follow-up continue for approximately 2 years at a minimum (Older & Searcy, 1990). Furthermore, it is recommended that compliance with the recovery plan and indicators of a healthy recovery be evidenced for 1 to 2 months before the frequency of follow-up sessions is decreased. For instance, if a patient who has been seen weekly is following his or her recovery plan and appears to be in recovery (as opposed to relapse), worker and patient should continue to meet weekly for at least once a month before agreeing to meet less often (Gray, 1989). The following frequency schedule is suggested: weekly sessions for the first 3 to 4 months, bimonthly sessions for the next 4 to 6 months, monthly sessions for the next 6 to 12 months, and quarterly or semiannual sessions for the last 12 to 24 months (Gray, 1989; Older & Searcy, 1990). However, the actual frequency should be determined by an assessment of the patient's compliance with the recovery plan and the degree to which he or she is bonding with self-help groups and appropriately using other support resources.

Clinical Instruments

Several examples of clinical instruments that can help social workers assess their patients' relapse risks and recovery plan compliance are included in the Appendix to this chapter. These instruments address situations that have been identified as obstacles to recovery, namely, high-risk situations, social instability, organic dysfunction, and lack of knowledge and training in relapse prevention.

CONCLUSION

Relapse prevention as a focus of substance abuse treatment is a relatively recent treatment component. Although this chapter does not offer an exhaustive survey of treatment approaches and interventions, it incorporates the work of several treatment practitioners, educators, and researchers to provide an understanding of the basic components and clinical approaches that aid in the prevention of relapse. While specific techniques vary, most treatment practitioners agree on the need to employ a comprehensive, holistic treatment philosophy that addresses the clients' biological, psychological, social, emotional, and spiritual needs.

In order to assess these needs throughout the treatment and recovery process, case management with extended structured follow-up is critical. However, because relapse continues to be prevalent in substance abuse treatment, and because much remains unknown about what works for which patients and what mechanisms are absolutely necessary in order for patients to maintain long-term recovery, continuing systematic study and clinical research are vital in helping social workers unravel this complicated and mysterious phenomenon.

APPENDIX. Clinical Instruments for Relapse Prevention

Inventory of Drinking Situations (IDS-100)
  and
Inventory of Drinking Situations User's Guide
Addiction Research Foundation
Department 897
33 Russell Street
Toronto, Ontario M5S 2S1, Canada

The Inventory of Drinking Situations (IDS) is a situation-specific measure of drinking that can be used to identify a client's high-risk situations for alcoholic relapse. It serves as a treatment planning tool, providing a profile of a client's areas of greatest drinking risk. Administration may be by paper-and-pencil questionnaire or computer interactive software. The 50-page User's Guide describes the development of the IDS and its use in clinical and research settings, presents reliability and validity information plus normative data, and provides guidelines for use in both paper-and-pencil and computer interactive formats.

Situational Confidence Questionnaire (SCQ-39)
  and
Situational Confidence Questionnaire (SCQ)—User's Guide
Addiction Research Foundation
Department 897
33 Russell Street
Toronto, Ontario M5S 2S1, Canada

The Situational Confidence Questionnaire (SCQ-39) is a situation-specific measure of efficacy expectations that is designed to assess self-efficacy in relation to a client's perceived ability to cope effectively with alcohol. Administration may be by paper-and-pencil questionnaire or computer interactive software. The 45-page User's Guide describes the development of the SCQ and presents guidelines for clinical and research applications. Reliability and validity data are summarized, and normative data are provided.

Relapse Prevention Workbook for Recovering Alcoholics
    and Drug Dependent Persons
Learning Publications, Inc.
5351 Gulf Drive
Holmes Beach, FL 34218

This workbook presents a number of exercises to help the client identify risk situations for drinking and to plan coping responses for those situations. Other topics covered include use of an emergency sobriety card, lifestyle balancing, and what to do if a relapse occurs.

Symbol Digit Modalities Test (SDMT)
Western Psychological Services
12031 Wilshire Boulevard
Los Angeles, CA 90025

This 5-minute test, which can be administered either orally or in written form, provides a measure of generalized effects of brain damage. In 90-second intervals, clients have the task of substituting a number for randomized presentations of geometric figures. It is not advisable to screen for brain dysfunction if a client is experiencing toxicity effects or postwithdrawal reaction.

Embedded Figures Test
Consulting Psychologists Press, Inc.
577 College Avenue
Palo Alto, CA 94306

This 23-item test may be administered in 20 to 40 minutes to assess broad dimensions of personal functioning as indicated by cognitive style. The construct applied to cognitive/perceptual style in this test is that of field independence/dependence. Field independence is highly correlated with a preference for individual interaction, while field dependence is highly correlated with a preference for group interaction. The test has three versions, each suited for group or individual administration to adults or children. This instrument can be helpful in deciding whether to assign clients to individual or group modalities.

Social Stability Index
Harvey Skinner, Ph.D.
Addiction Research Foundation
33 Russell Street
Toronto, Ontario M5S 2S1, Canada

This 7-item index was developed to provide an indication of the stability and support present in a person's life. It takes less than 5 minutes to administer and would be most effectively used in an interview format. This index is particularly helpful during the pretreatment and discharge planning phases of case management. The score derived from this index will aid in decisions regarding the appropriateness of inpatient versus outpatient treatment.

REFERENCES

Adelman, S., & Weiss, R. (1989). What is therapeutic about inpatient alcoholism treatment? *Hospital and Community Psychiatry, 40*(5), 515-520.

Alcoholics Anonymous. (1975). *Living sober.* New York: Alcoholics Anonymous World Services.

Annis, H., & Davis, C. (1989). Relapse prevention. In R. Hester & W. Miller (Eds.), *Handbook of alcoholism treatment approaches: Effective alternatives* (pp. 170-182). Elmsford, NY: Pergamon.

Ashley, A. (1988). Case management: The need to define goals. *Hospital and Community Psychiatry, 39*(5), 499-500.

Austin, C. (1983). Client assessment in context. In H. Weissman, I. Epstein, & A. Savage (Eds.), *Agency based social work* (pp. 83-96). Philadelphia: Temple University Press.

Chapman, P., & Huygens, I. (1988). An evaluation of three treatment programmes for alcoholism: An experimental study with 6 and 18 month follow-ups. *British Journal of Addiction, 83*(1), 67-81.

Daley, D. (1987). Relapse prevention with substance abusers: Clinical issues and myths. *Social Work, 32*(2), 138-142.

Dolan, J., & Olander, C. (1990, Summer). Grantmakers and the war on drugs. *Health Affairs,* pp. 202-208.

Edwards, D. (1982). Spouse participation in the treatment of alcoholism: Competition of treatment and recidivism. *Social Work with Groups, 5*(1), 41-48.

Foote, A., & Erfurt, J. (1990). Effects of EAP follow-up on prevention of relapse among substance abuse clients. *Journal of Studies on Alcohol, 51,* 241-248.

Gorski, T. (1980, November/December). Dynamics of relapse. *EAP Digest,* pp. 16-21, 45-49.

Gorski, T. (1986). Relapse prevention planning: A new recovery tool. *Alcohol Health and Research World, 11*(1), 6-11.

Gorski, T., & Miller, H. (1986). *Staying sober: A guide for relapse prevention.* Independence, MO: Independence Press.

Gray, M. (1989). Case management. In U.S. Department of Health and Human Services, *Drug abuse curriculum for employee assistance professionals* (pp. 1-94). Washington, DC: U.S. Government Printing Office.

Guiliani, D., & Schnoll, S. (1985). Clinical decision making in chemical dependence treatment: A programmatic model. *Journal of Substance Abuse Treatment, 2,* 203-208.

Hester, R., & Miller, W. (Eds.). (1989). *Handbook of alcoholism treatment approaches: Effective alternatives.* Elmsford, NY: Pergamon.

Ludwig, A. (1988). *Understanding the alcoholic's mind.* New York: Oxford University Press.

Marlatt, G. A., & George, W. (1984). Relapse prevention: Introduction and overview of the model. *British Journal of Addiction, 79,* 261-273.

Marlatt, G. A., & Gordon, J. R. (Eds.). (1985). *Relapse prevention: Maintenance strategies in the treatment of addictive behaviors.* New York: Guilford.

McAuliffe, W., & Ch'ien, J. (1986). Recovery training and self help: A relapse-prevention program for treatment of opiate addicts. *Journal of Substance Abuse Treatment, 3*, 9–20.

McCrady, B., & Irvin, S. (1989). Self-help groups. In R. Hester & W. Miller (Eds.), *Handbook of alcoholism treatment approaches: Effective alternatives* (pp. 153–169). Elmsford, NY: Pergamon.

Miller, W. (1989). Follow-up assessment. In R. Hester & W. Miller (Eds.), *Handbook of alcoholism treatment approaches: Effective alternatives* (pp. 81–89). Elmsford, NY: Pergamon.

O'Dwyer, P. (1984). Cost effective rehabilitation: A process of matching. *EAP Digest, 4*(2), 32–34.

Older, H., & Searcy, E. (1990). Assuring the continued recover of EAP clients through posttreatment aftercare. *EAPA Exchange, 20*(6), 22–24.

Roberts-DeGennaro, M. (1987, October). Developing case management as a practice model. *Social Casework* pp. 466–470.

Robinson, D. (1989). *Talking out of alcoholism.* London: Croom Helm.

Tournier, R. (1979). Alcoholics Anonymous as a treatment and as ideology. *Journal of Studies on Alcohol, 40*(3), 230–239.

Washton, A. (1986). Nonpharmacologic treatment of cocaine abuse. *Psychiatric Clinics of North America, 9*(3), 563–571

Washton, A. (1989). *Cocaine addiction: Treatment, recovery, and relapse prevention.* New York: Norton.

Index